Theory Test, Practical Test & Highway Code

Theory Test, Practical Test & Highway Code

Everything you need to know to help you pass your driving tests

Up to **£40 off** your
first 10 hours of lessons*
Call 0800 107 2045

AA

Published by AA Publishing (a trading name of AA Media Limited, whose registered
office is Fanum House, Basing View, Basingstoke, Hampshire RG21 4EA; registered
number 06112600).

© AA Media Limited 2016
Ninth edition

Previously published as *Complete Test.*

ISBN: 978-0-7495-7794-0

Printed in China by Leo Paper Products

A05410

For more driving products, visit AA Publishing at www.theaa.com/shop
For driving lessons, visit AA Driving School at www.theaa.com/driving-school

Contents

Getting your licence

You want to pass your driving test and take advantage of the freedom and mobility that driving a car can give you. The following three things will help you to achieve your goal.

- Acquire knowledge of the rules of the road by learning *The Highway Code*.
- Take the right attitude. Be careful, courteous and considerate to all other road users.
- Learn and understand the skills of driving by taking lessons from a trained and qualified driving instructor.

This book has been designed to help you become a careful and safe driver and help you take the first steps towards achieving your goal – preparing for your theory test.

Six essential steps to getting your licence

1 Get your provisional licence
You can apply online for your provisional licence at www.gov.uk/apply-first-provisional-driving-licence or apply using form D1 available from Post Offices.

The driving licence is issued as a photocard.

You must be at least 17 before you can legally begin learning to drive and you must be in possession of the correct licence documents. Take care when completing all the forms. Many licences cannot be issued for the required date because of errors or omissions on the application. You will need to provide proof of identity, such as a UK passport.

2 Learn The Highway Code
The Highway Code is essential reading for all drivers and not just those learning to drive. It sets out all the rules for good driving, as well as the rules for other road users such as pedestrians and motorcycle riders. When you have learned the rules you will be able to answer most of the questions in the theory test and be ready to start learning the driving skills you will need to pass your practical test.

3 Apply for and take the theory test
The driving test is in two parts, the theory test and the practical test. Once you have a valid provisional licence you may take the theory test at any time, but you must pass it before you are allowed to apply for the practical test. It is important, however, not to take your theory test too early in your course of practical lessons. This is because you need the experience of meeting real hazards while you are learning to drive, to help you pass the hazard perception element of the theory test.

You can book your theory test online or by phone. You will need your Driver and Vehicle Licensing Agency (DVLA) licence number and your debit or credit card details to hand.

Online: www.gov.uk/book-a-driving-theory-test
Enquiries and booking support: 0300 200 1122
Welsh speakers: 0300 200 1133
Textphone: 0300 200 1166
Lines are open Monday to Friday, from 8am to 4pm
Post: DVSA, PO Box 381, M50 3UW

4 Learn to drive

It is recommended that you learn to drive with an Approved Driving Instructor (ADI). Only an ADI may legally charge for providing tuition. A fully qualified ADI must display a green badge on the windscreen of the car while teaching you. Some trainee driving instructors display a pink badge on the windscreen.

Choose an instructor or driving school by asking friends or relatives for recommendations. Price is important, so find out whether the school offers any discounts for blocks or lessons paid in advance; if you decide to pay in advance, make sure the driving school is reputable. If lesson prices are very low, ask yourself 'why?' Check how long the lesson will last. Ask about the car you'll be learning to drive in. Is it modern and reliable? Is it insured? Does it have dual controls?

The most efficient and cost-effective way to learn to drive is to accept that there is no short-cut approach to learning the necessary skills. Agree with your instructor on a planned course of tuition suited to your needs, take regular lessons, and don't skip weeks and expect to pick up where you left off. Ensure the full official syllabus is covered and, as your skills develop, get as much driving practice on the road as possible with a relative or friend. Ensure they are legally able to supervise you; they must be over 21 years of age and have held a full driving licence for at least three years.

5 Apply for and take the practical test

Once you have passed the theory test, and with your instructor's guidance based on your progress, you can plan ahead for a suitable test date for the practical test. You can book your practical test online or by phone.

Online: www.gov.uk/book-practical-driving-test
Enquiries and booking support: 0300 200 1122
Welsh speakers: 0300 200 1133
Textphone: 0300 200 1144
Lines are open Monday to Friday, from 8am to 12pm
Post: DVSA, PO Box 280, Newcastle-upon-Tyne NE99 1FP

Introduction

Make sure you have the following details to hand when booking your practical test:

- Theory test pass certificate number
- driver number shown on your licence
- driving school code number (if known)
- your preferred date
- unacceptable days or periods
- if you can accept a test at short notice
- disability or any special circumstances
- your credit/debit card details (the person who books the test must be the cardholder).

If you need to, you can change your practical test appointment online.

Saturday and weekday evening tests are available at some driving test centres. The fee is higher than for a driving test during normal working hours on weekdays. Evening tests are available during the summer months only.

6 Apply for your full driving licence

If you have a photocard provisional driving licence issued after 1 March 2004, and pass your driving test, the examiner can issue your full driving licence immediately. The DVLA will send your new full licence by post within four weeks of passing your practical test.

If you don't have a photocard provisional driving licence, you need to send your Pass Certificate and your provisional licence to the DVLA in Swansea, within two years of passing your practical test.

After the practical test

Drivers may wish to enhance their basic skills and widen their experience by taking further training in the form of the Pass Plus scheme.

This is a six-module syllabus that covers town and rural driving, night driving, driving in adverse weather conditions and driving on dual carriageways and motorways. It offers you the opportunity to gain more driving experience with the help of an instructor. Insurance companies may be prepared to offer discounts to new drivers who have completed the course. There is no test to take at the end of the course.

More information

For more information on learning to drive, including the theory test, the practical test and Pass Plus, visit www.gov.uk/browse/driving.

How to use this book

This book is arranged in seven sections.

Part 1 explains what to expect and how to prepare for each part of the test: Theory and Practical.

This section explains how to take the theory test using a touch-screen computer and gives details of the clips used in the hazard perception part of the test. In the Practical section we have included information about the Driver's Record, which your instructor will complete after each lesson.

We tell you what to expect on the day you take your test, details of the documents you must have with you, and tell you what the examiner will be looking for in your general driving. We have also included information on the vehicle safety check questions, which forms part of the practical test.

Part 2 contains questions and answers for learner drivers set by a panel of driving experts, as an aid to help you pass your practical test. They are designed to test your knowledge of what is required before you even sit in the driver's seat. Topics include parallel parking, reversing and motorway driving.

Part 3 is designed to help you understand each of the 14 topics in the theory test. This section will tell you what type of questions you can expect in each section and we've included lots of helpful tips. Each topic is colour coded to its relevant section in Part 4 of this book, which contains all the revision Theory Questions from the Driver and Vehicle Standards Agency (DVSA).

Experience has taught us that learner drivers find particular theory questions difficult and are often confused when they see questions that are similar. Reading through the background to each topic, before looking at the questions, will help you to avoid the pitfalls and help you to group questions together, as you will often find several questions are asking the same thing in a slightly different way.

Part 4 contains revision questions for car drivers created by the DVSA. The questions in your live test will be unseen and different from the ones shown in this book.

The questions are arranged in topics, such as Safety Margins and Rules of the Road. You will be tested on a range of these topics when you take your touch-screen theory test. Each topic has its own colour band to help you find your way around.

Each question is accompanied by explanatory information to help you understand each question. Most of the theory test questions can be answered if you learn *The Highway Code*. However,

Introduction

you will only find the answers to some questions by talking to your driving instructor and learning about good driving practice on the road.

You'll find all the correct answers to the theory test questions in Part 6 (see pages 399–403), that way, you can easily test yourself to see what you are getting right and what you still need to work on.

Part 5 is a short glossary, which explains some of the more difficult words and terms used in the theory questions and

The Highway Code. It's in alphabetical order and you can use this to check if you're not sure what a chicane is, for example, or what brake fade means.

Part 6 has all the answers to the Theory Test questions.

Part 7 contains *The Highway Code* with its own index (according to rule number).

Part 1:
About the tests

Revising for the theory test

The theory test is all about making you a safer driver and it is a good idea to prepare for the theory test at the same time as you develop your skills behind the wheel for the practical test. By preparing for both tests at the same time, you will reinforce your knowledge and understanding of all aspects of driving and improve your chances of passing both tests first time.

Using the theory test revision questions

This book is designed to help you prepare for the multiple-choice questions part of the theory test and contains all the official revision questions. The test will consist of 50 unseen theory test questions based on the topics shown here (see pages 151–391). The real test questions are not published, but the questions in this book will help you revise for the test.

To help you study for the test, the questions are arranged into the theory test topics. Each topic has its own colour band to help you find your way through the book.

Start your revision by picking a topic; you don't have to study the topics in order. Study each question carefully to make sure you understand what it is asking you. Look carefully at any diagram or photograph before reading the explanatory information and deciding on your answer.

All the correct answers are given in Part 6 (see pages 399–403).

Remember
- Learning *The Highway Code* and taking lessons with an ADI (approved driving instructor) are the best way to prepare for your theory test.
- Don't attempt too many questions at once.
- Don't try to learn the questions and answers by heart; the real test questions are not available for you to practice and are different from the revision questions given in this book.

Questions marked **NI** are **not** found in theory tests in Northern Ireland.

1 Study the question carefully and make sure you understand what it is asking you

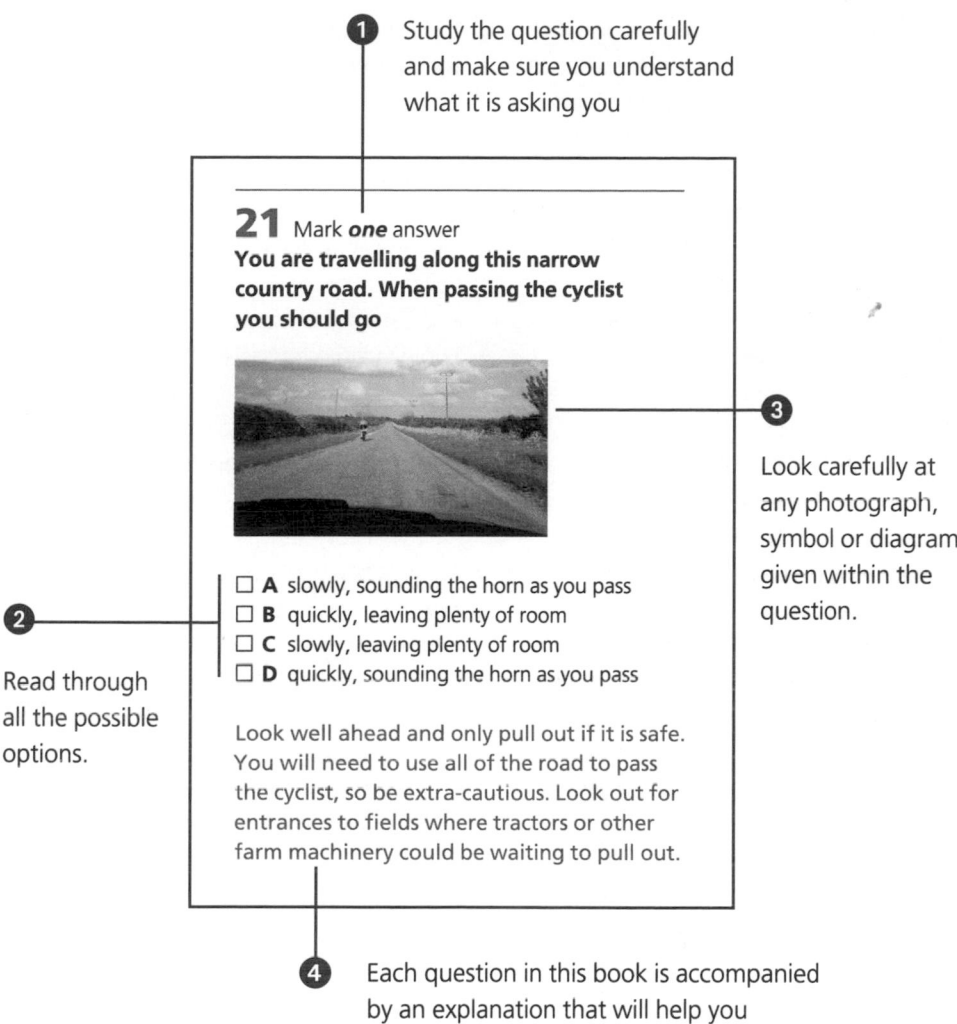

21 Mark *one* answer
You are travelling along this narrow country road. When passing the cyclist you should go

☐ **A** slowly, sounding the horn as you pass
☐ **B** quickly, leaving plenty of room
☐ **C** slowly, leaving plenty of room
☐ **D** quickly, sounding the horn as you pass

Look well ahead and only pull out if it is safe. You will need to use all of the road to pass the cyclist, so be extra-cautious. Look out for entrances to fields where tractors or other farm machinery could be waiting to pull out.

3 Look carefully at any photograph, symbol or diagram given within the question.

2 Read through all the possible options.

4 Each question in this book is accompanied by an explanation that will help you understand the theory behind the question and what answer may be appropriate. Make sure you read through this text before answering the question. This text will not appear in your actual theory test.

What to expect in the theory test

The theory test consists of two parts: 50 multiple-choice questions and hazard perception. You have to pass both parts in order to pass your theory test. You will receive your test scores at the end of the test. Even if you only failed on one part of the theory test, you still have to take both parts again next time.

Multiple-choice questions

You will have 57 minutes to complete the question part of the test using a touch-screen and all the questions are multiple-choice. The 50 questions appear on the screen one at a time and you can return to any of the questions within the 57 minutes to re-check or change your answers. You have to score a minimum of 43 out of 50 to pass. The Government may change the pass mark from time to time. Your driving school or the DVSA will be able to tell you if there has been a change.

Each question has four possible options. You must select the one correct answer. Don't worry about accidentally missing marking an answer because you'll be reminded that you haven't chosen an answer before moving on to the next question.

Study each question carefully and look carefully at any diagram, drawing or photograph. Before you look at the options given, decide what you think the correct answer might be. Read through the options and then select the answer that matches the one you had decided on. If you follow this system, you will avoid being confused by answers that appear to be similar.

You can answer the questions in any order you choose by moving forwards and backwards through the questions. You can also change your answer if necessary and flag questions you're unsure about, then go back to them later in the test. Your remaining time is shown on the screen.

Case study questions

Typically, five of the 50 questions will take the form of a case study. All five questions will be based on a single driving situation and appear one at time.

Case studies are designed to test that you not only know your car theory but also that you understand how to apply your knowledge when faced with a given driving situation.

The case study in your theory test could be based on any driving scenario and ask questions from a range of topics in the DVSA's database of questions.

The sample case study on the following pages demonstrates how the case study questions may appear in your live test, so you'll know what to expect.

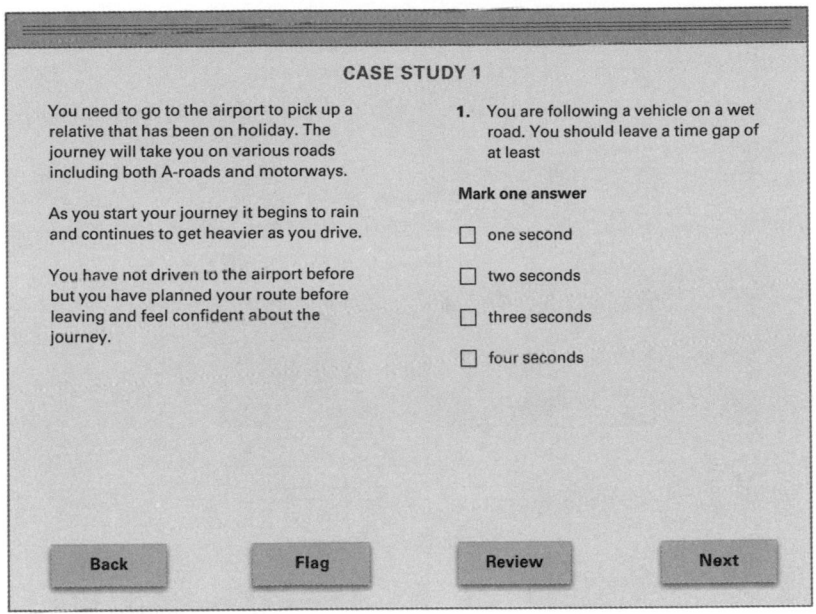

CASE STUDY 1

You need to go to the airport to pick up a relative that has been on holiday. The journey will take you on various roads including both A-roads and motorways.

As you start your journey it begins to rain and continues to get heavier as you drive.

You have not driven to the airport before but you have planned your route before leaving and feel confident about the journey.

1. You are following a vehicle on a wet road. You should leave a time gap of at least

Mark one answer

☐ one second

☐ two seconds

☐ three seconds

☐ four seconds

Back   Flag   Review   Next

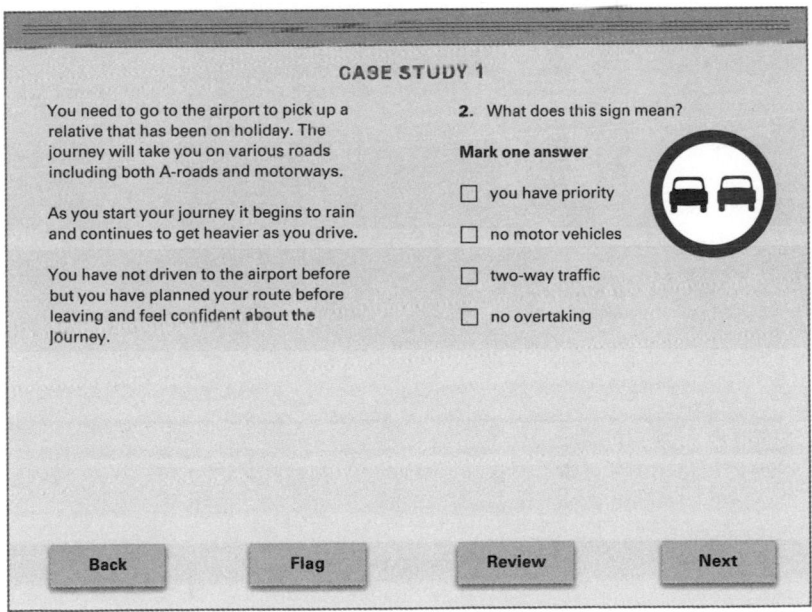

CASE STUDY 1

You need to go to the airport to pick up a relative that has been on holiday. The journey will take you on various roads including both A-roads and motorways.

As you start your journey it begins to rain and continues to get heavier as you drive.

You have not driven to the airport before but you have planned your route before leaving and feel confident about the journey.

2. What does this sign mean?

Mark one answer

☐ you have priority

☐ no motor vehicles

☐ two-way traffic

☐ no overtaking

Back   Flag   Review   Next

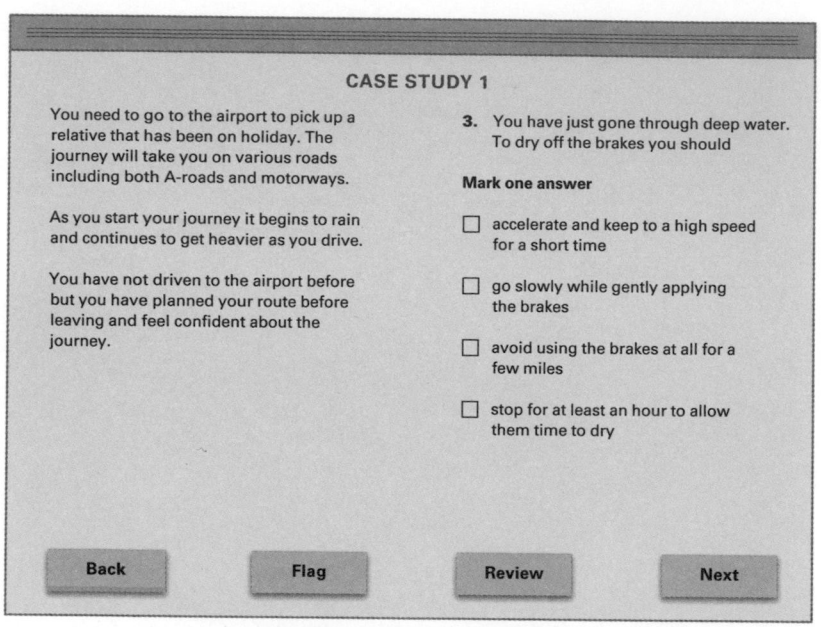

CASE STUDY 1

You need to go to the airport to pick up a relative that has been on holiday. The journey will take you on various roads including both A-roads and motorways.

As you start your journey it begins to rain and continues to get heavier as you drive.

You have not driven to the airport before but you have planned your route before leaving and feel confident about the journey.

3. You have just gone through deep water. To dry off the brakes you should

Mark one answer

☐ accelerate and keep to a high speed for a short time

☐ go slowly while gently applying the brakes

☐ avoid using the brakes at all for a few miles

☐ stop for at least an hour to allow them time to dry

Back   Flag   Review   Next

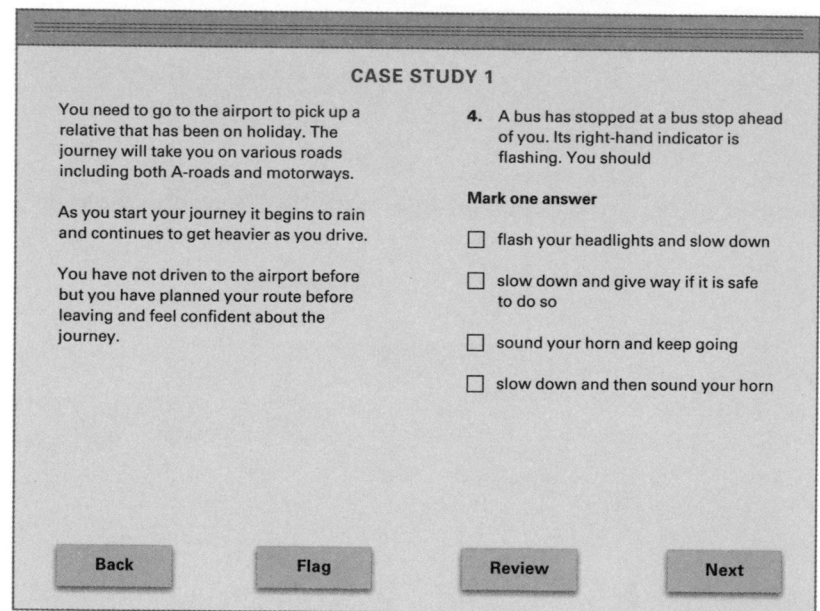

CASE STUDY 1

You need to go to the airport to pick up a relative that has been on holiday. The journey will take you on various roads including both A-roads and motorways.

As you start your journey it begins to rain and continues to get heavier as you drive.

You have not driven to the airport before but you have planned your route before leaving and feel confident about the journey.

4. A bus has stopped at a bus stop ahead of you. Its right-hand indicator is flashing. You should

Mark one answer

☐ flash your headlights and slow down

☐ slow down and give way if it is safe to do so

☐ sound your horn and keep going

☐ slow down and then sound your horn

Back   Flag   Review   Next

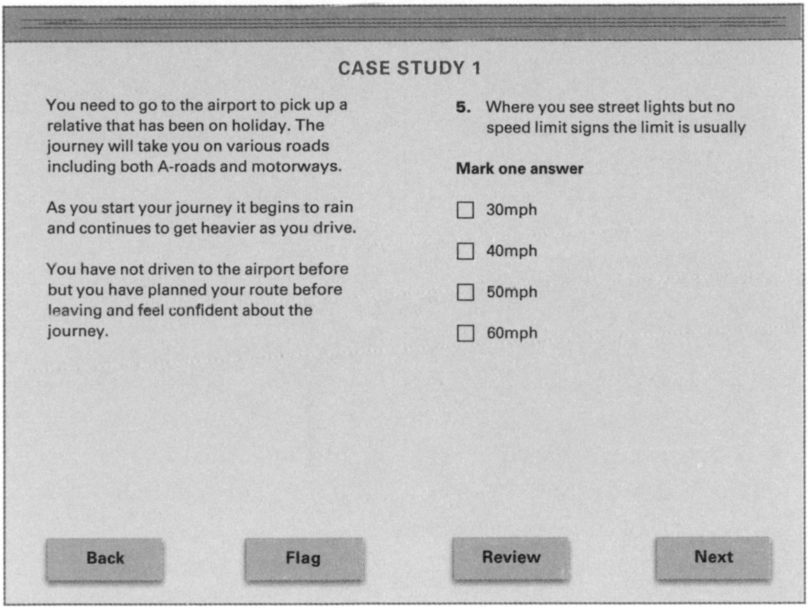

CASE STUDY 1

You need to go to the airport to pick up a relative that has been on holiday. The journey will take you on various roads including both A-roads and motorways.

As you start your journey it begins to rain and continues to get heavier as you drive.

You have not driven to the airport before but you have planned your route before leaving and feel confident about the journey.

5. Where you see street lights but no speed limit signs the limit is usually

Mark one answer

☐ 30mph

☐ 40mph

☐ 50mph

☐ 60mph

| Back | Flag | Review | Next |

Answers to sample case study questions: 1 D 2 D 3 B 4 B 5 A

Hazard perception

The clips element of the theory test is known as hazard perception. Its aim is to find out how good you are at noticing hazards developing on the road ahead. The test will also show how much you know about the risks to you as a driver, the risks to your passengers and the risks to other road users.

Who do you think have the most accidents – new or experienced drivers? New drivers have just had lessons, so they should remember how to drive safely, but in fact statistics show that new drivers have the most accidents.

Learner drivers need training in how to spot hazards because they are often so busy thinking about the car's controls that they forget to watch the road and traffic. Losing concentration for even a second could prove fatal to you or another road user.

Proper training can help you to recognize more of the hazards that you will meet when driving and to spot those hazards earlier, so you are less likely to have an accident.

Your driving instructor has been trained to help you learn hazard perception skills and can give you plenty of practice in what to look out for when driving, how to anticipate hazards, and what action to take to deal with hazards of all kinds.

What is a hazard?

A hazard is anything that might cause you to change speed or direction when driving. The hazard perception element of the Theory Test is about spotting developing hazards. This is one of the key skills of good driving and is also called anticipation. Anticipating hazards, such as car doors opening or children running into the road, means looking out for them in advance and taking the appropriate action.

As you get more driving experience you will start to learn about the times and places where you are most likely to meet hazards. An example of this is the rush hour. You know people take more risks when they are in a hurry. Maybe they have to drop their children at school before going to work. Perhaps they are late for a meeting or want to get home. So you have to be prepared for bad driving, for example another driver pulling out in front of you.

You won't be able to practise with the real clips used in the official test, of course, but training books and practice videos are widely available.

Taking the theory test: hazard perception

After answering the multiple-choice questions, you will be given a short break before you begin the hazard perception part of the test. The hazard perception test lasts for about 20 minutes. Before you start you will be given some instructions explaining how the test works; you'll also get a chance to practise with the computer and mouse before you start. This is to make sure that you know what to expect on the test and that you are happy with what you have to do.

Next you will see 14 clips of street scenes with traffic such as cars, pedestrians, cyclists, etc. The scenes are shot from the point of view of a driver in a car. You have to notice potential hazards that are developing on the road ahead – that is, problems that could lead to an incident. As soon as you notice a hazard developing, click the mouse. You will have plenty of time to see the hazard and the sooner you notice it, the more marks you score.

Each clip has at least one hazard in it but some clips may have more than one hazard. You have to score a minimum of 44 out of 75 to pass, but the pass mark may change so check with your instructor or the DSA before sitting your test.

Note that the computer has checks built in to show anyone trying to cheat – for example someone who keeps clicking the mouse all the time. Be aware that, unlike the theory test questions, you will not have an opportunity to go back to an earlier clip and change your response, so you need to concentrate throughout the test.

You responded to this clip in an unacceptable manner. You will score zero for this clip.

Above, top: Click the mouse when you spot potential hazards – the tractor emerging from the side road (ringed).

Above: You may see a warning screen similar to this one if the computer detects a clicking pattern or you click the mouse constantly.

What to expect in the practical test

The requirements for passing your test are a combination of practical skills and mental understanding. The open road can be a risky environment, and your test result will show whether you're ready to go out there alone or whether you need a little more practice first.

You'll be asked to sign a declaration that the insurance of your car is in order. Without this, the practical test can't proceed.

> Driving test standards are monitored so that whatever examiner you get, or whatever test centre you go to, you should get the same result. You might find a senior officer in the car as well as the examiner; he or she is not watching you, but checking that the examiner is doing his or her job properly.

The paperwork
You'll need to have with you:
- your signed photocard provisional driving licence. If your licence doesn't have a photo (i.e. an older-style paper licence) you'll need to bring a valid passport for photographic identity. No other forme of identification will be accepted.

- your theory test pass certificate
- your completed Driver's Record (if you have one) signed by your instructor.

Eyesight test
Your driving test begins with an eyesight test. You have to be able to read a new style number plate at a minimum distance of 20 metres (about 67 feet) or an old style number plate at 20.5 metres (about 67.5 feet). If you fail the eyesight test your driving test will stop at that point and you will have failed.

Vehicle safety checks
You will have to answer two vehicle safety check questions. The questions fall into three categories:
- identify
- tell me how you would check…
- show me how you would check…

These questions are designed to make sure that you know how to check that your vehicle is safe to drive.

If you turn up for your test in an unsuitable vehicle, you will forfeit your test fee.

Although some checks may require you to identify where fluid levels should be checked you will not be asked to touch a hot engine or physically check fluid levels. You may refer to vehicle information systems (if fitted) when answering questions on fluid levels and tyre pressures.

All vehicles differ slightly so it is important that you get to know all the safety systems and engine layout in the vehicle in which you plan to take your practical test.

Checks and observer on the test

Before you start the test, the examiner will check all of your documents and ask you to sign the marking sheet to declare that the car is insured and that you have lived in the UK for at least 185 days in the last 12 months. He or she will also ask if you would like your accompanying driver to accompany you on the test. This will mean that your accompanying driver (usually your driving instructor) would sit in the back of the car and observe. The accompanying driver would not be able to take part in the test or help you but will be in a better position to discuss the test afterwards and give advice.

On the practical test

During the test you will be expected to drive for about 40 minutes along normal roads following the directions of the examiner. The roads are selected so as to provide a range of different conditions and road situations and a varied density of traffic.

Your examiner will select suitable areas for you to carry out the set exercises. He or she will tell you to pull up and stop, and will then explain the exercise to you before you do it:

- you may or may not be asked to perform an emergency stop
- you will be asked to perform one reversing exercises selected by the examiner from: reversing round a corner; reverse parking (behind a parked car, or into a marked bay); turning in the road.

The examiner will be assessing:

- whether you are competent at controlling the car
- whether you are making normal progress for the roads you are on
- how you react to any hazards that occur in the course of the test
- whether you are noticing all traffic signs and signals and road markings, and reacting to them in the correct manner.

To pass the driving test, you must:

- not commit any serious fault, and
- commit fewer than 15 driving errors of a less serious nature.

If, during the test, you do not understand what the examiner says to you, ask him or her to repeat the instruction.

Once you have passed your test you will be driving independently without the help of someone giving you directions. This skill is examined during your practical test. In addition, the examiner will ask you to drive without junction-by-junction directions to assess if this skill has been learned. The examiner will continue to assess your driving skills but will not be assessing your ability to remember a route, so you can still ask the Examiner to confirm which direction you should be going in. Your driving instructor will help you to practise this skill.

If you are faced with an unusually difficult or hazardous situation in the course of your test that results in you making a driving fault, the examiner will take the circumstances into account when marking you that part of the test.

How to prepare for the practical test

Be sure that you are ready to take the test. This is where choosing a reliable qualified driving instructor is vital.

You should feel confident:
- about driving in all conditions
- that you know *The Highway Code*
- that you can make decisions on your own about how to cope with hazards, without having to wait for your instructor to tell you what to do.

Staying up-to-date

The government may change elements of the practical test from time to time. Your driving instructor or the Driver and Vehicle Standards Agency (DVSA) will be able to tell you if there has been a change.

Further information

For more practical information on learning to drive including the theory test, practical test and Pass Plus visit www.gov.uk/browse/driving.

Part 2:
The practical test questions and answers

The practical test

Good defensive driving depends on adopting the right attitude from the start. These questions will test your knowledge of what is required before you even sit in the driver's seat.

1

What do you need before you can drive on a public road?

Fill in the missing words

P__ __ __ __ __ __ __ __ __ __

__ __ __ __ __ __ __

2

The best way to learn is to have regular planned tuition with an ADI (Approved Driving Instructor).

An ADI is someone who has taken and passed all three driving instructor's

e __ __ __ __ __ __ __ __ __ __ __ and is on

the official r__ __ __ __ __ __ __

Complete the sentence

Answers on page 96

HINTS & TIPS

A fully qualified ADI should display a green certificate on the windscreen of their car. Ask to see it.

3

Anyone supervising a learner must be at least __ __ years old and must have held (and still hold) a full driving licence (motor car) for at least t__ __ __ __ years

Complete the sentence

4

Your tuition vehicle must display L-plates. Where should they be placed?

Answer _____

_____

_____

5

Young and inexperienced drivers are more vulnerable. Is this true or false?

Tick the correct box **True** ☐ **False** ☐

6

Showing responsibility to yourself and others is the key to being a safe driver. Ask yourself, would you ...

Tick the correct box

1 Want to drive with someone who has been drinking? **YES** ☐ **NO** ☐

2 Want to drive with someone who takes risks and puts other lives at risk? **YES** ☐ **NO** ☐

3 Want to drive with someone who does not concentrate? **YES** ☐ **NO** ☐

4 Want to drive with someone who drives too fast? **YES** ☐ **NO** ☐

7

Do you want to be a safe and responsible driver?

Tick the correct box **YES** ☐ **NO** ☐

8

You must pass a theory test before you can take the practical test. When would be the best time to sit this test?

Mark two answers

1. Before applying for a provisional licence. ☐
2. Just before taking the practical test. ☐
3. Some time during the early weeks of your driving lessons. ☐
4. After full study of available training materials. ☐

9

To use the controls safely you need to adopt a suitable driving position. There are a number of checks you should make.

Fill in the missing words

1 Check the h _ _ _ _ _ _ _ _ _ is on.
2 Check the d _ _ _ _ are shut.
3 Check your s _ _ is in the correct position.
4 Check the h _ _ _
  r _ _ _ _ _ _ _ _ is adjusted to give maximum protection.
5 Check the driving m _ _ _ _ _ _ are adjusted to give maximum rear view.
6 Check your s _ _ _ b _ _ _ _ is securely fastened.

10

Here is a list of functions and a list of controls.

Match each function to its control by placing the appropriate letter in the box

THE FUNCTIONS	THE CONTROLS
A To control the direction in which you want to travel	☐ The handbrake
B To slow or stop the vehicle	☐ The driving mirrors
C To increase or decrease the engine's speed	☐ The gear lever
D To give you a clear view behind	☐ The clutch
E To hold the vehicle still when it is stationary	☐ The steering wheel
F To enable you to change gear	☐ The foot-brake
G To enable you to make or break contact between the engine and the wheels	☐ The accelerator

Fill in the missing word

The accelerator can also be called the g _ _ pedal

Answers on page 96

11

Which foot should you use for each of these controls (in cars with a manual gearbox)?

R = Right foot   **L** = Left foot

The foot-brake ☐

The clutch ☐

The accelerator ☐

12

Are the following statements about steering true or false?

Tick the appropriate boxes

	True	False
1 I must keep both hands on the wheel at all times.	☐	☐
2 To keep good control I should feed the wheel through my hands.	☐	☐
3 I can place my hands at any position as long as I am comfortable.	☐	☐
4 When going round corners, it is best to cross my hands (hand over hand).	☐	☐
5 I should never take both hands off the wheel when the vehicle is moving.	☐	☐
6 To straighten up I should feed the wheel back through my hands.	☐	☐

13

Match each of the following functions to its control.

THE FUNCTIONS	THE CONTROLS
A To enable you to see the road ahead and other road users to see you without causing dazzle	☐ The direction indicators
B To show other road users which way you intend to turn	☐ Dipped beam
C To use only when visibility is 100 metres/yards or less	☐ Main beam
D To enable you to see further, but not to be used when there is oncoming traffic	☐ Rear fog lamp
E To warn other road users of your presence	☐ Horn
F To warn other road users when you are temporarily obstructing traffic	☐ Hazard lights

Answers on page 96

1

The following is a list of actions involved in moving off from rest. Number the boxes 1 to 9 to show the correct sequence

The first box has been filled in to give you a start

| 1 | **A** Press the clutch down fully |

[ ] **B** Check your mirrors

[ ] **C** Set the accelerator pedal

[ ] **D** Move the gear lever into 1st gear

[ ] **E** Decide whether you need to give a signal

[ ] **F** Let the clutch come to biting point and hold it steady

[ ] **G** Check your blind spot

[ ] **H** If safe, release the handbrake and let the clutch up a little more

[ ] **I** Press the accelerator pedal a little more and let the clutch up fully

Answers on page 97

2

The following is a list of actions required for stopping normally.
Number the boxes 1 to 9 to show the correct sequence.

The first box has been filled in to give you a start

1 **A** Check your mirrors

☐ **B** Take your foot off the accelerator pedal

☐ **C** Decide whether you need to signal and, if necessary, do so

☐ **D** Press the brake pedal, lightly at first and then more firmly

☐ **E** As the car stops, ease the pressure off the foot-brake
(except when you are on a slope)

☐ **F** Just before the car stops, press the clutch pedal right down

☐ **G** Put the gear lever into neutral

☐ **H** Apply the handbrake fully

☐ **I** Take both feet off the pedals

Answers on page 97

Gears enable you to select the power you need from the engine to perform a particular task.

3
Which gear gives you the most power?
Answer ☐

4
If you were travelling at 60mph on a clear road, which gear would you most likely select?
Answer ☐

5
When approaching and turning a corner, as shown in the diagram, which gear would you most likely use?
Answer ☐

6
You need to change gear to match your e_ _ _ _ _ speed to the speed at which your v_ _ _ _ _ _ is travelling. The s_ _ _ _ the engine is making will help you know w_ _ _ to change gear.
Complete the sentences

7
Number the boxes to show the correct sequence of actions required when changing up.
The first box has been filled in for you

☐1 **A** Place your left hand on the gear lever

☐ **B** Move the gear lever to the next highest position

☐ **C** Press the clutch pedal down fully and ease off the accelerator pedal

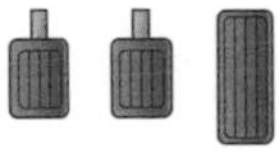

☐ **D** Let the clutch pedal come up fully and, at the same time, press the accelerator pedal

☐ **E** Put your left hand back on the steering wheel

Answers on page 97

8

Are the following statements about changing down true or false?

Tick the appropriate boxes

	True	False
1 I would stay in the highest gear as long as possible, even if my engine started to labour	☐	☐
2 I would change down early so that the engine helps to slow the car down	☐	☐
3 I would avoid using the foot-brake as much as possible	☐	☐
4 I would usually slow the car down by using the foot-brake first. Then, when I am at the required speed, I would change down to the appropriate gear	☐	☐
5 I would always change down through the gears so that I do not miss out any intermediate gears	☐	☐

Answers on page 98

HINTS & TIPS

In your driving test, you will be expected to show that you can control the car smoothly.
If you should stall, put the gears in neutral and the handbrake on, and start again.

9

When changing gear, I should look ...

1 Ahead ☐
2 At the gear lever ☐
3 At my feet ☐

Which is correct?

10

Do's and don'ts

Tick the appropriate boxes

	Do	Don't
1 Force the gear lever if there is any resistance	☐	☐
2 Rush the gear changes	☐	☐
3 Match your speed with the correct gear	☐	☐
4 Use the brakes, where necessary, to reduce speed before changing down	☐	☐
5 Listen to the sound of the engine	☐	☐
6 Take your eyes off the road when changing gear	☐	☐
7 Hold the gear lever longer than necessary	☐	☐
8 Coast with the clutch down or the gear lever in neutral	☐	☐

11

Which wheels turn when you turn the steering wheel?

A The front wheels

B The back wheels

Answer ☐

12

When you turn your steering wheel to the right, which way do your wheels turn?

A To the right

B To the left

Answer ☐

13

The steering lock is ...

A The locking mechanism that stops the steering wheel from moving when the ignition key is removed

B The angle through which the wheels turn when the steering wheel is turned

Answer ☐

14

Which wheels follow the shorter pathway?

A The front wheels

B The back wheels

Answer ☐

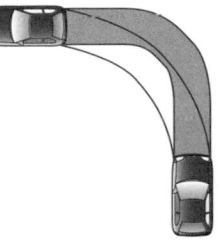

15

Which is the correct position for normal driving?

Put letter A, B or C in the box

Answer ☐

A   B   C

16

Which diagram shows the correct pathway when driving normally?

Put a letter A or B in the box

Answer ☐

A   B

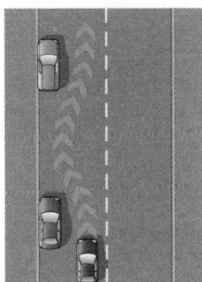

Answers on page 98

17

Pushing the clutch pedal down ...

A Releases the engine from the wheels
B Engages the engine with the wheels
Answer ☐

18

The point where the clutch plates meet is called the b_ _ _ _ _ point.

Fill in the missing word

19

By controlling the amount of contact between the clutch plates, it is possible to control the speed of the car.

Would you use this control ...

Tick the appropriate boxes

	Yes	No
1 When moving away from rest?	☐	☐
2 When manoeuvring the car in reverse gear?	☐	☐
3 When slowing down to turn a corner?	☐	☐
4 In very slow moving traffic?	☐	☐
5 To slow the car down?	☐	☐

HINTS ✓ & TIPS
Remember:
MSM stands for Mirror, Signal, Manoeuvre. Always use this routine when moving off, turning or overtaking.

Answers on page 98

1

A junction is a point where t __ __ o__ m__ __ __ r__ __ __ __ meet.

Complete the sentence

2

Here are five types of junction. Name them

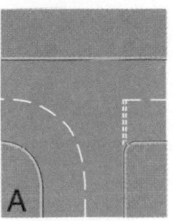

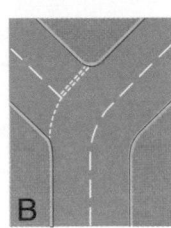

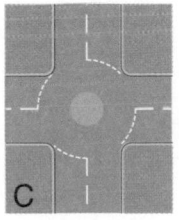

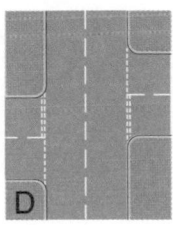

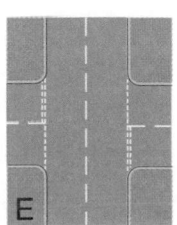

3

Match these road signs to the junctions shown opposite.

Put letters A, B, C, D and E in the boxes

1 ☐

2 ☐

3 ☐

4 ☐

5 ☐

4

What do these signs mean?

1 Stop and give way

2 Slow down, look, and proceed if safe

3 Give way to traffic on the major road

Put a number in each box

A ☐

B ☐

Answers on page 99

5

At every junction you should follow a safe routine.

Put the following into the correct order by numbering the boxes 1 to 5

Signal ☐ Speed ☐ Position ☐
Mirrors ☐ Look ☐

6

The diagram below shows a car turning right into a minor road. The boxes are numbered to show the correct sequence of actions.

Complete the sentence

At point 5 you should look and
a _ _ _ _ _ the situation,
d _ _ _ _ _ to go or wait,
and a _ _ accordingly.

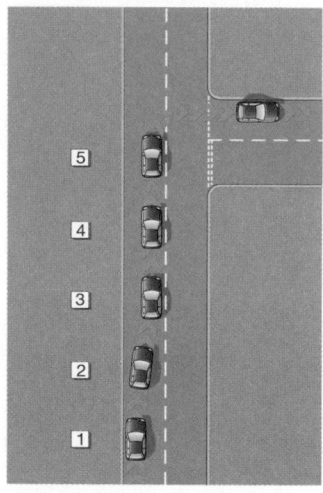

Answers on page 99

7

Turning left into a minor road. Which diagram below shows the best path to follow when driving a motor car A, B, C or D?

Answer ☐

A

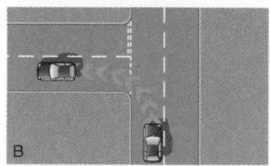

B

C

D

8

You turn into a side road. Pedestrians are already crossing it. Should you ...

Tick the appropriate box

A Sound your horn ☐
B Slow down and give way ☐
C Flash your lights ☐
D Wave them across ☐

9

Turning right into a minor road.
Which diagram shows the best path to
follow: A, B, C or D?

Answer ☐

10

These are the golden rules for emerging
from junctions.

Complete the sentences

1 Always use your m_ _ _ _ _ _ to
check the speed and p _ _ _ _ _ _ _ _
of vehicles behind.

2 Always cancel your s_ _ _ _ _ .

3 Speed up to a s_ _ _ speed after
joining the new road.

4 Keep a s_ _ _ d_ _ _ _ _ _ _
between you and the vehicle ahead.

5 Do not attempt to o_ _ _ _ _ _ _
until you can assess the new road.

Answers on page 99

11

All crossroads must be approached with caution.

Match actions 1, 2 and 3 listed below with these diagrams

Actions

1 Approach with caution, look well ahead and be prepared to stop. Remember other drivers may assume they have priority.

2 Look well ahead, slow down and be prepared to give way to traffic on the major road.

3 Look well ahead and into the side roads for approaching vehicles. Remember other drivers may not give you priority.

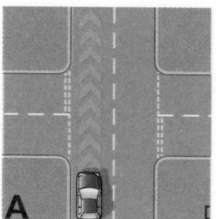

Answer ☐

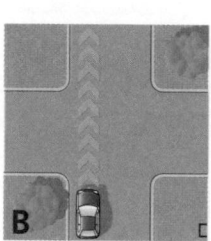

Answer ☐

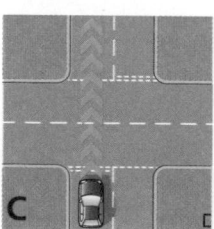

Answer ☐

12

Which of the following statements describes the correct procedure when approaching a roundabout?

Put letter A, B or C in the box

A The broken white line at a roundabout means I must stop and give way to traffic already on the roundabout.

B The broken white line at a roundabout means I must give priority to traffic already on the roundabout.

C The broken white line means I should give way to any traffic approaching from my immediate right.

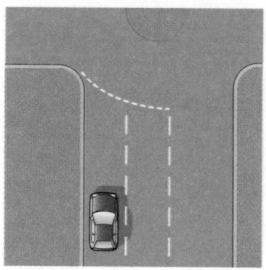

Answer ☐

HINTS & TIPS

At an unmarked crossroads, no one has priority.
Be extra-cautious at these junctions.

Answers on page 99

13

The following sentences give guidance on lane discipline on a roundabout.

Fill in the missing words

1 When turning left at a roundabout, I should stay in the _ _ _ _ hand lane and should stay in that lane throughout.

2 When going ahead at a roundabout, I should be in the _ _ _ _ hand lane, and should stay in that lane throughout, unless conditions dictate otherwise.

3 When turning right at a roundabout, I should approach in the r_ _ _ _ hand lane, or approach as if turning right at a junction, and stay in that lane throughout.

14

The letters A, B and C in the diagram mark places where you should signal.

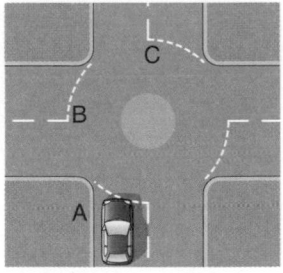

Complete the sentences

1 I would signal at **A** when turning _ _ _ _ _.

2 I would signal at **B** when g_ _ _ _ _

_ _ _ _ _.

3 I would signal at **A** and at **C** when turning _ _ _ _ _.

15

At a roundabout you should always use a safe routine.

Fill in the missing words

M_ _ _ _ _ _, s _ _ _ _ _,

p_ _ _ _ _ _ _, s_ _ _ _,

l_ _ _.

16

What does this sign mean?

Write 1, 2 or 3 in the box

1 Roundabout

2 Mini-roundabout

3 Vehicles may pass either side.

Answer ☐

HINTS ✔ & TIPS

Be careful at roundabouts where destinations are marked for each lane. Make sure you are in the correct lane for your destination.

Answers on page 99

1

It is safest to park off the road or in a car park whenever possible. If you have to park on the road, think ...

Fill in the missing words

1 Is it s_ _ _ ?

2 Is it c_ _ _ _ _ _ _ _ _ _ _?

3 Is it l_ _ _ _ ?

2

In this diagram four of the cars are parked illegally or without consideration of others.

Put the numbers of these cars in the boxes

☐ ☐ ☐ ☐

For reverse parallel parking manoeuvres, see pages 56–8.

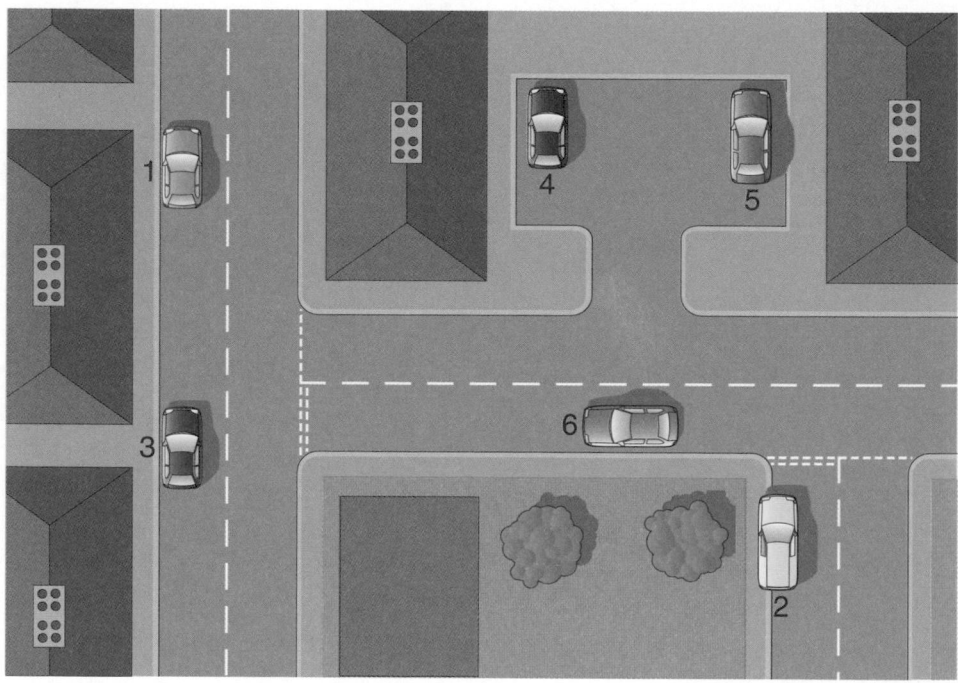

Answers on page 100

3

Check how well you know the rules about where you may and may not park. Are the following statements true or false?

Tick the appropriate boxes

	True	False
1 In a narrow street, I should park with two wheels up on the pavement to leave more room for other traffic.	☐	☐
2 I am allowed to park in a 'Disabled' space if all other spaces are full.	☐	☐
3 I should not park on the zig-zag lines near a zebra crossing.	☐	☐
4 Red lines painted on the road mean 'No Stopping'.	☐	☐

4

List three places not mentioned in Question 3 where you should *not* park.

1 _____
_____
_____
_____
_____
_____

2 _____
_____
_____
_____
_____
_____

3 _____
_____
_____
_____
_____
_____

HINTS ✔ & TIPS

Use your Highway Code to find out more about parking regulations

Answers on page 100

1

The diagram shows a stationary vehicle on the left-hand side of the road. Which should have priority, vehicle 1 or vehicle 2?

Answer ☐

2

This diagram shows a steep downward hill with an obstruction on the right-hand side of the road. Which vehicle should be given priority, vehicle 1 or vehicle 2?

Answer ☐

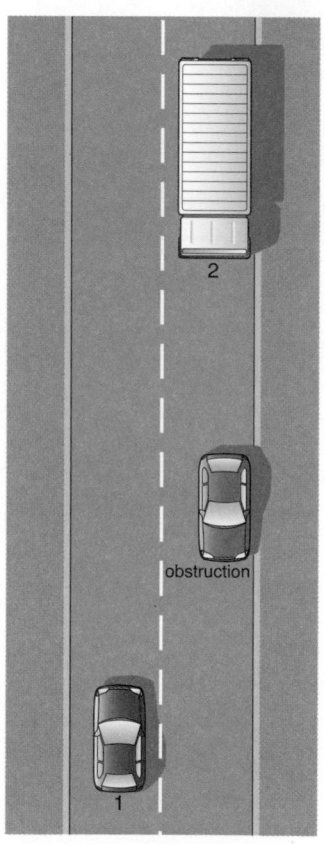

Answers on page 100

3

The diagram shows two vehicles, travelling in opposite directions, turning right at a crossroads.

Are these statements true or false?

Tick the appropriate boxes   **True False**

1 The safest route is to pass each other offside to offside. ☐ ☐

2 If the approaching vehicle flashes its headlamps, I should turn as quickly as possible. ☐ ☐

3 I should always try to get eye-to-eye contact with the driver of the other vehicle to determine which course to take. ☐ ☐

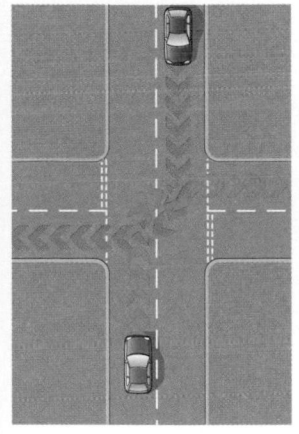

4

Which of the following factors, illustrated in the diagram, should be taken into consideration when turning right into a side road?

Tick the appropriate boxes   **YES NO**

1 The speed of the approaching vehicle (A) ☐ ☐

2 The roadworks ☐ ☐
3 The speed of vehicle B ☐ ☐
4 The cyclist ☐ ☐
5 Your speed (vehicle C) ☐ ☐
6 The pedestrians ☐ ☐
7 The car waiting to turn right (D) ☐ ☐

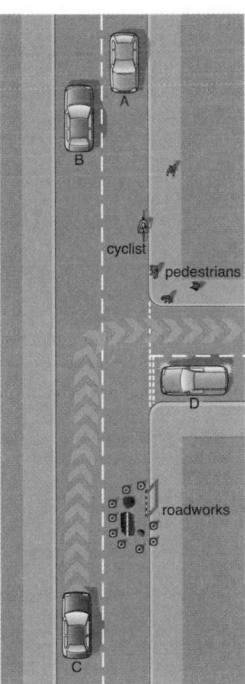

Answers on page 100

1

Are the following statements true or false when stopping in an emergency?

Tick the appropriate boxes   True   False

1 Stopping in an emergency ☐ ☐
increases the risk of skidding.

2 I should push the brake pedal ☐ ☐
down harder as I slow down.

3 It is important to react quickly. ☐ ☐

4 I should always remember ☐ ☐
to look in my mirrors as I
slow down.

5 I should signal left to tell ☐ ☐
other road users what I
am doing.

6 I should keep both hands ☐ ☐
on the wheel.

7 I should always check my ☐ ☐
mirrors and look round
before moving off.

2

Is the following statement true or false? An emergency stop will be carried out on every driving test

Tick the correct box   YES ☐   NO ☐

3

Cadence braking is a technique which can be used in very slippery conditions in an emergency.

Fill in the missing words

The technique requires you to p_ _ _ the brake pedal.

The procedure to follow is:

1 Apply m_ _ _ _ _ _ pressure.

2 Release the brake pedal just as the wheels are about to l_ _ _.

3 Then q_ _ _ _ _ _ apply the brakes again. Apply and release the brakes until the vehicle has stopped. This technique should only be used in emergency situations.

4

Anti-lock braking systems (ABS)* work in a similar way to cadence braking.

Fill in the missing words

When braking in an emergency, ABS brakes allow you to s_ _ _ _ and b_ _ _ _ at the same time. You do not have to p_ _ _ the brakes as you would in cadence braking. When using ABS you keep the p_ _ _ _ _ _ _ applied.

> **HINTS ✓ & TIPS**
> If a vehicle is travelling too close behind you, then increase the gap you have ahead. Always think for the driver behind.

Answers on page 101

Are these statements about ABS braking true or false?

Tick the appropriate boxes   True   False

1 Cars fitted with ABS braking ☐ ☐
cannot skid.

2 I do not need to leave as ☐ ☐
much room between me and
the car in front if I have ABS
brakes because I know I can
stop in a shorter distance.

**ABS is a registered trade mark of Bosch
(Germany). ABS stands for Anti-Blockiersystem.
The English translation is Anti-lock Braking System*

The distance taken for a car to reach stopping point divides into thinking distance and braking distance.

5

Could these factors affect thinking distance?

Tick the appropriate boxes   YES   NO

1 The condition of your tyres ☐ ☐
2 Feeling tired or unwell ☐ ☐
3 Speed of reaction ☐ ☐
4 Going downhill ☐ ☐

6

Most drivers' reaction time is well over ...

Tick the appropriate box

½ second ☐
1 second ☐
5 seconds ☐

7

Stopping distance depends partly on the speed at which the car is travelling.

Complete the sentences

1 At 30mph your overall stopping distance
will be __ __ metres or __ __ feet.

2 At 50mph your thinking distance will
be __ __ metres or __ __ feet.

3 At 70mph your overall stopping distance
will be __ __ metres or __ __ __ feet.

8

Stopping distance also varies according to road conditions.

Complete the sentences

In wet weather your vehicle will take
l __ __ __ __ __ to stop. You should
therefore allow m __ __ __ time.

9

Too many accidents are caused by drivers driving too close to the vehicle in front. A safe gap between you and the vehicle in front can be measured by noting a stationary object and counting in seconds the time that lapses between the vehicle in front passing that object and your own vehicle passing that object.

Complete the sentence

Only a fool b __ __ __ __ __ the t __ __
s __ __ __ __ __ rule.

Answers on page 101

1

Are these statements about moving off at an angle true or false?

Tick the appropriate boxes   True False

1 I should check my mirrors as ☐ ☐
  I am pulling out.

2 I should check my mirrors ☐ ☐
  and blindspot before I pull out.

3 I should move out as quickly ☐ ☐
  as possible.

4 The amount of steering ☐ ☐
  required will depend on how
  close I am to the vehicle in front.

5 I should look for oncoming ☐ ☐
  traffic.

6 As long as I am signalling, ☐ ☐
  people will know what I am
  doing. I will be able to pull out
  because somebody will let me in.

2

Are these statements about moving off uphill true or false?

Tick the appropriate boxes   True False

1 On an uphill gradient the car ☐ ☐
  will tend to roll back.

2 To stop the car rolling back I ☐ ☐
  need to use more acceleration.

3 I do not need to use the ☐ ☐
  handbrake.

4 The biting point may be ☐ ☐
  slightly higher.

5 I need to press the accelerator ☐ ☐
  pedal further down than
  when moving off on the level.

6 I need to allow more time ☐ ☐
  to pull away.

7 The main controls I use will ☐ ☐
  be the clutch pedal, the
  accelerator pedal and
  the handbrake.

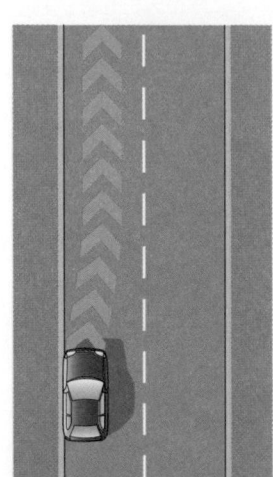

*Answers on
page 102*

3

Are these statements about moving off downhill true or false?

Tick the appropriate boxes

	True	False
1 The car will tend to roll forwards.	☐	☐
2 The main controls I use will be the handbrake, the clutch pedal and the accelerator pedal.	☐	☐
3 The only gear I can move off in is 1st gear.	☐	☐

	True	False
4 I should release the handbrake while keeping the foot-brake applied.	☐	☐
5 I should look round just before moving off.	☐	☐
6 I must not have my foot on the foot-brake as I start to release the clutch.	☐	☐

Answers on page 102

4

The following statements are about approaching a junction when going uphill or downhill. With which do you agree?

When going downhill ...	YES	NO
1 It is more difficult to slow down	☐	☐
2 Putting the clutch down will help slow the car down	☐	☐
3 The higher the gear, the greater the control	☐	☐
4 When changing gear you may need to use the foot-brake at the same time as the clutch	☐	☐

When going uphill ...	YES	NO
5 Early use of mirrors, signals, brakes, gears and steering will help to position the car correctly	☐	☐
6 You may need to use your handbrake more often	☐	☐
7 When you change gear, the car tends to slow down	☐	☐

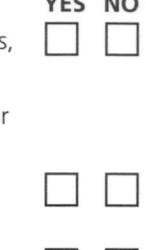

Answers on page 102

1

Before reversing there are three things to consider.

Fill in the missing words

1 Is it s_ _ _?
2 Is it c_ _ _ _ _ _ _ _ _ _?
3 Is it within the l_ _?

2

Are the following statements about reversing true or false?

Tick the appropriate boxes   **True**   **False**

1 Other road users should see what I am doing and wait for me. ☐ ☐

2 I should wave pedestrians on, so that I can get on with the manoeuvre more quickly. ☐ ☐

3 I should avoid being too hesitant. ☐ ☐

4 I should avoid making other road users slow down or change course. ☐ ☐

3

How should you hold the steering wheel when reversing left?
Which is correct?   Answer ☐

A   B   C

4

These statements are all about reversing.

Tick those which you think are correct

   True   **False**

1 My car will respond differently in reverse gear. ☐ ☐

2 My car will feel no different. ☐ ☐

3 Steering is not affected. The car responds the same as when going forward. ☐ ☐

4 The steering will feel different. I will have to wait for the steering to take effect. ☐ ☐

5

Which way will the rear of the car go when it is reversed? Left or right?

A   B

Answer _____   Answer _____

Answers on page 103

6

It is important to move the vehicle slowly when reversing.

Complete the sentence

Moving the vehicle slowly is safer because I have control and it allows me to carry out good o_ _ _ _ _ _ _ _ _ _ checks.

7

When reversing, good observation is vital. Where should you look?

Tick the correct answer

1 At the kerb ☐
2 Ahead ☐
3 Where your car is going ☐
4 Out of the back window ☐

8

Are these statements about reversing round a corner true or false?

Tick the correct boxes

	True	False
1 If the corner is sharp, I need to be further away from the kerb.	☐	☐
2 The distance from the kerb makes no difference.	☐	☐
3 I should try to stay reasonably close to the kerb all the way round.	☐	☐

9

Before reversing I should check ...

Tick the correct box

1 Behind me ☐
2 Ahead and to the rear ☐
3 My door mirrors ☐
4 All round ☐

10

Which position is the correct one in which to start steering?

A, B, C or D? Answer ☐

11

Which way should you steer?

Answer _____

12

What will happen to the front of the car?

Answer _____

Answers on page 103

13

Are these statements about steering when reversing round a corner true or false?

Tick the appropriate boxes   True False

1 The more gradual the corner, ☐ ☐
the less I have to steer.

2 I need to steer the same for ☐ ☐
every corner.

3 The sharper the corner, the ☐ ☐
more I have to steer.

14

**As I enter the new road, I should continue to keep a look-out for p_ _ _ _ _ _ _ _ _ _ and other r_ _ _ u_ _ _ _ _.
I should s_ _ _ if necessary.**

Complete the sentences

15

True or false? When reversing from a major road into a side road on the right, I have to move to the wrong side of the road.

Tick the correct box **True** ☐ **False** ☐

16

Which diagram shows the correct path to follow when moving to the right-hand side of the road? A or B?

Answer ☐

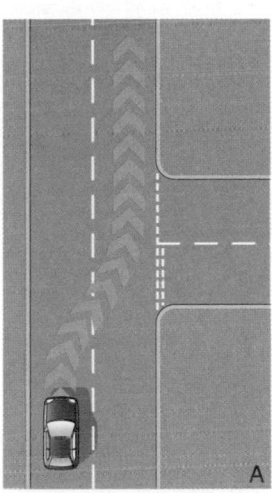

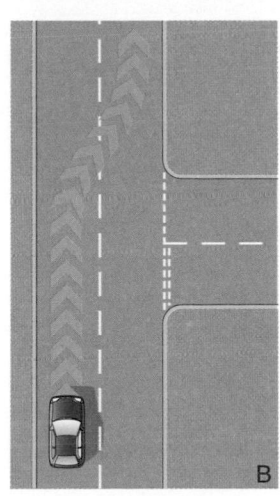

Answers on page 103

17

Which of the following correctly describes your sitting position for reversing to the right?

1 I will need to sit so that I can see over my right shoulder.

2 I will need to sit so that I can see over my right shoulder, ahead and to the left.

3 My position is the same as when reversing to the left.

Which statement is correct? 1, 2 or 3

Answer ☐

18

True or false? I may need to change my hand position on the wheel.

Tick the correct box **True** ☐ **False** ☐

19

True or false? It is easier to judge my position from the kerb when reversing to the right than when reversing to the left.

Tick the correct box **True** ☐ **False** ☐

20

Reversing to the right is more dangerous than reversing to the left because ...

1 I cannot see as well

2 I am on the wrong side of the road

3 I might get in the way of vehicles emerging from the side road

Which statement is correct – 1, 2 or 3?

Answer ☐

21

How far down the side road would you reverse before moving over to the left-hand side?

Which diagram is correct? A or B?

Answer ☐

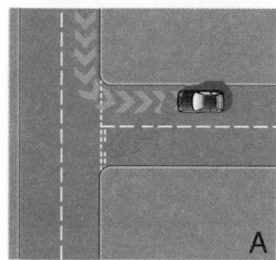

A

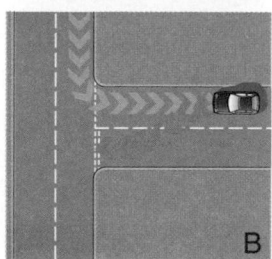

B

Answers on page 103

22

Look at the diagrams and decide which is safer.

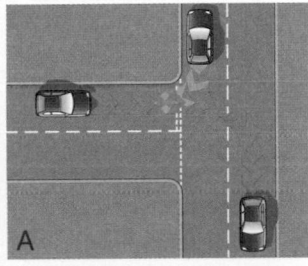

A Reversing into a side road

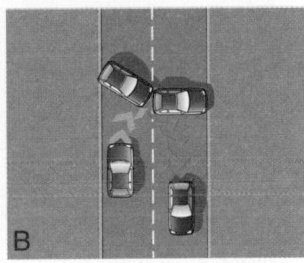

B Turning round in the road

Answer ☐

23

The secret of turning in the road is to move the vehicle s_ _ _ _ _ and steer b_ _ _ _ _ _.

Complete the sentence

24

I must be able to complete the manoeuvre in three moves: 1 forward, 2 reverse, 3 forward. True or false?

Tick the correct box   **True** ☐   **False** ☐

25

Before manoeuvring what should you take into consideration?

Tick the correct boxes

1 The size of your engine ☐
2 The width of the road ☐
3 The road camber ☐
4 The steering circle of your vehicle ☐
5 Parking restrictions ☐

26

Before moving forward, it is important to check a_ _ r_ _ _ _ for other road users.

Complete the sentence

> HINTS ✓ & TIPS
>
> When taking your test, you will be assessed on how well you can control the car; so don't rush your manoeuvres.

Answers on page 104

27

Turning in the road requires proper use of the steering wheel.

Answer the following questions…

1 When going forwards, which way should you steer?

Answer _____

2 Before you reach the kerb ahead, what should you do?

Answer _____

3 When reversing, which way should you steer?

Answer _____

4 Before you reach the kerb behind you, what should you do?

Answer _____

5 As you move forward again, which way should you steer to straighten up?

Answer _____

28

Reversing is a potentially dangerous manoeuvre. Good observation is essential.

Answer the following questions

1 If you are steering left when reversing, which shoulder should you look over?

Answer _____

2 As you begin to steer to the right, where should you look?

Answer _____

29

When parking between two cars …

1 The car is more manoeuvrable when driving forwards

2 The car is more manoeuvrable when reversing

3 There is no difference between going into the space forwards or reversing into it

Which statement is correct? 1, 2 or 3?

Answer ☐

HINTS ✔ **& TIPS**

In your driving test you may be asked to reverse into a parking bay at the test centre, or to park behind another car, using reverse gear. So make sure you practise these manoeuvres.

Answers on page 104

30

The diagram shows a car preparing to reverse into a parking space. Which position is the correct one in which to start steering left, A, B, C or D?

Answer ☐

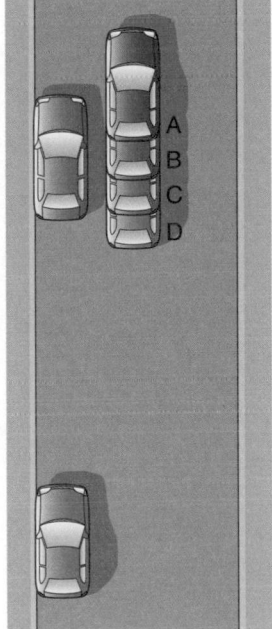

31

With practice you should be able to park in a gap ...

1 Your own car length

2 1½ times your own car length

3 2 times your own car length

4 2½ times your own car length

Answer ☐

32

Use the diagram to help you answer the following questions.

1 Which way would you steer?

Answer _____

2 At this point what would you try to line up with the offside (right-hand side) of your vehicle?

Answer _____

3 As you straighten up what do you have to be careful of?

Answer _____

4 What do you need to do to straighten up?

Answer _____

5 What would you need to do in order to position the vehicle parallel to the kerb?

Answer _____

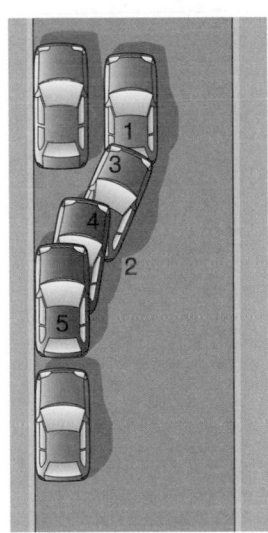

*Answers on
page 104*

33

True or false? During my driving test ...

Tick the correct boxes

	True	False
1 I will certainly be asked to perform the manoeuvre in Question 32	☐	☐
2 I have to be able to park in a tight space between two cars	☐	☐
3 It may be that only the lead car is present	☐	☐

34

When carrying out this manoeuvre, where is it important to look?

Answer _____

35

Look at the diagram and answer the following question.

Which bay should you use and why?

Answer _____

_____

_____

36

Why, wherever possible, should you choose to reverse into a parking bay?

Answer _____

_____

_____

_____

37

As well as being very aware of how c_ _ _ _ I am to the parked cars on either side, I should also be alert for cars moving near me from all d_ _ _ _ _ _ _ _ _, as well as the possibility of p_ _ _ _ _ _ _ _ _ _ walking around my car.

Complete the sentence

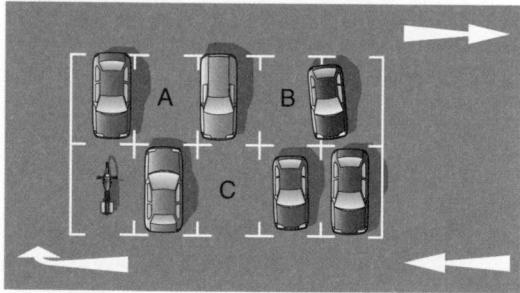

Answers on page 104

1

Traffic lights have three lights, red, amber, and green, which change from one to the other in a set order. Number the boxes 1 to 5 to show the correct order. The first answer has been filled in to give you a start.

☐ Amber   1 Red   ☐ Red and amber
☐ Red   ☐ Green

2

What do the colours mean?
Fill in the correct colour for each of the following
1 Go ahead if the way is clear.
Colour _____
2 Stop and wait.
Colour _____
3 Stop unless you have crossed the stop line or you are so close to it that stopping might cause an accident.
Colour _____
4 Stop and wait at the stop line.
Colour _____

3

Which of the following statements are true?
On approach to traffic lights you should ...
Tick the appropriate boxes
1 Speed up to get through before they change ☐

2 Be ready to stop ☐
3 Look for pedestrians ☐
4 Sound your horn to urge pedestrians to cross quickly ☐

4

Some traffic lights have green filters. Do they mean ...
1 You can filter in the direction of the arrow only when the main light is showing green?
2 You can filter even when the main light is not showing green?
Answer ☐

5

The diagram shows the three lanes at a set of traffic lights.
Which lane would you use for ...
1 Going ahead   Answer _____
2 Turning right   Answer _____
3 Turning left   Answer _____

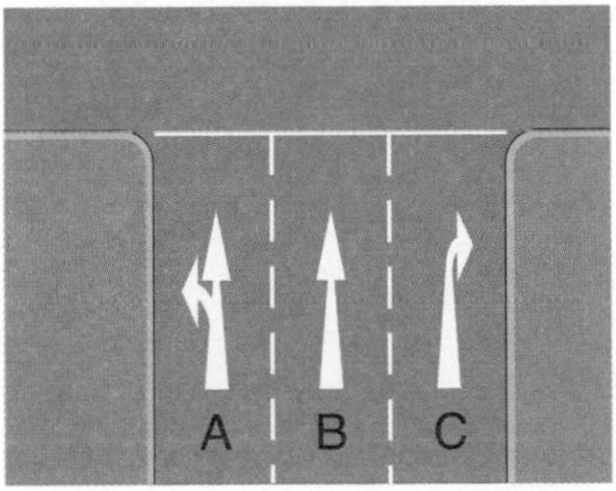

Answers on page 105

6

At some traffic lights and junctions you will see yellow criss-cross lines (box junctions). Can you ...

Tick the correct boxes

	Yes	No
1 Wait within them when going ahead if your exit is not clear?	☐	☐
2 Wait within them when going right if your exit is not clear?	☐	☐
3 Wait within them if there is oncoming traffic stopping you turning right but your exit is clear?	☐	☐

Answers on page 105

Pedestrians have certain rights of way at pedestrian crossings.

7

On approaching a zebra crossing, drivers will notice four features. Name them

1 _____

_____

2 _____

_____

3 _____

_____

4 _____

_____

8

Are these statements about pedestrian crossings true or false?

Tick the correct boxes

	True	False
1 I cannot park or wait on the zig-zag lines on the approach to a zebra crossing.	☐	☐
2 I cannot park or wait on the zig-zag lines on either side of the crossing.	☐	☐
3 I can overtake on the zig-zag lines on the approach to a crossing as long as the other vehicle is travelling slowly.	☐	☐
4 I must give way to a pedestrian once he/she has stepped on to the crossing.	☐	☐

5 If, on approach to a crossing, □ □
I intend to slow down or
stop, I may use a
slowing-down arm signal.

9

**On approaching a pelican crossing,
drivers will notice three key features.
Name them**

1 _____

_____

_____

_____

2 _____

_____

_____

_____

3 _____

_____

_____

_____

10

**If you see a pedestrian at a zebra
crossing or pelican crossing carrying a
white stick, do you think ...**

Tick the correct box

1 He/she has difficulty walking? □

2 He/she is visually impaired? □

11

**The traffic lights at a pelican crossing
have the same meaning as ordinary
traffic lights, but they do not have a red
and amber phase.**

1 What do they show instead of the red and
amber phase?

Answer _____

_____

2 What does the light mean?

Answer _____

_____

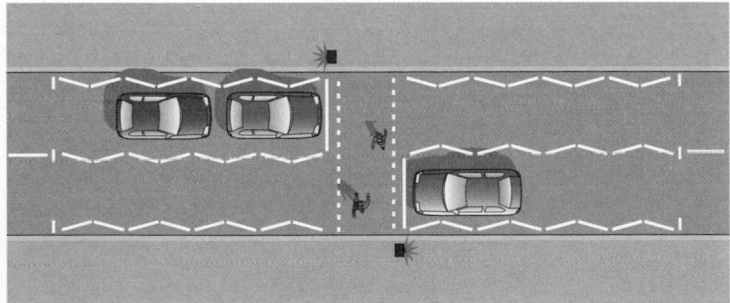

**Answers on pages 105–6**

12

What sound is usually heard at a pelican crossing when the green man is shown to pedestrians?

Answer _____

_____

_____

_____

13

Toucan and puffin crossings are similar to pelican crossings but with one main difference. Name it.

Answer _____

_____

_____

_____

14

As well as pedestrians, what other type of road users should you watch for at a toucan crossing?

Answer _____

_____

_____

_____

Answers on page 106

A level crossing is where the road crosses at a railway line. It is potentially dangerous and should be approached with caution.

15

Match each traffic sign below with its correct meaning.

1 Level crossing without gates or barriers ☐

2 Level crossing with lights ☐

3 Level crossing with gates or barriers ☐

4 Level crossing without lights ☐

16

If you break down on a level crossing, should you ...

Tick the appropriate boxes

1 Tell your passengers to wait in the vehicle while you go to get help? ☐

2 Get everybody out and clear of the crossing? ☐

3 Telephone the police? ☐

4 Telephone the signal operator? ☐

5 If there is still time, push your car clear of the crossing? ☐

One-way systems are where all traffic flows in the same direction.

1

Which of these signs means one-way traffic?

A

B

Answer ☐

2

Are these statements about one-way systems true or false?

Tick the correct boxes

	True	False
1 In one-way streets traffic can pass me on both sides.	☐	☐
2 Roundabouts are one-way systems.	☐	☐
3 For normal driving I should stay on the left.	☐	☐
4 I should look out for road markings and get in lane early.	☐	☐

As a rule, the more paint on the road, the more important the message.

3

Road markings are divided into three categories.

Fill in the missing words

1 Those which give

i _ _ _ _ _ _ _ _ _ _.

2 Those which give w _ _ _ _ _ _ _ _.

3 Those which give o _ _ _ _ _ _.

4

There are two main advantages which road markings have over other traffic signs. Name them.

1 _____

_____

2 _____

_____

Answers on page 106

5

What do these lines across the road mean?

1 Stop and give way
2 Give priority to traffic coming from the immediate right.
3 Give way to traffic coming from the right.
Answer ☐

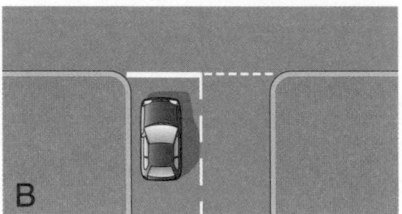

1 Give way to traffic on the major road.
2 Stop at the line and give way to traffic on the major road.
Answer ☐

6

Where you see double solid white lines painted along the centre of the road, what does this mean?
Tick any boxes you think are appropriate.
More than one answer may be correct.
1 I must not park or wait on the carriageway. ☐
2 I can park between 7pm and 7am. ☐
3 I must not overtake. ☐
4 I must not cross the white line except to turn right or in circumstances beyond my control. ☐

7

What is the purpose of these hatched markings (chevrons)?
Answer _____
_____

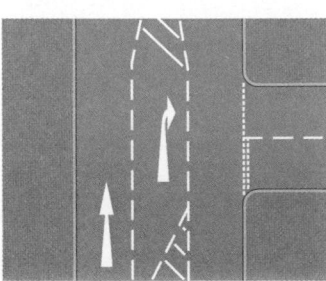

Answers on page 106

8

What does it mean if the chevrons are edged with a solid white line?

Answer _____

_____

The shape and colour of a sign will help you understand what it means.

9

Look at the sign shapes below and say whether each gives an order, a warning or information.

1

2

Answer _____ Answer _____

3

Answer _____

10

Complete the sentences

1 A circular sign with a blue background tells you what you m_ _ _ do.

2 A circular sign with a red border tells you what you m_ _ _ n_ _ do.

Answers on pages 106–7

11

What do these signs mean?

GIVE WAY

Answer _____

_____

_____

_____

STOP

Answer _____

_____

_____

12

Some junctions have a stop sign, others have a give way sign. *Complete the sentence*

A stop sign is usually placed at a junction where v_ _ _ _ _ is l_ _ _ _ _ _.

13

Information signs are colour-coded.

Match each of the following signs to its colouring.

A White letters on a brown background

B Black letters on a white background

C Black letters on a white background with a blue border

D White letters on a blue background with a white border

E White letters on a green background, yellow route numbers with a white border

☐ **M**otorway signs

☐ **P**rimary routes

☐ **O**ther routes

☐ **L**ocal places

☐ **T**ourist signs

1

Good observation is vital in today's busy traffic.

Complete the sentence

When using my mirrors I should try to make a mental note of the s_ _ _ _,
b_ _ _ _ _ _ _ _ and
i_ _ _ _ _ _ _ _ _ of the driver behind.

2

Driving in built-up areas is potentially dangerous.

Look at the diagram opposite

1 What action should the driver of car **A** take?

List four options

A _____

B _____

C _____

D _____

2 What action should the driver of car **B** take?

List four options

A _____

B _____

C _____

D _____

pedestrians

P

cyclist

B

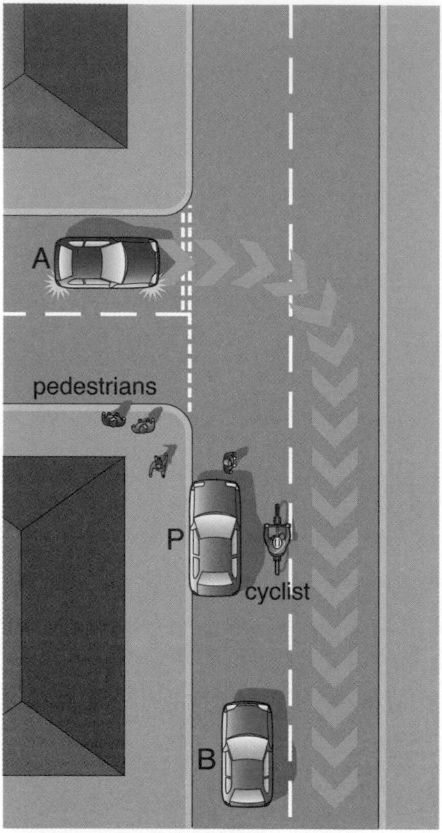

HINTS ✔ & TIPS

Observation means looking all around and seeing anything that matters. Don't stare at just one thing – keep your eyes moving.

Answers on pages 107–8

3

Motorcyclists are often less visible than other road users.

Complete this well-known phrase

Think once, think twice, think b__ __ __.

4

When you observe traffic following too close behind you, would you

Tick the correct box

1 Speed up to create a bigger gap? ☐

2 Touch your brake lights to warn the following driver? ☐

3 Keep to a safe speed, and keep checking the behaviour and intentions of the following driver? ☐

5

Some hazards are potential, others are actual and there all the time, such as a bend in the road.

A Name five more actual hazards

1 _____

_____

2 _____

_____

3 _____

_____

4 _____

_____

5 _____

_____

B Name five potential hazards, such as a dog off its lead

1 _____

_____

2 _____

_____

3 _____

_____

4 _____

_____

5 _____

_____

6

Modern driving requires full concentration. Are the following statements true or false?

Tick the correct boxes

	True	False
1 Carrying a mobile phone can reduce the stress of a long journey.	☐	☐
2 I must not use a hand-held phone while driving.	☐	☐
3 Conversation on a hands-free phone can still distract my attention.	☐	☐
4 I should pull up in a safe place to make or receive calls.	☐	☐

Answers on page 108

7

When driving, all the following actions have something in common.

What is it?

Reading a map

Eating

Changing a cassette

Listening to loud music

Answer _____

_____

_____

_____

One of the features of driving on the open road is taking bends properly.

8

As a rule you should be travelling at the correct s_ _ _ _, using the correct g_ _ _, and be in the correct p_ _ _ _ _ _ _.

9

Should you brake ...

Tick the appropriate box

1 Before you enter the bend?

2 As you enter the bend?

3 While negotiating the bend?

10

Which way does force push a car on a bend?

A Inwards or **B** Outwards

Answer ☐

11

What happens to the weight of the car when you use the brakes?

A It is thrown forwards

B It remains even

C It is thrown back

Answer ☐

Answers on page 108

12

When you approach a bend, what position should you be in?

Complete the sentences

A On a right-hand bend I should keep
to the _____
_____

B On a left-hand bend I should keep
to the_____
_____

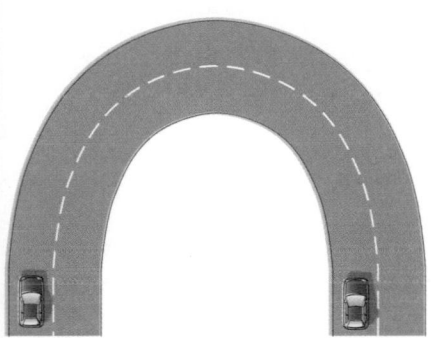

Overtaking is a potentially dangerous manoeuvre.

13

Before overtaking, consider whether it is really n__ __ __ __ __ __ __ __.

Fill in the missing word

Always use the safety routine when overtaking.

Put these actions into their correct sequence by putting numbers 1 to 7, as seen in the diagram, in the boxes

☐ Signal ☐ Mirrors ☐ Look
☐ Position ☐ Mirrors ☐ Speed
☐ Manoeuvre

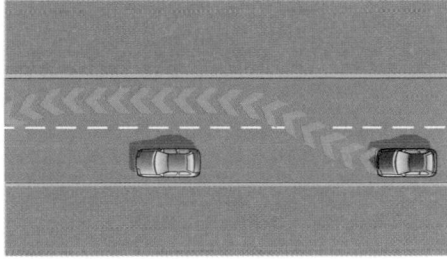

14

What is the minimum amount of clearance you should give a cyclist or motor cyclist?

Answer _____
_____

Answers on pages 108–9

15

There are four situations in which you may, with caution, overtake on the left-hand side of the car in front.

Name them

1 _____
_____
_____

2 _____
_____
_____

3 _____
_____
_____

4 _____
_____
_____

16

List four places where it would be dangerous to overtake.

1 _____
_____
_____

2 _____
_____
_____

3 _____
_____
_____

4 _____
_____
_____

17

Dual carriageways can appear similar to motorways, but there are important differences. Which of the following statements apply to dual carriageways?

Tick the relevant boxes

1 Reflective studs are not used. ☐

2 Cyclists are allowed. ☐

3 The speed limit is always 60mph. ☐

4 You cannot turn right to enter or leave a dual carriageway. ☐

5 Milk floats and slow moving farm vehicles are prohibited. ☐

18

When turning right from a minor road on to a dual carriageway, where would you wait ...

A When there is a wide central reserve?

Answer _____
_____

B When the central reserve is too narrow for your car?

Answer _____
_____

19

When travelling at 70mph on a dual carriageway, which lane would you use?

Answer _____

Answers on pages 109–10

20

What do these signs mean?

A

Answer _____

B

Answer _____

C

Answer _____

21

Which of the signs in Question 20 (see opposite) would you expect to see on a dual carriageway?

Answer _____

_____

_____

_____

22

Why is it important to plan your movements especially early when leaving a dual carriageway to the right (see diagram below)?

Answer _____

_____

_____

_____

Answers on page 110

1

Cars fitted with automatic transmission select the gear depending on the road speed and the load on the engine. They therefore have no c_ _ _ _ _ _ pedal.

Fill in the missing word

2

The advantages of an automatic car are ...

1 _____
   _____

2 _____
   _____

3

The gear selector has the same function as a manual selector, but what function do each of the following have?

P   Park_____
    _____

R   Reverse_____
    _____

N   Neutral_____
    _____

D   Drive_____
    _____

3   3rd_____
    _____

2   2nd_____
    _____

1   1st_____
    _____

4

Automatic cars have a device called a kickdown. Is its function ...

Tick the correct box

1 To select a higher gear? ☐

2 To select a lower gear manually? ☐

3 To provide quick acceleration when needed? ☐

5

When driving an automatic car, would you select a lower gear ...

Tick the appropriate boxes

	Yes	No
1 To control speed when going down a steep hill?	☐	☐
2 To slow the car down in normal driving?	☐	☐
3 When going uphill?	☐	☐
4 To overtake, in certain circumstances?	☐	☐
5 When manoeuvring?	☐	☐
6 Before stopping?	☐	☐

6

An automatic car has two foot pedals, the foot-brake and the accelerator.

For normal driving, which foot would you use ...

1 For the brake?
Answer _____

2 For the accelerator?
Answer _____

Answers on pages 110–11

7

When you are driving an automatic car, using one foot to control both pedals is preferable to using both the left and the right foot. Why?

Answer _____

_____

8

Some cars with automatic transmission have a tendency to 'creep'.

Which gears allow the car to creep?

Answer _____

_____

9

When driving an automatic car, would you use the handbrake ...

Tick the correct box

1 More than in a manual car? ☐

2 The same? ☐

3 Less? ☐

10

In which position should the gear selector be when you are starting the engine?

Answer _____

or _____

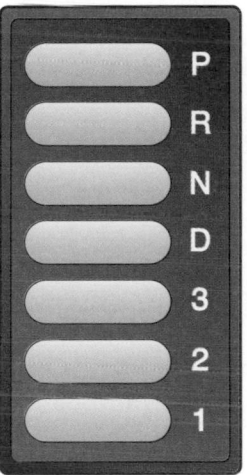

11

As you approach a bend, an automatic car will sometimes change up because there is less pressure on the accelerator. What should you do to prevent this happening?

Tick the correct box

1 Slow down before the bend and accelerate gently as you turn. ☐

2 Brake as you go round the bend. ☐

3 Brake and accelerate at the same time. ☐

HINTS & TIPS

Remember – if you haven't got your foot on the brake when you select Drive in an automatic car, the vehicle may begin to move forward

Answers on page 111

1

There are many myths and misunderstandings surrounding the driving test.

Are the following true or false?

Tick the correct boxes **True False**

1 The driving test is designed ☐ ☐
to see whether I can drive
around a test route without
making any mistakes.

2 The driving test is designed ☐ ☐
to see whether I can drive
safely under various traffic
conditions.

3 I do not need to know any ☐ ☐
of The Highway Code.

4 The examiner has a set ☐ ☐
allocation of passes
each week.

5 I may be expected to drive ☐ ☐
up to the maximum national
speed limit, where appropriate.

2

The length of the normal driving test is approximately ...

Tick the correct box

1 60 minutes ☐

2 90 minutes ☐

3 40 minutes ☐

3

If, during the test, you do not understand what the examiner says to you, you would take a guess because you must not talk to him or her.

Is this statement true or false?

Tick the correct box **True** ☐ **False** ☐

4

You may have heard people say that it is easier to pass the driving test in certain parts of the country.

Tick the correct box **Yes No**

Do you agree with this ☐ ☐
statement?

5

If you fail your test, you can take it again. Which of the following statements is correct?

Tick the correct box(es)

1 If you fail the test, you can apply straight
away for another appointment. ☐

2 If you fail the test you have to wait a
month before you can apply for another
appointment. ☐

3 You can re-take your test, subject to
appointment availability, any time. ☐

4 You have to wait 10 working days before
you can re-take the test. ☐

Answers on page 111

6

Before the practical part of your test, the examiner will test your eyesight. This is done by asking you to read a new-style number plate at a distance of ...

Tick the correct box

1 30.5 metres (100 feet) ☐

2 20 metres (67 feet) ☐

3 40.5 metres (133 feet) ☐

7

What will happen if you fail your eyesight test?

Answer _____

_____

8

It is essential that you take both sections of your p_ _ _ _ _ _ _ _ _ _ l_ _ _ _ _ _ to the test centre.

9

The examiner will expect you to drive without making any mistakes. Do you think this statement is true or false?

Tick the correct box **True** ☐ **False** ☐

10

When reversing, are you allowed to undo your seat belt?

Tick the correct box **Yes** ☐ **No** ☐

11

If you fail your test, what will the examiner do?

1 _____

_____

2 _____

_____

12

When you have passed your driving test, what are you entitled to do?

1 _____

_____

2 _____

_____

3 _____

_____

13

I have within the last month passed my test. Can I supervise a learner driver?

Tick the correct box **Yes** ☐ **No** ☐

Answers on page 112

14

When you have passed your test, what will the Examiner do with your provisional licence?

Answer _____

_____

15

While you are waiting for your full licence to be sent to you, can you drive legally?

Tick the correct box   **Yes** ☐   **No** ☐

16

It is recommended that you take further tuition once you have passed your test, especially on motorway driving.

Complete the sentence

As a learner driver you will not have experienced the special r__ __ __ __ that apply on the motorway and the h__ __ __ s__ __ __ __ of the other traffic.

17

While taking your driving test, you should drive ...

Tick the correct box

1 Especially carefully, keeping about 5mph below the speed limit ☐

2 As you would normally drive with your instructor ☐

3 With confidence, keeping at or just over the speed limit, to show that you can really drive ☐

18

Can you take a driving test if you are deaf?

Tick the correct box   **Yes** ☐   **No** ☐

Answers on page 112

The driving test ensures that all drivers reach a minimum standard.

1

Do you think that learning to drive ends with passing the test?

Tick the correct box   Yes ☐   No ☐

2

What knowledge and skills are not necessarily assessed in the present driving test?

List three

1 _____

_____

2 _____

_____

3 _____

_____

3

Which of these statements do you think best describes advanced driving?

Tick the correct box

1 Advanced driving is learning to handle your car to its maximum performance. ☐

2 Advanced driving is learning to drive defensively with courtesy and consideration to others. ☐

3 Advanced driving is learning to drive fast. ☐

4

Some people have difficulty in driving at night.
Which age group would you expect, in general, to experience most difficulties?

Tick the correct box

1 Older people ☐

2 Younger people ☐

5

Once you have passed your driving test, your licence is usually valid until you reach __ __ years of age.

Complete the sentence

6

There are particular circumstances under which you are required to take a driving test again. Name them

Answer _____

_____

_____

HINTS ✓ & TIPS

Driving is a skill you can improve for the rest of your life; consider further training after the test.

Answers on page 113

7

Motorways are designed to enable traffic to travel faster in greater safety. Compared to other roads, are they statistically ...

Tick the correct box

1 Safer? ☐

2 Less safe? ☐

3 No different? ☐

8

Are the following groups allowed on the motorway?

Tick the correct boxes

1 Provisional licence holders ☐

2 Motor cycles over 50cc ☐

3 Pedestrians ☐

4 HGV learner drivers ☐

5 Newly qualified drivers with less than three months' experience ☐

6 Motor cycles under 125cc ☐

7 Cyclists ☐

9

There are some routine checks you should carry out on your car before driving on the motorway.
Name four of them

1 _____

_____

2 _____

_____

3 _____

_____

4 _____

_____

10

On the motorway, if something falls from either your own or another vehicle, should you ...

Tick the correct box

1 Flash your headlights to inform other drivers? ☐

2 Pull over, put your hazard warning lights on and quickly run on to the motorway to collect the object? ☐

3 Pull over on to the hard shoulder, use the emergency telephone to call the police? ☐

4 Flag another motorist down to get help? ☐

Answers on page 113

11

Which colour do you associate with motorway signs?

Tick the correct box

1 Black lettering on a white background ☐

2 White lettering on a green background ☐

3 White lettering on a blue background ☐

12

At night or in poor weather conditions, your headlights will pick out reflective studs. Match the colour of the studs to their function by placing the appropriate letter in the box.

A Amber **B** Red **C** Green **D** White

1 Marks the edge of the hard shoulder ☐

2 Marks the edge of the central reservation ☐

3 Marks the lane lines ☐

4 Marks exits and entrances ☐

13

Do the broken lines at the end of the acceleration lane mean ...

Tick the correct box

1 The edge of the carriageway? ☐

2 Other traffic should let you in? ☐

3 Give way to traffic already on the carriageway? ☐

14

If you see congestion ahead, is it legal to use your hazard warning lights to warn drivers behind you?

Tick the correct box   **Yes** ☐   **No** ☐

15

What is the most common cause of accidents on motorways?

Tick the correct box

1 Vehicles breaking down ☐

2 Drivers falling asleep ☐

3 Drivers travelling too fast, too close to the vehicle in front ☐

4 Fog ☐

16

Are the following statements true or false?

I can use the hard shoulder ...

Tick the correct boxes   **True**   **False**

1 To take a short break ☐ ☐

2 To stop and read a map ☐ ☐

3 To allow the children to stretch their legs ☐ ☐

4 To pull over in an emergency ☐ ☐

5 To answer a phone call ☐ ☐

Answers on pages 113–14

17

In normal driving on the motorway, you should overtake ...

Tick the correct box

1 On the right
2 On the left
3 On either side

Driving at night can cause problems.

18

Which of these statements do you think is correct?

Tick the correct box

1 Street lighting and my car's headlights mean that I can see just as well as in the daylight. Therefore driving at night is just like driving in the daylight.

2 At night I have to rely on my car's headlights and any additional lighting. Therefore I cannot see as far or drive as fast as in the daylight.

19

At dusk and dawn what action should you take to compensate for driving a dark coloured car?

Answer _____

_____

20

When driving after dark in a built-up area, should you use ...

Tick the correct box

1 Dipped headlights?
2 Side or dim-dipped lights?

21

The Highway Code says you should not use your horn in a built-up area between 11.30pm and 7am.

What is the exception to that rule?

Answer _____

_____

22

The diagram below illustrates two vehicles parked at night on a two-way road.

Which one is parked correctly?

Tick the correct box

A ☐   B ☐

Answers on page 114

23

Certain groups of road users are particularly vulnerable at night. Name two of them

1 _____

2 _____

24

Under what circumstances would you use dipped headlights during the day?

Answer _____

_____

and then complete the sentence

S__ __ and b__ s__ __ __.

25

When you are waiting at a junction after dark, your brake lights might d__ __ __ __ __ the driver behind. It is better to use your h__ __ __ __ __ __ __ __.

Complete the sentences

Certain weather conditions can create hazardous driving conditions in the summer as well as in the winter.

26

Which of the following causes greatest danger to drivers?

Tick the correct box

1 Snow ☐

2 Ice ☐

3 Heavy rain ☐

4 Not being able to see properly ☐

27

In wet weather conditions your tyres can lose their grip. You should allow at least d__ __ __ __ __ the distance between you and the car in front that you allow on a dry road.

Fill in the missing word

28

In very wet conditions there is a danger of a build-up of water between your tyres and the road. This is called a__ __ __ __ __ __ __ __ __.

Fill in the missing word

Answers on page 114

29

How can you prevent a build-up of water occurring?

S__ __ __ d__ __ __ .

30

How should you deal with floods?

Tick the correct box

1 Drive through as fast as possible to avoid stopping ☐

2 Drive through slowly in 1st gear, slipping the clutch to keep the engine speed high ☐

3 Drive through in the highest gear possible, slipping the clutch to keep the engine speed high ☐

31

Will less tread on your tyres ...

Tick the correct box

1 Increase your braking distance? ☐

2 Decrease your braking distance? ☐

32

When the tyres lose contact with the road, the steering will feel v__ __ __ l__ __ __ __.

Complete the sentence

33

After you have driven through a flood, should you check ...

Tick the correct box

1 Your speedometer? ☐

2 Your brakes? ☐

3 Your oil? ☐

34

There are certain key precautions you should take when driving in fog.

Complete the following sentences

1 S__ __ __ d__ __ __.

2 Ensure you are able to s__ __ __ within the distance you can see to be clear.

3 Use your w__ __ __ __ __ __ __ __ __ w__ __ __ __ __.

4 Use your d__ __ __ __ __ __ __ and your h__ __ __ __ __ r__ __ __ w__ __ __ __ __ __ __ __ __.

35

Under what circumstances should you use your rear fog lights?
When visibility is less than _____ metres/feet.

Fill in the correct number

Answers on page 114

36

When you are following another vehicle in fog, should you ...

Tick the correct box

1 Follow closely behind because it will help you see where you are going? ☐
2 Leave plenty of room between you and the vehicle in front? ☐

37

When you are following another vehicle in fog, should you use ...

Tick the correct box

1 Main beam headlights? ☐
2 Dipped headlights? ☐

38

Extra precautions are needed when dealing with a junction in fog.

Complete the following sentences

1 Open your w_ _ _ _ _ _ _ and switch off your a_ _ _ _ s_ _ _ _ _ _. L_ _ _ _ _ for other vehicles.
2 Signal e_ _ _ _ .
3 Use your b_ _ _ _ _ _. The light will a_ _ _ _ _ following vehicles.
4 Use your h_ _ _ _ if you think it will w_ _ _ other road users.

39

Is the following statement about anti-lock brakes true or false?
Anti-lock brakes will stop me skidding when driving on snow or ice.

Tick the correct box True ☐ False ☐

40

When driving in snow or ice you should gently test your b_ _ _ _ _ from time to time.

Fill in the missing word

41

In order to slow down when driving on snow or ice you should ...

Fill in the missing words

1 Use your brakes g_ _ _ _ .
2 Get into a l_ _ _ _ _ g_ _ _ earlier than normal.
3 Allow your speed to d_ _ _ _ and use b_ _ _ _ _ gently and early.

42

On snow or ice, braking distances can increase by ...

Tick the correct box

1 10 times ☐
2 5 times ☐
3 20 times ☐
4 15 times ☐

Answers on page 115

43

When going downhill in snow, what would you do to help you slow down?

Answer _____

_____

44

When cornering in snow or ice, what should you avoid doing?

Answer _____

_____

45

How can you reduce the risk of wheel spin?

Answer _____

_____

46

Three important factors cause a skid. Name them.

1 _____

_____

_____

2 _____

_____

_____

3 _____

_____

_____

47

Some everyday driving actions, especially in poor weather, can increase the risk of skidding.

Fill in the missing words

1 S_ _ _ _ _ _ down.

2 S_ _ _ _ _ _ _ up.

3 T_ _ _ _ _ _ corners.

4 Driving u_ _ _ _ _ and

  d_ _ _ _ _ _ _.

HINTS & TIPS

If you realise that your car is starting to skid, ease off the brake and accelerator, then steer smoothly in the same direction as the skid.

Answers on page 115

All vehicles need routine attention and maintenance to keep them in good working order. Neglecting maintenance can be costly and dangerous.

1

With which of these statements do you agree?

Tick the correct box

1 Allowing the fuel gauge to drop too low is bad for the engine. ☐

2 In modern cars the fuel level makes little difference. ☐

2

What do you put into the engine to lubricate the moving parts?

Answer _____

_____

_____

3

How frequently should you check your oil level?

Tick the correct box

1 Once a month ☐

2 Once a year ☐

3 Every time you fill up with fuel ☐

4

The engine is often cooled by a mixture of w_ _ _ _ _ and a_ _ _ _ _ f_ _ _ _ _.

Some engines are a_ _ cooled.

Complete the sentence

5

How frequently should you test your brakes?

Tick the correct box

1 Daily ☐

2 Monthly ☐

3 Weekly ☐

4 When I use them ☐

6

Incorrectly adjusted headlamps can cause d_ _ _ _ _ to other road users.

Complete the sentence

7

All headlamps, indicators and brake lights should be kept in good working order. It is also important that they are kept c_ _ _ _ _ .

Fill in the missing word

Answers on page 115

8

**Tyres should be checked for
u_ _ _ _ _ wear and tyre walls
for b_ _ _ _ _ and c_ _ _.**

Complete the sentence

9

**The legal requirement for tread depth is
not less than ...**

Tick the correct box

1 1.4mm

2 1.6mm

3 2mm

10

**What should you do if your brakes feel
slack or spongy?**

Answer _____

_____

_____

11

Vehicle breakdowns could result from ...

Fill in the missing words

1 N_ _ _ _ _ _ _ of the vehicle

2 Lack of r_ _ _ _ _ _ _

  c_ _ _ _ _

3 Little or no

  p_ _ _ _ _ _ _ _ _ _ _

  maintenance

4 A_ _ _ _ of the vehicle

Answers on page 115

12

**It is advisable to carry a warning
triangle.**

1 On a straight road how far back should
it be placed?

Tick the correct box

45 metres/yards

200 metres/yards

150 metres/yards

2 On a dual carriageway, how far back
should it be placed? At least ...

Tick the correct box

200 metres/yards

150 metres/yards

450 metres/yards

13

**If you use a warning triangle, is it worth
putting your hazard lights on as well?**

Tick the correct box Yes ☐ No ☐

14

**If your vehicle breaks down on a
motorway, should you ...**

Tick the correct box

1 Gently brake, put your hazard lights on
and seek assistance? ☐

2 Pull over to the central reservation as far to
the right as possible? ☐

3 Pull over safely on to the hard shoulder
as far away from the carriageway as
possible? ☐

15

If your vehicle has broken down on the motorway, should you tell your passengers to ...

Tick the correct box

1 Stay in the vehicle while you seek assistance? ☐

2 Wait by the car on the hard shoulder but watch for other vehicles? ☐

3 Get out of the vehicle and wait on the embankment away from the hard shoulder? ☐

16

The marker posts at the side of all motorways have a picture of a telephone handset.

How can you tell which way to walk to reach the nearest telephone?

Answer _____

_____

_____

17

When you use the emergency telephone on a motorway, what will the operator ask you?

1 _____
_____
_____

2 _____
_____
_____

3 _____
_____
_____

4 _____
_____
_____

18

Disabled drivers cannot easily get to an emergency telephone. How can they summon help?

1 _____
_____
_____

2 _____
_____
_____

Answers on page 116

19

If you break down when travelling alone, there are three things you are advised NOT to do.

Complete the sentences

1 Do not ask p__ __ __ __ __ __
m__ __ __ __ __ __ __ __ for help.

2 Do not accept help from anyone you
d__ n__ __ k__ __ __ (except the
emergency services or a breakdown
service).

3 Do not l__ __ __ __ you vehicle
l__ __ __ __ __ than necessary.

20

If I am first or one of the first to arrive at the scene of an accident, should I ...

Tick the correct boxes

	True	False
1 Always move injured people away from vehicles?	☐	☐
2 Tell the ambulance personnel or paramedics what I think is wrong with those injured?	☐	☐
3 Give casualties something warm to drink?	☐	☐
4 Switch off hazard warning lights?	☐	☐
5 Switch off vehicle engines?	☐	☐
6 Inform the police of the accident?	☐	☐

Answers on page 116

21

If you are involved in an accident, what MUST you do?

Answer _____

_____

_____

22

If you are involved in an accident and nobody is injured, do you have to call the police?

Tick the correct box   **Yes** ☐   **No** ☐

23

What information do you need to exchange if you are involved in an accident?

1 _____
_____
_____

2 _____
_____
_____

3 _____
_____
_____

4 _____
_____
_____

5 _____
_____
_____

24

If you thought you had a fire in your car's engine, what action would you take?

1 _____
_____
_____

2 _____
_____
_____

3 _____
_____
_____

25

There are three items of emergency equipment it is wise to carry in your car.

Fill in the missing words

1 F_ _ _ _ _ A_ _ kit.

2 F_ _ _ _
   e_ _ _ _ _ _ _ _ _ _ _ _ _.

3 W_ _ _ _ _ _ _ t_ _ _ _ _ _

26

When you rejoin a motorway from the hard shoulder, should you ...

Tick the correct box

1 Signal right and join when there is safe gap? ☐

2 Keep your hazard lights on and drive down the hard shoulder until there is a safe gap? ☐

3 Use the hard shoulder to build up speed and join the carriageway when safe? ☐

27

Fuel combustion causes waste products. One of these is a gas called

c_ _ _ _ _ d_ _ _ _ _ _.

This is a major cause of the

g_ _ _ _ _ _ _ _ _ effect.

Complete the sentences

28

How much does transport contribute to the production of carbon dioxide in the country (expressed as a percentage of the total production)?

Tick the correct box

1 10 per cent ☐
2 25 per cent ☐
3 50 per cent ☐
4 20 per cent ☐

Answers on page 117

29

The MOT test checks the roadworthiness of a vehicle.

Does it include an exhaust emission test?

Tick the correct box   **YES** ☐   **NO** ☐

30

A catalytic convertor stops the emission of carbon dioxide.

Tick the correct box   **True** ☐   **False** ☐

31

Which uses up more fuel?

Tick the correct box

1 A car travelling at 50mph ☐
2 A car travelling at 70mph ☐

32

There are some measures car drivers can take to help reduce damage to the environment.

List five

1 _____

_____

2 _____

_____

3 _____

_____

4 _____

_____

5 _____

_____

Before buying a used car it is best to decide what you want the car for and how much you can afford.

33

There are three main sources of supply for used vehicles. You can buy from a d_ _ _ _ _, at an a_ _ _ _ _ _ _ or p_ _ _ _ _ _ _ _.

Complete the sentence

34

When reading a glowing description of a used car, what should you first consider?

Answer _____

_____

_____

Answers on page 117

35

Are these statements about buying
a used car through a dealer or at an
auction true or false?

Tick the correct boxes   True   False

1 It is often cheaper to buy a   ☐   ☐
car at an auction than
through a dealer.

2 I have the same legal rights   ☐   ☐
when I buy at an auction as
when I buy from a dealer.

3 I should always read the   ☐   ☐
terms and conditions of
trade before I buy a car
at an auction.

4 The best way to select a   ☐   ☐
used car dealer is by
recommendation.

36

Cars bought through a dealer often have
a warranty.
What should you check?

1 _____
_____
_____

2 _____
_____
_____

37

When you test drive a vehicle, you
should make sure that it is t_ _ _ _,
has a current M_ _ certificate
(if applicable) and that all
i_ _ _ _ _ _ _ _ _ requirements are
complied with.

Complete the sentence

38

There are some important items that
you should check on before you buy a
used car.
List three

1 _____
_____
_____

2 _____
_____
_____

3 _____
_____
_____

39

Do you think the following statement is
true or false?
It is advisable to have my vehicle
examined by a competent and unbiased
expert before I buy.

Tick the correct box   **True** ☐   **False** ☐

Answers on page 117

Particular difficulties are encountered when towing a caravan or trailer. There are some very good courses which will help you master the skills required.

1

People can underestimate the length of the total combination of car and caravan or trailer.

Is the overall length usually ...

Tick the correct box

1 Twice the length of a normal car? ☐

2 Three times the length of a normal car? ☐

2

What additional fixtures should you attach to your car to help you see more clearly?

1 _____

_____

_____

3

When towing you will need more distance than normal to overtake. Is it ...

Tick the correct box

1 Twice the normal distance? ☐

2 Three times the normal distance? ☐

3 Four times the normal distance? ☐

4

A device called a s_____ will make the combination safer to handle.

Fill in the missing word

5

The stability of the caravan will depend on how you load it. Should heavy items be loaded ...

Tick the correct box

1 At the front? ☐

2 At the rear? ☐

3 Over the axle(s)? ☐

6

There are special restrictions for vehicles which are towing.

A What is the speed limit on a dual carriageway?

Tick the correct box

1 50mph ☐

2 60mph ☐

3 70mph ☐

B What is the speed on a single

Answers on page 118

carriageway?

Tick the correct box

1 40mph ☐
2 50mph ☐
3 60mph ☐

7

There are some important checks you should make before starting off.
List four

1 _____

  _____

2 _____

  _____

3 _____

  _____

4 _____

  _____

8

If you decide to stop to take a break, before allowing anyone to enter the caravan you should lower the

j_ _ _ _ _ w_ _ _ _ and

c_ _ _ _ _ s_ _ _ _ _ _ _.

Fill in the missing words

Many people now take their car abroad or hire a vehicle when on holiday.

9

Motoring organisations such as the Automobile Association can help you plan and organise your trip.
The AA can provide advice on travel and v_ _ _ _ _ _ insurance.
They will also help you organise the d_ _ _ _ _ _ _ _ that you will need.

Fill in the missing words

10

Before travelling to Europe, you should always ...

Complete the sentences

1 Plan the r_ _ _ _ _ you wish to take.
2 Know the local m_ _ _ _ _ _ _ _

  r_ _ _ _ _ _ _ _ _ _.

Answers on page 118

11

It is essential that your vehicle should be checked thoroughly.
List four of the routine checks you should make

1 _____
_____
_____

2 _____
_____
_____

3 _____
_____
_____

4 _____
_____
_____

12

In most European countries you are advised to carry your d_ _ _ _ _ _ _
l_ _ _ _ _ _ _ on you.

Complete the sentence

13

What do the letters IDP stand for?
Answer _____
_____
_____

14

Where might you need an IDP?
Answer _____
_____
_____

15

In most European countries what age do you have to be to drive?

Tick the correct box
1 ☐ 21 **2** ☐ 18 **3** ☐ 16

16

Some European countries can require you to carry additional emergency equipment.
List four of the items you are recommended to carry

1 _____
_____
_____

2 _____
_____
_____

3 _____
_____
_____

4 _____
_____
_____

Answers on page 118

Answers to questions

Answers to questions

INTRODUCTION TO LEARNING TO DRIVE

Questions on pages 28–9

A1 A current, signed, full or provisional licence for the category of vehicle that you are driving

A2 examinations
register

A3 21 years old
three years

A4 To the front and rear. It is important not to place them in windows where they could restrict good vision.

A5 True

A6 You should have answered No to all the questions.

A7 Yes. This should be the ambition of every driver.

A8 3, 4

ADJUSTING YOUR DRIVING POSITION

Questions on page 29

A9 **1** handbrake
2 doors
3 seat
4 head restraint
5 mirrors
6 seat belt

INTRODUCTION TO VEHICLE CONTROLS

Questions on pages 29–30

A10 The handbrake E
The driving mirrors D
The gear lever F
The clutch G
The steering wheel A
The foot-brake B
The accelerator C
gas

A11 The foot-brake R
The clutch L
The accelerator R

A12 **1** False. You will need one hand to change gear or use other controls.
2 True
3 False. The best position is quarter to three or ten to two.
4 False. It is safest to feed the wheel through your hands.
5 True
6 True

A13 The direction indicators B
Dipped beam A
Main beam D
Rear fog lamp C
Horn E
Hazard lights F

Section 2

MOVING OFF

Questions on page 31

A1 **A** 1
    B 5
    C 3
    D 2
    E 6
    F 4
    G 7
    H 8
    I 9

STOPPING (NORMALLY)

Questions on page 32

A2 **A** 1
    B 3
    C 2
    D 4
    E 6
    F 5
    G 8
    H 7
    I 9

GEAR CHANGING

Questions on pages 33–4

A3 1st gear

A4 5th, or 4th if the car has a 4-speed gear box

A5 Usually 2nd gear, but 1st if you need to go very slowly or 3rd if the corner is sweeping and you can take it safely at a higher speed

A6 engine
    vehicle
    sound
    when

A7 **A** 1
    B 3
    C 2
    D 4
    E 5

A8 **1** False. This will cause the engine to labour.

2 False. It is good practice to use the brakes to slow the car down. Using the transmission causes wear and tear which can be very costly. Also, the brakes are more effective.

3 False

4 True

5 False. It is good practice to miss out the unwanted gears and select the gear most appropriate to your road speed.

A9 **1**

A10 **1** Don't

2 Don't

3 Do

4 Do

5 Do

6 Don't

7 Don't

8 Don't

STEERING

Questions on page 35

A11 **A**, except in a few cars fitted with four-wheel steering (in which case all four wheels will move)

A12 **A**

A13 **B**

A14 **B**

ROAD POSITIONING

Questions on page 35

A15 **C** well to the left but not too close to the kerb

A16 **B**. Avoid swerving in and out. It is unnecessary and confuses other drivers.

CLUTCH CONTROL

Questions on page 36

A17 **A**

A18 biting

A19 **1** Yes

2 Yes

3 No

4 Yes

5 No

Section 3

JUNCTIONS
Questions on pages 37–9

A1 two or more roads

A2 **A** T-junction
B Y-junction
C Roundabout
D Staggered crossroads
E Crossroads

A3 **1** E
2 C
3 B
4 D
5 A

A4 **A** 1
B 3

A5 **1** Mirrors
2 Signal
3 Position
4 Speed
5 Look

A6 assess
decide
act

A7 **A**

A8 **B**

A9 **D**

A10 **1** mirrors, position
2 signal
3 safe
4 safe distance
5 overtake

CROSSROADS
Questions on page 40

A11 **A 3** Crossroads. Priority for traffic on the major road. Never assume other drivers will give you priority.
B 1 Unmarked crossroads
C 2 Crossroads with give way lines at the end of your road. Give way to traffic on the major road.

ROUNDABOUTS
Questions on pages 40–1

A12 **C**

A13 **1** Left
2 Left
3 Right. Remember to use the MSM routine before signalling left to turn off.

A14 **1** Left
2 Going ahead
3 Right

A15 mirrors
signal
position
speed
look

A16 **2**

Section 4

PARKING (ON THE ROAD)
Questions on pages 42–3

A1 **1** safe
   2 considerate
   3 legal
A2 Cars 1, 2, 3, 6
A3 **1** False
   2 False
   3 True
   4 True
A4 Any of the following:
   at a bus stop
   at a school entrance
   opposite a junction
   on a bend
   on the brow of a hill
   on a Clearway
   on a motorway
   at night facing oncoming traffic
   in a residents' parking zone.

Section 5

PASSING STATIONARY VEHICLES AND OBSTRUCTIONS

Questions on page 44
A1 Vehicle 2
A2 Vehicle 2, even though the obstruction is on the right. Where safe, when travelling downhill be prepared to give priority to vehicles (especially heavy vehicles) that are coming uphill.

MEETING AND CROSSING THE PATH OF OTHER VEHICLES
Questions on pages 45

A3 **1** True
   2 False. Always consider whether it is safe. Are there dangers the other driver cannot see? Remember, flashing headlamps has the same meaning as sounding the horn. It is a warning: 'I am here!' Sometimes it is taken to mean: 'I am here and I am letting you pass.'
   3 True
A4 **1** Yes
   2 Yes
   3 No
   4 Yes
   5 Yes
   6 Yes
   7 Yes

Section 6

STOPPING IN AN EMERGENCY
Questions on pages 46–7

A1 **1** True
2 True
3 True
4 False. Looking in the mirror should not be necessary. You should know what is behind you.
5 False
6 True
7 True

A2 False. An emergency stop will be conducted randomly on only some tests. You must always know how to stop safely in an emergency.

A3 pump
1 maximum
2 lock
3 quickly

A4 steer
brake
pump
pressure
1 False. Other elements beyond braking can cause skidding e.g. acceleration or going too fast into a bend.
2 False. Although you may stop in a shorter distance, you still need to leave the correct distance to allow yourself time to react and vehicles behind you time to stop.

STOPPING DISTANCES
Questions on page 47

A5 **1** No
2 Yes
3 Yes
4 No

A6 ½ second

A7 **1** 23 metres/75 feet
2 15 metres/50 feet
3 96 metres/315 feet

A8 longer
more

A9 breaks
two-second

Answers to questions

Section 7

MOVING OFF AT AN ANGLE

Question on page 48

A1 **1** False. You should check your mirrors and blindspot before moving out. Keep alert for other traffic as you pull out and stop if necessary.
2 True
3 False. Move out slowly and carefully.
4 True. The closer you are, the greater the angle.
5 True. As you move out, you are likely to move on to the right-hand side of the road and into conflict with oncoming vehicles.
6 False. You should signal only if it helps or warns other road users. Signalling gives you no right to pull out.

MOVING OFF UPHILL

Question on page 48

A2 **1** True
2 False. Using the accelerator pedal will not move the car forwards.
3 False. As your feet will be using the clutch pedal and the accelerator pedal you need to use the handbrake to stop the car rolling back.
4 True
5 True
6 True
7 True

MOVING OFF DOWNHILL

Question on page 49

A3 **1** True
2 False. Almost certainly you will need to use the foot-brake.
3 False. It is often better to move off in 2nd gear.
4 True. This will stop the car rolling forwards.
5 True
6 False. You will need to have your foot on the foot-brake to stop the car rolling forwards.

APPROACHING JUNCTIONS UPHILL AND DOWNHILL

Question on page 50

A4 The following statements are correct: 1, 4, 5, 6, 7

Section 8

REVERSING

Questions on pages 51–2

A1   safe
         convenient
         law
A2   **1** False
         2 False
         3 True
         4 True
A3   **A**
A4   **1, 4**
A5   Car A: to the left
         Car B: to the right
A6   observation

REVERSING INTO A SIDE ROAD ON THE LEFT

Questions on pages 52–3

A7   **3**
A8   **1** True
         2 False
         3 True
A9   **4**
A10 **C**
A11 Left

A12 The front of the car will swing out to the right
A13 **1** True
         2 False
         3 True
A14 pedestrians
         road users
         stop

REVERSING INTO A SIDE ROAD ON THE RIGHT

Questions on pages 53–54

A15 True
A16 **B**
A17 **2**
A18 True. You may need to place your left hand at 12 o'clock and lower your right hand.
A19 True
A20 **2**
A21 **B**

TURNING IN THE ROAD

Questions on pages 55–6

A22 A

A23 slowly
briskly

A24 False, but you should try to complete the manoeuvre in as few moves as possible.

A25 2, 3, 4

A26 all round

A27 **1** Right
2 Steer briskly left
3 Left
4 Steer briskly right
5 Right

A28 **1** Left
2 Over your right shoulder to where the car is going

REVERSE PARALLEL PARKING

Questions on pages 56–8

A29 2

A30 **C**, in line with the rear of the parked vehicle

A31 2

A32 **1** To the left
2 The nearside headlamp of the vehicle towards which you are reversing
3 Clipping the rear offside of the lead car
4 Take off the left lock
5 Steer to the right and then take off the right lock as you get straight

A33 **1** False
2 False
3 True. You will be expected to be able to complete the exercise within approximately two car lengths.

A34 All round, particularly for pedestrians and oncoming vehicles

A35 **C**. The other bay widths are reduced by parked vehicles. This may make opening doors a squeeze.

A36 Allows you to make best use of the area in front of the bay. Gives you a better view when driving out of the space

A37 close
directions
pedestrians

Section 9

TRAFFIC LIGHTS AND YELLOW BOX JUNCTIONS

Questions on pages 59–60

A1 **1** red
  2 red and amber
  3 green
  4 amber
  5 red

A2 **1** green
  2 red and amber
  3 amber
  4 red

A3 **1** False
  2 True
  3 True
  4 False. Pedestrians who are already crossing have priority.

A4 **2**

A5 **1** Lane A or B
  2 Lane C
  3 Lane A

A6 **1** No. If your exit is blocked you should not enter a yellow box junction.
  2 No. If your exit is blocked you should not enter a yellow box junction.
  3 Yes

PEDESTRIAN CROSSINGS

Questions on pages 60–2

A7 **1** Zig-zag lines
  2 Flashing yellow beacons on both sides of the road
  3 Black and white stripes on the crossing
  4 A give way line

A8 **1** True
  2 True. You must not park or wait on the zig-zag lines on either side of the crossing.
  3 False. You must not overtake on the zig-zag lines on approach to the crossing.
  4 True
  5 True. A slowing down arm signal should be used. It helps pedestrians understand what you intend to do. They cannot see your brake lights.

A9 **1** Traffic lights
  2 Zig-zag lines
  3 A white stop line

A10 **2** A white stick means the pedestrian is visually impaired. A white stick with two reflector bands means the pedestrian may be deaf as well as visually impaired.

Answers to questions

A11 **1** Flashing amber
2 You must give way to pedestrians on the crossing, but if it is clear you may go on.
A12 A bleeping tone. This sounds when the red light shows to drivers and helps visually impaired pedestrians know when it is safe to cross.
A13 There is no flashing amber light sequence. The light sequence is the same as normal traffic lights.
A14 cyclists

LEVEL CROSSINGS
Questions on page 62

A15 **A** 3
B 1
C 2
D 4
A16 **2**
4
5

ONE-WAY SYSTEMS
Questions on page 63

A1 **A** is the correct sign for a one-way street.
B tells you 'Ahead only'.
A2 **1** True
2 True
3 True
4 True

ROAD MARKINGS
Questions on pages 63–5

A3 information
warnings
orders
A4 **1** They can be seen when other signs may be hidden
2 They give a continuing message
A5 **A** 2
B 2
A6 **1, 4**
A7 They are used to separate potentially dangerous streams of traffic.
A8 You must not enter the hatched area.

TRAFFIC SIGNS

Questions on pages 65

A9   **1** Warning
2 Order
3 Information
A10 **1** must
2 must not
A11 **1** You must give way to traffic on the major road. Delay your entry until it is safe to join the major road.
2 You must stop (even if the road is clear). Wait until you can enter the new road safely.
A12 vision is limited
A13 Motorway signs D
Primary routes F
Other routes B
Local places C
Tourist signs A

ROAD OBSERVATION

Questions on pages 66–8

A1   speed
behaviour
intentions
A2   **1** Observe that the view into the new road is restricted.
The driver should ...
Move forward slowly, to get a better view.
Note the pedestrian who may walk in front of or behind car **A**.
Note the pedestrian waiting to cross.
Allow the cyclist to pass.
Once in position to see car **B**, stop and give way.
2 Observe that the parked car restricts the view into and out of the side road.
The driver should ...

Answers to questions

Slow down on approach to parked car **P**.

Take up position to gain a better view and be more visible to car **A** and the pedestrian.

Slow down in case the pedestrian walks out from behind the parked car **P**.

Consider signal to pass parked car **P**.

Look carefully into minor road. Note the actions of car **A**. Be prepared to stop.

A3 bike

A4 3

A5 A

  1 Junctions
  2 Hump-back bridges
  3 Concealed entrances
  4 Dead ground
  5 Narrow lanes

  B

  1 Children playing
  2 Horses
  3 Pedestrians
  4 Especially elderly and young cyclists
  5 Other vehicles

A6 **1** True. The ability to advise those at your destination of delays can help to reduce the worry of late arrivals
  2 True
  3 True
  4 True

A7 All are distracting and upset concentration, and should not be carried out while driving.

DEALING WITH BENDS
Questions on pages 68–9

A8 speed
  gear
  position

A9 1

A10 B

A11 A

A12 **A** On a right-hand bend keep to the left. This will help to improve your view.

  B On a left-hand bend keep to the centre of the lane. Do not move to the centre of the road to get a better view. A vehicle travelling in the opposite direction may be taking the bend wide.

OVERTAKING

Questions on pages 69–70

A13 necessary
1 Mirrors
2 Position
3 Speed
4 Look
5 Mirrors
6 Signal
7 Manoeuvre

A14 About the width of a small car, more in windy or poor weather conditions

A15 1 The vehicle in front is signalling and positioned to turn right
2 You are using the correct lane to turn left at a junction
3 Traffic is moving slowly in queues and the traffic on the right is moving more slowly than you are
4 You are in a one-way street

A16 1 On approach to a junction
2 The brow of a hill
3 The approach to a bend
4 Where there is dead ground.
NB These are examples. Be guided by The Highway Code.

DUAL CARRIAGEWAYS

Questions on pages 70–1

A17 **2** Statements 1, 3, 4 and 5 do not apply:
1 Reflective studs are used on some dual carriageways.
3 The speed limit is subject to local conditions and may vary from 40mph up to the national speed limit.
4 You can turn right on to and off dual carriageways unlike motorways, where all traffic enters and leaves on the left.
5 You may find slow moving vehicles sometimes displaying a flashing amber light.

A18 **A** You would cross over the first carriageway then wait in the gap in the central reservation. Be careful, if you are towing or if your vehicle is long, that you do not cause other road users to change course or slow down.

B You would wait until there is a gap in the traffic long enough for you safely to clear the first carriageway and emerge into the second.

A19 The speed limit applies to all lanes. Use the first lane to travel in and the second for overtaking.

A20 **A** Dual carriageway ends
B Road narrows on both sides
C Two-way traffic straight ahead

A21 **A** and **C**

A22 Traffic is moving much faster, and one or more lanes will have to be crossed.

Section 12

DRIVING AN AUTOMATIC CAR
Questions on pages 72–3

A1 Clutch

A2 **1** Driving is easier
2 There is more time to concentrate on the road

A3 Park – Locks the transmission. This should be selected only when the vehicle is stationary.
Reverse – Enables the car to go backwards, as in a manual car.
Neutral – Has the same function as in a manual car. The engine is not in contact with the driving wheels.
Drive – Is used for driving forwards. It automatically selects the most appropriate gear.
3rd – Has the same function as manual gears
2nd – Has the same function as manual gears
1st – Has the same function as manual gears

A4 **3**

A5 **1** Yes

 2 No

 3 Yes, if you needed extra control

 4 You would probably use kickdown, but possibly in certain circumstances you would manually select a lower gear

 5 Yes, maybe using 1st gear

 6 No. Use the brakes

A6 **1** The right foot

 2 The right foot

A7 It stops you trying to control the brake and accelerator at the same time. It encourages early release of the accelerator and progressive braking.

A8 Drive, reverse, all forward gears.

A9 **1** You should apply the handbrake every time you stop. Otherwise you have to keep your foot on the foot-brake.

A10 Park (P) or Neutral (N)

A11 1

Section 13

THE DRIVING TEST

Questions on pages 74–6

A1 **1** False

 2 True

 3 False

 4 False

 5 True

A2 3

A3 False. If you did not hear clearly or did not understand what the examiner said, you should ask him or her to repeat the instruction. If you have any problem with your hearing, it is advisable to tell the examiner at the start of the test.

A4 No. The standard test does not vary. The test result should be the same wherever it is taken.

A5 1, 4

A6 2

A7 The test will not proceed. You have failed not only the eyesight section, but the whole test. Remember, if you wear glasses or contact lenses, to wear them for the eyesight test and for the rest of the driving test.

A8 provisional licence

A9 False. You can make some less serious faults and still reach the required standard.

A10 Yes, but remember to do it up again when you have completed the exercise.

A11 **1** Give you a verbal explanation of the main reasons for failure

2 Write out a form for you to take away showing you your main errors

A12 **1** Drive unsupervised

2 Drive on a motorway

3 Drive without L-plates

A13 No. You must have had at least three years' driving experience (and be over 21 years of age).

A14 The Examiner will keep your provisional licence and arrange for DVLA to send your full licence to you.

A15 Yes. It is a good idea to keep a note of your driver number and the date you passed your test.

A16 rules
high speed

A17 **2** The examiner will expect you to drive normally. You should abide by all speed limits and drive according to road and traffic conditions.

A18 Yes. The examiner will be skilled in giving instructions and directions to deaf candidates.

Section 14

BEYOND THE TEST

Questions on page 77

A1 No
A2 **1** Bad weather driving
2 Night-time driving
3 Motorway driving
4 Skid control ... and more
A3 2
A4 **1,** although people of any age can find it difficult to drive at night
A5 70
A6 There are certain serious driving offences which carry the penalty of disqualification. In order to regain a full licence, the disqualified driver has to apply for a provisional licence and take an extended test. If, because of certain illnesses, you have been unable to drive for 10 years, you will be required to take the test again in order to gain a full licence.
For new drivers: the accumulation of six or more penalty points within two years of passing the test will mean reverting to a provisional licence and re-sitting the test.

MOTORWAY DRIVING

Questions on pages 78–80

A7 1
A8 **1** No
2 Yes
3 No
4 Yes
5 Yes
6 Yes
7 No
A9 **1** Oil
2 Water
3 Fuel
4 Tyre pressures
These are just some of the checks; for more information, refer to your car's manual.
A10 **3** You should never attempt to retrieve anything from the carriageway.
A11 3
A12 **B** Amber
A Red
D Green
C White
A13 3
A14 Yes

A15 3

A16 1 False

2 False

3 False

4 True

5 False

A17 **1**, except when traffic is moving slowly in queues and the queue on the right is travelling more slowly

SAFE NIGHT DRIVING

Questions on pages 80–1

A18 2

A19 Switch on earlier, switch off later.

A20 **1**. It helps others to see you.

A21 If you are stationary, to avoid danger from a moving vehicle.

A22 **A**. Always park with the flow of traffic. You will show red reflectors to vehicles travelling in your direction.

A23 1 Pedestrians ⎱
2 Cyclists ⎰ two of these
3 Motorcyclists

A24 In poor weather conditions – see and be seen

A25 dazzle
handbrake

ALL-WEATHER DRIVING

Questions on pages 81–4

A26 4

A27 double

A28 aquaplaning

A29 Slow down
Allow time for the tread patterns to disperse the water.

A30 2

A31 1

A32 very light

A33 2

A34 1 Slow down
2 stop
3 windscreen wipers
4 demister, heated rear windscreen

A35 100 metres/328 feet

A36 2

A37 2

A38 **1** windows, audio system.
Listen
2 early
3 brakes, alert
4 horn, warn

A39 False, because your tyres are not in contact with the road

A40 brakes

A41 **1** gently
2 lower gear
3 drop, brakes

A42 1

A43 If possible, control your speed before reaching the hill. Select a low gear early.

A44 Using your brakes

A45 Avoid harsh acceleration

A46 **1** The driver
2 The vehicle
3 The road conditions

A47 **1** Slowing
2 Speeding
3 Turning
4 uphill, downhill

Section 15

VEHICLE CARE
Questions on pages 85–6

A1 1

A2 Oil

A3 3

A4 Water, anti-freeze, air

A5 1

A6 dazzle

A7 clean

A8 uneven, bulges, cuts

A9 2

A10 Get them checked as quickly as possible

BREAKDOWNS, ACCIDENTS AND EMERGENCIES
Questions on pages 86–9

A11 **1** Neglect
2 routine checks
3 preventative
4 abuse

A12 **1** 45 metres/yards
2 At least 150 metres/yards

A13 Yes. Try to give as much warning as possible.

A14 3

A15 3

A16 Under the drawing of the handset is an arrow which points to the nearest telephone.

A17 **1** The emergency number (painted on the box)
2 Vehicle details (make, registration mark, colour)
3 Membership details of your motoring organisation
4 Details of the fault

A18 **1** By displaying a Help pennant
2 By using a mobile telephone

A19 **1** passing motorists
2 do not know
3 leave, longer

A20 **1** False. Do not move injured people unless they are in danger.
2 False. Tell them the facts, not what you think is wrong.
3 False. Do not give those injured anything to eat or drink. Keep them warm and reassure them.
4 False. Keep hazard lights on to warn other drivers.
5 True. Switch off engines. Put out cigarettes.
6 True, in the case of injury.

A21 Stop

A22 No

A23 **1** The other driver's name, address and contact number
2 The registration numbers of all vehicles involved
3 The make of the other car
4 The other driver's insurance details
5 If the driver is not the owner, the owner's details.

A24 **1** Pull up quickly

2 Get all passengers out

3 Call assistance

A25 **1** First aid

2 Fire extinguisher

3 Warning triangle

A26 **3**

THE MOTOR CAR AND THE ENVIRONMENT

Questions on pages 89–90

A27 carbon dioxide, greenhouse

A28 **4**

A29 Yes

A30 False. A catalytic convertor reduces the level of carbon monoxide, nitrogen oxide and hydrocarbons by up to 90 per cent. Carbon dioxide is still produced.

A31 **2**

A32 Eight measures are listed here:

1 Make sure your vehicle is in good condition and regularly serviced.

2 Make sure tyres are correctly inflated. Under-inflated tyres waste fuel.

3 Avoid harsh braking.

4 Buy a fuel-efficient vehicle.

5 Use the most appropriate gear.

6 Use your accelerator sensibly and avoid harsh acceleration.

7 Use unleaded fuel.

8 Dispose of waste oil, old batteries and used tyres sensibly.

BUYING A USED CAR

Questions on pages 90–1

A33 dealer, auction, privately

A34 Why is it being sold?

A35 **1** True

2 False

3 True

4 True

A36 **1** What is covered

2 The length of the agreement

A37 taxed, MOT, insurance

A38 Four items to check are listed here:

1 Mileage

2 Has it been involved in any accidents?

3 Number of owners

4 Is there any hire purchase or finance agreement outstanding?

A39 True. The AA offers a national inspection scheme.

Section 16

TOWING A CARAVAN OR TRAILER
Questions on pages 92–3

A1 1

A2 Exterior towing mirrors, to give you a good view

A3 2

A4 stabilizer

A5 3

A6 **A** 2

B 2

A7 Seven checks are listed here:

1 Is the caravan or trailer loaded correctly?

2 Is it correctly hitched up to your vehicle?

3 Are the lights and indicators working properly?

4 Is the braking system working correctly?

5 Is the jockey wheel assembly fully retracted?

6 Are tyre pressures correct?

7 Are all windows, doors and roof lights closed?

A8 jockey wheel, corner steadies

DRIVING IN EUROPE
Questions on pages 93–4

A9 vehicle, documents

A10 **1** route

2 motoring regulations

A11 Here are five routine checks:

1 Tyres, including spare. Always carry a spare tyre.

2 Tool kit and jack.

3 Lamps and brake lights.

4 Fit deflectors to your headlamps to prevent dazzle to other drivers approaching on the left.

5 Check you have an extra exterior mirror on the left.

A12 driving licence

A13 International Driving Permit

A14 Some non-EU countries

A15 2

A16 Five items are listed here:

1 Spare lamps and bulbs

2 Warning triangle

3 First aid kit

4 Fire extinguisher

5 Emergency windscreen

Part 3: Understanding the theory behind the test

Contents

Section 1
Alertness

The first section in the theory test revision questions is headed ALERTNESS. Alertness is a short section and is a good place to start.

- Alertness means being wide awake and concentrating on what you are doing – driving – not being distracted by mobile phones or loud music.
- Alertness means looking out for hazards.
- Alertness means noticing all road signs and road markings, and acting on the instructions and information they give.

Are you fit to drive?
'Fit' can mean:
- Did you have any alcoholic drinks before you set out?
- Are you under the influence of illegal substances (drugs)?
- Are you feeling groggy or unwell?
- Are you taking prescription medicine that could affect your ability to control the car?
- Are you too tired to drive?

It's unwise to set out on a journey if you're not well, on the basis of 'I'll see how I go – I'll probably be all right':
- Your reactions are likely to be slower.
- You may be unable to judge distances properly.
- Your actions may be less well co-ordinated than usual and it's not legal.

If you are tired, open the window for a few moments to let in some fresh air. If you drive when you are too tired, you risk falling asleep

at the wheel – an all too common cause of serious accidents. Driving for long stretches on a motorway at night can be especially dangerous. If you sense that you are losing your concentration, then take a break at a motorway service station. Plan your journey ahead, giving yourself plenty of time for rest stops – at least every couple of hours.

Tackling the questions
Look at the questions in the Alertness section. You'll see that the Alertness questions are all about these
- anticipation
- observation
- signalling
- reversing
- using your mirrors
- concentration
- getting distracted
- feeling sleepy
- using mobile phones

DID YOU KNOW?
The main causes of distraction are:
- Loud music in the car
- Passengers (usually children)
- Events happening outside (such as accidents)
- Using a mobile phone

Now test yourself on the questions on pages 152–60

Section 2
Attitude

The government road safety organisations believe that the ATTITUDE of learner drivers is extremely important for road safety.

Attitude means
- Your frame of mind when you get in the car
- How you react when you meet hazards on the road
- How you behave towards other drivers

Attitude is a very important part of being a good driver. Your attitude when you are driving plays a big part in ensuring your safety and that of other road users.

Do you aim to be a careful and safe driver or a fast and skilful driver? If you don't want to end up as another road accident statistic, then carefully and safely is the way to go.

Remember that a car is not an offensive weapon, and often people don't realise what a potentially lethal machine they are in control of when they get behind the wheel. You only have to think about this to understand the importance of your attitude when driving.

You'll see that questions in this section are concerned with encouraging you to be a careful and safe driver, and cover:
- Tailgating
- Consideration for other road users, including pedestrians, buses, slow-moving vehicles and horse riders
- Driving at the right speed for the conditions
- When to flash headlights
- The right place, time and way to overtake

And remembering a few dos and don'ts will help you achieve the right attitude for driving and make passing this section of the test much easier.

Good drivers do
- drive at the right speed and for the road and traffic conditions
- observe speed limits
- overtake only when it is safe to do so
- park in correct and safe places
- wait patiently if the driver in front is a learner or elderly or hesitant
- look out for vulnerable road users such as cyclists, pedestrians and children
- concentrate on their driving at all times
- plan their journey so that they have plenty of time to get to their destination

Good drivers don't
- allow themselves to become involved in road rage
- break speed limits
- drive too fast, particularly in wet, foggy or icy weather
- accelerate or brake too harshly
- overtake and 'cut in', forcing others to brake sharply
- put pressure on other drivers by driving too close behind them (this is called 'tailgating'), flashing headlights or gesturing
- allow their attention to be distracted by passengers, mobile phones or loud music, or what is happening on the road, such as staring at an accident

Tailgating

Driving excessively close behind another vehicle is known as tailgating – and it's dangerous! The car in front may stop suddenly (to avoid hitting a child or animal that has dashed out into the road, for example); when this happens the car following runs the risk of crashing into it.

You should always leave enough space between your vehicle and the one in front, so that you can stop safely if the driver in front suddenly slows down or stops.

Rear-end shunts account for a large percentage of all accidents on the road. In these situations, the driver of the car behind is almost always judged to be the guilty party.

So tailgating is potentially expensive as well as dangerous.

Another time when drivers are tempted to tailgate is when attempting to pass a large, slow-moving vehicle. However, keeping well back will improve your view of the road ahead, so that you're better able to judge when it's safe to overtake and the driver of the large vehicle will also be able to see you.

Useful tip

If you are being followed too closely by another driver you should slow down and increase the distance between your vehicle and the one in front. If you slow down or have to stop suddenly, the driver behind may crash into you, but you will have increased your stopping distance and will not be pushed into the vehicle in front of you.

Always remember

- Expect the unexpected, and make provision for the potential errors of other drivers – everyone makes mistakes sometimes.
- Don't create unnecessary stress for other drivers by showing your frustration in an aggressive manner.

If you are driving at the right speed for the road and weather conditions and a driver behind tries to overtake, you should pull back a bit from the vehicle in front so that if the driver behind insists on overtaking, there is less risk of an accident.

Do not try to stop the car behind from overtaking. Do not move into the middle of the road or move up close to the car in front. These actions could be very dangerous.

You should not give confusing signals such as indicating left or waving the other driver on.

Now test yourself on the questions on pages 161–72

Section 3
Safety and your vehicle

When you go through this section you will notice that the questions are a bit of a mixture. They cover a number of topics about SAFETY, including:

- Understanding the controls of your vehicle
- What the car's warning lights tell you
- Tyres – correct inflation, pressures and tread depths
- When to use hazard warning lights
- Passenger safety
- The environment
- Security and crime prevention

Many of the questions in this section are to do with 'legal requirements' and rules regarding parking your car and using lights. Look up all the sections in *The Highway Code* that deal with parking rules. Find out the rules for red routes, white lines and zigzag lines as well as yellow lines.

use your lights, including your hazard warning lights.

A confusing question

One of the most confusing questions in this section asks what kind of driving results in high fuel consumption. The answer, of course, is **bad** driving – especially harsh braking and acceleration. This means you will use more fuel than you should and therefore cause more damage to the environment than is necessary.

BUT many people read the word 'high' as meaning 'good' – as in a level of driving skill – and so pick the wrong answer.

Don't let it be you...

Now test yourself on the questions on pages 173–97

Seat belts

If any of your passengers are young people under 14, you are responsible for making sure that they wear seat belts. You are responsible for them by law, even if you are still a learner driver yourself.

Tips for this section

Learn *The Highway Code* and you will be able to answer most of the questions in this section. In particular make sure you know the rules regarding seat belts, tyres, and when to

Section 4
Safety margins

Experienced drivers are usually better than new or learner drivers at leaving good SAFETY MARGINS. Learner drivers find it harder to keep their vehicle at a safe distance from the one in front. Therefore the questions in this section cover
• safe stopping distances
and
• safe separation distances (these are the same as safety margins)

What is a safety margin?

A safety margin is the space that you need to leave between your vehicle and the one in front so that you will not crash into it if it slows downs or stops suddenly. They are also called 'separation distances' and are an important part of anticipating road and traffic hazards. When you are learning to drive, you can feel pressured to speed up by drivers behind you.

Don't let other drivers make you cut down on your safety margins. Stay a safe distance behind the vehicle in front. Then you will have time to anticipate and react to hazards.

The two-second rule

In traffic that's moving at normal speed, allow at least a two-second gap between you and the vehicle in front.

Stopping distances

Many people who are taking their theory test get confused about this. You will notice that some of the questions ask for your overall stopping distance and others ask for your braking distance. These are different.

Overall stopping distance or stopping distance is not the same as braking distance. Stopping distance is made up of thinking distance + braking distance.

In other words, the time it takes to notice that there's a hazard ahead plus the time it takes to brake to deal with it.

Thinking distance

Thinking distance is sometimes called reaction time or reaction distance. If you are driving at 30mph, your thinking distance will be 30 feet (9 metres). That means your vehicle will travel 30 feet (9 metres) before you start braking.

The link between stopping distance and safety margins

You should always leave enough space between your vehicle and the one in front. If the other driver has to slow down suddenly or stop without warning, you need to be able to stop safely. The space is your safety margin.

Safety margins for other vehicles

Long vehicles and motorcycles need more room to stop – in other words, you must leave a bigger safety margin when following a long vehicle or motorbike. When driving behind a long vehicle, pull back to increase your separation distance and your safety margin so that you get a better view of the road ahead – there could be hazards developing and if you are too close he will be unable to see you in his rear view mirror. Strong winds can blow

Thinking Distance   **Braking Distance**

20 mph

6 metres + 6 metres

= 12 metres (40 feet) or 3 car lengths

30 mph

9 metres + 14 metres

= 23 metres (75 feet) or 6 car lengths

40 mph

12 metres + 24 metres

= 36 metres (118 feet) or 9 car lengths

50 mph

15 metres + 38 metres

= 53 metres (175 feet) or 13 car lengths

60 mph

18 metres + 55 metres

= 73 metres (240 feet) or 18 car lengths

70 mph

21 metres + 75 metres

= 96 metres (315 feet) or 24 car lengths

lorries and motorbikes off course. So leave a bigger safety margin.

Different conditions and safety margins

You may find that one or more questions in your theory test might be about driving in 'different conditions'. These questions aim to make sure you know what adjustments you should make to your driving when either road conditions are different from normal, for example, when parts of the road are closed off for roadworks or weather conditions affect your driving.

Roadworks

You should always take extra care when you see a sign warning you that there are roadworks ahead. Remember, roadworks are a hazard and you have to anticipate them.

If you see the driver in front of you slowing down, take this as a sign that you should do the same – even if you can't see a hazard ahead. You still need to keep a safe distance from him. Harassing the driver in front by 'tailgating' is both wrong and dangerous and so is overtaking to fill the gap. It's especially important that you know what to do when you see a sign for roadworks ahead on a motorway.

- There may be a lower speed limit than normal – keep to it.
- Use your mirrors and indicators, and get into the correct lane in plenty of time.
- Don't overtake the queue and then force your way in at the last minute (this is an example of showing an inconsiderate attitude to other road users).

- Always keep a safe distance from the vehicle in front.

Weather conditions

In bad weather (often called 'adverse' weather), you need to increase your safety margins.

When it's raining you need to leave at least twice as much distance between you and the vehicle in front. When there's ice on the road leave an even bigger gap because your stopping distance increases tenfold.

It's amazing how often drivers go too fast in bad weather. In adverse weather motorways have lower speed limits, but some drivers don't take any notice of them.

When it's icy you should multiply your two-second gap by ten.

Questions that look alike

There are a number of questions about anti-lock brakes in this section. Lots of questions look the same. Some are easy and some are hard. Some of them appear to be the same but they are not.

The questions test two things – your knowledge of the rules of the road and your understanding of words to do with driving.

> **Now test yourself on the questions on pages 198–211**

Section 5
Hazard awareness

How often does a motorist protest that the accident happened before they had time to realise the person they hit was there? Some accidents will inevitably happen, but part of your instructor's job while teaching you to drive is to help you learn to anticipate problems before they happen.

What is the difference between Hazard Awareness and Hazard Perception?

- Hazard Awareness and Hazard Perception mean the same thing.
- Hazard Perception is the name for the part of the theory test that uses video clips. This test is about spotting developing hazards. One of the key skills of good driving, this is called anticipation.
- Anticipating hazards means looking out for them in advance and taking action now.
- Hazard Awareness is about being alert whenever you are driving.

That is why some of the questions in the HAZARD AWARENESS section deal with things that might make you less alert. For example feeling tired, feeling ill, taking medicines prescribed by your doctor, drinking alcohol or taking illegal drugs.

Other questions in Hazard Awareness cover noticing road and traffic signs as well as road markings, what to do at traffic lights and when to slow down for hazards ahead.

Why are young male drivers more at risk?

New drivers have a greater than average chance of being involved in accidents. Statistics show that young male drivers have the most accidents.

- Maybe it's because when they first get their licence they want to show off to other drivers.
- Some people think that driving much too fast will earn them 'respect' from their friends.
- Some people think that they are such good drivers that the rules of the road should not apply to them.

Whatever the reason – drivers who don't watch out for hazards are at risk of being involved in an accident. The problem has a lot to do with people's attitude to driving. You'll find more about this aspect of driving in the Attitude part of the theory test.

We've already said that young drivers often don't learn to anticipate hazards until they are older and more experienced. The Hazard Perception test aims to 'fill the gap' in hazard perception for young drivers and other new drivers by making sure they have some proper training to make up for their lack of experience.

This should make them safer drivers when they start out on the road alone.

Looking for clues to hazards developing on the road

As you get more driving experience you will start to learn about the times and places where you are most likely to meet hazards. Think about some of these examples.

Rush hour

You know that people take more risks when driving in the rush hour. Maybe they have to drop their children off at school before going to work. Maybe they are late for a business meeting. So you have to be prepared for bad driving, such as other drivers pulling out in front of you.

Dustbin day

Drivers in a hurry may get frustrated if they are held up in traffic because of a hazard such as a dustcart. They may accelerate and pull out to overtake even though they cannot see clearly ahead. You should not blindly follow the lead of another driver. Check for yourself that there are no hazards ahead.

School children

Young children are often not very good at judging how far away a car is from them, and may run into the road unexpectedly. Always be on the lookout for hazards near a school entrance.

Parked cars

Imagine you are driving on a quiet one-way street with cars parked down each side of the road. You wouldn't expect to meet any vehicles coming the other way – but what about children playing? They might run out into the road after a football. It would be difficult to see them because of the parked cars, until they were in the road in front of you.

More examples of hazards

So, what kinds of hazards are we talking about? And what should you do about them?

Road markings and road signs sometimes highlight likely hazards for you.

The list below gives some of the hazards you should look out for when driving along a busy street in town.

After each hazard there are some ideas about what you should be looking out for, and what to do next.

- You see a bus which has stopped in a lay-by ahead.
There may be some pedestrians hidden by the bus who are trying to cross the road, or the bus may signal to pull out. Be ready to slow down and stop.

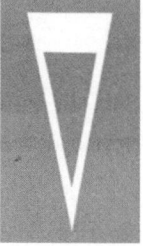

- You see a white triangle painted on the road surface ahead.
This is a hazard warning sign. It tells you that there is a 'Give Way' junction just ahead. Slow down and be ready to stop.

- You see a sign for a roundabout on the road ahead.
Anticipate that other drivers may need to change lane, and be ready to leave them enough room.

- You come to some road works where the traffic is controlled by temporary traffic lights. *Watch out for drivers speeding to get through before the lights change.*

- You look in your rear view mirror and see an emergency vehicle with flashing lights coming up behind you. *An emergency vehicle wants to pass, so get ready to pull over when it's safe.*

- You see a small child standing with an adult near the edge of the pavement. *Check if the child is safely holding the adult's hand. Be ready to stop safely if the child suddenly steps into the road.*

- You notice dustbins or rubbish bags put out on the pavement. *The dustcart could be around the next corner, or the bin men could be crossing the road with bags of rubbish. Be ready to slow down and stop if necessary.*

- You hear a siren. *Look all around to find out where the emergency vehicle is. You may have to pull over to let it pass.*

You will find out more about the different types of hazards you may encounter, including what to look for when driving on narrow country roads, or in bad (adverse) weather conditions, in the Vehicle Handling section of this book.

Always expect the unexpected
Don't forget that not all hazards can be anticipated. There are bound to be some you haven't expected.

Red flashing warning lights
Level crossings, ambulance stations, fire stations and swing bridges all have red lights that flash on and off to warn you when you must stop.

Observation

Another word for taking in information through our eyes is observation. Observation is one of the three key skills needed in hazard perception. The three skills are

- observation
- anticipation
- planning

An easy way to remember this is **O A P** for

Observe
Anticipate
Plan

Talk to yourself!

It's a good idea to 'talk to yourself' when you're learning to drive – and even after you've passed your test. Talk about all the things you see that could be potential hazards. Your driving instructor might suggest this as a way of making you concentrate and notice hazards ahead.

Even if you don't talk out loud, you can do a 'running commentary' in your head on everything you see around you as you drive.

For example, you might say to yourself – 'I am following a cyclist and the traffic lights ahead are red. *When the lights change I will allow him/her plenty of time and room to move off.'*
or
'The dual carriageway ahead is starting to look very busy. There is a sign showing that the right lane is closing in 800 yards. *I must get ready to check my mirrors and, if safe to do so, drop back to allow other vehicles to move into the left-hand lane ahead of me.'*

Note: Don't forget the mirrors! This way, you will notice more hazards, and you will learn to make more sense of the information that your eyes are taking in.

Learn your road signs!
Notice the information at the bottom of the first page of traffic signs in *The Highway Code*. It explains that you won't find every road sign shown here.

You can buy a copy of *Know Your Road Signs* from a bookshop to see some of the extra signs that are not in *The Highway Code*.

Note: In Wales, some road signs include the Welsh spelling as well as the English, and in Scotland some signs are written using Gaelic spelling. You'll also see some 'old-style' road signs around, which are slightly different too.

Scanning the road

Learner drivers tend to look straight ahead of their car and may not notice all the hazards that might be building up on both sides. You will spot more hazards when driving if you train yourself to scan the road.

- Practise looking up and ahead as far as possible.
- Use all your mirrors to look out for hazards too.
- Don't forget that you have 'blind spots' when driving – work out where they are and find safe ways of checking all round for hazards.
- Ask your driving instructor to help you with all of this.

How is learning to scan the road going to help me pass my theory test?
- The idea of the hazard perception element of the test is to encourage you to get some real experience of driving before you take the theory test.
- If you meet real hazards on the road and learn how to anticipate them, you'll learn how to pass the hazard perception element of the test.
- In the video test you may not be able to look all around you as you would when driving a car; but the clips will be as realistic as possible in giving you a wide 'view' of the road ahead.

Observation questions

Study some of the pictures in the Hazard Awareness section.

They include photographs of scenes such as

- a cyclist at traffic lights, seen from the viewpoint of a driver in a car behind the cyclist

- what you see as a driver when you are approaching a level crossing

- what you see when coming up to a 'blind bend'

- a view of the road ahead with traffic building up where one lane is closing.

Look out for situations like these when you are out driving with your instructor, and use the practice to improve your hazard awareness.

As well as photographs, there are pictures of road and traffic signs.

What do these signs mean?

What actions should you take when you see these signs?

- If you are not sure, look them up in *The Highway Code*.

- Think about why the square yellow sign with the two children is in the Vehicle Markings section and not with the rest of the road signs.

Now test yourself on the questions on pages 212–36

Section 6
Vulnerable road users

Today's new vehicles are becoming safer all the time for the driver inside the car, but sadly this is not always the case for the pedestrian or cyclist outside. Many road users who are not driving cars have nothing to protect them if they are in an accident with a motor vehicle.

The questions in the VULNERABLE ROAD USERS section deal with the following:
• why different types of road users are vulnerable
• what you as a driver must do to keep them safe

Who are vulnerable road users?
The following are all vulnerable road users and you must drive with extra care when you are near vulnerable road users.
– pedestrians
– children
– elderly people
– people with disabilities
– cyclists
– motorcycle riders
– horse riders
– learner drivers and new drivers
– animals being herded along the road

Cyclists
Give cyclists plenty of room. Remember to keep well back from cyclists when you are coming up to a junction or a roundabout because you cannot be sure what they are going to do. On the roundabout they may go in any direction – left, right or straight ahead. They are allowed to stay in the left lane and

signal right if they are going to continue round. Leave them enough room to cross in front of you if they need to. Turn to the section headed Vulnerable Road Users in the theory test questions to see some pictures of this. You must also give way to cyclists at toucan crossings and in cycle lanes (see the rules for cyclists set out in *The Highway Code*).

Look out for cyclists!
• It can be hard to see cyclists in busy town traffic.
• It can also be hard to see them coming when you are waiting to turn out at a junction. They can be hidden by other vehicles.

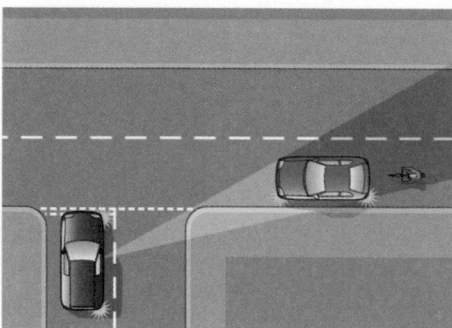

Always be on the lookout for cyclists.

Especially, check your mirror to make sure you do not trap a cyclist on your left when you are turning left into a side road. Check your blind spots for cyclists, too.

Controlling your vehicle near cyclists
When you are following a cyclist, you must be able to drive as slowly as they do, and keep

your vehicle under control. Only overtake when you can allow them plenty of room, and it is safe to do so.

Cycle lanes

Cycle lanes are reserved for cyclists and car drivers should not use them. A cycle lane is marked by a white line on the road. A solid white line means you must not drive or park in the cycle lane during the hours it is in use. A broken white line means that you should drive or park in it only if there is no alternative. You should not park there at any time when there are waiting restrictions.

When you overtake a cyclist, a motorcyclist or a horse rider, give them at least as much room as you would give a car.

Cyclists and motorcycle riders

Cyclists and motorcycle riders are more at risk than car drivers because

- they are more affected by strong winds, or by turbulence caused by other vehicles
- they are more affected by an uneven road surface, and they may have to move out suddenly to avoid a pothole
- car drivers often cannot see them

Pedestrians

Pedestrians most at risk include elderly people and children. Elderly people and others who cannot move easily may be slower to cross roads – you must give them plenty of time. Children don't have a sense of danger on the road; they can't tell how close a car is, or how fast it is going. They may run out into the road without looking. Or they may step out behind you when you are reversing – you may not see them because they are small.

People who are unable to see and/or hear

A person who is blind will usually carry a white stick to alert you to their presence. If the stick has a red band, this means that the person is also deaf, so will have no warning of an approaching car either visually or from engine noise.

When to give way to pedestrians

At any pedestrian crossing, if a pedestrian has started to cross, wait until they have reached the other side. Do not harass them by revving your engine or edging forward.

At a crossing with lights (pelican, toucan or puffin crossings), pedestrians have priority once they have started to cross even if, when on a pelican crossing, the amber lights start flashing.

Once a pedestrian has stepped on to a zebra crossing, you must stop and wait for them to cross.

Note: It is courteous to stop at a zebra crossing if a pedestrian is waiting to cross.

When you take your practical driving test, you must stop for any pedestrians who are waiting on the pavement at a zebra crossing even if they haven't stepped on to the crossing yet. However, you must not wave to them to cross.

If you want to turn left into a side road and pedestrians have already started to cross the side road on foot, wait for them to finish crossing. People on foot have priority over car drivers.

DID YOU KNOW?

If a car hits a pedestrian at 40mph, the pedestrian will probably be killed. Even at 35mph, 50% of pedestrians hit by cars will be killed.

At 20mph, pedestrians have a better chance of surviving. This is why you will find 20mph limits and other things to slow traffic in some residential streets and near school entrances.

Other types of vulnerable road users

Be prepared to slow down for animals, learner drivers, and other more unusual hazards such as people walking along the road in organised groups (for example, on a demonstration, or a sponsored walk). There are rules in *The Highway Code* that walkers must follow. But even if they break the rules, make sure you keep to them.

Animals

Drive slowly past horses or other animals. Allow them plenty of space on the road. Don't frighten them by sounding your horn or revving your engine.

If you see a flock of sheep or a herd of cattle blocking the road, you must
- stop
- switch off your engine
- and wait until they have left the road

People riding horses on the road are often children, so you need to take extra care; when you see two riders abreast, it may well be that the one on the outside is shielding a less experienced rider.

Traffic signs

Look up the Traffic Signs and Vehicle Markings sections in *The Highway Code* and find the following signs
- pedestrians walking in the road ahead (no pavement)
- cycle lane and pedestrian route
- advance warning of school crossing patrol ahead
- school crossing patrol
- elderly or disabled people crossing
- sign on back of school bus or coach

Now test yourself on the questions on pages 237–56

Section 7
Other types of vehicle

We have already come across some of the other types of vehicle that share the road with you and your car including motorbikes and bicycles. The questions in this part of the theory test are mostly about long vehicles such as lorries. However, you also need to know what to do about

- buses
- caravans
- trams
- tractors and other farm vehicles
- special vehicles for disabled drivers (powered invalid carriages)
- slow vehicles such as road gritters
- motorway repair vehicles

Important points to remember about these types of vehicle
- Many of them can only move very slowly.
- They cannot easily stop or change direction.

The driver's field of vision may be restricted – this means that car drivers have to allow them plenty of room.

Motorcycles

- Motorcycles are easily blown off course by strong winds. If you see a motorcyclist overtaking a high-sided vehicle such as a lorry, keep well back. The lorry may shield the motorcyclist from the wind as it is overtaking, but then a sudden gust could blow the motorcyclist off course.
- It can be hard to see a motorcyclist when you are waiting at a junction. Always look out for them.

- If you see a motorcyclist looking over their shoulder, it could mean that they will soon give a signal to turn right. This applies to cyclists too. Keep back to give them plenty of room.
- Motorcyclists and cyclists sometimes have to swerve to avoid hazards such as bumps in the road, patches of ice and drain covers. As before – give them plenty of room.

Long vehicles

- Like cyclists, long vehicles coming up to roundabouts may stay in the left lane even if they intend to turn right. This is because they need lots of room to manoeuvre. Keep well back so they have room to turn.
- Take great care when overtaking long or high-sided vehicles. Before you pull out to overtake, make sure you have a clear view of the road ahead.
- A long vehicle that needs to turn left off a major road into a minor road may prepare to do so by moving out towards the centre of the road, or by moving across to the other side.

If you're following them
- Give way, and don't try to overtake – on the right or the left.
- You might need to slow down and stop while the driver of the long vehicle makes the turn.

Buses and trams

- Always give way to buses when they signal to pull out.
- Always give way to trams as they cannot steer to avoid you.
- Don't try to overtake a tram.

Trams are **quiet** vehicles – you cannot rely on approaching engine noise to warn you that a tram is coming.

Take extra care when you see this sign, because trams are sometimes allowed to go when car drivers are not.

Tractors and slow-moving vehicles

- Always be patient if you are following a slow vehicle.

Drivers of slow vehicles will usually try to find a safe place to pull in to let the traffic go past. In the meantime you should keep well back, so that you can see the road ahead. Allow a safe distance in case they slow down or stop.

Slow vehicles are not allowed on motorways because they cannot keep up with the fast-moving traffic. Vehicles not allowed on motorways include

- motorcycles under 50cc
- bicycles
- tractors and other farm vehicles
- powered invalid carriages

Now test yourself on the questions on pages 257–64

Section 8
Vehicle handling

The questions in this section test how much you know about controlling your vehicle on different road surfaces and in different weather.

Your control is affected by

- the road surface – is it rough or smooth? Are there any holes or bumps? Are there any 'traffic-calming' measures, such as humps or chicanes?
- the weather conditions – you have to drive in different ways when there is fog, snow, ice or heavy rain.

Other questions in this section cover driving on country roads – on narrow and one-way roads, humpback bridges, steep hills, fords. Other questions need practical knowledge, for example, on engine braking, brake fade, and coasting your vehicle – use the Glossary.

This section also has some questions on overtaking and parking.

Road surface

The condition of the road surface can affect the way your vehicle handles. Your vehicle handles better on a smooth surface than on a surface that is damaged, bumpy or full of holes. If you have to drive on an uneven surface, keep your speed down so that you have full control of your vehicle, even if your steering wheel is jolted.

Take care also where there are tramlines on the road. The layout of the road affects the way your vehicle handles.

You may have to adjust your driving for traffic-calming measures, such as traffic humps (sometimes called 'sleeping policemen') and chicanes. These are double bends that have been put into the road layout to slow the traffic down. The sign before the chicane tells you who has priority.

Traffic calming measures are often used in residential areas or near school entrances to make it safer for pedestrians.

Weather conditions

Bad weather (adverse weather) such as heavy rain, ice or snow affects the way your vehicle handles. If you drive too fast in adverse weather, your tyres may lose their grip on the road when you try to brake. This means the car may skid or 'aquaplane'. Aquaplaning means sliding out of control on a wet surface.

Driving in snow

In snow, the best advice is do not drive at all unless you really have to make a journey. If you have to drive in snowy conditions, leave extra time for your journey and keep to the main roads. You can fit snow chains to your tyres to increase their grip in deep snow.

Driving in fog

In fog your field of vision can be down to a few metres. Your vehicle is fitted with fog lights to help you see and be seen in fog. But you must know how and when to use them. Look up the three rules about fog lights in *The Highway Code*. You'll see that the key points to remember are:

- Don't dazzle other road users with your fog lights.
- Switch them off as soon as you can see better (as soon as the fog starts to clear).

> **Remember the two-second rule**
> You should double the two-second gap to four seconds when driving in rain, and increase the gap by as much as ten times when there is ice on the road.

Country driving

If you have had most of your driving lessons in a town, you need to know how to drive on narrow country roads. Some are only wide enough for one vehicle ('single-track'), and some are on very steep hills.

Your control of the gears, clutch and brakes will be important if you have to follow a tractor very slowly up a hill. On a steep downward slope you have to make sure your vehicle does not 'run away'.

On country roads you might find humpback bridges and fords. The signs below warn you of these hazards.

- Find out what you must do first after you have driven through a ford.

Technical knowledge

We have already mentioned engine braking. Understanding how engine braking works is part of good vehicle handling.

Note: If you press the footbrake constantly on a long hill, you may get brake fade. If you're not sure, check what that means in the Glossary near the back of this book.

Use the gears to control your vehicle on a downhill slope (or 'gradient'). If you put the vehicle in 'neutral', or drive with the clutch down (called coasting), your vehicle will increase speed beyond what is safe and will not be under proper control.

This sign warns you of a steep hill downwards.

- Travelling in neutral for long distances (known as coasting) is wrong and dangerous – you should not be tempted to do it and it doesn't save fuel.

Remember that if there is sudden heavy rain after a dry hot spell, the road surface can get very slippery.

Now test yourself on the questions on pages 265–79

Section 9
Motorway rules

Learner drivers aren't allowed on motorways, so you can't get experience of what it's like to drive on them until you've passed your test. However, you do need to know all about MOTORWAY RULES before taking your practical test, and your theory test will most likely include a question about motorways.

As soon as you pass your driving test you will be legally allowed to drive on motorways. You need to know all the motorway rules in advance, so that you are confident and ready to cope with motorway driving when you pass your test.

There are some major roads and dual carriageways that learners can drive on which are very much like motorways. You may drive on some of these fast roads during your driving test, so that your examiner can see how well you cope with hazards at higher speeds.

When driving on these fast roads you will need some of the very same skills that you will need for motorway driving – for example, using lanes properly, knowing when it is safe to overtake, and controlling your vehicle at speed.

If you are learning to drive with a driving school, you will have the chance to book a motorway lesson with your instructor after you have passed your test. It makes sense to take up this offer before you drive on a motorway alone for the first time.

Motorways and other roads

- On a motorway traffic is moving at high speed all the time.
- All lanes are in use.
- No stopping is allowed on a motorway – traffic only slows or comes to a stop because of accidents or other types of hold-up.
- Some road users are not allowed on motorways. These include
- pedestrians, cyclists and learner drivers
- horses and other animals
- motorcycles under 50cc
- slow-moving vehicles, tractors and farm vehicles and invalid carriages
- You always enter and leave a motorway on the left, via a slip road.
- To the left of the inside lane (left-hand lane) on a motorway is the hard shoulder. You can only drive on this in an emergency.
- Special signs and signals are used on motorways. These include signs above the road on overhead gantries, signs on the central reservation, and amber and red flashing lights.

Checks before your journey

Be extra careful about doing all your regular checks before you set out on a motorway journey. You cannot stop on the motorway to fix small problems, and no one wants to break down in the middle of fast traffic.

Always check

- oil and coolant levels, screen wash container
- tyres and tyre pressures
- fuel gauge
- that all mirrors and windows are free of dirt and grease
- that the horn works

Many of these checks are legally necessary, as well as important for your safety.

How to move on to a motorway

- Join the motorway by building up your speed on the slip road to match the speed of traffic in the left lane of the motorway.
- Use MSM (Mirrors – Signal – Manoeuvre) and move into the flow of traffic when it is safe to do so.

Changing lanes and overtaking

Driving on a motorway needs all the skills you have learned about anticipation and forward planning.

You should

- make good use of all mirrors, and check your blind spots
- signal to move out in plenty of time
- look out for hazards ahead in the lane you want to move to
- not go ahead if it will force another vehicle to brake or swerve
- keep a safe distance from the vehicle in front

Take a break

When you drive on motorways you will sometimes see signs that say 'Tiredness can kill – take a break!' This is very good advice. Motorways are monotonous – boring to drive, with long stretches of road that look the same for miles. A major cause of accidents is drivers falling asleep at the wheel. Plan your journey so that you have time to get out, stretch your legs and have a drink or snack.

The rules you need to know

- Keep to the left-hand lane unless you are overtaking and move back to the left lane as soon as it is safe to do so. Sometimes you need to stay in the centre lane for a time – for example, when a line of lorries is travelling up a hill in the left lane. Stay in the centre lane until you have passed the hazard, then signal left and return to the left lane.
- NEVER reverse, park, walk or drive in the wrong direction on a motorway.
- Don't exceed the speed limit. This is normally 70mph, but lower speed limits may be signed when the road is busy, or in bad weather.
- Keep to the correct separation distance (see Safety Margins).
- Don't overtake on the left.
  If traffic is moving slowly in all three lanes you may find that the lane on the left is moving faster than the one to its right for a short time. Or the left lane may be signed for traffic turning off at the next junction only. But these are exceptions to the rule.
- If luggage falls from your vehicle, do not get out to pick it up. Stop at the next emergency phone and tell the Highways Agency or the police. Posts on the edge of the motorway show the way to the nearest emergency phone. You should use these phones rather than your mobile phone, because the emergency phone connects directly to the Highways Agency or the police and tells them exactly where you are calling from on the motorway.
- Don't stop on the hard shoulder except in an emergency. The hard shoulder is an extremely dangerous place, as many as one in eight road deaths happen there.

Traffic signs and road markings

Light signals

In *The Highway Code* you'll find the light signals only seen on motorways. Signs above the roadway or on the central reservation are activated as needed to warn of accidents, lane

closures or weather conditions. Overhead gantries display arrows or red crosses showing which lanes are open or closed to traffic and which lanes to move to

 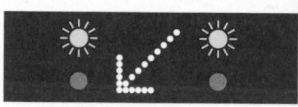

when motorways merge or diverge. They may also show temporary speed limits.

Direction signs

Direction signs on motorways are blue and those on other major roads are green – other direction signs are white with black print.

Reflective studs

It's useful to know the colours of studs on a motorway; this can help in working out which part of the road you're on if it's dark or foggy. White studs mark lanes or the centre of the road and red studs mark the left edge of the carriageway.

Amber studs are used alongside the central reservation and green studs mark the entry to a slip road.

Note: These markings are also found on some dual carriageways.

Using the hard shoulder
- Stop as far to the left as possible and, if you can, near an emergency phone.
- Emergency phones are situated 1 mile  apart and have blue and white marker posts every 100 metres. An arrow on the posts points the direction of the nearest phone.
  - If you are using a mobile phone you can identify your location from the number on the post.
- Switch on your hazard warning lights.
- Use the left-hand door to get out of the vehicle, and make sure your passengers do too.
- Get everyone away from the road – if possible, behind the barrier or up the bank.
- Leave animals in the vehicle unless they aren't safe there.
- Phone the Highways Agency or the police with full details of where you are, then go back and wait in a safe place near your vehicle.

Now test yourself on the questions on pages 280–97

Section 10
Rules of the road

'Rules of the Road' is a good way to describe what is in *The Highway Code*.

The questions that come under this heading in the theory test include several on road signs and road markings. There are many more road sign questions in the section on Road and Traffic Signs. Several of the topics listed in this section have already come up.

Other questions in this section cover
- speed limits
- overtaking
- parking
- lanes and roundabouts
- clearways
- box junctions
- crossroads
- pedestrian crossings
- towing caravans and trailers

Speed limits
Driving too fast for the road, traffic or weather conditions causes accidents. Make sure that you keep below the speed limit shown on the signs for the road that you are on.

| 30mph in a built-up area | 50mph on a long, twisty country road | or as low as 20mph in a residential area with speed humps or traffic-calming measures |

The national speed limit for cars on a dual carriageway is 70mph.
This is also the maximum speed for motorway driving.

National speed limit

When you leave a built-up area you will usually see this sign.

- This sign tells you that the national speed limit for this type of road applies here.
- The national speed limit for cars on a normal road (single carriageway outside a built-up area) is 60mph. So on this road you must drive below 60mph even if it is straight and empty.

Street lights usually mean that a 30mph limit applies, unless there are signs showing other limits.

The right speed for the conditions

If it is raining or there is snow and ice on the road or if you are driving in a high wind you will have to drive more slowly than the maximum speed limit. This will keep you and other road users safe.

- Remember – you have to double the time you allow for stopping and braking in wet weather. Allow even more time in snow and ice.
- You need to be extra careful when driving in fog.

The right speed for your vehicle

Some other vehicles have lower speed limits than cars. You can find out more about speed limits from the table in *The Highway Code*.

Parking rules

There are some general rules about parking that all drivers should know.

- Whenever you can, you should use off-street car parks, or parking bays. These are marked out with white lines on the road.
- Never park where your vehicle could be a danger to other road users.

Look for special signs that tell you that you cannot park there at certain times of the day or that only certain people may park in that place. Examples include signs showing bus lanes, cycle lanes, residents' parking zones and roads edged with red or yellow lines.

Blue badges are given to people with disabilities. Do not park in a space reserved for a driver with a disability, even if that is the only place left to park. A driver with a disability may need to park there. You will break the law if you park in that space.

Parking at night
- If you park at night on a road that has a speed limit higher than 30mph, you must switch on your parking lights. You must switch on your parking lights even if you have parked in a lay-by on this type of road.
- When parking at night, always park facing in the same direction as the traffic flow.
- If your vehicle has a trailer, you must switch on parking lights, even if the road has a 30mph speed limit.

Where not to park
You are not permitted to park
- on the pavement
- at a bus stop
- in front of someone's drive
- opposite a traffic island
- near a school entrance
- on a pedestrian crossing (or inside the zigzag lines either side of it)
- near a junction
- on a clearway
- on a motorway

Now test yourself on the questions on pages 298–315

Section 11
Road and traffic signs

When you look up the chapter on ROAD AND TRAFFIC SIGNS in the theory test questions you will see that it takes up a lot of pages. This is because most of the questions have a picture of a road sign or marking. You will also see that a lot of questions ask 'What does this sign mean?'

But however differently the questions are worded, it all comes down to how well you know *The Highway Code*. You can try to learn as much of *The Highway Code* as possible, but there are other ways you can get to know the road signs.

As you walk or drive around, look at the road signs you see in the street, and the different markings painted on the road surface.

On foot
Look at the signs and signals that all road users must obey, whether they are in a car or walking. For example, when you use a pedestrian crossing, check what kind of crossing it is (such as a pelican, toucan or zebra crossing).

Check whether you know the following
- What are the rules for pedestrians and drivers coming up to the crossing?
- What kinds of crossings are controlled by traffic lights?
- What is different about a zebra crossing?

During your driving lessons

If you are having a driving lesson look well ahead so that you see all the signs that tell you what to do next. Obey them in good time.

During your test

When you take your test the examiner will tell you when to move off, when to make a turn and when to carry out one of the set manoeuvres. The examiner will expect you to watch out for lane markings on the road, and signs giving directions, and to decide how to react to these yourself.

Signs

If you see several signs all on the same post, it can be confusing. The general rule is to start at the top and read down the post. The sign at the top tells you about the first hazard you have to look out for.

If you are a passenger in a car on a motorway, look at the motorway signs, because you need to know them, even though you can't drive on a motorway yet yourself.

Check that you can answer the following:
What colour are the signs at the side of the motorway?
What do the light signals above the road tell you?
What signs tell you that you are coming to an exit?

Shapes of signs

Road and traffic signs come in three main shapes. Get to know them. You must learn what the signs mean.

Circles
Signs in circles tell you to do (blue) or not do (red) something – they give orders.

Triangles
Signs in triangles tell you of a hazard ahead – they give warnings.

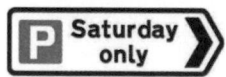

Rectangles
Signs in rectangles tell you about where you are or where you are going – they give information.

There is only one sign which is octagonal – that is, it has eight sides. This is the sign for STOP. The eight-sided shape makes the sign stand out.

Now test yourself on the questions on pages 316–55

Section 12
Documents

This is quite a short section in the theory test questions. It is also different from the other sections, because it does not deal with either your driving skills or knowledge of *The Highway Code*.

It covers all the paperwork and the laws that you need to know about when you start learning to drive.

In this section there are questions about
- driving licences
- insurance
- MOT certificate
- Vehicle Excise Duty (road tax)
- Vehicle Registration Document (log book)

This section also covers who can supervise a learner driver and changes you must tell the licensing authority about.

Driving licence

If you are learning to drive, you'll need a provisional licence.
- You must have a valid licence to drive legally.
- The driving licence consists of a photocard (see example, above) – keep it with you at all times.
- Your signature appears on the licence.
- Take good care of your provisional licence. If you lose it by mistake, you can get another one but you will have to pay a fee, and wait for the new licence to come.
- When you pass your test you can apply for a full licence.

Insurance

You must have a valid insurance certificate that covers you at least for third party liability. If you are learning with a driving school, you are covered by their insurance while you are in the driving school car. When you are in your own or anybody else's car, you must have insurance. Third party insurance cover usually comes as 'Third Party, Fire and Theft'. It is a basic insurance policy that will pay for repairs to another person's car and allows you to claim on the other driver's insurance if you are in an accident that was not your fault. If you have comprehensive insurance, the policy will pay for repairs to your vehicle even when the accident was your fault.

MOT certificate

Cars and motorcycles must have their first MOT test three years (four years in Northern Ireland) after they are new and first registered. After that, they must have an MOT test every year.

The MOT test checks that your vehicle
- is roadworthy – that is, all the parts work properly and the vehicle is safe to drive
- keeps to the legal limits for exhaust emissions – that is, the level of poisons in the gas that comes from the exhaust

If your vehicle is more than three years old you must not drive it without a valid MOT certificate – unless you are on your way to get an MOT and you have booked it in advance.

Vehicle Excise Duty

Vehicle Excise Duty is the tax that the government charges you to drive your vehicle on the roads. It is also sometimes called road tax.

To drive or keep a vehicle on the road you must get vehicle tax. The DVLA will send you a reminder when your tax is due to expire. When you buy a vehicle, any existing tax cannot be transferred with the vehicle.

Your vehicle must have valid insurance cover before you can tax it. If required, it will also need to have a valid MOT certificate. You can tax your vehicle online, by phone or at certain post offices.

If you want to keep a vehicle off the public road you must inform the DVLA by completing a Statutory Off Road Vehicle Notification (SORN). It is an offence not to do so. You then won't have to pay vehicle excise duty (road tax). The SORN is valid until your vehicle is taxed, sold or scrapped.

Vehicle Registration Certificate

The Vehicle Registration Certificate has all the important details about you and your vehicle, such as the make and model of the vehicle. It also has your name and address as the registered keeper of the vehicle. It is a record of the vehicle's history and is sometimes called 'the log book'.

DVLA

The Driver and Vehicle Licensing Agency is known as the DVLA. You must tell the DVLA if you are going to keep your car off road and are not renewing your vehicle excise duty (car tax), when you buy or sell a car and if you change your name or your address.

This is because your details go on to the Vehicle Registration Certificate and you are legally responsible for the vehicle (car tax, parking fines, etc) until you have notified the DVLA that it is off road or you have sold it.

Supervising a learner driver

As a learner driver you cannot drive on your own. If you are not with your driving instructor, you must be supervised by a person who is at least 21 years old, has a full licence for the kind of car you drive and has had that licence for at least three years. Note that if a person has a licence to drive an automatic car only, they cannot supervise a learner in a manual car.

Now test yourself on the questions on pages 356–66

Section 13
Incidents, accidents and emergencies

The questions in this section are about helping anyone who is hurt in a road accident. Some people think they might do more harm than good if they try to help. But if you have a basic knowledge of first aid you won't panic and if you are first on the scene at an accident, you could even save a life. Look up 'First Aid on the road' in *The Highway Code*.

The theory test questions in this section cover
- what to do when warning lights come on in your vehicle
- what to do if you break down
- safety equipment to carry with you
- when to use hazard warning lights
- what to do – and what not to do – at the scene of an accident
- what to do in tunnels

Basic first aid
What to do at an accident scene
- Check that you are not putting yourself in danger before you go to help somebody else. You may need to warn other drivers of the accident.
- Check all vehicle engines are switched off.
- Make sure no one is smoking.
- Move people who are not injured to a safe place. If the accident has happened on a motorway, if possible get uninjured people away from the hard shoulder, behind the barrier or on to the bank.
- Call the emergency services. You will need to tell them exactly where you are, and how many vehicles are involved in the accident.

On motorways, use the emergency phone which connects directly to the Highways Agency or the police and tells them exactly where you are.
- Do not move injured people – unless there is a risk of fire or of an explosion.
- Give essential first aid to injured people (see Annexe 7 of *The Highway Code* in this book).
- Stay there until the emergency services arrive.

Other ways to help
- Do speak in a calm way to the injured person.
- Do try to keep them warm and as comfortable as possible.
- Do not give them anything to drink.
- Do not give them a cigarette.
- Don't let injured people wander into the road.

Advice on safety if you break down
If you are on a non-motorway road
- Try to get your vehicle off the main road. At least, get it right to the side of the road or on to the verge.
- If the vehicle is in a place where it might be hit by another vehicle, get any passengers out and to a safer place.
- Switch on the hazard warning lights to warn other drivers.
- If you have a red warning triangle, place it at least 45 metres behind your car to warn other traffic (but don't use it on a motorway).
- If you are a member of a motoring organisation, call them and tell them where you are and what has happened. Wait with your vehicle until the patrol arrives.

If you are on a motorway

- If possible, leave the motorway at the next exit. If you can't get that far, drive on to the hard shoulder. Stop far over to the left, and switch on your hazard warning lights.
- Get everyone out of the vehicle, using the nearside doors (but leave pets in the vehicle). Get them to sit on the bank, well away from the traffic.
- Use the nearest orange emergency phone to call the emergency services and tell them where you are and what has happened (for your safety, face the oncoming traffic while you are on the phone).
- Go back to your vehicle and wait on the bank near by until help arrives.
- Do not cross the motorway on foot or try to do repairs yourself – even changing a wheel. This is too dangerous on a motorway.

DID YOU KNOW?
Before driving into a tunnel you should tune into a local radio station and listen to the traffic reports in case there are any accidents or problems in the tunnel.

Now test yourself on the questions on pages 367–86

Section 14
Vehicle loading

This last section, called VEHICLE LOADING, is the shortest of all. It covers a mixture of the following

- how to load your vehicle safely
- using a roof rack
- towing caravans and trailers
- child restraints and safety locks

When you have passed your test you can tow a trailer, if the combined weight of the vehicle and trailer is less than 3,500kg. So you need to know the rules about towing.

Towing

When you get your first full driving licence, check it to see how much you are allowed to tow. Do not tow any trailer that comes to more than that weight. The weight of a trailer should be no more than 85% of the weight of the car that is to pull it. But it is best to stay well below that top weight, because towing a trailer will affect the way your vehicle handles. When you are towing, you need to allow more room when overtaking and more time to brake and stop.

When you are turning at a roundabout or junction you will need to think about where you are on the road.

When towing a heavy load, you might need to blow your tyres up to more than the normal pressures. Check your vehicle's handbook for advice. Remember to change back to the normal tyre pressures when you finish your journey.

Roof racks

If you attach a roof rack to your car, it will make a difference to the way in which your vehicle handles. Any load that is carried on a roof rack must be tied down securely.

- The roof rack makes your vehicle taller, so more vulnerable to strong winds.
- You will increase your fuel consumption.
- You need to change the way you drive to allow for the extra weight.

To find out more, look up the parts of *The Highway Code* that deal with 'Loads and Towing'.

Loading a trailer

If the weight of the load is arranged properly, this should cut down the risk of losing control, swerving and snaking.

- Try to spread the weight evenly when you load your trailer. Do not put more weight towards the front, or the back, or to one side.
- It is against the law to have a load that is sticking out in a dangerous way.
- Don't forget that if you park a vehicle with a trailer overnight, it must have lights.

A vehicle towing a trailer

- must not go over a maximum speed limit of 60mph
- must not use the right (outside) lane on a motorway

If you are going to buy a trailer, make sure it fits your car's tow bar. Tow bars must keep to EU regulations, and must have electric sockets to connect to the lights on the trailer.

Snaking

'Snaking' means moving from side to side. A caravan will snake if it is not properly attached or loaded, or if the car pulling it is going too fast.

If you are towing a caravan or trailer and it starts to snake

- slow down – stop pressing the accelerator (do not brake suddenly)
- get back in control of the steering
- then brake gently

You are responsible for passengers in your vehicle

There are also questions in the Vehicle Loading section about the safety of passengers. As the driver, you are responsible for making sure your vehicle is not overloaded – and this applies to people and animals as well as to luggage. Remember that all passengers must wear a seat belt (unless they have a medical certificate saying they should not wear one) and that all children under the age of 14 must wear a seat belt or be strapped into a child seat or other 'restraint' suitable for their age. (See the section on 'Child Restraints' in *The Highway Code*).

Children

Children must not sit in the space behind the back seat of a hatchback car, and no passengers should sit in a caravan while it is being towed.

Pets

Pets should be kept under careful control. You might keep them and you safe with a special harness, or if they are kept behind a screen in a hatchback which would stop them being thrown forward in the event of an accident.

Now test yourself on the questions on pages 387–90

Part 3: Theory test revision questions

Contents | Page

1 Mark *one* answer
Before you make a U-turn in the road, you should

☐ **A** give an arm signal as well as using your indicators
☐ **B** signal so that other drivers can slow down for you
☐ **C** look over your shoulder for a final check
☐ **D** select a higher gear than normal

If you want to make a U-turn, slow down and ensure that the road is clear in both directions. Make sure that the road is wide enough to carry out the manoeuvre safely.

---

2 Mark *one* answer
As you approach this bridge you should

☐ **A** move to the right
☐ **B** slow down
☐ **C** change gear
☐ **D** keep to 30mph

You should slow down and be cautious. The bridge is narrow and there may not be enough room for you to pass an oncoming vehicle at this point. There is also no footpath, so there may be pedestrians in the road.

3 Mark *one* answer
In which of these situations should you avoid overtaking?

☐ **A** Just after a bend
☐ **B** In a one-way street
☐ **C** On a 30mph road
☐ **D** Approaching a dip in the road

As you begin to think about overtaking, ask yourself if it's really necessary. If you can't see well ahead stay back and wait for a safer place to pull out.

---

4 Mark *one* answer
This road marking warns

☐ **A** drivers to use the hard shoulder
☐ **B** overtaking drivers there is a bend to the left
☐ **C** overtaking drivers to move back to the left
☐ **D** drivers that it is safe to overtake

You should plan your overtaking to take into account any hazards ahead. In this picture the marking indicates that you are approaching a junction. You will not have time to overtake and move back into the left safely.

5 Mark *one* answer
Your mobile phone rings while you are travelling. You should

- ☐ **A** stop immediately
- ☐ **B** answer it immediately
- ☐ **C** pull up in a suitable place
- ☐ **D** pull up at the nearest kerb

The safest option is to switch off your mobile phone before you set off, and use a message service. Even hands-free systems are likely to distract your attention. Don't endanger other road users. If you need to make a call, pull up in a safe place when you can, you may need to go some distance before you can find one. It's illegal to use a hand-held mobile or similar device when driving or riding, except in a genuine emergency.

6 Mark *one* answer
Why are these yellow lines painted across the road?

- ☐ **A** To help you choose the correct lane
- ☐ **B** To help you keep the correct separation distance
- ☐ **C** To make you aware of your speed
- ☐ **D** To tell you the distance to the roundabout

These lines are often found on the approach to a roundabout or a dangerous junction. They give you extra warning to adjust your speed. Look well ahead and do this in good time.

7 Mark *one* answer
You are approaching traffic lights that have been on green for some time. You should

- ☐ **A** accelerate hard
- ☐ **B** maintain your speed
- ☐ **C** be ready to stop
- ☐ **D** brake hard

The longer traffic lights have been on green, the greater the chance of them changing. Always allow for this on approach and be prepared to stop.

8 Mark *one* answer
Which of the following should you do before stopping?

- ☐ **A** Sound the horn
- ☐ **B** Use the mirrors
- ☐ **C** Select a higher gear
- ☐ **D** Flash your headlights

Before pulling up check the mirrors to see what is happening behind you. Also assess what is ahead and make sure you give the correct signal if it helps other road users.

9 Mark *one* answer
When following a large vehicle you should keep well back because this

- ☐ **A** allows you to corner more quickly
- ☐ **B** helps the large vehicle to stop more easily
- ☐ **C** allows the driver to see you in the mirrors
- ☐ **D** helps you to keep out of the wind

If you're following a large vehicle but are so close to it that you can't see the exterior mirrors, the driver can't see you.
Keeping well back will also allow you to see the road ahead by looking past either side of the large vehicle.

10 Mark *one* answer
When you see a hazard ahead you should use the mirrors. Why is this?

☐ **A** Because you will need to accelerate out of danger
☐ **B** To assess how your actions will affect following traffic
☐ **C** Because you will need to brake sharply to a stop
☐ **D** To check what is happening on the road ahead

You should be constantly scanning the road for clues about what is going to happen next. Check your mirrors regularly, particularly as soon as you spot a hazard. What is happening behind may affect your response to hazards ahead.

---

11 Mark *one* answer
You are waiting to turn right at the end of a road. Your view is obstructed by parked vehicles. What should you do?

☐ **A** Stop and then move forward slowly and carefully for a proper view
☐ **B** Move quickly to where you can see so you only block traffic from one direction
☐ **C** Wait for a pedestrian to let you know when it is safe for you to emerge
☐ **D** Turn your vehicle around immediately and find another junction to use

At junctions your view is often restricted by buildings, trees or parked cars. You need to be able to see in order to judge a safe gap. Edge forward slowly and keep looking all the time. Don't cause other road users to change speed or direction as you emerge.

12 Mark *one* answer
Objects hanging from your interior mirror may

☐ **A** restrict your view
☐ **B** improve your driving
☐ **C** keep you focused
☐ **D** help your concentration

Ensure that you can see clearly through the windscreen of your vehicle. Stickers or hanging objects could affect your field of vision or draw your eyes away from the road.

---

13 Mark *one* answer
Which of the following may cause loss of concentration on a long journey?

☐ **A** Keeping fresh air circulating
☐ **B** Arguing with a passenger
☐ **C** Stopping regularly to rest
☐ **D** Pulling up to tune the radio

You should not allow yourself to be distracted when driving. You need to concentrate fully in order to be safe on the road. Loud music could mask other sounds, such as the audible warning of an emergency vehicle. Any distraction which causes you to take your hands off the steering wheel or your eyes off the road could be dangerous.

14 Mark *one* answer
On a long motorway journey boredom can cause you to feel sleepy. You should

- ☐ **A** play some loud music
- ☐ **B** stop on the hard shoulder for a rest
- ☐ **C** drive faster to complete your journey sooner
- ☐ **D** ensure a supply of fresh air into your vehicle

Plan your journey to include suitable rest stops. You should take all possible precautions against feeling sleepy while driving. Any lapse of concentration could have serious consequences.

15 Mark *one* answer
You're driving at dusk. You should switch your lights on

- ☐ **A** when you see other traffic
- ☐ **B** so others can see you
- ☐ **C** only when others have done so
- ☐ **D** only when street lights are lit

Your headlights and tail lights help others on the road to see you. It may be necessary to turn on your lights during the day if visibility is reduced, for example due to heavy rain. In these conditions the light might fade before the street lights are timed to switch on. Be seen to be safe.

16 Mark *one* answer
You're most likely to lose concentration when driving if you

- ☐ **A** use a mobile phone
- ☐ **B** check road signs
- ☐ **C** switch on the heated rear window
- ☐ **D** look at the door mirrors

Using a mobile phone distracts your attention away from driving. Distractions caused by mobile phones are known to be potentially dangerous. Avoid being distracted by your phone by turning it off before you start driving.

17 Mark *one* answer
What's most likely to distract you while you're driving?

- ☐ **A** Using a mobile phone
- ☐ **B** Using the windscreen wipers
- ☐ **C** Using the demisters
- ☐ **D** Checking the mirrors

It's easy to be distracted. Planning your journey before you set off is important. A few sensible precautions are to tune your radio to stations in your area of travel, take planned breaks, and plan your route. Except for emergencies, it's illegal to use a hand-held mobile phone while driving. Even using a hands-free kit can severely distract your attention.

18 Mark *one* answer
You should ONLY use a mobile phone when

☐ **A** receiving a call
☐ **B** suitably parked
☐ **C** driving at less than 30mph
☐ **D** driving an automatic vehicle

It is illegal to use a hand-held mobile phone while driving, except in a genuine emergency. Even using hands-free kit can distract your attention. Park in a safe and convenient place before receiving or making a call or using text messaging. Then you will also be free to take notes or refer to papers.

19 Mark *one* answer
You are driving on a wet road. You have to stop your vehicle in an emergency. You should

☐ **A** apply the handbrake and footbrake together
☐ **B** keep both hands on the wheel
☐ **C** select reverse gear
☐ **D** give an arm signal

As you drive, look well ahead and all around so that you're ready for any hazards that might occur. There may be occasions when you have to stop in an emergency. React as soon as you can whilst keeping control of the vehicle.

20 Mark *one* answer
When you're moving off from behind a parked car you should

☐ **A** give a signal after moving off
☐ **B** check both interior and exterior mirrors
☐ **C** look round after moving off
☐ **D** use the exterior mirrors only

Before moving off you should use both the interior and exterior mirrors to check if the road is clear. Look around to check the blind spots and give a signal if it's necessary to warn other road users of your intentions.

21 Mark *one* answer
You are travelling along this narrow country road. When passing the cyclist you should go

☐ **A** slowly, sounding the horn as you pass
☐ **B** quickly, leaving plenty of room
☐ **C** slowly, leaving plenty of room
☐ **D** quickly, sounding the horn as you pass

Look well ahead and only pull out if it is safe. You will need to use all of the road to pass the cyclist, so be extra-cautious. Look out for entrances to fields where tractors or other farm machinery could be waiting to pull out.

22 Mark *one* answer

Your vehicle is fitted with a hand-held telephone. To use the telephone you should

- ☐ **A** reduce your speed
- ☐ **B** find a safe place to stop
- ☐ **C** steer the vehicle with one hand
- ☐ **D** be particularly careful at junctions

Your attention should be on your driving at all times. Except in a genuine emergency never attempt to use a hand-held phone while on the move. It's illegal and very dangerous. Your eyes could wander from the road and at 60mph your vehicle will travel about 27 metres (89 feet) every second.

23 Mark *one* answer

To answer a call on your mobile phone while travelling you should

- ☐ **A** reduce your speed wherever you are
- ☐ **B** stop in a proper and convenient place
- ☐ **C** keep the call time to a minimum
- ☐ **D** slow down and allow others to overtake

No phone call is important enough to risk endangering lives. It's better to switch your phone off completely when driving. If you must be contactable plan your route to include breaks so you can catch up on messages in safety. Always choose a safe and convenient place to take a break, such as a lay-by or service area.

24 Mark *one* answer

You lose your way on a busy road. What is the best action to take?

- ☐ **A** Stop at traffic lights and ask pedestrians
- ☐ **B** Shout to other drivers to ask them the way
- ☐ **C** Turn into a side road, stop and check a map
- ☐ **D** Check a map, and keep going with the traffic flow

It's easy to lose your way in an unfamiliar area. If you need to check a map or ask for directions, first find a safe place to stop.

25 Mark *one* answer

Windscreen pillars can obstruct your view. You should take particular care when

- ☐ **A** driving on a motorway
- ☐ **B** driving on a dual carriageway
- ☐ **C** approaching a one-way street
- ☐ **D** approaching bends and junctions

Windscreen pillars can obstruct your view, particularly at bends and junctions. Look out for other road users, particularly cyclists and pedestrians, as they can be hard to see.

26 Mark *one* answer

You cannot see clearly behind when reversing. What should you do?

- ☐ **A** Open your window to look behind
- ☐ **B** Open the door and look behind
- ☐ **C** Look in the nearside mirror
- ☐ **D** Ask someone to guide you

If you want to turn your car around try to find a place where you have good all-round vision. If this isn't possible and you're unable to see clearly, then get someone to guide you.

27 Mark *one* answer

What does the term 'blind spot' mean for a driver?

- ☐ **A** An area covered by your right-hand mirror
- ☐ **B** An area not covered by your headlights
- ☐ **C** An area covered by your left-hand mirror
- ☐ **D** An area not covered by your mirrors

Modern vehicles provide the driver with well-positioned mirrors which are essential to safe driving. However, they cannot see every angle of the scene behind and to the sides of the vehicle. This is why it is essential that you check over your shoulder, so that you are aware of any hazards not reflected in your mirrors.

28 Mark *one* answer

Your vehicle is fitted with a hands-free phone system. Using this equipment whilst driving

- ☐ **A** is quite safe as long as you slow down
- ☐ **B** could distract your attention from the road
- ☐ **C** is recommended by The Highway Code
- ☐ **D** could be very good for road safety

Using a hands-free system doesn't mean that you can safely drive and use a mobile phone. This type of mobile phone can still distract your attention from the road. As a driver, it is your responsibility to keep yourself and other road users safe at all times.

29 Mark *one* answer

Using a hands-free phone is likely to

- ☐ **A** improve your safety
- ☐ **B** increase your concentration
- ☐ **C** reduce your view
- ☐ **D** divert your attention

Unlike someone in the car with you, the person on the other end of the line is unable to see the traffic situations you are dealing with. They will not stop speaking to you even if you are approaching a hazardous situation. You need to be concentrating on your driving all of the time, but especially so when dealing with a hazard.

30 Mark *one* answer

What is the safest way to use a mobile phone in your vehicle?

- ☐ **A** Use hands-free equipment
- ☐ **B** Find a suitable place to stop
- ☐ **C** Drive slowly on a quiet road
- ☐ **D** Direct your call through the operator

It's illegal to use a hand-held mobile phone while driving, except in genuine emergencies. Even using hands-free kit is very likely to take your mind off your driving. If the use of a mobile causes you to drive in a careless or dangerous manner, you could be prosecuted for those offences. The penalties include an unlimited fine, disqualification and up to two years' imprisonment.

31 Mark *one* answer

Your mobile phone rings while you are on the motorway. Before answering you should

- ☐ **A** reduce your speed to 30mph
- ☐ **B** pull up on the hard shoulder
- ☐ **C** move into the left-hand lane
- ☑ **D** stop in a safe place

When driving on motorways, you can't just pull up to answer your mobile phone. Do not stop on the hard shoulder or slip road. To avoid being distracted it's safer to switch it off when driving. If you need to be contacted plan your journey to include breaks at service areas so you can pick up any messages when you stop.

32 Mark *one* answer

You are turning right onto a dual carriageway. What should you do before emerging?

- ☐ **A** Stop, apply the handbrake and then select a low gear
- ☐ **B** Position your vehicle well to the left of the side road
- ☐ **C** Check that the central reservation is wide enough for your vehicle
- ☐ **D** Make sure that you leave enough room for a vehicle behind

Before emerging right onto a dual carriageway make sure that the central reserve is deep enough to protect your vehicle. If it's not, you should treat it as one road and check that it's clear in both directions before pulling out. Neglecting to do this could place part or all of your vehicle in the path of approaching traffic and cause a collision.

33 Mark *one* answer

You are waiting to emerge from a junction. The windscreen pillar is restricting your view. What should you be particularly aware of?

- ☐ **A** Lorries
- ☐ **B** Buses
- ☑ **C** Motorcyclists
- ☐ **D** Coaches

Windscreen pillars can completely block your view of pedestrians, motorcyclists and pedal cyclists. You should particularly watch out for these road users; don't just rely on a quick glance. Where possible make eye contact with them so you can be sure they have seen you too.

34 Mark *one* answer

When emerging from junctions, which is most likely to obstruct your view?

- ☐ **A** Windscreen pillars
- ☐ **B** Steering wheel
- ☐ **C** Interior mirror
- ☐ **D** Windscreen wipers

Windscreen pillars can block your view, particularly at junctions. Those road users most at risk of not being seen are cyclists, motorcyclists and pedestrians. Never rely on just a quick glance.

35 Mark *one* answer

Your vehicle is fitted with a navigation system. How should you avoid letting this distract you while driving?

- ☐ **A** Keep going and input your destination into the system
- ☐ **B** Keep going as the system will adjust to your route
- ☐ **C** Stop immediately to view and use the system
- ☐ **D** Stop in a safe place before using the system

Vehicle navigation systems can be useful when driving on unfamiliar routes. However they can also distract you and cause you to lose control if you look at or adjust them while driving. Pull up in a convenient and safe place before adjusting them.

36 Mark *one* answer

You are driving on a motorway and want to use your mobile phone. What should you do?

- ☐ **A** Try to find a safe place on the hard shoulder
- ☐ **B** Leave the motorway and stop in a safe place
- ☐ **C** Use the next exit and pull up on the slip road
- ☐ **D** Move to the left lane and reduce your speed

Except in a genuine emergency you MUST NOT use your mobile phone when driving. If you need to use it leave the motorway and find a safe place to stop. Even a hands-free phone can distract your attention. Use your voicemail to receive calls. Driving requires all of your attention, all of the time.

37 Mark one answer

You must not use a hand-held phone while driving. Using a hands-free system

- ☐ **A** is acceptable in a vehicle with power steering
- ☐ **B** will significantly reduce your field of vision
- ☐ **C** will affect your vehicle's electronic systems
- ☐ **D** is still likely to distract your attention from the road

While driving your concentration is required all the time. Even using a hands-free kit can still distract your attention from the road. Any distraction, however brief, is potentially dangerous and could cause you to lose control. Except in a genuine emergency, it is an offence to use a hand-held phone while driving.

38 Mark *one* answer

At a pelican crossing the flashing amber light means you MUST

- ☐ **A** stop and wait for the green light
- ☐ **B** stop and wait for the red light
- ☐ **C** give way to pedestrians waiting to cross
- ☐ **D** give way to pedestrians already on the crossing

Pelican crossings are signal-controlled crossings operated by pedestrians. Push-button controls change the signals. Pelican crossings have no red-and-amber stage before green. Instead, they have a flashing amber light, which means you MUST give way to pedestrians already on the crossing, but if it is clear, you may continue.

39 Mark *one* answer

You should never wave people across at pedestrian crossings because

- ☐ **A** there may be another vehicle coming
- ☐ **B** they may not be looking
- ☐ **C** it is safer for you to carry on
- ☐ **D** they may not be ready to cross

If people are waiting to use a pedestrian crossing, slow down and be prepared to stop. Don't wave them across the road since another driver may not have seen them, not have seen your signal and may not be able to stop safely.

40 Mark *one* answer

'Tailgating' means

- ☐ **A** using the rear door of a hatchback car
- ☐ **B** reversing into a parking space
- ☐ **C** following another vehicle too closely
- ☐ **D** driving with rear fog lights on

'Tailgating' is used to describe this dangerous practice, often seen in fast-moving traffic and on motorways. Following the vehicle in front too closely is dangerous because it

- restricts your view of the road ahead
- leaves you no safety margin if the vehicle in front slows down or stops suddenly.

41 Mark *one* answer

Following this vehicle too closely is unwise because

- ☐ **A** your brakes will overheat
- ☐ **B** your view ahead is increased
- ☐ **C** your engine will overheat
- ☐ **D** your view ahead is reduced

Staying back will increase your view of the road ahead. This will help you to see any hazards that might occur and allow you more time to react.

42 Mark *one* answer
You are following a vehicle on a wet road. You should leave a time gap of at least

- ☐ **A** one second
- ☐ **B** two seconds
- ☐ **C** three seconds
- ☐ **D** four seconds

Wet roads will reduce your tyres' grip on the road. The safe separation gap of at least two seconds in dry conditions should be doubled in wet weather.

43 Mark *one* answer
A long, heavily-laden lorry is taking a long time to overtake you. What should you do?

- ☐ **A** Speed up
- ☐ **B** Slow down
- ☐ **C** Hold your speed
- ☐ **D** Change direction

A long lorry with a heavy load will need more time to pass you than a car, especially on an uphill stretch of road. Slow down and allow the lorry to pass.

44 Mark *one* answer
Which vehicle will use a blue flashing beacon?

- ☐ **A** Motorway maintenance
- ☐ **B** Bomb disposal
- ☐ **C** Snow plough
- ☐ **D** Breakdown recovery

Emergency vehicles use blue flashing lights. If you see or hear one, move out of its way as soon as it's safe and legal to do so.

45 Mark *one* answer
Which of these services can display a blue flashing beacon?

- ☐ **A** Coastguard
- ☐ **B** Doctor's car
- ☐ **C** Gritting lorry
- ☐ **D** Animal ambulance

Emergency vehicles often travel at high speed. You should help their progress by pulling over and allowing them to pass. Do so safely and legally. Don't stop suddenly or in a dangerous position.

46 Mark *one* answer
When being followed by an ambulance showing a flashing blue beacon you should

- ☐ **A** pull over as soon as safely possible to let it pass
- ☐ **B** accelerate hard to get away from it
- ☐ **C** maintain your speed and course
- ☐ **D** brake harshly and immediately stop in the road

Pull over in a place where the ambulance can pass safely. Check that there are no bollards or obstructions in the road that will prevent it from doing so.

47 Mark *one* answer
What type of emergency vehicle is fitted with a green flashing beacon?

☐ **A** Fire engine
☐ **B** Road gritter
☐ **C** Ambulance
☐ **D** Doctor's car

A green flashing beacon on a vehicle means the driver or passenger is a doctor on an emergency call. Give way to them if it's safe to do so. Be aware that the vehicle may be travelling quickly or may stop in a hurry.

48 Mark *one* answer
A flashing green beacon on a vehicle means

☐ **A** police on non-urgent duties
☐ **B** doctor on an emergency call
☐ **C** road safety patrol operating
☐ **D** gritting in progress

If you see a vehicle with a flashing green beacon approaching, allow it to pass when you can do so safely. Be aware that someone's life could depend on the driver making good progress through traffic.

49 Mark *one* answer
Diamond-shaped signs give instructions to

☐ **A** tram drivers
☐ **B** bus drivers
☐ **C** lorry drivers
☐ **D** taxi drivers

These signs only apply to trams. They are directed at tram drivers but you should know their meaning so that you're aware of the priorities and are able to anticipate the actions of the driver.

50 Mark *one* answer
On a road where trams operate, which of these vehicles will be most at risk from the tram rails?

☐ **A** Cars
☐ **B** Cycles
☐ **C** Buses
☐ **D** Lorries

The narrow wheels of a bicycle can become stuck in the tram rails, causing the cyclist to stop suddenly, wobble or even lose balance altogether. The tram lines are also slippery which could cause a cyclist to slide or fall off.

51 Mark *one* answer
What should you use your horn for?

☐ **A** To alert others to your presence
☐ **B** To allow you right of way
☐ **C** To greet other road users
☐ **D** To signal your annoyance

Your horn must not be used between 11.30pm and 7am in a built-up area or when you are stationary, unless a moving vehicle poses a danger. Its function is to alert other road users to your presence.

52 Mark *one* answer
You are in a one-way street and want to turn right. You should position yourself

☐ **A** in the right-hand lane
☐ **B** in the left-hand lane
☐ **C** in either lane, depending on the traffic
☐ **D** just left of the centre line

If you're travelling in a one-way street and wish to turn right you should take up a position in the right-hand lane. This will enable other road users not wishing to turn to proceed on the left. Indicate your intention and take up your position in good time.

53 Mark *one* answer
You wish to turn right ahead. Why should you take up the correct position in good time?

☐ **A** To allow other drivers to pull out in front of you
☐ **B** To give a better view into the road that you're joining
☐ **C** To help other road users know what you intend to do
☐ **D** To allow drivers to pass you on the right

If you wish to turn right into a side road take up your position in good time. Move to the centre of the road when it's safe to do so. This will allow vehicles to pass you on the left. Early planning will show other traffic what you intend to do.

54 Mark *one* answer
At which type of crossing are cyclists allowed to ride across with pedestrians?

☐ **A** Toucan
☐ **B** Puffin
☐ **C** Pelican
☐ **D** Zebra

A toucan crossing is designed to allow pedestrians and cyclists to cross at the same time. Look out for cyclists approaching the crossing at speed.

55 Mark *one* answer
You are travelling at the legal speed limit. A vehicle comes up quickly behind, flashing its headlights. You should

☐ **A** accelerate to make a gap behind you
☐ **B** touch the brakes sharply to show your brake lights
☐ **C** maintain your speed to prevent the vehicle from overtaking
☐ **D** allow the vehicle to overtake

Don't enforce the speed limit by blocking another vehicle's progress. This will only lead to the other driver becoming more frustrated. Allow the other vehicle to pass when you can do so safely.

56 Mark *one* answer
You should ONLY flash your headlights to other road users

☐ **A** to show that you are giving way
☐ **B** to show that you are about to turn
☐ **C** to tell them that you have right of way
☐ **D** to let them know that you are there

You should only flash your headlights to warn others of your presence. Don't use them to greet others, show impatience or give priority to other road users. They could misunderstand your signal.

57 Mark *one* answer
You are approaching unmarked crossroads. How should you deal with this type of junction?

☐ **A** Accelerate and keep to the middle
☐ **B** Slow down and keep to the right
☐ **C** Accelerate looking to the left
☑ **D** Slow down and look both ways

Be extra-cautious, especially when your view is restricted by hedges, bushes, walls and large vehicles etc. In the summer months these junctions can become more difficult to deal with when growing foliage may obscure your view.

58 Mark *one* answer
You are approaching a pelican crossing. The amber light is flashing. You must

☐ **A** give way to pedestrians who are crossing
☐ **B** encourage pedestrians to cross
☐ **C** not move until the green light appears
☐ **D** stop even if the crossing is clear

While the pedestrians are crossing don't encourage them to cross by waving or flashing your headlights: other road users may misunderstand your signal. Don't harass them by creeping forward or revving your engine.

59 Mark *one* answer

The conditions are good and dry. You could use the 'two-second rule'

☐ **A** before restarting the engine after it has stalled
☐ **B** to keep a safe gap from the vehicle in front
☐ **C** before using the 'Mirror-Signal-Manoeuvre' routine
☐ **D** when emerging on wet roads

To measure this, choose a fixed reference point such as a bridge, sign or tree. When the vehicle ahead passes the object, say to yourself 'Only a fool breaks the two-second rule.' If you reach the object before you finish saying this, you're TOO CLOSE.

60 Mark *one* answer

At a puffin crossing, which colour follows the green signal?

☐ **A** Steady red
☐ **B** Flashing amber
☐ **C** Steady amber
☐ **D** Flashing green

Puffin crossings have infra-red sensors which detect when pedestrians are crossing and hold the red traffic signal until the crossing is clear. The use of a sensor means there is no flashing amber phase as there is with a pelican crossing.

61 Mark *one* answer

You are in a line of traffic. The driver behind you is following very closely. What action should you take?

☐ **A** Ignore the following driver and continue to travel within the speed limit
☐ **B** Slow down, gradually increasing the gap between you and the vehicle in front
☐ **C** Signal left and wave the following driver past
☐ **D** Move over to a position just left of the centre line of the road

If the driver behind is following too closely there's a danger they will collide with the back of your car if you stop suddenly. You can reduce this risk by slowing down and increasing your safety margin ahead. This reduces the chance that you will have to stop suddenly and you can spread your braking out over a greater distance. This is an example of defensive driving.

62 Mark *one* answer

A vehicle has a flashing green beacon. What does this mean?

☐ **A** A doctor is answering an emergency call
☐ **B** The vehicle is slow-moving
☐ **C** It is a motorway police patrol vehicle
☐ **D** The vehicle is carrying hazardous chemicals

A doctor attending an emergency may show a green flashing beacon on their vehicle. Give way to them when you can do so safely as they will need to reach their destination quickly. Be aware that they might pull over suddenly.

63 Mark *one* answer

A bus has stopped at a bus stop ahead of you. Its right-hand indicator is flashing. You should

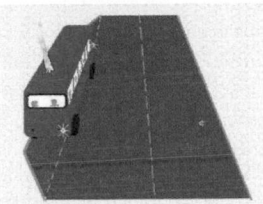

- ☐ **A** flash your headlights and slow down
- ☐ **B** slow down and give way if it is safe to do so
- ☐ **C** sound your horn and keep going
- ☐ **D** slow down and then sound your horn

Give way to buses whenever you can do so safely, especially when they signal to pull away from bus stops. Look out for people leaving the bus and crossing the road.

64 Mark *one* answer

You are driving on a clear night. There is a steady stream of oncoming traffic. The national speed limit applies. Which lights should you use?

- ☐ **A** Full beam headlights
- ☐ **B** Sidelights
- ☐ **C** Dipped headlights
- ☐ **D** Fog lights

Use the full beam headlights only when you can be sure that you won't dazzle other road users.

65 Mark *one* answer

You are driving behind a large goods vehicle. It signals left but steers to the right. You should

- ☐ **A** slow down and let the vehicle turn
- ☐ **B** drive on, keeping to the left
- ☐ **C** overtake on the right of it
- ☐ **D** hold your speed and sound your horn

Large, long vehicles need extra room when making turns at junctions. They may move out to the right in order to make a left turn. Keep well back and don't attempt to pass on the left.

66 Mark *one* answer

You are driving along this road. The red van cuts in close in front of you. What should you do?

- ☐ **A** Accelerate to get closer to the red van
- ☐ **B** Give a long blast on the horn
- ☐ **C** Drop back to leave the correct separation distance
- ☐ **D** Flash your headlights several times

There are times when other drivers make incorrect or ill-judged decisions. Be tolerant and try not to retaliate or react aggressively. Always consider the safety of other road users, your passengers and yourself.

67 Mark *one* answer
You are waiting in a traffic queue at night. To avoid dazzling following drivers you should

- ☐ **A** apply the handbrake only
- ☐ **B** apply the footbrake only
- ☐ **C** switch off your headlights
- ☐ **D** use both the handbrake and footbrake

You should consider drivers behind as brake lights can dazzle. However, if you are driving in fog it's safer to keep your foot on the footbrake. In this case it will give the vehicle behind extra warning of your presence.

68 Mark *one* answer
You are driving in traffic at the speed limit for the road. The driver behind is trying to overtake. You should

- ☐ **A** move closer to the car ahead, so the driver behind has no room to overtake
- ☐ **B** wave the driver behind to overtake when it is safe
- ☐ **C** keep a steady course and allow the driver behind to overtake
- ☐ **D** accelerate to get away from the driver behind

Keep a steady course to give the driver behind an opportunity to overtake safely. If necessary, slow down. Reacting incorrectly to another driver's impatience can lead to danger.

69 Mark *one* answer
A bus lane on your left shows no times of operation. This means it is

- ☐ **A** not in operation at all
- ☐ **B** only in operation at peak times
- ☑ **C** in operation 24 hours a day
- ☐ **D** only in operation in daylight hours

Don't drive or park in a bus lane when it's in operation. This can cause disruption to traffic and delays to public transport.

70 Mark *one* answer
You're driving along a country road. A horse and rider are approaching. What should you do?

- ☐ **A** Increase your speed
- ☐ **B** Sound your horn
- ☐ **C** Flash your headlights
- ☐ **D** Drive slowly past

It's important that you reduce your speed. Passing too closely at speed could startle the horse and unseat the rider.

71 Mark *one* answer

A person herding sheep asks you to stop. You should

☐ **A** ignore them as they have no authority
☐ **B** stop and switch off your engine
☐ **C** continue on but drive slowly
☐ **D** try and get past quickly

Allow the sheep to clear the road before you proceed. Animals are unpredictable and startle easily; they could turn and run into your path or into the path of another moving vehicle.

72 Mark *one* answer

When overtaking a horse and rider you should

☐ **A** sound your horn as a warning
☐ **B** go past as quickly as possible
☐ **C** flash your headlights as a warning
☐ **D** go past slowly and carefully

Horses can become startled by the sound of a car engine or the rush of air caused by passing too closely. Keep well back and only pass when it is safe; leave them plenty of room. You may have to use the other side of the road to go past: if you do, first make sure there is no oncoming traffic.

73 Mark *one* answer

You are approaching a zebra crossing. Pedestrians are waiting to cross. You should

☐ **A** give way to the elderly and infirm only
☐ **B** slow down and prepare to stop
☐ **C** use your headlights to indicate they can cross
☐ **D** wave at them to cross the road

Look out on the approach especially for children and older pedestrians. They may walk across without looking. Zebra crossings have flashing amber beacons on both sides of the road, black and white stripes on the crossing and white zigzag markings on both sides of the crossing. Where you can see pedestrians waiting to cross, slow down and prepare to stop.

74 Mark *one* answer

A vehicle pulls out in front of you at a junction. What should you do?

☐ **A** Swerve past it and sound your horn
☐ **B** Flash your headlights and drive up close behind
☐ **C** Slow down and be ready to stop
☐ **D** Accelerate past it immediately

Try to be ready for the unexpected. Plan ahead and learn to anticipate hazards. You'll then give yourself more time to react to any problems that might occur.

Be tolerant of the behaviour of other road users who don't behave correctly.

75 Mark *one* answer

You stop for pedestrians waiting to cross at a zebra crossing. They do not start to cross. What should you do?

☐ **A** Be patient and wait
☐ **B** Sound your horn
☐ **C** Carry on
☐ **D** Wave them to cross

If you stop for pedestrians and they don't start to cross don't wave them across or sound your horn. This could be dangerous if another vehicle is approaching which hasn't seen or heard your signal.

---

76 Mark *one* answer

You are following this lorry. You should keep well back from it to

☐ **A** give you a good view of the road ahead
☐ **B** stop following traffic from rushing through the junction
☐ **C** prevent traffic behind you from overtaking
☐ **D** allow you to hurry through the traffic lights if they change

By keeping well back you will increase your width of vision around the rear of the lorry. This will allow you to see further down the road and be prepared for any hazards.

77 Mark *one* answer

You are approaching a red light at a puffin crossing. Pedestrians are on the crossing. The red light will stay on until

☐ **A** you start to edge forward on to the crossing
☐ **B** the pedestrians have reached a safe position
☐ **C** the pedestrians are clear of the front of your vehicle
☐ **D** a driver from the opposite direction reaches the crossing

The electronic device will automatically detect that the pedestrians have reached a safe position. Don't proceed until the green light shows it is safe for vehicles to do so.

---

78 Mark *one* answer

Which instrument panel warning light would show that headlights are on full beam?

☐ A    ☐ B

☐ C    ☐ D

You should be aware of where all the warning lights and visual aids are on the vehicle you are driving. If you are driving a vehicle for the first time you should take time to check all the controls.

79 Mark *one* answer
At puffin crossings, which light will not show to a driver?

☐ **A** Flashing amber   ☐ **B** Red
☐ **C** Steady amber   ☐ **D** Green

A flashing amber light is shown at pelican crossings, but puffin crossings are different. They are controlled electronically and automatically detect when pedestrians are on the crossing. The phase is shortened or lengthened according to the position of the pedestrians.

80 Mark *one* answer
You should leave at least a two-second gap between your vehicle and the one in front when conditions are

☐ **A** wet   ☐ **B** good
☐ **C** damp   ☐ **D** foggy

In good, dry conditions an alert driver, who's driving a vehicle with tyres and brakes in good condition, needs to keep a distance of at least two seconds from the car in front.

81 Mark *one* answer
You are driving at night on an unlit road behind another vehicle. You should

☐ **A** flash your headlights
☐ **B** use dipped beam headlights
☐ **C** switch off your headlights
☐ **D** use full beam headlights

If you follow another vehicle with your headlights on full beam they could dazzle the driver. Leave a safe distance and ensure that the light from your dipped beam falls short of the vehicle in front.

82 Mark *one* answer
You are driving a slow-moving vehicle on a narrow winding road. You should

☐ **A** keep well out to stop vehicles overtaking dangerously
☐ **B** wave following vehicles past you if you think they can overtake quickly
☐ **C** pull in safely when you can, to let following vehicles overtake
☐ **D** give a left signal when it is safe for vehicles to overtake you

Try not to hold up a queue of traffic. Other road users may become impatient and this could lead to reckless actions. If you're driving a slow-moving vehicle and the road is narrow, look for a safe place to pull in. DON'T wave other traffic past since this could be dangerous if you or they haven't seen an oncoming vehicle.

83 Mark *one* answer
A loose filler cap on your diesel fuel tank will

☐ **A** make the engine difficult to start
☐ **B** make roads slippery for other road users
☐ **C** improve your vehicle's fuel consumption
☐ **D** increase the level of exhaust emissions

Diesel fuel is especially slippery if spilled on a wet road. At the end of a dry spell of weather you should be aware that the road surfaces may have a high level of diesel spillage that hasn't been washed away by rain.

Section 2 – Attitude

84 Mark *one* answer
To avoid spillage after refuelling, you should make sure that

- ☐ **A** your tank is only three quarters full
- ☐ **B** you have used a locking filler cap
- ☐ **C** you check your fuel gauge is working
- ☑ **D** your filler cap is securely fastened

When learning to drive it is a good idea to practise filling your car with fuel. Ask your instructor if you can use a petrol station and fill the fuel tank yourself. You need to know where the filler cap is located on the car you are driving in order to park on the correct side of the pump. Take care not to overfill the tank or spill fuel. Make sure you secure the filler cap as soon as you have replaced the fuel nozzle.

85 Mark *one* answer
If your vehicle uses diesel fuel, take extra care when refuelling. Diesel fuel when spilt is

- ☐ **A** sticky
- ☐ **B** odourless
- ☐ **C** clear
- ☑ **D** slippery

If you are using diesel, or are at a pump which has a diesel facility, be aware that there may be spilt fuel on the ground. Fuel contamination on the soles of your shoes may cause them to slip when using the foot pedals.

86 Mark *one* answer
What style of driving causes increased risk to everyone?

- ☐ **A** Considerate
- ☐ **B** Defensive
- ☐ **C** Competitive
- ☐ **D** Responsible

Competitive driving increases the risks to everyone and is the opposite of responsible, considerate and defensive driving. Defensive driving is about questioning the actions of other road users and being prepared for the unexpected. Don't be taken by surprise.

87 Mark *one* answer
Young, inexperienced and newly qualified drivers can often be involved in crashes. This is due to

- ☐ **A** being too cautious at junctions
- ☐ **B** driving in the middle of their lane
- ☐ **C** showing off and being competitive
- ☐ **D** staying within the speed limit

Newly qualified, and particularly young drivers, are more vulnerable in the first year after passing the test. Inexperience plays a part in this but it's essential to have the correct attitude. Be responsible and always show courtesy and consideration to other road users.

88 Mark *one* answer
What's badly affected if the tyres are under-inflated?

☐ **A** Braking
☐ **B** Indicating
☐ **C** Changing gear
☐ **D** Parking

Your tyres are your only contact with the road. To prevent problems with braking and steering keep your tyres free from defects; they must have sufficient tread depth and be correctly inflated. Correct tyre pressures help reduce the risk of skidding and provide a safer and more comfortable drive or ride.

89 Mark *one* answer
You must NOT sound your horn

☐ **A** between 10pm and 6am in a built-up area
☐ **B** at any time in a built-up area
☐ **C** between 11.30pm and 7am in a built-up area
☐ **D** between 11.30pm and 6am on any road

Vehicles can be noisy. Every effort must be made to prevent excessive noise, especially in built-up areas at night. Don't
 • rev the engine
 • sound the horn
unnecessarily.
It is illegal to sound your horn in a built-up area between 11.30pm and 7am, except when another vehicle poses a danger.

90 Mark *one* answer
The pictured vehicle is 'environmentally friendly' because it is powered by

☐ **A** gravity
☐ **B** diesel
☐ **C** electricity
☐ **D** unleaded petrol

Trams are powered by electricity and therefore don't emit exhaust fumes. They also ease traffic congestion by offering drivers an alternative to using their car.

91 Mark *one* answer
Supertrams or Light Rapid Transit (LRT) systems are environmentally friendly because

☐ **A** they use diesel power
☐ **B** they use quieter roads
☐ **C** they use electric power
☐ **D** they do not operate during rush hour

This means that they do not emit toxic fumes, which add to city pollution problems. They are also a lot quieter and smoother to ride on.

92 Mark *one* answer

'Red routes' in major cities have been introduced to

- ☐ **A** raise the speed limits
- ☒ **B** help the traffic flow
- ☐ **C** provide better parking
- ☐ **D** allow lorries to load more freely

Traffic jams today are often caused by the volume of traffic. However, inconsiderate parking can lead to the closure of an inside lane or traffic having to wait for oncoming vehicles. Driving slowly in traffic increases fuel consumption and causes a build-up of exhaust fumes.

93 Mark *one* answer

Road humps, chicanes, and narrowings are

- ☐ **A** always at major road works
- ☐ **B** used to increase traffic speed
- ☐ **C** at toll-bridge approaches only
- ☐ **D** traffic calming measures

Traffic calming measures help keep vehicle speeds low in congested areas where there are pedestrians and children. A pedestrian is much more likely to survive a collision with a vehicle travelling at 20mph than at 40mph.

94 Mark *one* answer

The purpose of a catalytic converter is to reduce

- ☐ **A** fuel consumption
- ☐ **B** the risk of fire
- ☐ **C** toxic exhaust gases
- ☐ **D** engine wear

Catalytic converters are designed to reduce a large percentage of toxic emissions. They work more efficiently when the engine has reached its normal working temperature.

95 Mark *one* answer

Catalytic converters are fitted to make the

- ☐ **A** engine produce more power
- ☐ **B** exhaust system easier to replace
- ☐ **C** engine run quietly
- ☐ **D** exhaust fumes cleaner

Harmful gases in the exhaust system pollute the atmosphere. These gases are reduced by up to 90% if a catalytic converter is fitted. Cleaner air benefits everyone, especially people who live or work near congested roads.

96 Mark *one* answer

It is essential that tyre pressures are checked regularly. When should this be done?

- ☐ **A** After any lengthy journey
- ☐ **B** After travelling at high speed
- ☐ **C** When tyres are hot
- ☐ **D** When tyres are cold

When you check the tyre pressures do so when the tyres are cold. This will give you a more accurate reading. The heat generated from a long journey will raise the pressure inside the tyre.

97 Mark *one* answer
When should you NOT use your horn in a built-up area?

- ☐ **A** Between 8pm and 8am
- ☐ **B** Between 9pm and dawn
- ☐ **C** Between dusk and 8am
- ☐ **D** Between 11.30pm and 7am

By law you must not sound your horn in a built-up area between 11.30pm and 7am. The exception to this is when another road user poses a danger.

98 Mark *one* answer
You will use more fuel if your tyres are

- ☐ **A** under-inflated
- ☐ **B** of different makes
- ☐ **C** over-inflated
- ☐ **D** new and hardly used

Check your tyre pressures frequently normally once a week. If pressures are lower than those recommended by the manufacturer, there will be more 'rolling resistance'. The engine will have to work harder to overcome this, leading to increased fuel consumption.

99 Mark *one* answer
How should you dispose of a used car battery?

- ☐ **A** Bury it in your garden
- ☐ **B** Put it in the dustbin
- ☐ **C** Take it to a local authority site
- ☐ **D** Leave it on waste land

Batteries contain acid, which is hazardous, and they must be disposed of safely. This means taking them to an appropriate disposal site.

100 Mark *one* answer
What is most likely to cause high fuel consumption?

- ☐ **A** Poor steering control
- ☐ **B** Accelerating around bends
- ☐ **C** Staying in high gears
- ☐ **D** Harsh braking and accelerating

Accelerating and braking gently and smoothly will help to save fuel, reduce wear on your vehicle and is better for the environment.

101 Mark *one* answer
The fluid level in your battery is low. What should you top it up with?

- ☐ **A** Battery acid
- ☐ **B** Distilled water
- ☐ **C** Engine oil
- ☐ **D** Engine coolant

Some modern batteries are maintenance-free. Check your vehicle handbook and, if necessary, make sure that the plates in each battery cell are covered.

102 Mark *one* answer
You are parked on the road at night. Where must you use parking lights?

- ☐ **A** Where there are continuous white lines in the middle of the road
- ☐ **B** Where the speed limit exceeds 30mph
- ☐ **C** Where you are facing oncoming traffic
- ☐ **D** Where you are near a bus stop

When parking at night, park in the direction of the traffic. This will enable other road users to see the reflectors on the rear of your vehicle. Use your parking lights if the speed limit is over 30mph.

103 Mark *one* answer

Motor vehicles can harm the environment. This has resulted in

☐ **A** less use of electrical vehicles
☐ **B** improved public transport
☐ **C** raised speed limits
☐ **D** air pollution

Exhaust emissions are harmful to health. Together with vibration from heavy traffic, this can result in damage to buildings. Most petrol and diesel fuels come from a non-renewable source. Anything you can do to reduce your use of these fuels will help the environment.

104 Mark *one* answer

What can cause excessive or uneven tyre wear?

☐ **A** A faulty gearbox
☐ **B** A faulty braking system
☐ **C** A faulty electrical system
☐ **D** A faulty exhaust system

If you see that parts of the tread on your tyres are wearing before others, it may indicate a brake, steering or suspension fault. Regular servicing will help to detect faults at an early stage and this will avoid the risk of minor faults becoming serious or even dangerous.

105 Mark *one* answer

You need to top up your battery. What level should you fill to?

☐ **A** The top of the battery
☐ **B** Half-way up the battery
☐ **C** Just below the cell plates
☒ **D** Just above the cell plates

Top up the battery with distilled water and make sure each cell plate is covered.

106 Mark *one* answer

You are parking on a two-way road at night. The speed limit is 40mph. You should park on the

☐ **A** left with parking lights on
☐ **B** left with no lights on
☐ **C** right with parking lights on
☐ **D** right with dipped headlights on

At night all vehicles must display parking lights when parked on a road with a speed limit greater than 30mph. They should be close to the kerb, facing in the direction of the traffic flow and not within a distance as specified in The Highway Code.

107 Mark *one* answer

Before starting a journey it is wise to plan your route. How can you do this?

☐ **A** Look at a map
☐ **B** Contact your local garage
☐ **C** Look in your vehicle handbook
☐ **D** Check your vehicle registration document

Planning your journey before you set out can help to make it much easier, more pleasant and may help to ease traffic congestion. Look at a map to help you to do this. You may need different scale maps depending on where and how far you're going. Printing or writing out the route can also help.

108 Mark *one* answer   **NI**

Before starting a journey, where can you get help to plan your route?

☐ **A** your local filling station
☐ **B** a motoring organisation
☐ **C** the Driver and Vehicle Licensing Agency
☐ **D** your vehicle manufacturer

Most motoring organisation websites allow you to create a detailed plan of your trip, showing directions and distances. Some also include advice on rest and fuel stops. The Traffic England website will give you information on roadworks and accidents, along with expected delay times.

109 Mark *one* answer

How can you plan your route before starting a long journey?

☐ **A** Check your vehicle's workshop manual
☐ **B** Ask your local garage
☐ **C** Use a route planner on the internet
☐ **D** Consult your travel agents

Various route planners are available on the internet. Most of them give you various options allowing you to choose the most direct, quickest or scenic route. They can also include rest and fuel stops and distances. Print them off and take them with you.

110 Mark *one* answer

Planning your route before setting out can be helpful. How can you do this?

☐ **A** Look in a motoring magazine
☐ **B** Only visit places you know
☐ **C** Try to travel at busy times
☐ **D** Print or write down the route

Print or write down your route before setting out. Some places are not well signed so using place names and road numbers may help you avoid problems en route. Try to get an idea of how far you're going before you leave. You can also use it to re-check the next stage at each rest stop.

111 Mark *one* answer
Why is it a good idea to plan your journey to avoid busy times?

- ☐ **A** You will have an easier journey
- ☐ **B** You will have a more stressful journey
- ☐ **C** Your journey time will be longer
- ☐ **D** It will cause more traffic congestion

No one likes to spend time in traffic queues. Try to avoid busy times related to school or work travel. As well as moving vehicles you should also consider congestion caused by parked cars, buses and coaches around schools.

112 Mark *one* answer
Planning your journey to avoid busy times has a number of advantages. One of these is

- ☐ **A** your journey will take longer
- ☐ **B** you will have a more pleasant journey
- ☐ **C** you will cause more pollution
- ☐ **D** your stress level will be greater

Having a pleasant journey can have safety benefits. You will be less tired and stressed and this will allow you to concentrate more on your driving or riding.

113 Mark *one* answer
It is a good idea to plan your journey to avoid busy times. This is because

- ☐ **A** your vehicle will use more fuel
- ☐ **B** you will see less road works
- ☐ **C** it will help to ease congestion
- ☐ **D** you will travel a much shorter distance

Avoiding busy times means that you are not adding needlessly to traffic congestion. Other advantages are that you will use less fuel and feel less stressed.

114 Mark *one* answer
By avoiding busy times when travelling

- ☐ **A** you are more likely to be held up
- ☐ **B** your journey time will be longer
- ☐ **C** you will travel a much shorter distance
- ☐ **D** you are less likely to be delayed

If possible, avoid the early morning and late afternoon and early evening 'rush hour'. Doing this should allow you to travel in a more relaxed frame of mind, concentrate solely on what you're doing and arrive at your destination feeling less stressed.

115 Mark *one* answer
It can help to plan your route before starting a journey. Why should you also plan an alternative route?

- ☐ **A** Your original route may be blocked
- ☐ **B** Your maps may have different scales
- ☐ **C** You may find you have to pay a congestion charge
- ☐ **D** Because you may get held up by a tractor

It can be frustrating and worrying to find your planned route is blocked by roadworks or diversions. If you have planned an alternative you will feel less stressed and more able to concentrate fully on your driving or riding. If your original route is mostly on motorways it's a good idea to plan an alternative using non-motorway roads. Always carry a map with you just in case you need to refer to it.

116 Mark *one* answer

As well as planning your route before starting a journey, you should also plan an alternative route. Why is this?

- ☐ **A** To let another driver overtake
- ☑ **B** Your first route may be blocked
- ☐ **C** To avoid a railway level crossing
- ☐ **D** In case you have to avoid emergency vehicles

It's a good idea to plan an alternative route in case your original route is blocked for any reason. You're less likely to feel worried and stressed if you've got an alternative in mind. This will enable you to concentrate fully on your driving or riding. Always carry a map that covers the area you will travel in.

117 Mark *one* answer

You are making an appointment and will have to travel a long distance. You should

- ☐ **A** allow plenty of time for your journey
- ☐ **B** plan to go at busy times
- ☐ **C** avoid all national speed limit roads
- ☐ **D** prevent other drivers from overtaking

Always allow plenty of time for your journey in case of unforeseen problems. Anything can happen, punctures, breakdowns, road closures, diversions etc. You will feel less stressed and less inclined to take risks if you are not 'pushed for time'.

118 Mark *one* answer

Rapid acceleration and heavy braking can lead to

- ☐ **A** reduced pollution
- ☐ **B** increased fuel consumption
- ☐ **C** reduced exhaust emissions
- ☐ **D** increased road safety

Using the controls smoothly can reduce fuel consumption by about 15% as well as reducing wear and tear on your vehicle. Plan ahead and anticipate changes of speed well in advance. This will reduce the need to accelerate rapidly or brake sharply.

119 Mark *one* answer

What percentage of all emissions does road transport account for?

- ☐ **A** 10%
- ☐ **B** 20%
- ☐ **C** 30%
- ☐ **D** 40%

Transport is an essential part of modern life but it does have environmental effects. In heavily populated areas traffic is the biggest source of air pollution. Eco-safe driving and riding will reduce emissions and can make a surprising difference to local air quality.

120 Mark *one* answer
Which of these, if allowed to get low, could cause you to crash?

☐ **A** Anti-freeze level
☐ **B** Brake fluid level
☐ **C** Battery water level
☐ **D** Radiator coolant level

You should carry out frequent checks on all fluid levels but particularly brake fluid. As the brake pads or shoes wear down the brake fluid level will drop. If it drops below the minimum mark on the fluid reservoir, air could enter the hydraulic system and lead to a loss of braking efficiency or complete brake failure.

121 Mark *one* answer
New petrol-engined cars must be fitted with catalytic converters. The reason for this is to

☐ **A** control exhaust noise levels
☐ **B** prolong the life of the exhaust system
☐ **C** allow the exhaust system to be recycled
☑ **D** reduce harmful exhaust emissions

We should all be concerned about the effect traffic has on our environment. Fumes from vehicles are polluting the air around us. Catalytic converters act like a filter, removing some of the toxic waste from exhaust gases.

122 Mark *one* answer
What can cause heavy steering?

☐ **A** Driving on ice
☐ **B** Badly worn brakes
☐ **C** Over-inflated tyres
☐ **D** Under-inflated tyres

If your tyre pressures are low this will increase the drag on the road surface and make the steering feel heavy. Your vehicle will also use more fuel. Incorrectly inflated tyres can affect the braking, cornering and handling of your vehicle to a dangerous level.

123 Mark *one* answer
Driving with under-inflated tyres can affect

☐ **A** engine temperature
☐ **B** fuel consumption
☐ **C** the gearbox
☐ **D** oil pressure

Keeping your vehicle's tyres correctly inflated is a legal requirement. Your vehicle will use less fuel and have a shorter stopping distance with correctly inflated tyres.

124 Mark *one* answer
Excessive or uneven tyre wear can be caused by faults in the

☐ **A** gearbox   ☐ **B** engine
☐ **C** suspension   ☐ **D** exhaust system

Uneven wear on your tyres can be caused by the condition of your vehicle. Having it serviced regularly will ensure that the brakes, steering and wheel alignment are maintained in good order.

125 Mark *one* answer
The main cause of brake fade is

☐ **A** the brakes overheating
☐ **B** air in the brake fluid
☐ **C** oil on the brakes
☐ **D** the brakes out of adjustment

If your vehicle is fitted with drum brakes they can get hot and lose efficiency. This happens when they're used continually, such as on a long, steep, downhill stretch of road. Using a lower gear will assist the braking and help prevent the vehicle gaining momentum.

126 Mark *one* answer
Your anti-lock brakes warning light stays on. You should

☐ **A** check the brake fluid level
☐ **B** check the footbrake free play
☐ **C** check that the handbrake is released
☐ **D** have the brakes checked immediately

Consult the vehicle handbook or garage before driving the vehicle. Only drive to a garage if it is safe to do so. If you're not sure get expert help.

127 Mark *one* answer
While driving, this warning light on your dashboard comes on. It means

☐ **A** a fault in the braking system
☐ **B** the engine oil is low
☐ **C** a rear light has failed
☐ **D** your seat belt is not fastened

Don't ignore this warning light. A fault in your braking system could have dangerous consequences.

128 Mark *one* answer
It is important to wear suitable shoes when you are driving. Why is this?

☐ **A** To prevent wear on the pedals
☐ **B** To maintain control of the pedals
☐ **C** To enable you to adjust your seat
☐ **D** To enable you to walk for assistance if you break down

When you're going to drive, ensure that you're wearing suitable clothing.
   Comfortable shoes will ensure that you have proper control of the foot pedals.

129 Mark *one* answer

What will reduce the risk of neck injury resulting from a collision?

☐ **A** An air-sprung seat
☐ **B** Anti-lock brakes
☐ **C** A collapsible steering wheel
☑ **D** A properly adjusted head restraint

If you're involved in a collision, head restraints will reduce the risk of neck injury. They must be properly adjusted. Make sure they aren't positioned too low, in a crash this could cause damage to the neck.

130 Mark *one* answer

You are testing your suspension. You notice that your vehicle keeps bouncing when you press down on the front wing. What does this mean?

☐ **A** Worn tyres
☐ **B** Tyres under-inflated
☐ **C** Steering wheel not located centrally
☐ **D** Worn shock absorbers

If you find that your vehicle bounces as you drive around a corner or bend in the road, the shock absorbers might be worn. Press down on the front wing and, if the vehicle continues to bounce, take it to be checked by a qualified mechanic.

131 Mark *one* answer

A roof rack fitted to your car will

☐ **A** reduce fuel consumption
☐ **B** improve the road handling
☐ **C** make your car go faster
☐ **D** increase fuel consumption

If you are carrying anything on a roof rack, make sure that any cover is securely fitted and does not flap about while driving. Aerodynamically designed roof boxes are available which reduce wind resistance and, in turn, fuel consumption.

132 Mark *one* answer

It is illegal to drive with tyres that

☐ **A** have been bought second-hand
☐ **B** have a large deep cut in the side wall
☐ **C** are of different makes
☐ **D** are of different tread patterns

When checking your tyres for cuts and bulges in the side walls, don't forget the inner walls (i.e. those facing each other under the vehicle).

133 Mark *one* answer

The legal minimum depth of tread for car tyres over three quarters of the breadth is

☐ **A** 1mm   ☐ **B** 1.6mm
☐ **C** 2.5mm   ☐ **D** 4mm

Tyres must have sufficient depth of tread to give them a good grip on the road surface. The legal minimum for cars is 1.6mm.

This depth should be across the central three quarters of the breadth of the tyre and around the entire circumference.

134 Mark *one* answer

You are carrying two 13-year-old children and their parents in your car. Who is responsible for seeing that the children wear seat belts?

- [ ] **A** The children's parents
- [x] **B** You, the driver
- [ ] **C** The front-seat passenger
- [ ] **D** The children

Seat belts save lives and reduce the risk of injury. If you are carrying passengers under 14 years of age it's your responsibility as the driver to ensure that their seat belts are fastened or they are seated in an approved child restraint.

135 Mark *one* answer

When a roof rack is not in use it should be removed. Why is this?

- [ ] **A** It will affect the suspension
- [ ] **B** It is illegal
- [ ] **C** It will affect your braking
- [x] **D** It will waste fuel

We are all responsible for the environment we live in. If each driver takes responsibility for conserving fuel, together it will make a difference.

136 Mark *one* answer

How can drivers help the environment?

- [ ] **A** By accelerating harshly
- [x] **B** By accelerating gently
- [ ] **C** By using leaded fuel
- [ ] **D** By driving faster

Rapid acceleration and heavy braking lead to increased
- fuel consumption
- wear

on your vehicle.
Having your vehicle regularly serviced will maintain its efficiency, produce cleaner emissions and reduces the risk of a breakdown.

137 Mark *one* answer

You can avoid wasting fuel by

- [x] **A** having your vehicle serviced regularly
- [ ] **B** revving the engine in the lower gears
- [ ] **C** keeping an empty roof rack on your vehicle
- [ ] **D** driving at higher speeds where possible

If you don't have your vehicle serviced regularly, the engine won't burn all the fuel efficiently. This will cause increased fuel consumption and an increase in the amount of harmful emissions it produces.

138 Mark *one* answer
To reduce the volume of traffic on the roads you could

- ☐ **A** drive in a bus lane
- ☑ **B** use a car with a smaller engine
- ☐ **C** walk or cycle on short journeys
- ☐ **D** travel by car at all times

Walking or cycling are good ways to get exercise. Using public transport also gives the opportunity for exercise if you walk to the railway station or bus stop. Leave the car at home whenever you can.

139 Mark *one* answer
What is most likely to waste fuel?

- ☐ **A** Reducing your speed
- ☐ **B** Driving on motorways
- ☐ **C** Using different brands of fuel
- ☐ **D** Under-inflated tyres

Wasting fuel costs you money and also causes unnecessary pollution. Ensuring your tyres are correctly inflated, avoiding carrying unnecessary weight and removing a roof rack that's not in use, will all help to reduce your fuel consumption.

140 Mark *one* answer
What can you do to help the environment?

- ☑ **A** Cycle when possible
- ☐ **B** Drive on under-inflated tyres
- ☐ **C** Only use your car for short journeys
- ☐ **D** Use the brakes heavily

Although the car is a convenient form of transport it can also cause damage to health and the environment, especially when used on short journeys. Before you travel consider other types of transport. Walking and cycling are better for your health and public transport can be quicker, more convenient and less stressful than driving.

141 Mark *one* answer
To help protect the environment you should NOT

- ☐ **A** remove your roof rack when unloaded
- ☐ **B** use your car for very short journeys
- ☐ **C** walk, cycle, or use public transport
- ☐ **D** empty the boot of unnecessary weight

Try not to use your car as a matter of routine. For shorter journeys, consider walking or cycling instead – this is much better for both you and the environment.

142 Mark *one* answer
What does the law require you to keep in good condition?

☐ **A** Gears
☐ **B** Transmission
☐ **C** Door locks
☐ **D** Seat belts

Unless exempt, you and your passengers must wear a seat belt (or suitable child restraint). The seat belts in your car must be in good condition and working properly; they will be checked during its MOT test.

143 Mark *one* answer
Driving at 70mph uses more fuel than driving at 50mph by up to

☐ **A** 10%
☐ **B** 30%
☐ **C** 75%
☐ **D** 100%

Your vehicle will use less fuel if you avoid heavy acceleration. The higher the engine revs, the more fuel you will use. Using the same gear, a vehicle travelling at 70mph will use up to 30% more fuel to cover the same distance, than at 50mph. However, don't travel so slowly that you inconvenience or endanger other road users.

144 Mark *one* answer
Your vehicle pulls to one side when braking. You should

☐ **A** change the tyres around
☐ **B** consult your garage as soon as possible
☐ **C** pump the pedal when braking
☐ **D** use your handbrake at the same time

The brakes on your vehicle must be effective and properly adjusted. If your vehicle pulls to one side when braking, take it to be checked by a qualified mechanic. Don't take risks.

145 Mark *one* answer
Unbalanced wheels on a car may cause

☐ **A** the steering to pull to one side
☐ **B** the steering to vibrate
☐ **C** the brakes to fail
☐ **D** the tyres to deflate

If your wheels are out of balance it will cause the steering to vibrate at certain speeds. It is not a fault that will rectify itself. You will have to take your vehicle to a garage or tyre fitting firm as this is specialist work.

146 Mark *one* answer
Turning the steering wheel while your car is stationary can cause damage to the

☐ **A** gearbox   ☐ **B** engine
☐ **C** brakes   ☐ **D** tyres

Turning the steering wheel when the car is not moving is known as dry steering. It can cause unnecessary wear to the tyres and steering mechanism.

147 Mark *one* answer
**You have to leave valuables in your car.
It would be safer to**

- ☐ **A** put them in a carrier bag
- ☐ **B** park near a school entrance
- ☐ **C** lock them out of sight
- ☐ **D** park near a bus stop

If you have to leave valuables in your car, always lock them out of sight. If you can see them, so can a thief.

148 Mark *one* answer
How could you deter theft from your car when leaving it unattended?

- ☐ **A** Leave valuables in a carrier bag
- ☐ **B** Lock valuables out of sight
- ☐ **C** Put valuables on the seats
- ☐ **D** Leave valuables on the floor

If you can see valuables in your car so can a thief. If you can't take them with you lock them out of sight or you risk losing them, as well as having your car damaged.

149 Mark *one* answer.
Which of the following may help to deter a thief from stealing your car?

- ☐ **A** Always keeping the headlights on
- ☐ **B** Fitting reflective glass windows
- ☐ **C** Always keeping the interior light on
- ☐ **D** Etching the car number on the windows

Having your car registration number etched on all your windows is a cheap and effective way to deter professional car thieves.

150 Mark *one* answer
Which of the following should not be kept in your vehicle?

- ☐ **A** The car dealer's details
- ☐ **B** The owner's manual
- ☐ **C** The service record
- ☐ **D** The vehicle registration document

Never leave the vehicle registration document inside your car. This document would help a thief dispose of your car more easily.

151 Mark *one* answer
What should you do when leaving your vehicle?

- ☐ **A** Put valuable documents under the seats
- ☐ **B** Remove all valuables
- ☐ **C** Cover valuables with a blanket
- ☐ **D** Leave the interior light on

When leaving your vehicle unattended it is best to take valuables with you. If you can't, then lock them out of sight in the boot. If you can see valuables in your car, so can a thief.

152 Mark *one* answer
Which of these is most likely to deter the theft of your vehicle?

- ☐ **A** An immobiliser
- ☐ **B** Tinted windows
- ☐ **C** Locking wheel nuts
- ☐ **D** A sun screen

An immobiliser makes it more difficult for your vehicle to be driven off by a thief. It is a particular deterrent to opportunist thieves.

153 Mark *one* answer
When parking and leaving your car, what should you do to make it more secure?

- ☐ **A** Park under a shady tree
- ☐ **B** Turn the wheels towards the kerb
- ☐ **C** Park in a quiet road
- ☐ **D** Engage the steering lock

When you leave your car always engage the steering lock. This increases the security of your vehicle, as the ignition key is needed to release the steering lock.

154 Mark *one* answer
When leaving your vehicle parked and unattended you should

- ☐ **A** park near a busy junction
- ☐ **B** park in a housing estate
- ☐ **C** remove the key and lock it
- ☐ **D** leave the left indicator on

An unlocked car is an open invitation to thieves. Leaving the keys in the ignition not only makes your car easy to steal, it could also invalidate your insurance.

155 Mark *one* answer
What will improve fuel consumption?

- ☐ **A** Reducing your speed
- ☐ **B** Rapid acceleration
- ☐ **C** Late and harsh braking
- ☐ **D** Driving in lower gears

Harsh braking, frequent gear changes and harsh acceleration increase fuel consumption. An engine uses less fuel when travelling at a constant low speed.

You need to look well ahead so you're able to anticipate hazards early. Easing off the accelerator and timing your approach, at junctions, for example, can reduce the fuel consumption of your vehicle.

156 Mark *one* answer
You service your own vehicle. How should you get rid of the old engine oil?

- ☐ **A** Take it to a local authority site
- ☐ **B** Pour it down a drain
- ☐ **C** Tip it into a hole in the ground
- ☐ **D** Put it into your dustbin

It is illegal to pour engine oil down any drain. Oil is a pollutant and harmful to wildlife. Dispose of it safely at an authorised site.

157 Mark *one* answer
Why do MOT tests include a strict exhaust emission test?

☐ **A** To recover the cost of expensive garage equipment

☐ **B** To help protect the environment against pollution

☐ **C** To discover which fuel supplier is used the most

☐ **D** To make sure diesel and petrol engines emit the same fumes

Emission tests are carried out to ensure your vehicle's engine is operating efficiently. This ensures the pollution produced by the engine is kept to a minimum. If your vehicle is not serviced regularly, it may fail the annual MOT test.

158 Mark *one* answer
To reduce the damage your vehicle causes to the environment you should

☐ **A** use narrow side streets

☐ **B** brake harshly

☐ **C** use busy routes

☐ **D** anticipate well ahead

By looking well ahead and recognising hazards in good time, you can avoid last-minute harsh braking. Watch the traffic flow and look well ahead for potential hazards so you can control your speed accordingly. Avoid over-revving the engine and accelerating harshly as this increases wear to the engine and uses more fuel.

159 Mark *one* answer
Your vehicle has a catalytic converter. Its purpose is to reduce

☐ **A** exhaust noise

☐ **B** fuel consumption

☐ **C** exhaust emissions

☐ **D** engine noise

Catalytic converters reduce the harmful gases given out by the engine. The gases are changed by a chemical process as they pass through a special filter.

160 Mark *one* answer
A properly serviced vehicle will result in

☐ **A** reduced insurance premiums

☐ **B** lower vehicle excise duty (road tax)

☐ **C** better fuel economy

☐ **D** slower journey times

All vehicles need to be serviced to keep working efficiently; an efficient engine uses less fuel and produces less harmful emissions than an engine running inefficiently. Keeping the vehicle serviced to the manufacturers schedule should also keep it reliable and reduce the chance of it breaking down.

161 Mark *one* answer
You enter a road where there are road humps. What should you do?

- ☐ **A** Maintain a reduced speed throughout
- ☐ **B** Accelerate quickly between each one
- ☐ **C** Always keep to the maximum legal speed
- ☐ **D** Drive slowly at school times only

The humps are there for a reason – to reduce the speed of the traffic. Don't accelerate harshly between them as this means you will only have to brake harshly to negotiate the next hump. Harsh braking and accelerating uses more fuel.

162 Mark *one* answer
When should you especially check the engine oil level?

- ☐ **A** Before a long journey
- ☐ **B** When the engine is hot
- ☐ **C** Early in the morning
- ☐ **D** Every 6,000 miles

During long journeys an engine can use more oil than on shorter trips. Insufficient oil is potentially dangerous: it can lead to excessive wear and expensive repairs.

Most cars have a dipstick to allow the oil level to be checked. If not, you should refer to the vehicle's handbook. Also make checks on
- fuel
- water
- tyres.

163 Mark *one* answer
You are having difficulty finding a parking space in a busy town. You can see there is space on the zigzag lines of a zebra crossing. Can you park there?

- ☐ **A** No, unless you stay with your car
- ☐ **B** Yes, in order to drop off a passenger
- ☐ **C** Yes, if you do not block people from crossing
- ☐ **D** No, not in any circumstances

It's an offence to park there. You will be causing an obstruction by obscuring the view of both pedestrians and drivers.

164 Mark *one* answer
When leaving your car unattended for a few minutes you should

- ☐ **A** leave the engine running
- ☐ **B** switch the engine off but leave the key in
- ☐ **C** lock it and remove the key
- ☐ **D** park near a traffic warden

Always switch off the engine, remove the key and lock your car, even if you are only leaving it for a few minutes.

165 Mark *one* answer
When parking and leaving your car for a few minutes you should

- ☐ **A** leave it unlocked
- ☐ **B** lock it and remove the key
- ☐ **C** leave the hazard warning lights on
- ☐ **D** leave the interior light on

Always remove the key and lock your car even if you only leave it for a few minutes.

166 Mark *one* answer

When leaving your vehicle where should you park if possible?

☐ **A** Opposite a traffic island
☐ **B** In a secure car park
☐ **C** On a bend
☐ **D** At or near a taxi rank

Whenever possible leave your car in a secure car park. This will help stop thieves.

---

167 Mark *one* answer

Where would parking your vehicle cause an obstruction?

☐ **A** Alongside a parking meter
☐ **B** In front of a property entrance
☐ **C** On your driveway
☐ **D** In a marked parking space

Don't park your vehicle where it may obstruct an access to a business or property. Think carefully before you slow down and stop. Look at road markings and signs to ensure that you aren't parking illegally.

168 Mark *one* answer

Where would parking cause an obstruction to others?

☐ **A** Near the brow of a hill
☐ **B** In a lay-by
☐ **C** Where the kerb is raised
☐ **D** On your driveway

Think about the effect your parking will have on other road users. Don't forget that not all vehicles are the size of a car. Large vehicles will need more room to pass and might need more time too. Parking out of the view of traffic, such as before the brow of a hill, causes unnecessary risks. Think before you park.

---

169 Mark *one* answer

You are away from home and have to park your vehicle overnight. Where should you leave it?

☐ **A** Opposite another parked vehicle
☐ **B** In a quiet road
☐ **C** Opposite a traffic island
☐ **D** In a secure car park

When leaving your vehicle unattended, use a secure car park whenever possible.

170 Mark *one* answer
The most important reason for having a properly adjusted head restraint is to

☐ **A** make you more comfortable
☐ **B** help you to avoid neck injury
☐ **C** help you to relax
☐ **D** help you to maintain your driving position

The restraint should be adjusted so that it gives maximum protection to the head and neck. This will help in the event of a rear-end collision.

171 Mark *one* answer
A driver causes more damage to the environment by

☐ **A** choosing a fuel-efficient vehicle
☐ **B** having their vehicle regularly serviced
☐ **C** driving in as high a gear as possible
☐ **D** making a lot of short journeys

Avoid using your car for short journeys. On a short journey the engine is unlikely to warm up fully and will therefore be running less efficiently; this will result in it using more fuel and producing higher levels of harmful emissions.

172 Mark *one* answer
As a driver, you can help reduce pollution levels in town centres by

☐ **A** driving more quickly
☐ **B** over-revving in a low gear
☐ **C** walking or cycling
☐ **D** driving short journeys

Using a vehicle for short journeys means the engine does not have time to reach its normal running temperature. When an engine is running below its normal running temperature it produces increased amounts of pollution. Walking and cycling do not create pollution and have health benefits as well.

173 Mark *one* answer
How can you reduce the chances of your car being broken into when leaving it unattended?

☐ **A** Take all valuables with you
☐ **B** Park near a taxi rank
☐ **C** Place any valuables on the floor
☐ **D** Park near a fire station

When leaving your car take all valuables with you if you can, otherwise lock them out of sight.

174 Mark *one* answer
How can you help to prevent your car radio being stolen?

☐ **A** Park in an unlit area
☐ **B** Hide the radio with a blanket
☐ **C** Park near a busy junction
☐ **D** Install a security-coded radio

A security-coded radio can deter thieves as it is likely to be of little use when removed from the vehicle.

175 Mark *one* answer

You are parking your car. You have some valuables which you are unable to take with you. What should you do?

- ☐ **A** Park near a police station
- ☐ **B** Put them under the driver's seat
- ☐ **C** Lock them out of sight
- ☐ **D** Park in an unlit side road

Your vehicle is like a shop window for thieves. Either remove all valuables or lock them out of sight.

176 Mark *one* answer

Wherever possible, which one of the following should you do when parking at night?

- ☐ **A** Park in a quiet car park
- ☐ **B** Park in a well-lit area
- ☐ **C** Park facing against the flow of traffic
- ☐ **D** Park next to a busy junction

If you are away from home, try to avoid leaving your vehicle unattended in poorly-lit areas. If possible park in a secure, well-lit car park.

177 Mark *one* answer

How can you lessen the risk of your vehicle being broken into at night?

- ☐ **A** Leave it in a well-lit area
- ☐ **B** Park in a quiet side road
- ☐ **C** Don't engage the steering lock
- ☐ **D** Park in a poorly-lit area

Having your vehicle broken into or stolen can be very distressing and inconvenient. Avoid leaving your vehicle unattended in poorly-lit areas.

178 Mark *one* answer

To help keep your car secure you could join a

- ☐ **A** vehicle breakdown organisation
- ☐ **B** vehicle watch scheme
- ☐ **C** advanced driver's scheme
- ☐ **D** car maintenance class

The vehicle watch scheme helps reduce the risk of having your car stolen. By displaying high visibility vehicle watch stickers in your car you are inviting the police to stop your vehicle if seen in use between midnight and 5am.

179 Mark *one* answer

On a vehicle, where would you find a catalytic converter?

- ☐ **A** In the fuel tank
- ☐ **B** In the air filter
- ☐ **C** On the cooling system
- ☐ **D** On the exhaust system

Although carbon dioxide is still produced, a catalytic converter reduces the toxic and polluting gases by up to 90%. Unleaded fuel must be used in vehicles fitted with a catalytic converter.

180 Mark *one* answer
When leaving your car to help keep it secure you should

- ☐ **A** leave the hazard warning lights on
- ☐ **B** lock it and remove the key
- ☐ **C** park on a one-way street
- ☐ **D** park in a residential area

To help keep your car secure when you leave it, you should always remove the key from the ignition, lock it and take the key with you. Don't make it easy for thieves.

181 Mark *one* answer
You will find that driving smoothly can

- ☐ **A** reduce journey times by about 15%
- ☐ **B** increase fuel consumption by about 15%
- ☐ **C** reduce fuel consumption by about 15%
- ☐ **D** increase journey times by about 15%

Not only will you save about 15% of your fuel by driving smoothly, but you will also reduce the amount of wear and tear on your vehicle as well as reducing pollution. You will also feel more relaxed and have a more pleasant journey.

182 Mark *one* answer
You can save fuel when conditions allow by

- ☐ **A** using lower gears as often as possible
- ☐ **B** accelerating sharply in each gear
- ☐ **C** using each gear in turn
- ☐ **D** missing out some gears

Missing out intermediate gears when appropriate, helps to reduce the amount of time spent accelerating and decelerating – the time when your vehicle uses most fuel.

183 Mark *one* answer
How can driving in an eco-safe manner help protect the environment?

- ☐ **A** Through the legal enforcement of speed regulations
- ☐ **B** By increasing the number of cars on the road
- ☐ **C** Through increased fuel bills
- ☐ **D** By reducing exhaust emissions

Eco-safe driving is all about becoming a more environmentally-friendly driver. This will make your journeys more comfortable as well as considerably reducing your fuel bills and reducing emissions that can damage the environment.

184 Mark *one* answer
What does eco-safe driving achieve?

- ☐ **A** Increased fuel consumption
- ☐ **B** Improved road safety
- ☐ **C** Damage to the environment
- ☐ **D** Increased exhaust emissions

The emphasis is on hazard awareness and planning ahead. By looking well ahead you will have plenty of time to deal with hazards safely and won't need to brake sharply. This will also reduce damage to the environment.

185 Mark *one* answer
How can missing out some gear changes save fuel?

- ☐ **A** By reducing the amount of time you are accelerating
- ☐ **B** Because there is less need to use the footbrake
- ☐ **C** By controlling the amount of steering
- ☐ **D** Because coasting is kept to a minimum

Missing out some gears helps to reduce the amount of time you are accelerating and this saves fuel. You don't always need to change up or down through each gear. As you accelerate between each gear more fuel is injected into the engine than if you had maintained constant acceleration. Fewer gear changes means less fuel used.

186 Mark *one* answer
Missing out some gears saves fuel by reducing the amount of time you spend

- ☐ **A** braking
- ☐ **B** coasting
- ☐ **C** steering
- ☐ **D** accelerating

It is not always necessary to change up or down through each gear. Missing out intermediate gears helps to reduce the amount of time you are accelerating. Because fuel consumption is at its highest when accelerating this can save fuel.

187 Mark *one* answer
You are checking your trailer tyres. What is the legal minimum tread depth over the central three quarters of its breadth?

- ☐ **A** 1mm
- ☐ **B** 1.6mm
- ☐ **C** 2mm
- ☐ **D** 2.6mm

Trailers and caravans may be left in storage over the winter months and tyres can deteriorate. It's important to check their tread depth and also the pressures and general condition. The legal tread depth applies to the central three quarters of its breadth over its entire circumference.

188 Mark *one* answer
Fuel consumption is at its highest when you are

- ☐ **A** braking
- ☐ **B** coasting
- ☐ **C** accelerating
- ☐ **D** steering

Always try to use the accelerator smoothly. Taking your foot off the accelerator allows the momentum of the car to take you forward, especially when going downhill. This can save a considerable amount of fuel without any loss of control over the vehicle.

189 Mark *one* answer

Car passengers MUST wear a seat belt/ restraint if one is available, unless they are

☐ **A** under 14 years old
☐ **B** under 1.5 metres (5 feet) in height
☐ **C** sitting in the rear seat
☐ **D** exempt for medical reasons

If you have adult passengers it is their responsibility to wear a seat belt, but you should still remind them to use them as they get in the car. It is your responsibility to ensure that all children in your car are secured with an appropriate restraint.

190 Mark *one* answer

Car passengers MUST wear a seat belt if one is available, unless they are

☐ **A** in a vehicle fitted with air bags
☐ **B** travelling within a congestion charging zone
☐ **C** sitting in the rear seat
☐ **D** exempt for medical reasons

When adult passengers are travelling in a vehicle, it is their own responsibility to wear a seat belt. However, you should still remind them to use a seat belt.

191 Mark *one* answer

You are driving the children of a friend home from school. They are both under 14 years old. Who is responsible for making sure they wear a seat belt or approved child restraint where required?

☐ **A** An adult passenger
☐ **B** The children
☐ **C** You, the driver
☐ **D** Your friend

Passengers should always be secured and safe. Children should be encouraged to fasten their seat belts or approved restraints themselves from an early age so that it becomes a matter of routine. As the driver you must check that they are fastened securely. It's your responsibility.

192 Mark *one* answer

You have too much oil in your engine. What could this cause?

☐ **A** Low oil pressure
☐ **B** Engine overheating
☐ **C** Chain wear
☐ **D** Oil leaks

Too much oil in the engine will create excess pressure and could damage engine seals and cause oil leaks. Any excess oil should be drained off.

193 Mark *one* answer

You are carrying a 5-year-old child in the back seat of your car. They are under 1.35 metres (4 feet 5 inches). A correct child restraint is NOT available. They MUST

- ☐ **A** sit behind the passenger seat
- ☐ **B** use an adult seat belt
- ☐ **C** share a belt with an adult
- ☐ **D** sit between two other children

Usually a correct child restraint MUST be used. In a few exceptional cases if one is not available an adult seat belt MUST be used. In a collision unrestrained objects and people can cause serious injury or even death.

---

194 Mark *one* answer

You are carrying a child using a rear-facing baby seat. You want to put it on the front passenger seat. What MUST you do before setting off?

- ☐ **A** Deactivate all front and rear airbags
- ☐ **B** Make sure any front passenger airbag is deactivated
- ☐ **C** Make sure all the child safety locks are off
- ☐ **D** Recline the front passenger seat

You MUST deactivate any frontal passenger airbag when using a rear-facing baby seat in a front passenger seat. It is ILLEGAL if you don't. If activated in a crash it could cause serious injury or death. Ensure you follow the manufacturers instructions. In some cars this is now done automatically.

195 Mark *one* answer

You are carrying an 11-year-old child in the back seat of your car. They are under 1.35 metres (4 feet 5 inches) in height. You MUST make sure that

- ☐ **A** they sit between two belted people
- ☐ **B** they can fasten their own seat belt
- ☐ **C** a suitable child restraint is available
- ☐ **D** they can see clearly out of the front window

It is your responsibility as a driver to ensure that children are secure and safe in your vehicle. Make sure you are familiar with the rules. In a few very exceptional cases when a child restraint is not available, an adult seat belt MUST be used. Child restraints and seat belts save lives!

---

196 Mark *one* answer

You are parked at the side of the road. You will be waiting for some time for a passenger. What should you do?

- ☐ **A** Switch off the engine
- ☐ **B** Apply the steering lock
- ☐ **C** Switch off the radio
- ☐ **D** Use your headlights

If your vehicle is stationary and is likely to remain so for some time, switch off the engine. We should all try to reduce global warming and pollution.

197 Mark *one* answer
You are using a rear-facing baby seat. You want to put it on the front passenger seat which is protected by a frontal airbag. What MUST you do before setting off?

☑ **A** Deactivate the airbag
☐ **B** Turn the seat to face sideways
☐ **C** Ask a passenger to hold the baby
☐ **D** Put the child in an adult seat belt

If the airbag activates near a baby seat, it could cause serious injury or even death to the child. It is illegal to fit a rear-facing baby seat into a passenger seat protected by an active frontal airbag. You MUST secure it in a different seat or deactivate the relevant airbag. Follow the manufacturers advice when fitting a baby seat.

198 Mark *one* answer
You are carrying a five-year-old child in the back seat of your car. They are under 1.35 metres (4 feet 5 inches) in height. They MUST use an adult seat belt ONLY if

☐ **A** a correct child restraint is not available
☐ **B** it is a lap type belt
☐ **C** they sit between two adults
☐ **D** it can be shared with another adult

You should make all efforts to ensure a correct child restraint is used, with very few exceptions. If in specific circumstances one is not available, then an adult seat belt MUST be used. Unrestrained objects, including people, can be thrown violently around in a collision, and may cause serious injury or even death!

199 Mark *one* answer
You are leaving your vehicle parked on a road unattended. When may you leave the engine running?

☐ **A** If you will be parking for less than five minutes
☐ **B** If the battery keeps going flat
☐ **C** When parked in a 20mph zone
☐ **D** Never if you are away from the vehicle

When you leave your vehicle parked on a road, switch off the engine and secure the vehicle. Make sure there aren't any valuables visible, shut all the windows, lock the vehicle, set the alarm if it has one and use an anti-theft device such as a steering wheel lock.

200 Mark *one* answer
Braking distances on ice can be

☐ **A** twice the normal distance
☐ **B** five times the normal distance
☐ **C** seven times the normal distance
☐ **D** ten times the normal distance

In icy and snowy weather, your stopping
distance will increase by up to ten times
compared to good, dry conditions.
   Take extra care when braking,
accelerating and steering, to cut down
the risk of skidding.

201 Mark *one* answer
**Freezing conditions will affect the distance
it takes you to come to a stop. You should
expect stopping distances to increase
by up to**

☐ **A** two times
☐ **B** three times
☐ **C** five times
☐ **D** ten times

Your tyre grip is greatly reduced on icy roads
and you need to allow up to ten times the
normal stopping distance.

202 Mark *one* answer
**In windy conditions you need to take extra
care when**

☐ **A** using the brakes
☐ **B** making a hill start
☐ **C** turning into a narrow road
☐ **D** passing pedal cyclists

You should always give cyclists plenty of
room when overtaking. When it's windy, a
sudden gust could blow them off course.

203 Mark *one* answer
**When approaching a right-hand bend you
should keep well to the left. Why is this?**

☐ **A** To improve your view of the road
☐ **B** To overcome the effect of the road's slope
☐ **C** To let faster traffic from behind overtake
☐ **D** To be positioned safely if you skid

Doing this will give you an earlier view
around the bend and enable you to see any
hazards sooner.
   It also reduces the risk of collision with an
oncoming vehicle that may have drifted over
the centre line while taking the bend.

204 Mark *one* answer
**You have just gone through deep water. To
dry off the brakes you should**

☐ **A** accelerate and keep to a high speed for a
short time
☐ **B** go slowly while gently applying the brakes
☐ **C** avoid using the brakes at all for a few miles
☐ **D** stop for at least an hour to allow them
time to dry

Water on the brakes will act as a lubricant,
causing them to work less efficiently. Using
the brakes lightly as you go along will dry
them out.

205 Mark *one* answer
In very hot weather the road surface can become soft. What will this affect?

☐ **A** The suspension
☐ **B** The exhaust emissions
☐ **C** The fuel consumption
☒ **D** The tyre grip

If the road surface becomes very hot it can soften. Tyres are unable to grip onto a soft surface as well as they can a firm dry one. Take care when cornering and braking.

206 Mark *one* answer
Where are you most likely to be affected by a side wind?

☐ **A** On a narrow country lane
☐ **B** On an open stretch of road
☐ **C** On a busy stretch of road
☐ **D** On a long, straight road

In windy conditions, care must be taken on exposed roads. A strong gust of wind can blow you off course. Watch out for other road users who are particularly likely to be affected, such as cyclists, motorcyclists, high-sided lorries and vehicles towing trailers.

207 Mark *one* answer
In good conditions, what is the typical stopping distance at 70mph?

☐ **A** 53 metres (175 feet)
☐ **B** 60 metres (197 feet)
☐ **C** 73 metres (240 feet)
☒ **D** 96 metres (315 feet)

Note that this is the typical stopping distance. It will take at least this distance to think, brake and stop in good conditions. In poor conditions it will take much longer.

208 Mark *one* answer
What is the shortest overall stopping distance on a dry road at 60mph?

☐ **A** 53 metres (175 feet)
☒ **B** 58 metres (190 feet)
☐ **C** 73 metres (240 feet)
☐ **D** 96 metres (315 feet)

This distance is the equivalent of 18 car lengths. Try pacing out 73 metres and then look back. It's probably further than you think.

209 Mark *one* answer

You are following a vehicle at a safe distance on a wet road. Another driver overtakes you and pulls into the gap you have left. What should you do?

☐ **A** Flash your headlights as a warning
☐ **B** Try to overtake safely as soon as you can
☐ **C** Drop back to regain a safe distance
☐ **D** Stay close to the other vehicle until it moves on

Wet weather will affect the time it takes for you to stop and can affect your control. Your speed should allow you to stop safely and in good time. If another vehicle pulls into the gap you've left, ease back until you've regained your stopping distance.

210 Mark *one* answer

You are travelling at 50mph on a good, dry road. What is your typical overall stopping distance?

☐ **A** 36 metres (118 feet)
☐ **B** 53 metres (175 feet)
☐ **C** 75 metres (245 feet)
☐ **D** 96 metres (315 feet)

Even in good conditions it will usually take you further than you think to stop. Don't just learn the figures, make sure you understand how far the distance is.

211 Mark *one* answer

You are on a good, dry, road surface. Your brakes and tyres are good. What is the typical overall stopping distance at 40mph?

☐ **A** 23 metres (75 feet)
☐ **B** 36 metres (118 feet)
☐ **C** 53 metres (175 feet)
☐ **D** 96 metres (315 feet)

Stopping distances are affected by a number of variable factors. These include the type, model and condition of your vehicle, road and weather conditions, and your reaction time. Look well ahead for hazards and leave enough space between you and the vehicle in front. This should allow you to pull up safely if you have to, without braking sharply.

212 Mark *one* answer

What should you do when overtaking a motorcyclist in strong winds?

☐ **A** Pass close
☐ **B** Pass quickly
☐ **C** Pass wide
☐ **D** Pass immediately

In strong winds riders of two-wheeled vehicles are particularly vulnerable. When you overtake them allow plenty of room. Always check to the left as you pass.

213 Mark *one* answer
You are overtaking a motorcyclist in strong winds? What should you do?

☐ **A** Allow extra room
☐ **B** Give a thank you wave
☐ **C** Move back early
☐ **D** Sound your horn

It is easy for motorcyclists to be blown off course. Always give them plenty of room if you decide to overtake, especially in strong winds. Decide whether you need to overtake at all. Always check to the left as you pass.

---

214 Mark *one* answer
Overall stopping distance is made up of thinking and braking distance. You are on a good, dry road surface with good brakes and tyres. What is the typical BRAKING distance from 50mph?

☐ **A** 14 metres (46 feet)
☐ **B** 24 metres (80 feet)
☐ **C** 38 metres (125 feet)
☐ **D** 55 metres (180 feet)

Be aware this is just the braking distance. You need to add the thinking distance to this to give the OVERALL STOPPING DISTANCE. At 50mph the typical thinking distance will be 15 metres (50 feet), plus a braking distance of 38 metres (125 feet), giving an overall stopping distance of 53 metres (175 feet). The distance could be greater than this depending on your attention and response to any hazards. These figures are a general guide.

215 Mark *one* answer
In heavy motorway traffic the vehicle behind you is following too closely. How can you lower the risk of a collision?

☐ **A** Increase your distance from the vehicle in front
☐ **B** Operate the brakes sharply
☐ **C** Switch on your hazard lights
☐ **D** Move onto the hard shoulder and stop

On busy roads traffic may still travel at high speeds despite being close together. Don't follow too closely to the vehicle in front. If a driver behind seems to be 'pushing' you, gradually increase your distance from the vehicle in front by slowing down gently. This will give you more space in front if you have to brake, and lessen the risk of a collision involving several vehicles.

216 Mark *one* answer

You are following other vehicles in fog. You have your lights on. What else can you do to reduce the chances of being in a collision?

- ☐ **A** Keep close to the vehicle in front
- ☐ **B** Use your main beam instead of dipped headlights
- ☐ **C** Keep up with the faster vehicles
- ☐ **D** Reduce your speed and increase the gap in front

When it's foggy use dipped headlights. This will help you see and be seen by other road users. If visibility is seriously reduced consider using front and rear fog lights if you have them. Keep a sensible speed and don't follow the vehicle in front too closely. If the road is wet and slippery you'll need to allow twice the normal stopping distance.

217 Mark *one* answer

When entering a contraflow system, you should

- ☐ **A** choose an appropriate lane in good time
- ☐ **B** switch lanes at any time to make progress
- ☐ **C** increase speed to pass through quickly
- ☐ **D** follow other motorists closely to avoid long queues

In a contraflow system you'll be travelling close to oncoming traffic and sometimes in narrow lanes. You should get into the correct lane in good time, obey the temporary speed limit signs and keep a safe separation distance from the vehicle ahead.

218 Mark *one* answer

What is the most common cause of skidding?

- ☐ **A** Worn tyres
- ☐ **B** Driver error
- ☐ **C** Other vehicles
- ☐ **D** Pedestrians

A skid happens when the driver changes the speed or direction of their vehicle so suddenly that the tyres can't keep their grip on the road.

Remember that the risk of skidding on wet or icy roads is much greater than in dry conditions.

219 Mark *one* answer

You are driving on an icy road. How can you avoid wheel-spin?

- ☑ **A** Drive at a slow speed in as high a gear as possible
- ☐ **B** Use the handbrake if the wheels start to slip
- ☐ **C** Brake gently and repeatedly
- ☐ **D** Drive in a low gear at all times

If you're travelling on an icy road extra caution will be required to avoid loss of control. Keeping your speed down and using the highest gear possible will reduce the risk of the tyres losing their grip on this slippery surface.

220 Mark *one* answer

Skidding is mainly caused by

- ☐ **A** the weather
- ☐ **B** the driver
- ☐ **C** the vehicle
- ☐ **D** the road

You should always consider the conditions and drive accordingly.

221 Mark *one* answer
You're driving in freezing conditions. What should you do when approaching a sharp bend?

☐ **A** Coast into the bend
☐ **B** Gently apply your handbrake
☐ **C** Firmly use your footbrake
☐ **D** Slow down before you reach the bend

Harsh use of the accelerator, brakes or steering are likely to lead to skidding, especially on slippery surfaces. Avoid steering and braking at the same time.

In icy conditions it's very important that you constantly assess what's ahead, so that you can take appropriate action in plenty of time.

222 Mark *one* answer
You are turning left on a slippery road. The back of your vehicle slides to the right. You should

☐ **A** brake firmly and not turn the steering wheel
☐ **B** steer carefully to the left
☐ **C** steer carefully to the right
☐ **D** brake firmly and steer to the left

Steer into the skid but be careful not to overcorrect with too much steering. Too much movement may lead to a skid in the opposite direction. Skids don't just happen, they are caused. The three important factors in order are: the driver, the vehicle and the road conditions.

223 Mark *one* answer
Before starting a journey in freezing weather you should clear ice and snow from your vehicle's

☐ **A** aerial
☐ **B** windows
☐ **C** bumper
☐ **D** boot

Only travel if you have to. Making unnecessary journeys in bad weather can increase the risk of having a collision. It's important that you can see and be seen. Make sure any snow or ice is cleared from lights, mirrors, number plates and windows.

224 Mark *one* answer
You are trying to move off on snow. You should use

☐ **A** the lowest gear you can
☐ **B** the highest gear you can
☐ **C** a high engine speed
☐ **D** the handbrake and footbrake together

If you attempt to move off in a low gear, such as first, the engine will rev at a higher speed. This could cause the wheels to spin and dig further into the snow.

225 Mark *one* answer
When driving in falling snow you should

- ☐ **A** brake firmly and quickly
- ☐ **B** be ready to steer sharply
- ☐ **C** use sidelights only
- ☐ **D** brake gently in plenty of time

Braking on snow can be extremely dangerous. Be gentle with both the accelerator and brake to prevent wheel-spin.

---

226 Mark *one* answer
The MAIN benefit of having four-wheel drive is to improve

- ☐ **A** road holding
- ☐ **B** fuel consumption
- ☐ **C** stopping distances
- ☐ **D** passenger comfort

By driving all four wheels there is improved grip, but this does not replace the skills you need to drive safely. The extra grip helps road holding when travelling on slippery or uneven roads.

---

227 Mark *one* answer
You are about to go down a steep hill. To control the speed of your vehicle you should

- ☐ **A** select a high gear and use the brakes carefully
- ☐ **B** select a high gear and use the brakes firmly
- ☐ **C** select a low gear and use the brakes carefully
- ☐ **D** select a low gear and avoid using the brakes

When going down a steep hill your vehicle will speed up. This will make it more difficult for you to stop. Select a lower gear to give you more engine braking and control. Use this in combination with careful use of the brakes.

228 Mark *one* answer
What should you do when parking your vehicle facing downhill?

- ☐ **A** Turn the steering wheel towards the kerb
- ☐ **B** Park close to the bumper of another car
- ☐ **C** Park with two wheels on the kerb
- ☐ **D** Turn the steering wheel away from the kerb

Turning the wheels towards the kerb will allow it to act as a chock, preventing any forward movement of the vehicle. It will also help to leave it in gear, or select 'Park' if you have an automatic.

---

229 Mark *one* answer
You are driving in a built-up area. You approach a speed hump. You should

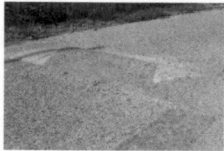

- ☐ **A** move across to the left-hand side of the road
- ☐ **B** wait for any pedestrians to cross
- ☐ **C** slow your vehicle right down
- ☐ **D** stop and check both pavements

Many towns have speed humps to slow down traffic. Slow down when driving over them. If you go too fast they may affect your steering and suspension, causing you to lose control or even damaging it. Be aware of pedestrians in these areas.

230 Mark *one* answer
You are on a long, downhill slope. What should you do to help control the speed of your vehicle?

☐ **A** Select neutral
☐ **B** Select a lower gear
☐ **C** Grip the handbrake firmly
☐ **D** Apply the parking brake gently

Selecting a low gear when travelling downhill will help you to control your speed. The engine will assist the brakes and help prevent your vehicle gathering speed.

231 Mark *one* answer
Anti-lock brakes prevent wheels from locking. This means the tyres are less likely to

☐ **A** aquaplane
☐ **B** skid
☐ **C** puncture
☐ **D** wear

If an anti-lock braking system is fitted it activates automatically when maximum braking pressure is applied or when it senses that the wheels are about to lock. It prevents the wheels from locking so you can continue to steer the vehicle during braking. It does not remove the need for good driving practices such as anticipation and correct speed for the conditions.

232 Mark *one* answer
Anti-lock brakes reduce the chances of a skid occurring particularly when

☐ **A** driving down steep hills
☐ **B** braking during normal driving
☐ **C** braking in an emergency
☐ **D** driving on good road surfaces

The anti-lock braking system will operate when the brakes have been applied harshly. It will reduce the chances of your car skidding, but it is not a miracle cure for careless driving.

233 Mark *one* answer
Vehicles fitted with anti-lock brakes

☐ **A** are impossible to skid
☐ **B** can be steered while you are braking
☐ **C** accelerate much faster
☐ **D** are not fitted with a handbrake

Preventing the wheels from locking means that the vehicle's steering and stability can be maintained, leading to safer stopping. However, you must ensure that the engine does not stall, as this could disable the power steering. Look in your vehicle handbook for the correct method when stopping in an emergency.

234 Mark *one* answer

Anti-lock brakes may not work as effectively if the road surface is

☐ **A** dry
☐ **B** loose
☐ **C** firm
☐ **D** smooth

Poor contact with the road surface could cause one or more of the tyres to lose grip on the road. This is more likely to happen when braking in poor weather conditions and when the road has a loose or uneven surface.

235 Mark *one* answer

Anti-lock brakes are of most use when you are

☐ **A** braking gently
☐ **B** driving on worn tyres
☐ **C** braking excessively
☐ **D** driving normally

Anti-lock brakes will not be required when braking normally. Looking well down the road and anticipating possible hazards could prevent you having to brake late and harshly. Knowing that you have anti-lock brakes is not an excuse to drive in a careless or reckless way.

236 Mark *one* answer

Driving a vehicle fitted with anti-lock brakes allows you to

☐ **A** brake harder because it is impossible to skid
☐ **B** drive at higher speeds
☐ **C** steer and brake at the same time
☐ **D** pay less attention to the road ahead

When stopping in an emergency anti-lock brakes will help you continue to steer when braking. In poor weather conditions this may be less effective. You need to depress the clutch pedal to prevent the car stalling as most power steering systems use an engine-driven pump and will only operate when the engine is running. Look in your vehicle handbook for the correct method when stopping in an emergency.

237 Mark *one* answer

Anti-lock brakes can greatly assist with

☐ **A** a higher cruising speed
☐ **B** steering control when braking
☐ **C** control when accelerating
☐ **D** motorway driving

If the wheels of your vehicle lock they will not grip the road and you will lose steering control. In good conditions the anti-lock system will prevent the wheels locking and allow you to retain steering control.

238 Mark *one* answer
You are driving a vehicle fitted with anti-lock brakes. You need to stop in an emergency. You should apply the footbrake

- ☐ **A** slowly and gently
- ☐ **B** slowly but firmly
- ☐ **C** rapidly and gently
- ☑ **D** rapidly and firmly

Look well ahead down the road as you drive and give yourself time and space to react safely to any hazards. You may have to stop in an emergency due to a misjudgement by another driver or a hazard arising suddenly such as a child running out into the road. In this case, if your vehicle has anti-lock brakes, you should apply the brakes immediately and keep them firmly applied until you stop.

---

239 Mark *one* answer
Your vehicle has anti-lock brakes, but they may not always prevent skidding. This is most likely to happen when driving

- ☐ **A** in foggy conditions
- ☐ **B** at night on unlit roads
- ☐ **C** on loose road surfaces
- ☐ **D** on dry tarmac

On gravel or loose surfaces anti-lock brakes (ABS) may be ineffective. ABS may also be ineffective in very wet weather when water can build up between the tyre and the road surface. This is known as aquaplaning.

240 Mark *one* answer
You are driving along a country road. You see this sign. AFTER dealing safely with the hazard you should always

- ☐ **A** check your tyre pressures
- ☐ **B** switch on your hazard warning lights
- ☐ **C** accelerate briskly
- ☐ **D** test your brakes

Deep water can affect your brakes, so you should check that they're working properly before you build up speed again. Before you do this, remember to check your mirrors and consider what's behind you.

---

241 Mark *one* answer
You are driving in heavy rain. Your steering suddenly becomes very light. You should

- ☐ **A** steer towards the side of the road
- ☐ **B** apply gentle acceleration
- ☐ **C** brake firmly to reduce speed
- ☐ **D** ease off the accelerator

If the steering becomes light in these conditions it is probably due to a film of water that has built up between your tyres and the road surface. Easing off the accelerator should allow your tyres to displace the film of water and they should then regain their grip on the road.

242 Mark *one* answer
The roads are icy. You should drive slowly

- ☐ **A** in the highest gear possible
- ☐ **B** in the lowest gear possible
- ☐ **C** with the handbrake partly on
- ☐ **D** with your left foot on the brake

Driving at a slow speed in a high gear will reduce the likelihood of wheel-spin and help your vehicle maintain the best possible grip.

243 Mark *one* answer
You are driving along a wet road. How can you tell if your vehicle is aquaplaning?

- ☐ **A** The engine will stall
- ☐ **B** The engine noise will increase
- ☐ **C** The steering will feel very heavy
- ☐ **D** The steering will feel very light

If you drive at speed in very wet conditions your steering may suddenly feel 'light'. This means that the tyres have lifted off the surface of the road and are skating on the surface of the water. This is known as aquaplaning. Reduce speed by easing off the accelerator, but don't brake until your steering returns to normal.

244 Mark *one* answer
What would suggest you're driving on ice?

- ☐ **A** There's less wind noise
- ☐ **B** There's less tyre noise
- ☐ **C** There's less transmission noise
- ☐ **D** There's less engine noise

Drive extremely carefully when the roads are icy. When travelling on ice, tyres make virtually no noise and the steering feels light and unresponsive.

In icy conditions be very gentle when braking, accelerating and steering.

245 Mark *one* answer
You are driving along a wet road. How can you tell if your vehicle's tyres are losing their grip on the surface?

- ☐ **A** The engine will stall
- ☐ **B** The steering will feel very heavy
- ☐ **C** The engine noise will increase
- ☐ **D** The steering will feel very light

If you drive at speed in very wet conditions your steering may suddenly feel lighter than usual. This means that the tyres have lifted off the surface of the road and are skating on the surface of the water. This is known as aquaplaning. Reduce speed but don't brake until your steering returns to a normal feel.

246 Mark *one* answer
Your overall stopping distance will be much longer when driving

- ☐ **A** in the rain
- ☐ **B** in fog
- ☐ **C** at night
- ☐ **D** in strong winds

Extra care should be taken in wet weather as, on wet roads, your stopping distance could be double that necessary for dry conditions.

247 Mark *one* answer

You have driven through a flood. What is the first thing you should do?

☐ **A** Stop and check the tyres
☐ **B** Stop and dry the brakes
☐ **C** Check your exhaust
☑ **D** Test your brakes

Before you test your brakes you must check for following traffic. If it is safe, gently apply the brakes to clear any water that may be covering the braking surfaces.

248 Mark *one* answer

You are on a fast, open road in good conditions. For safety, the distance between you and the vehicle in front should be

☐ **A** a two-second time gap
☐ **B** one car length
☐ **C** 2 metres (6 feet 6 inches)
☐ **D** two car lengths

One useful method of checking that you've allowed enough room between you and the vehicle in front is the two-second rule.

To check for a two-second time gap, choose a stationary object ahead, such as a bridge or road sign. When the car in front passes the object say 'Only a fool breaks the two-second rule'. If you reach the object before you finish saying it you're too close.

249 Mark *one* answer

How can you use your vehicle's engine as a brake?

☐ **A** By changing to a lower gear
☐ **B** By selecting reverse gear
☐ **C** By changing to a higher gear
☐ **D** By selecting neutral gear

When driving on downhill stretches of road selecting a lower gear gives increased engine braking. This will prevent excess use of the brakes, which become less effective if they overheat.

250 Mark *one* answer

Anti-lock brakes are most effective when you

☐ **A** keep pumping the foot brake to prevent skidding
☐ **B** brake normally, but grip the steering wheel tightly
☑ **C** brake promptly and firmly until you have slowed down
☐ **D** apply the handbrake to reduce the stopping distance

Releasing the brake before you have slowed right down will disable the system. If you have to brake in an emergency ensure that you keep your foot firmly on the brake pedal until the vehicle has stopped.

251 Mark *one* answer
Your car is fitted with anti-lock brakes. You need to stop in an emergency. You should

- [ ] **A** brake normally and avoid turning the steering wheel
- [ ] **B** press the brake pedal promptly and firmly until you have stopped
- [ ] **C** keep pushing and releasing the foot brake quickly to prevent skidding
- [ ] **D** apply the handbrake to reduce the stopping distance

Keep pressure on the brake pedal until you have come to a stop. The anti-lock mechanism will activate automatically if it senses the wheels are about to lock.

252 Mark *one* answer
When would an anti-lock braking system start to work?

- [ ] **A** After the parking brake has been applied
- [ ] **B** Whenever pressure on the brake pedal is applied
- [ ] **C** Just as the wheels are about to lock
- [ ] **D** When the normal braking system fails to operate

The anti-lock braking system has sensors that detect when the wheels are about to lock. It releases the brakes momentarily to allow the wheels to revolve and grip, then automatically reapplies them. This cycle is repeated several times a second to maximise braking performance.

253 Mark *one* answer
Anti-lock brakes will take effect when

- [ ] **A** you do not brake quickly enough
- [ ] **B** maximum brake pressure has been applied
- [ ] **C** you have not seen a hazard ahead
- [ ] **D** speeding on slippery road surfaces

If your car is fitted with anti-lock brakes they will take effect when you use them very firmly in an emergency. The system will only activate when it senses the wheels are about to lock.

254 Mark *one* answer
You are on a wet motorway with surface spray. You should use

- [ ] **A** hazard flashers
- [ ] **B** dipped headlights
- [ ] **C** rear fog lights
- [ ] **D** sidelights

When surface spray reduces visibility switch on your dipped headlights. This will help other road users to see you.

255 Mark *one* answer
Your vehicle is fitted with anti-lock brakes. To stop quickly in an emergency you should

- ☐ **A** brake firmly and pump the brake pedal on and off
- ☐ **B** brake rapidly and firmly without releasing the brake pedal
- ☐ **C** brake gently and pump the brake pedal on and off
- ☐ **D** brake rapidly once, and immediately release the brake pedal

Once you have applied the brake keep your foot firmly on the pedal. Releasing the brake and reapplying it will disable the anti-lock brake system.

256 Mark *one* answer
Travelling for long distances in neutral (known as coasting)

- ☐ **A** improves the driver's control
- ☐ **B** makes steering easier
- ☑ **C** reduces the driver's control
- ☐ **D** uses more fuel

Coasting is the term used when the clutch is held down, or the gear lever is in neutral, and the vehicle is allowed to freewheel. This reduces the driver's control of the vehicle. When you coast, the engine can't drive the wheels to pull you through a corner. Coasting also removes the assistance of engine braking that helps to slow the car.

257 Mark *one* answer
How can you tell when you are driving over black ice?

- ☐ **A** It is easier to brake
- ☐ **B** The noise from your tyres sounds louder
- ☐ **C** You will see tyre tracks on the road
- ☐ **D** Your steering feels light

Sometimes you may not be able to see that the road is icy. Black ice makes a road look damp. The signs that you're travelling on black ice can be that
- the steering feels light
- the noise from your tyres suddenly goes quiet.

258 Mark *one* answer
What should you do when driving in fog?

- ☐ **A** Use side lights only
- ☐ **B** Position close to the centre line
- ☐ **C** Allow more time for your journey
- ☐ **D** Keep close to the car in front

Don't venture out if your journey is not necessary. If you have to travel and someone is expecting you at the other end, let them know that you'll be taking longer than usual for your journey. This will stop them worrying if you don't turn up on time and will also take the pressure off you, so you don't feel you have to rush.

259 Mark *one* answer

Where would you expect to see these markers?

- ☐ **A** On a motorway sign
- ☐ **B** On a railway bridge
- ☐ **C** On a large goods vehicle
- ☐ **D** On a diversion sign

These markers must be fitted to vehicles over 13 metres long, large goods vehicles, and rubbish skips placed in the road. They are reflective to make them easier to see in the dark.

---

260 Mark *one* answer

What is the main hazard shown in this picture?

- ☐ **A** Vehicles turning right
- ☐ **B** Vehicles doing U-turns
- ☐ **C** The cyclist crossing the road
- ☐ **D** Parked cars around the corner

Look at the picture carefully and try to imagine you're there. The cyclist in this picture appears to be trying to cross the road. You must be able to deal with the unexpected, especially when you're approaching a hazardous junction. Look well ahead to give yourself time to deal with any hazards.

261 Mark *one* answer

Which road user has caused a hazard?

- ☐ **A** The parked car (arrowed A)
- ☐ **B** The pedestrian waiting to cross (arrowed B)
- ☐ **C** The moving car (arrowed C)
- ☐ **D** The car turning (arrowed D)

The car arrowed A is parked within the area marked by zigzag lines at the pedestrian crossing. Parking here is illegal. It also

- blocks the view for pedestrians wishing to cross the road
- restricts the view of the crossing for approaching traffic.

---

262 Mark *one* answer

What should the driver of the car approaching the crossing do?

- ☐ **A** Continue at the same speed
- ☐ **B** Sound the horn
- ☐ **C** Drive through quickly
- ☐ **D** Slow down and get ready to stop

Look well ahead to see if any hazards are developing. This will give you more time to deal with them in the correct way. The man in the picture is clearly intending to cross the road. You should be travelling at a speed that allows you to check your mirror, slow down and stop in good time. You shouldn't have to brake harshly.

263 Mark *one* answer
What should the driver of the grey car (arrowed) be especially aware of?

- ☐ **A** The uneven road surface
- ☐ **B** Traffic following behind
- ☐ **C** Doors opening on parked cars
- ☐ **D** Empty parking spaces

When passing parked cars, there's a risk that a driver or passenger may not check before opening the door into the road. A defensive driver will drive slowly and be looking for people who may be about to get out of their car.

264 Mark *one* answer
You see this sign ahead. You should expect the road to

- ☐ **A** go steeply uphill
- ☐ **B** go steeply downhill
- ☐ **C** bend sharply to the left
- ☐ **D** bend sharply to the right

Adjust your speed in good time and select the correct gear for your speed. Going too fast into the bend could cause you to lose control.

Braking late and harshly while changing direction reduces your vehicle's grip on the road, and is likely to cause a skid.

265 Mark *one* answer
You are approaching this cyclist. You should

- ☐ **A** overtake before the cyclist gets to the junction
- ☐ **B** flash your headlights at the cyclist
- ☐ **C** slow down and allow the cyclist to turn
- ☐ **D** overtake the cyclist on the left-hand side

Keep well back and allow the cyclist room to take up the correct position for the turn. Don't get too close behind or try to squeeze past.

266 Mark *one* answer
Why must you take extra care when turning right at this junction?

- ☐ **A** Road surface is poor
- ☐ **B** Footpaths are narrow
- ☐ **C** Road markings are faint
- ☐ **D** There is reduced visibility

You may have to pull forward slowly until you can see up and down the road. Be aware that the traffic approaching the junction can't see you either. If you don't know that it's clear, don't go.

267 Mark *one* answer

When approaching this bridge you should give way to

- ☐ **A** bicycles
- ☐ **B** buses
- ☐ **C** motorcycles
- ☐ **D** cars

A double-deck bus or high-sided lorry will have to take up a position in the centre of the road so that it can clear the bridge. There is normally a sign to indicate this.

Look well down the road, through the bridge and be aware you may have to stop and give way to an oncoming large vehicle.

268 Mark *one* answer

What type of vehicle could you expect to meet in the middle of the road?

- ☐ **A** Lorry
- ☐ **B** Bicycle
- ☐ **C** Car
- ☐ **D** Motorcycle

The highest point of the bridge is in the centre so a large vehicle might have to move to the centre of the road to allow it enough room to pass under the bridge.

269 Mark *one* answer

At this blind junction you must stop

- ☐ **A** behind the line, then edge forward to see clearly
- ☐ **B** beyond the line at a point where you can see clearly
- ☐ **C** only if there is traffic on the main road
- ☐ **D** only if you are turning to the right

The 'stop' sign has been put here because there is a poor view into the main road. You must stop because it will not be possible to assess the situation on the move, however slowly you are travelling.

270 Mark *one* answer

A driver pulls out of a side road in front of you. You have to brake hard. You should

- ☐ **A** ignore the error and stay calm
- ☐ **B** flash your lights to show your annoyance
- ☐ **C** sound your horn to show your annoyance
- ☐ **D** overtake as soon as possible

Where there are a number of side roads, be alert. Be especially careful if there are a lot of parked vehicles because they can make it more difficult for drivers emerging to see you. Try to be tolerant if a vehicle does emerge and you have to brake quickly. Don't react aggressively.

271 Mark *one* answer
An elderly person's driving ability could be affected because they may be unable to

☐ **A** obtain car insurance
☐ **B** understand road signs
☐ **C** react very quickly
☐ **D** give signals correctly

Be tolerant of older drivers. Poor eyesight and hearing could affect the speed with which they react to a hazard and may cause them to be hesitant.

272 Mark *one* answer
You have just passed these warning lights. What hazard would you expect to see next?

☐ **A** A level crossing with no barrier
☐ **B** An ambulance station
☑ **C** A school crossing patrol
☐ **D** An opening bridge

These lights warn that children may be crossing the road to a nearby school. Slow down so that you're ready to stop if necessary.

273 Mark *one* answer
You are planning a long journey. Do you need to plan rest stops?

☐ **A** Yes, you should plan to stop every half an hour
☐ **B** Yes, regular stops help concentration
☐ **C** No, you will be less tired if you get there as soon as possible
☐ **D** No, only fuel stops will be needed

Try to plan your journey so that you can take rest stops. It's recommended that you take a break of at least 15 minutes after every two hours of driving or riding. This should help to maintain your concentration.

274 Mark *one* answer
A driver does something that upsets you. You should

☐ **A** try not to react
☐ **B** let them know how you feel
☐ **C** flash your headlights several times
☐ **D** sound your horn

There are times when other road users make a misjudgement or mistake. When this happens try not to get annoyed and don't react by showing anger. Sounding your horn, flashing your headlights or shouting won't help the situation. Good anticipation will help to prevent these incidents becoming collisions.

275 Mark *one* answer

The red lights are flashing. What should you do when approaching this level crossing?

- ☐ **A** Go through quickly
- ☐ **B** Go through carefully
- ☐ **C** Stop before the barrier
- ☐ **D** Switch on hazard warning lights

At level crossings the red lights flash before and when the barrier is down. At most crossings an amber light will precede the red lights. You must stop behind the white line unless you have already crossed it when the amber light comes on. NEVER zigzag around half-barriers.

---

276 Mark *one* answer

You are approaching crossroads. The traffic lights have failed. What should you do?

- ☐ **A** Brake and stop only for large vehicles
- ☐ **B** Brake sharply to a stop before looking
- ☐ **C** Be prepared to brake sharply to a stop
- ☐ **D** Be prepared to stop for any traffic.

When approaching a junction where the traffic lights have failed, you should proceed with caution. Treat the situation as an unmarked junction and be prepared to stop.

277 Mark *one* answer

What should the driver of the red car (arrowed) do?

- ☐ **A** Wave the pedestrians who are waiting to cross
- ☐ **B** Wait for the pedestrian in the road to cross
- ☐ **C** Quickly drive behind the pedestrian in the road
- ☐ **D** Tell the pedestrian in the road she should not have crossed

Some people might take longer to cross the road. They may be older or have a disability. Be patient and don't hurry them by showing your impatience. They might have poor eyesight or not be able to hear traffic approaching. If pedestrians are standing at the side of the road, don't signal or wave them to cross. Other road users may not have seen your signal and this could lead the pedestrians into a hazardous situation.

278 Mark *one* answer

You are following a slower-moving vehicle on a narrow country road. There is a junction just ahead on the right. What should you do?

- ☐ **A** Overtake after checking your mirrors and signalling
- ☐ **B** Stay behind until you are past the junction
- ☐ **C** Accelerate quickly to pass before the junction
- ☐ **D** Slow down and prepare to overtake on the left

You should never overtake as you approach a junction. If a vehicle emerged from the junction while you were overtaking, a dangerous situation could develop very quickly.

279 Mark *one* answer

What should you do as you approach this overhead bridge?

- ☐ **A** Move out to the centre of the road before going through
- ☐ **B** Find another route, this is only for high vehicles
- ☐ **C** Be prepared to give way to large vehicles in the middle of the road
- ☐ **D** Move across to the right-hand side before going through

Oncoming large vehicles may need to move to the middle of the road so that they can pass safely under the bridge. There will not be enough room for you to continue and you should be ready to stop and wait.

280 Mark *one* answer

Why are mirrors often slightly curved (convex)?

- ☐ **A** They give a wider field of vision
- ☐ **B** They totally cover blind spots
- ☐ **C** They make it easier to judge the speed of following traffic
- ☐ **D** They make following traffic look bigger

Although a convex mirror gives a wide view of the scene behind, you should be aware that it will not show you everything behind or to the side of the vehicle. Before you move off you will need to check over your shoulder to look for anything not visible in the mirrors.

281 Mark *one* answer

You see this sign on the rear of a slow-moving lorry that you want to pass. It is travelling in the middle lane of a three-lane motorway. You should

- ☐ **A** cautiously approach the lorry then pass on either side
- ☐ **B** follow the lorry until you can leave the motorway
- ☐ **C** wait on the hard shoulder until the lorry has stopped
- ☐ **D** approach with care and keep to the left of the lorry

This sign is found on slow-moving or stationary works vehicles. If you wish to overtake, do so on the left, as indicated. Be aware that there might be workmen in the area.

282 Mark *one* answer

You think the driver of the vehicle in front has forgotten to cancel their right indicator. You should

- ☐ **A** flash your lights to alert the driver
- ☐ **B** sound your horn before overtaking
- ☐ **C** overtake on the left if there is room
- ☐ **D** stay behind and not overtake

The driver may be unsure of the location of a junction and turn suddenly. Be cautious and don't attempt to overtake.

283 Mark *one* answer

What is the main hazard the driver of the red car (arrowed) should be aware of?

- ☐ **A** Glare from the sun may affect the driver's vision
- ☐ **B** The black car may stop suddenly
- ☐ **C** The bus may move out into the road
- ☐ **D** Oncoming vehicles will assume the driver is turning right

If you can do so safely give way to buses signalling to move off at bus stops. Try to anticipate the actions of other road users around you. The driver of the red car should be prepared for the bus pulling out. As you approach a bus stop look to see how many passengers are waiting to board. If the last one has just got on, the bus is likely to move off.

284 Mark *one* answer

This yellow sign on a vehicle indicates this is

- ☐ **A** a broken-down vehicle
- ☐ **B** a school bus
- ☐ **C** an ice cream van
- ☐ **D** a private ambulance

Buses which carry children to and from school may stop at places other than scheduled bus stops. Be aware that they might pull over at any time to allow children to get on or off. This will normally be when traffic is heavy during rush hour.

285 Mark *one* answer
What hazard should you be aware of when driving along this street?

- ☐ **A** Glare from the sun
- ☐ **B** Lack of road markings
- ☐ **C** Children running out between vehicles
- ☐ **D** Large goods vehicles

On roads where there are many parked vehicles you might not be able to see children between parked cars and they may run out into the road without looking.

286 Mark *one* answer
What is the main hazard you should be aware of when following this cyclist?

- ☐ **A** The cyclist may move to the left and dismount
- ☐ **B** The cyclist may swerve out into the road
- ☐ **C** The contents of the cyclist's carrier may fall onto the road
- ☐ **D** The cyclist may wish to turn right at the end of the road

When following a cyclist be aware that they have to deal with the hazards around them. They may wobble or swerve to avoid a pothole in the road or see a potential hazard and change direction suddenly. Don't follow them too closely or rev your engine impatiently.

287 Mark *one* answer
A driver's behaviour has upset you. It may help if you

- ☐ **A** stop and take a break
- ☐ **B** shout abusive language
- ☐ **C** gesture to them with your hand
- ☐ **D** follow their car, flashing your headlights

Tiredness may make you more irritable than you would be normally. You might react differently to situations because of it. If you feel yourself becoming tense, take a break.

288 Mark *one* answer
In areas where there are traffic calming measures you should

☐ **A** travel at a reduced speed
☐ **B** always travel at the speed limit
☐ **C** position in the centre of the road
☐ **D** only slow down if pedestrians are near

Traffic calming measures such as road humps, chicanes and narrowings are intended to slow you down. Maintain a reduced speed until you reach the end of these features. They are there to protect pedestrians. Kill your speed!

289 Mark *one* answer
When approaching this hazard why should you slow down?

☐ **A** Because of the level crossing
☐ **B** Because it's hard to see to the right
☐ **C** Because of approaching traffic
☐ **D** Because of animals crossing

You should be slowing down and selecting the correct gear in case you have to stop at the level crossing. Look for the signals and be prepared to stop if necessary.

290 Mark *one* answer
Why are place names painted on the road surface?

☐ **A** To restrict the flow of traffic
☐ **B** To warn you of oncoming traffic
☐ **C** To enable you to change lanes early
☐ **D** To prevent you changing lanes

The names of towns and cities may be painted on the road at busy junctions and complex road systems. Their purpose is to let you move into the correct lane in good time, allowing traffic to flow more freely.

291 Mark *one* answer
Some two-way roads are divided into three lanes. Why are these particularly dangerous?

☐ **A** Traffic in both directions can use the middle lane to overtake
☐ **B** Traffic can travel faster in poor weather conditions
☐ **C** Traffic can overtake on the left
☐ **D** Traffic uses the middle lane for emergencies only

If you intend to overtake you must consider that approaching traffic could be planning the same manoeuvre. When you have considered the situation and have decided it is safe, indicate your intentions early. This will show the approaching traffic that you intend to pull out.

292 Mark *one* answer

You are on a dual carriageway. Ahead you see a vehicle with an amber flashing light. What could this be?

- ☐ **A** An ambulance
- ☐ **B** A fire engine
- ☐ **C** A doctor on call
- ☐ **D** A disabled person's vehicle

An amber flashing light on a vehicle indicates that it is slow-moving. Battery powered vehicles used by disabled people are limited to 8mph. It's not advisable for them to be used on dual carriageways where the speed limit exceeds 50mph. If they are then an amber flashing light must be used.

293 Mark *one* answer

What does this signal from a police officer mean to oncoming traffic?

- ☐ **A** Go ahead
- ☐ **B** Stop
- ☐ **C** Turn left
- ☐ **D** Turn right

Police officers may need to direct traffic, for example, at a junction where the traffic lights have broken down. Check your copy of The Highway Code for the signals that they use.

294 Mark *one* answer

Why should you be cautious when going past this stationary bus?

- ☐ **A** There is traffic approaching in the distance
- ☐ **B** The driver may open the door
- ☐ **C** People may cross the road in front of it
- ☐ **D** The road surface will be slippery

A stationary bus at a bus stop can hide pedestrians who might try to cross the road just in front of it. Drive at a speed that will enable you to respond safely if you have to.

295 Mark *one* answer

You should NOT overtake

- ☐ **A** on a single carriageway
- ☐ **B** on a one-way street
- ☐ **C** approaching a junction
- ☐ **D** travelling up a long hill

You should overtake only when it's really necessary and you can see it's clear ahead. Look out for road signs and markings that show it's illegal or would be unsafe to overtake, for example approaching junctions or bends. In many cases overtaking is unlikely to significantly improve your journey time.

296 Mark *one* answer
What is an effect of drinking alcohol?

- ☐ **A** Poor judgement of speed
- ☐ **B** A loss of confidence
- ☐ **C** Faster reactions
- ☐ **D** Greater awareness of danger

Alcohol will severely reduce your ability to drive or ride safely and there are serious consequences if you're caught over the drink drive limit. It's known that alcohol can
- affect your judgement
- cause overconfidence
- reduced coordination and control.

297 Mark *one* answer
What does the solid white line at the side of the road indicate?

- ☐ **A** Traffic lights ahead
- ☐ **B** Edge of the carriageway
- ☐ **C** Footpath on the left
- ☐ **D** Cycle path

The continuous white line shows the edge of the carriageway. It can be especially useful when visibility is restricted, for example at night or in bad weather. It is discontinued where it crosses junctions, lay-bys etc.

298 Mark *one* answer
You are driving towards this level crossing. What would be the first warning of an approaching train?

- ☐ **A** Both half barriers down
- ☐ **B** A steady amber light
- ☐ **C** One half barrier down
- ☐ **D** Twin flashing red lights

The steady amber light will be followed by twin flashing red lights that mean you must stop. An alarm will also sound to alert you to the fact that a train is approaching.

299 Mark *one* answer
You are behind this cyclist. When the traffic lights change, what should you do?

- ☐ **A** Try to move off before the cyclist
- ☐ **B** Allow the cyclist time and room
- ☐ **C** Turn right but give the cyclist room
- ☐ **D** Tap your horn and drive through first

Hold back and allow the cyclist to move off. In some towns, junctions have special areas marked across the front of the traffic lane. These allow cyclists to wait for the lights to change and move off ahead of other traffic.

300 Mark *one* answer
While driving, you see this sign ahead. You should

- [ ] **A** stop at the sign
- [x] **B** slow, but continue around the bend
- [ ] **C** slow to a crawl and continue
- [ ] **D** stop and look for open farm gates

Drive around the bend at a steady speed in the correct gear. Be aware that you might have to stop for approaching trains.

301 Mark *one* answer
When the traffic lights change to green the white car should

- [x] **A** wait for the cyclist to pull away
- [ ] **B** move off quickly and turn in front of the cyclist
- [ ] **C** move close up to the cyclist to beat the lights
- [ ] **D** sound the horn to warn the cyclist

If you are waiting at traffic lights, check all around you before you move away, as cyclists often filter through waiting traffic. Allow the cyclist to move off safely.

302 Mark *one* answer
You intend to turn left at the traffic lights. Just before turning you should

- [ ] **A** check your right mirror
- [ ] **B** move close up to the white car
- [ ] **C** straddle the lanes
- [ ] **D** check for bicycles on your left

Check your nearside for cyclists before moving away. This is especially important if you have been in a stationary queue of traffic and are about to move off, as cyclists often try to filter past on the nearside of stationary vehicles.

303 Mark *one* answer
You should reduce your speed when driving along this road because

- [x] **A** there is a staggered junction ahead
- [ ] **B** there is a low bridge ahead
- [ ] **C** there is a change in the road surface
- [ ] **D** the road ahead narrows

Traffic could be turning off ahead of you, to the left or right.

Vehicles turning left will be slowing down before the junction and any vehicles turning right may have to stop to allow oncoming traffic to clear. Be prepared for this as you might have to slow down or stop behind them.

304 Mark *one* answer

You are driving at 60mph. As you approach this hazard you should

- ☐ **A** maintain your speed
- ☐ **B** reduce your speed
- ☐ **C** take the next right turn
- ☐ **D** take the next left turn

There could be stationary traffic ahead, waiting to turn right. Other traffic could be emerging and it may take time for them to gather speed.

305 Mark *one* answer

What might you expect to happen in this situation?

- ☐ **A** Traffic will move into the right-hand lane
- ☐ **B** Traffic speed will increase
- ☑ **C** Traffic will move into the left-hand lane
- ☐ **D** Traffic will not need to change position

Be courteous and allow the traffic to merge into the left-hand lane.

306 Mark *one* answer

You are driving on a road with several lanes. You see these signs above the lanes. What do they mean?

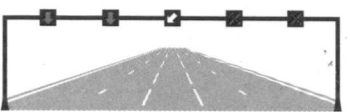

- ☐ **A** The two right lanes are open
- ☐ **B** The two left lanes are open
- ☐ **C** Traffic in the left lanes should stop
- ☐ **D** Traffic in the right lanes should stop

If you see a red cross above your lane it means that there is an obstruction ahead. You will have to move into one of the lanes which is showing the green light. If all the lanes are showing a red cross, then you must stop.

307 Mark *one* answer

You are invited to a pub lunch. You know that you will have to drive in the evening. What is your best course of action?

- ☐ **A** Avoid mixing your alcoholic drinks
- ☐ **B** Not drink any alcohol at all
- ☐ **C** Have some milk before drinking alcohol
- ☐ **D** Eat a hot meal with your alcoholic drinks

Alcohol will stay in the body for several hours and may make you unfit to drive later in the day. Drinking during the day will also affect your performance at work or study.

308 Mark *one* answer

You have been convicted of driving whilst unfit through drink or drugs. You will find this is likely to cause the cost of one of the following to rise considerably. Which one?

☐ **A** Road fund licence
☑ **B** Insurance premiums
☐ **C** Vehicle test certificate
☐ **D** Driving licence

You have shown that you are a risk to yourself and others on the road. For this reason insurance companies may charge you a higher premium.

309 Mark *one* answer

What advice should you give to a driver who has had a few alcoholic drinks at a party?

☐ **A** Have a strong cup of coffee and then drive home
☐ **B** Drive home carefully and slowly
☑ **C** Go home by public transport
☐ **D** Wait a short while and then drive home

Drinking black coffee or waiting a few hours won't make any difference. Alcohol takes time to leave the body.

A driver who has been drinking should go home by public transport or taxi. They might even be unfit to drive the following morning.

310 Mark *one* answer

You have been taking medicine for a few days which made you feel drowsy. Today you feel better but still need to take the medicine. You should only drive

☐ **A** if your journey is necessary
☐ **B** at night on quiet roads
☐ **C** if someone goes with you
☐ **D** after checking with your doctor

Take care – it's not worth taking risks. Always check with your doctor to be really sure. You may not feel drowsy now, but the medicine could have an effect on you later in the day.

311 Mark *one* answer

You are about to return home from holiday when you become ill. A doctor prescribes drugs which are likely to affect your driving. You should

☐ **A** drive only if someone is with you
☐ **B** avoid driving on motorways
☐ **C** not drive yourself
☐ **D** never drive at more than 30mph

Find another way to get home even if this proves to be very inconvenient. You must not put other road users, your passengers or yourself at risk.

312 Mark *one* answer
During periods of illness your ability to drive may be impaired. You MUST

☐ **A** see your doctor each time before you drive
☐ **B** only take smaller doses of any medicines
☐ **C** be medically fit to drive
☐ **D** take all your medicines with you when you drive

Be responsible and only drive if you are fit to do so. Some medication can affect your concentration and judgement when dealing with hazards. It may also cause you to become drowsy or even fall asleep. Driving while taking such medication is highly dangerous.

313 Mark *one* answer
You feel drowsy when driving. You should

☐ **A** stop and rest as soon as possible
☐ **B** turn the heater up to keep you warm and comfortable
☐ **C** close the car windows to help you concentrate
☐ **D** continue with your journey but drive more slowly

You'll be putting other road users at risk if you continue to drive when drowsy. Pull over and stop in a safe place. If you're driving a long distance, think about finding some accommodation so you can get some sleep before continuing your journey.

314 Mark *one* answer
You're driving along a motorway and become tired. You should

☐ **A** pull up on the hard shoulder and change drivers
☐ **B** leave the motorway at the next exit and rest
☐ **C** increase your speed and turn up the radio volume
☐ **D** close all your windows and set heating to warm

Plan your journey to include rest stops. This should ensure you don't become tired while driving and you arrive at your destination in good time.

315 Mark *one* answer
You are taking drugs that are likely to affect your driving. What should you do?

☐ **A** Seek medical advice before driving
☐ **B** Limit your driving to essential journeys
☐ **C** Only drive if accompanied by a full licence-holder
☐ **D** Drive only for short distances

Check with your doctor or pharmacist if you think that the drugs you're taking are likely to make you feel drowsy or impair your judgement.

316 Mark *one* answer

You are about to drive home. You feel very tired and have a severe headache. You should

☐ **A** wait until you are fit and well before driving

☐ **B** drive home, but take a tablet for headaches

☐ **C** drive home if you can stay awake for the journey

☐ **D** wait for a short time, then drive home slowly

All your concentration should be on your driving. Any pain you feel will distract you and you should avoid driving when drowsy. The safest course of action is to wait until you have rested and feel better.

317 Mark *one* answer

If you are feeling tired it is best to stop as soon as you can. Until then you should

☐ **A** increase your speed to find a stopping place quickly

☐ **B** ensure a supply of fresh air

☐ **C** gently tap the steering wheel

☐ **D** keep changing speed to improve concentration

If you're going on a long journey plan your route before you leave. This will help you to be decisive at intersections and junctions, plan rest stops and have an idea of how long the journey will take.

Make sure your vehicle is well-ventilated to stop you becoming drowsy. You need to maintain concentration so that your judgement is not impaired.

318 Mark *one* answer

Driving long distances can be tiring. You can prevent this by

☐ **A** eating a large meal before driving

☐ **B** having regular refreshment breaks

☐ **C** playing loud music in the car

☐ **D** completing the journey without stopping

Long-distance driving can be boring. This, coupled with a stuffy, warm vehicle, can make you feel tired. Make sure you take rest breaks to keep yourself awake and alert. Stop in a safe place before you get to the stage of fighting sleep.

319 Mark *one* answer

You go to a social event and need to drive a short time after. What precaution should you take?

☐ **A** Avoid drinking alcohol on an empty stomach

☐ **B** Drink plenty of coffee after drinking alcohol

☐ **C** Avoid drinking alcohol completely

☐ **D** Drink plenty of milk before drinking alcohol

This is always going to be the safest option. Just one drink could put you over the limit and dangerously impair your judgement and reactions.

320 Mark *one* answer
You take some cough medicine given to you by a friend. What should you do before driving?

- ☐ **A** Ask your friend if taking the medicine affected their driving
- ☐ **B** Drink some strong coffee one hour before driving
- ☐ **C** Check the label to see if the medicine will affect your driving
- ☐ **D** Drive a short distance to see if the medicine is affecting your driving

Never drive if you have taken drugs, without first checking what the side effects might be. They might affect your judgement and perception, and therefore endanger lives.

321 Mark *one* answer
You take the wrong route and find you are on a one-way street. You should

- ☐ **A** reverse out of the road
- ☐ **B** turn round in a side road
- ☑ **C** continue to the end of the road
- ☐ **D** reverse into a driveway

Never reverse or turn your vehicle around in a one-way street. This is highly dangerous. Carry on and find another route, checking the direction signs as you drive. If you need to check a map, first stop in a safe place.

322 Mark *one* answer
What will be a serious distraction from driving?

- ☐ **A** Looking at road maps
- ☐ **B** Switching on your demister
- ☐ **C** Using your windscreen washers
- ☐ **D** Looking in your wing mirror

Looking at road maps while driving is very dangerous. If you aren't sure of your route, stop in a safe place and check the map. You must not allow anything to take your attention away from the road while you're driving.

323 Mark *one* answer
You are driving along this road. The driver on the left is reversing from a driveway. You should

- ☐ **A** move to the opposite side of the road
- ☐ **B** drive through as you have priority
- ☐ **C** sound your horn and be prepared to stop
- ☐ **D** speed up and drive through quickly

White lights at the rear of a car show that it is about to reverse. Sound your horn to warn of your presence and reduce your speed as a precaution.

324 Mark *one* answer
You have been involved in an argument before starting your journey. This has made you feel angry. You should

☐ **A** start to drive, but open a window
☐ **B** drive slower than normal and turn your radio on
☐ **C** have an alcoholic drink to help you relax before driving
☐ **D** calm down before you start to drive

If you are feeling upset or angry you should wait until you have calmed down before setting out on a journey.

325 Mark *one* answer
You start to feel tired while driving. What should you do?

☐ **A** Increase your speed slightly
☐ **B** Decrease your speed slightly
☐ **C** Find a less busy route
☐ **D** Pull over at a safe place to rest

If you start to feel tired, stop at a safe place for a rest break.

Every year many fatal incidents are caused by drivers falling asleep at the wheel.

326 Mark *one* answer
You are driving on this dual carriageway. Why may you need to slow down?

☐ **A** There is a broken white line in the centre
☐ **B** There are solid white lines either side
☐ **C** There are roadworks ahead of you
☐ **D** There are no footpaths

Look well ahead and read any road signs as you drive. They are there to inform you of what is ahead. In this case you may need to slow right down and change direction.

Make sure you can take whatever action is necessary in plenty of time. Check your mirrors so you know what is happening around you before you change speed or direction.

327 Mark *one* answer
You have just been overtaken by this motorcyclist who is cutting in sharply. You should

☐ **A** sound the horn   ☐ **B** brake firmly
☐ **C** keep a safe gap   ☐ **D** flash your lights

If another vehicle cuts in too sharply, ease off the accelerator and drop back to allow a safe separation distance. Try not to overreact by braking sharply or swerving, as you could lose control. If vehicles behind you are too close or unprepared, it could lead to a crash.

328 Mark *one* answer

You are about to drive home. You cannot find the glasses you need to wear. You should

- ☐ **A** drive home slowly, keeping to quiet roads
- ☐ **B** borrow a friend's glasses and use those
- ☐ **C** drive home at night, so that the lights will help you
- ☐ **D** find a way of getting home without driving

Don't be tempted to drive if you've lost or forgotten your glasses. You must be able to see clearly when driving.

329 Mark *one* answer

What's a common effect of drinking alcohol?

- ☐ **A** Colour blindness
- ☐ **B** Increased confidence
- ☐ **C** Faster reactions
- ☐ **D** Increased concentration

Alcohol can increase confidence to a point where a driver's behaviour might become 'out of character'. Someone who normally behaves sensibly might suddenly enjoy taking risks. Never let yourself or your friends get into this situation.

330 Mark *one* answer

How does alcohol affect you?

- ☐ **A** It speeds up your reactions
- ☐ **B** It increases your awareness
- ☐ **C** It improves your co-ordination
- ☐ **D** It reduces your concentration

Concentration and good judgement are needed at all times to be a good, safe driver. Don't put yourself or others at risk by drinking and driving.

331 Mark *one* answer

Your doctor has given you a course of medicine. Why should you ask how it will affect you?

- ☐ **A** Drugs make you a better driver by quickening your reactions
- ☐ **B** You will have to let your insurance company know about the medicine
- ☐ **C** Some types of medicine can cause your reactions to slow down
- ☐ **D** The medicine you take may affect your hearing

Always check the label of any medication container. The contents might affect your driving. If you aren't sure, ask your doctor or pharmacist.

332 Mark *one* answer

You are on a motorway. You feel tired. You should

☐ **A** carry on but go slowly
☐ **B** leave the motorway at the next exit
☐ **C** complete your journey as quickly as possible
☐ **D** stop on the hard shoulder

If you do feel tired and there's no service station for many miles, leave the motorway at the next exit. Find a road off the motorway where you can pull up and stop safely.

333 Mark *one* answer

You find that you need glasses to read vehicle number plates at the required distance. When MUST you wear them?

☐ **A** Only in bad weather conditions
☐ **B** At all times when driving
☐ **C** Only when you think it necessary
☐ **D** Only in bad light or at night time

Have your eyesight tested before you start your practical training. Then, throughout your driving life, have checks periodically to ensure that your eyes haven't deteriorated.

334 Mark *one* answer

What would help to keep you alert during a long journey?

☐ **A** Using the heater to keep the car warm
☐ **B** Keeping off the motorways and using country roads
☐ **C** Making sure that you get plenty of fresh air
☐ **D** Drinking a sugary drink while driving

Make sure that the vehicle you're driving is well ventilated. A warm, stuffy atmosphere will make you feel drowsy. Opening a window and turning down the heating can help you to remain alert on a long journey.

335 Mark *one* answer

Which of the following types of glasses should NOT be worn when driving at night?

☐ **A** Half-moon
☐ **B** Round
☐ **C** Bi-focal
☐ **D** Tinted

If you are driving at night or in poor visibility, tinted lenses will reduce the efficiency of your vision, by reducing the amount of available light reaching your eyes.

336 Mark *one* answer

Drinking any amount of alcohol is likely to

☐ **A** affect your judgement of speed
☐ **B** increase the speed of your reactions
☐ **C** lower your driving confidence
☐ **D** improve your awareness of danger

If you're going to drive, the safest option is not to drink at all. Your judgement will be seriously impaired and it's not worth the risk to yourself and other road users.

337 Mark *one* answer
What can seriously affect your ability to concentrate?

- ☑ **A** Drugs
- ☐ **B** Busy roads
- ☐ **C** Tinted windows
- ☐ **D** Contact lenses

Both recreational drugs and prescribed medicine can affect your concentration. It's also now an offence to drive with certain drugs in your body and a positive test could lead to a conviction.

338 Mark *one* answer
As a driver you find that your eyesight has become very poor. Your optician says they cannot help you. The law says that you should tell

- ☐ **A** the licensing authority
- ☐ **B** your own doctor
- ☐ **C** the local police station
- ☐ **D** another optician

This will have a serious effect on your judgement and concentration. If you cannot meet the eyesight requirements you must tell DVLA (or DVA in Northern Ireland).

339 Mark *one* answer
When should you use hazard warning lights?

- ☐ **A** When you are double-parked on a two-way road
- ☐ **B** When your direction indicators are not working
- ☐ **C** When warning oncoming traffic that you intend to stop
- ☐ **D** When your vehicle has broken down and is causing an obstruction

Hazard warning lights are an important safety feature and should be used if you have broken down and are causing an obstruction. Don't use them as an excuse to park illegally such as when using a cash machine or post box. You may also use them on motorways to warn traffic behind you of danger ahead.

340 Mark *one* answer
You want to turn left at this junction. The view of the main road is restricted. What should you do?

- ☐ **A** Stay well back and wait to see if something comes
- ☐ **B** Build up your speed so that you can emerge quickly
- ☐ **C** Stop and apply the handbrake even if the road is clear
- ☐ **D** Approach slowly and edge out until you can see more clearly

You should slow right down, and stop if necessary, at any junction where the view is restricted. Edge forward until you can see properly. Only then can you decide if it is safe to go.

341 Mark *one* answer
When may you use hazard warning lights?

☐ **A** To park alongside another car
☐ **B** To park on double yellow lines
☐ **C** When you are being towed
☐ **D** When you have broken down

Hazard warning lights may be used to warn other road users when you have broken down and are causing an obstruction, or are on a motorway and want to warn following traffic of a hazard ahead. Don't use them when being towed or when parking illegally.

342 Mark *one* answer
Hazard warning lights should be used when vehicles are

☐ **A** broken down and causing an obstruction
☐ **B** faulty and moving slowly
☐ **C** being towed along a road
☐ **D** reversing into a side road

Don't use hazard lights as an excuse for illegal parking. If you do use them, don't forget to switch them off when you move away. There must be a warning light on the control panel to show when the hazard lights are in operation.

343 Mark *one* answer
When driving a car fitted with automatic transmission what would you use 'kick down' for?

☐ **A** Cruise control
☑ **B** Quick acceleration
☐ **C** Slow braking
☐ **D** Fuel economy

'Kick down' selects a lower gear, enabling the vehicle to accelerate faster.

344 Mark *one* answer
You're driving along this motorway. It's raining. When following this lorry you should

☐ **A** allow at least a two-second gap
☐ **B** move left and drive on the hard shoulder
☐ **C** move right and stay in the right-hand lane
☑ **D** be aware of spray reducing your vision

The usual two-second time gap will increase to four seconds when the roads are wet. If you stay well back you'll
• be able to see past the vehicle
• be out of the spray thrown up by the lorry's tyres
• give yourself more time to stop if the need arises
• increase your chances of being seen by the lorry driver.

345 Mark *one* answer

You are driving towards this left-hand bend. What dangers should you be aware of?

- ☐ **A** A vehicle overtaking you
- ☐ **B** No white lines in the centre of the road
- ☐ **C** No sign to warn you of the bend
- ☐ **D** Pedestrians walking towards you

Pedestrians walking on a road with no pavement should walk against the direction of the traffic. You can't see around this bend: there may be hidden dangers. Always keep this in mind so you give yourself time to react if a hazard does arise.

346 Mark *one* answer

Ahead of you, traffic in the left-hand lane is slowing. You should

- ☐ **A** slow down, keeping a safe separation distance
- ☐ **B** accelerate past the vehicles in the left-hand lane
- ☐ **C** pull up on the left-hand verge
- ☐ **D** move across and continue in the right-hand lane

Allow the traffic to merge into the nearside lane. Leave enough room so that you can maintain a safe separation distance, even if vehicles pull in ahead of you.

347 Mark *one* answer

As a provisional licence holder, you mustn't drive a motor car

- ☐ **A** at more than 40mph
- ☐ **B** with passengers in the rear seats
- ☐ **C** on the motorway
- ☐ **D** between 11:30pm and 7am

When you've passed your practical test you'll be able to drive on a motorway. It's recommended that you have instruction on motorway driving before you venture out on your own. Ask your instructor about this.

348 Mark *one* answer

You're not sure if your cough medicine will affect your ability to drive safely. What should you do?

- ☐ **A** Take your medicine with food
- ☐ **B** Check the medicine label
- ☐ **C** Drive if you feel alright
- ☐ **D** Ask a friend or relative for advice

If you're taking medicine or drugs prescribed by your doctor, check to ensure that they won't make you drowsy. If you forget to ask at the time of your visit to the surgery, check with your pharmacist. Some over-the-counter medication can also cause drowsiness. Read the label and don't drive if you're affected.

349 Mark *one* answer
For which of these may you use hazard warning lights?

☐ **A** When driving on a motorway to warn traffic behind of a hazard ahead
☐ **B** When you are double-parked on a two-way road
☐ **C** When your direction indicators are not working
☐ **D** When warning oncoming traffic that you intend to stop

Hazard warning lights are an important safety feature. Use them when driving on a motorway to warn traffic behind you of danger ahead. You should also use them if your vehicle has broken down and is causing an obstruction.

350 Mark *one* answer
You are waiting to emerge at a junction. Your view is restricted by parked vehicles. What can help you to see traffic on the road you are joining?

☐ **A** Looking for traffic behind you
☐ **B** Reflections of traffic in shop windows
☐ **C** Making eye contact with other road users
☐ **D** Checking for traffic in your interior mirror

When your view is restricted into the new road you must still be completely sure it is safe to emerge. Try to look for traffic through the windows of the parked cars or the reflections in shop windows. Keep looking in all directions as you slowly edge forwards until you can see it is safe.

351 Mark *one* answer
After passing your driving test, you suffer from ill health. This affects your driving. You MUST

☐ **A** inform your local police station
☐ **B** avoid using motorways
☐ **C** always drive accompanied
☐ **D** inform the licensing authority

The licensing authority won't automatically take away your licence without investigation. For advice, contact the Driver and Vehicle Licensing Agency (or DVA in Northern Ireland).

352 Mark *one* answer
Why should the junction on the left be kept clear?

☐ **A** To allow vehicles to enter and emerge
☐ **B** To allow the bus to reverse
☐ **C** To allow vehicles to make a U-turn
☐ **D** To allow vehicles to park

You should always try to keep junctions clear. If you are in queuing traffic make sure that when you stop you leave enough space for traffic to flow in and out of the junction.

353 Mark *one* answer

Your motorway journey seems boring and you feel drowsy. What should you do?

☐ **A** Stop on the hard shoulder for a sleep
☐ **B** Open a window and stop as soon as it's safe and legal
☐ **C** Speed up to arrive at your destination sooner
☐ **D** Slow down and let other drivers overtake

Never stop on the hard shoulder to rest. If there is no service station for several miles, leave the motorway at the next exit and find somewhere safe and legal to pull over.

---

354 Mark *one* answer

You are driving on a motorway. The traffic ahead is braking sharply because of an incident. How could you warn traffic behind you?

☐ **A** Briefly use the hazard warning lights
☐ **B** Switch on the hazard warning lights continuously
☐ **C** Briefly use the rear fog lights
☐ **D** Switch on the headlights continuously

The only time you are permitted to use your hazard warning lights while moving is if you are on a motorway or dual carriageway and you need to warn other road users, particularly those behind, of a hazard or obstruction ahead. Only use them long enough to ensure your warning has been seen.

355 Mark *one* answer

Which sign means that there may be people walking along the road?

☐ A  ☐ B

☐ C  ☐ D

Always check the road signs. Triangular signs are warning signs and they'll keep you informed of hazards ahead and help you to anticipate any problems. There are a number of different signs showing pedestrians. Learn the meaning of each one.

---

356 Mark *one* answer

You are turning left at a junction. Pedestrians have started to cross the road. You should

☐ **A** go on, giving them plenty of room
☐ **B** stop and wave at them to cross
☐ **C** blow your horn and proceed
☐ **D** give way to them

If you're turning into a side road, pedestrians already crossing the road have priority and you should give way to them. Don't wave them across the road, sound your horn, flash your lights or give any other misleading signal. Other road users may misinterpret your signal and this may lead the pedestrians into a dangerous situation. If a pedestrian is slow or indecisive be patient and wait. Don't hurry them across by revving your engine.

357 Mark *one* answer

You are turning left from a main road into a side road. People are already crossing the road into which you are turning. You should

☐ **A** continue, as it is your right of way
☐ **B** signal to them to continue crossing
☐ **C** wait and allow them to cross
☐ **D** sound your horn to warn them of your presence

Always check the road into which you are turning. Approaching at the correct speed will allow you enough time to observe and react.

Give way to any pedestrians already crossing the road.

358 Mark *one* answer

You are at a road junction, turning into a minor road. There are pedestrians crossing the minor road. You should

- ☐ **A** stop and wave the pedestrians across
- ☐ **B** sound your horn to let the pedestrians know that you are there
- ☐ **C** give way to the pedestrians who are already crossing
- ☐ **D** carry on; the pedestrians should give way to you

Always look into the road into which you are turning. If there are pedestrians crossing, give way to them, but don't wave or signal to them to cross. Signal your intention to turn as you approach.

359 Mark *one* answer

You are turning left into a side road. What hazards should you be especially aware of?

- ☐ **A** One-way street
- ☐ **B** Pedestrians
- ☐ **C** Traffic congestion
- ☐ **D** Parked vehicles

Make sure that you have reduced your speed and are in the correct gear for the turn. Look into the road before you turn and always give way to any pedestrians who are crossing.

360 Mark *one* answer

You intend to turn right into a side road. Just before turning you should check for motorcyclists who might be

- ☐ **A** overtaking on your left
- ☐ **B** following you closely
- ☐ **C** emerging from the side road
- ☐ **D** overtaking on your right

Never attempt to change direction to the right without first checking your right-hand mirror. A motorcyclist might not have seen your signal and could be hidden by the car behind you. This action should become a matter of routine.

361 Mark *one* answer

A toucan crossing is different from other crossings because

- ☐ **A** moped riders can use it
- ☐ **B** it is controlled by a traffic warden
- ☐ **C** it is controlled by two flashing lights
- ☐ **D** cyclists can use it

Toucan crossings are shared by pedestrians and cyclists and they are shown the green light together. Cyclists are permitted to cycle across.

The signals are push-button operated and there is no flashing amber phase.

362 Mark *one* answer
How will a school crossing patrol signal you to stop?

- ☐ **A** By pointing to children on the opposite pavement
- ☐ **B** By displaying a red light
- ☐ **C** By displaying a stop sign
- ☐ **D** By giving you an arm signal

If a school crossing patrol steps out into the road with a stop sign you must stop. Don't wave anyone across the road and don't get impatient or rev your engine.

363 Mark *one* answer
Where would you see this sign?

- ☐ **A** In the window of a car taking children to school
- ☐ **B** At the side of the road
- ☐ **C** At playground areas
- ☐ **D** On the rear of a school bus or coach

Vehicles that are used to carry children to and from school will be travelling at busy times of the day. If you're following a vehicle with this sign be prepared for it to make frequent stops. It might pick up or set down passengers in places other than normal bus stops.

364 Mark *one* answer
Which sign tells you that pedestrians may be walking in the road as there is no pavement?

☐ **A**   ☐ **B**

☐ **C**   ☐ **D**

Give pedestrians who are walking at the side of the road plenty of room when you pass them. They may turn around when they hear your engine and unintentionally step into the path of your vehicle.

365 Mark *one* answer
What does this sign mean?

- ☐ **A** No route for pedestrians and cyclists
- ☐ **B** A route for pedestrians only
- ☐ **C** A route for cyclists only
- ☐ **D** A route for pedestrians and cyclists

This sign shows a shared route for pedestrians and cyclists: when it ends, the cyclists will be rejoining the main road.

366 Mark *one* answer
You see a pedestrian with a white stick and red band. This means that the person is

☐ **A** physically disabled
☐ **B** deaf only
☐ **C** blind only
☐ **D** deaf and blind

If someone is deaf as well as blind, they may be carrying a white stick with a red reflective band. You can't see if a pedestrian is deaf. Don't assume everyone can hear you approaching.

367 Mark *one* answer
What action would you take when elderly people are crossing the road?

☐ **A** Wave them across so they know that you have seen them
☐ **B** Be patient and allow them to cross in their own time
☐ **C** Rev the engine to let them know that you are waiting
☐ **D** Tap the horn in case they are hard of hearing

Be aware that older people might take a long time to cross the road. They might also be hard of hearing and not hear you approaching. Don't hurry older people across the road by getting too close to them or revving your engine.

368 Mark *one* answer
You see two elderly pedestrians about to cross the road ahead. You should

☐ **A** expect them to wait for you to pass
☐ **B** speed up to get past them quickly
☐ **C** stop and wave them across the road
☐ **D** be careful, they may misjudge your speed

Older people may have impaired hearing, vision, concentration and judgement. They may also walk slowly and so could take a long time to cross the road.

369 Mark *one* answer
You are coming up to a roundabout. A cyclist is signalling to turn right. What should you do?

☐ **A** Overtake on the right
☐ **B** Give a horn warning
☐ **C** Signal the cyclist to move across
☑ **D** Give the cyclist plenty of room

If you're following a cyclist who's signalling to turn right at a roundabout leave plenty of room. Give them space and time to get into the correct lane.

370 Mark *one* answer
Which of these should you allow extra room when overtaking?

☐ **A** Lorry
☐ **B** Tractor
☐ **C** Bicycle
☐ **D** Road-sweeping vehicle

Don't pass cyclists too closely as
• they may need to veer around a pothole or other obstacle
• be buffeted by side wind
• be made unsteady by your vehicle.
Always leave as much room as you would for a car, and don't cut in front of them.

371 Mark *one* answer

Why should you look particularly for motorcyclists and cyclists at junctions?

- [ ] **A** They may want to turn into the side road
- [ ] **B** They may slow down to let you turn
- [x] **C** They are harder to see
- [ ] **D** They might not see you turn

Cyclists and motorcyclists are smaller than other vehicles and so are more difficult to see. They can easily become hidden from your view by cars parked near a junction.

372 Mark *one* answer

You are waiting to come out of a side road. Why should you watch carefully for motorcycles?

- [ ] **A** Motorcycles are usually faster than cars
- [ ] **B** Police patrols often use motorcycles
- [ ] **C** Motorcycles are small and hard to see
- [ ] **D** Motorcycles have right of way

If you're waiting to emerge from a side road watch out for motorcycles: they're small and can be difficult to see. Be especially careful if there are parked vehicles restricting your view, there might be a motorcycle approaching.
IF YOU DON'T KNOW, DON'T GO.

373 Mark *one* answer

In daylight, an approaching motorcyclist is using a dipped headlight. Why?

- [ ] **A** So that the rider can be seen more easily
- [ ] **B** To stop the battery overcharging
- [ ] **C** To improve the rider's vision
- [ ] **D** The rider is inviting you to proceed

A motorcycle can be lost from sight behind another vehicle. The use of the headlight helps to make it more conspicuous and therefore more easily seen.

374 Mark *one* answer

Motorcyclists should wear bright clothing mainly because

- [ ] **A** they must do so by law
- [ ] **B** it helps keep them cool in summer
- [ ] **C** the colours are popular
- [ ] **D** drivers often do not see them

Motorcycles are small vehicles and can be difficult to see. If the rider wears bright clothing it can make it easier for other road users to see them approaching, especially at junctions.

375 Mark *one* answer

There is a slow-moving motorcyclist ahead of you. You are unsure what the rider is going to do. You should

- [ ] **A** pass on the left
- [ ] **B** pass on the right
- [ ] **C** stay behind
- [ ] **D** move closer

If a motorcyclist is travelling slowly it may be that they are looking for a turning or entrance. Be patient and stay behind them in case they need to make a sudden change of direction.

376 Mark *one* answer
Motorcyclists will often look round over their right shoulder just before turning right. This is because

- [ ] **A** they need to listen for following traffic
- [ ] **B** motorcycles do not have mirrors
- [ ] **C** looking around helps them balance as they turn
- [ ] **D** they need to check for traffic in their blind area

If you see a motorcyclist take a quick glance over their shoulder, this could mean they are about to change direction. Recognising a clue like this helps you to be prepared and take appropriate action, making you safer on the road.

377 Mark *one* answer
Which is the most vulnerable road user at road junctions?

- [ ] **A** Car driver
- [ ] **B** Tractor driver
- [ ] **C** Lorry driver
- [ ] **D** Motorcyclist

Pedestrians and riders on two wheels can be harder to see than other road users. Make sure you look for them, especially at junctions. Good effective observation, coupled with appropriate action, can save lives.

378 Mark *one* answer
Motorcyclists are particularly vulnerable

- [ ] **A** when moving off
- [ ] **B** on dual carriageways
- [ ] **C** at junctions
- [ ] **D** on motorways

Another road user failing to see a motorcyclist is a major cause of collisions at junctions. Wherever streams of traffic join or cross there's the potential for this type of incident to occur.

379 Mark *one* answer
You're approaching a roundabout. There are horses just ahead of you. What should you do?

- [ ] **A** sound your horn as a warning
- [ ] **B** treat them like any other vehicle
- [ ] **C** give them plenty of room
- [ ] **D** accelerate past as quickly as possible

Horse riders often keep to the outside of the roundabout even if they're turning right. Give them plenty of room and remember that they may have to cross lanes of traffic.

380 Mark *one* answer
As you approach a pelican crossing the lights change to green. Elderly people are halfway across. You should

☐ **A** wave them to cross as quickly as they can
☐ **B** rev your engine to make them hurry
☐ **C** flash your lights in case they have not heard you
☐ **D** wait because they will take longer to cross

Even if the lights turn to green, wait for them to clear the crossing. Allow them to cross the road in their own time, and don't try to hurry them by revving your engine.

381 Mark *one* answer
There are flashing amber lights under a school warning sign. What action should you take?

☐ **A** Reduce speed until you are clear of the area
☐ **B** Keep up your speed and sound the horn
☐ **C** Increase your speed to clear the area quickly
☐ **D** Wait at the lights until they change to green

The flashing amber lights are switched on to warn you that children may be crossing near a school. Slow down and take extra care as you may have to stop.

382 Mark *one* answer
These road markings must be kept clear to allow

☐ **A** school children to be dropped off
☐ **B** for teachers to park
☐ **C** school children to be picked up
☐ **D** a clear view of the crossing area

The markings are there to show that the area must be kept clear to allow an unrestricted view for
• approaching drivers and riders
• children wanting to cross the road.

383 Mark *one* answer
Where would you see this sign?

☐ **A** Near a school crossing
☐ **B** At a playground entrance
☐ **C** On a school bus
☐ **D** At a 'pedestrians only' area

Watch out for children crossing the road from the other side of the bus.

384 Mark *one* answer
You are following two cyclists. They approach a roundabout in the left-hand lane. In which direction should you expect the cyclists to go?

☐ **A** Left
☐ **B** Right
☐ **C** Any direction
☐ **D** Straight ahead

Cyclists approaching a roundabout in the left-hand lane may be turning right but may not have been able to get into the correct lane due to the heavy traffic. They may also feel safer keeping to the left all the way round the roundabout. Be aware of them and give them plenty of room.

385 Mark *one* answer
You are travelling behind a moped. You want to turn left just ahead. You should

☐ **A** overtake the moped before the junction
☐ **B** pull alongside the moped and stay level until just before the junction
☐ **C** sound your horn as a warning and pull in front of the moped
☐ **D** stay behind until the moped has passed the junction

Passing the moped and turning into the junction could mean that you cut across the front of the rider. This might force them to slow down, stop or even lose control. Slow down and stay behind the moped until it has passed the junction and you can then turn safely.

386 Mark *one* answer
You see a horse rider as you approach a roundabout. They are signalling right but keeping well to the left. You should

☐ **A** proceed as normal
☐ **B** keep close to them
☐ **C** cut in front of them
☐ **D** stay well back

Allow the horse rider to enter and exit the roundabout in their own time. They may feel safer keeping to the left all the way around the roundabout. Don't get up close behind or alongside them. This is very likely to upset the horse and create a dangerous situation.

387 Mark *one* answer
How would you react to drivers who appear to be inexperienced?

☐ **A** Sound your horn to warn them of your presence
☑ **B** Be patient and prepare for them to react more slowly
☐ **C** Flash your headlights to indicate that it is safe for them to proceed
☐ **D** Overtake them as soon as possible

Learners might not have confidence when they first start to drive. Allow them plenty of room and don't react adversely to their hesitation. We all learn from experience, but new drivers will have had less practice in dealing with all the situations that might occur.

388 Mark *one* answer

You are following a learner driver who stalls at a junction. You should

- ☐ **A** be patient as you expect them to make mistakes
- ☐ **B** stay very close behind and flash your headlights
- ☐ **C** start to rev your engine if they take too long to restart
- ☐ **D** immediately steer around them and drive on

Learning is a process of practice and experience. Try to understand this and tolerate those who are at the beginning of this process.

389 Mark *one* answer

You are on a country road. What should you expect to see coming towards you on YOUR side of the road?

- ☐ **A** Motorcycles
- ☐ **B** Bicycles
- ☐ **C** Pedestrians
- ☐ **D** Horse riders

On a quiet country road always be aware that there may be a hazard just around the next bend, such as a slow-moving vehicle or pedestrians. Pedestrians are advised to walk on the right-hand side of the road if there is no pavement, so they may be walking towards you on your side of the road.

390 Mark *one* answer

You are turning left into a side road. Pedestrians are crossing the road near the junction. You must

- ☐ **A** wave them on
- ☐ **B** sound your horn
- ☐ **C** switch on your hazard lights
- ☐ **D** wait for them to cross

Check that it's clear before you turn into a junction. If there are pedestrians crossing they have priority, so let them cross in their own time.

391 Mark *one* answer

You are following a car driven by an elderly driver. You should

- ☐ **A** expect the driver to drive badly
- ☐ **B** flash your lights and overtake
- ☐ **C** be aware that the driver's reactions may not be as fast as yours
- ☐ **D** stay very close behind but be careful

You must show consideration to other road users. The reactions of older drivers may be slower and they might need more time to deal with a situation. Be tolerant and don't lose patience or show your annoyance.

392 Mark *one* answer
You are following a cyclist. You wish to turn left just ahead. You should

- ☐ **A** overtake the cyclist before the junction
- ☐ **B** pull alongside the cyclist and stay level until after the junction
- ☐ **C** hold back until the cyclist has passed the junction
- ☐ **D** go around the cyclist on the junction

Make allowances for cyclists. Allow them plenty of room. Don't try to overtake and then immediately turn left. Be patient and stay behind them until they have passed the junction.

393 Mark *one* answer
A horse rider is in the left-hand lane approaching a roundabout. You should expect the rider to

- ☐ **A** go in any direction
- ☐ **B** turn right
- ☐ **C** turn left
- ☐ **D** go ahead

Horses and their riders will move more slowly than other road users. They might not have time to cut across heavy traffic to take up positions in the offside lane. For this reason a horse and rider may approach a roundabout in the left-hand lane, even though they're turning right.

394 Mark *one* answer
Powered vehicles used by disabled people are small and hard to see. How do they give early warning when on a dual carriageway?

- ☐ **A** They will have a flashing red light
- ☐ **B** They will have a flashing green light
- ☐ **C** They will have a flashing blue light
- ☐ **D** They will have a flashing amber light.

Powered vehicles used by disabled people are small, low, hard to see and travel very slowly. On a dual carriageway a flashing amber light will warn other road users.

395 Mark *one* answer
You should never attempt to overtake a cyclist

- ☐ **A** just before you turn left
- ☐ **B** on a left-hand bend
- ☐ **C** on a one-way street
- ☐ **D** on a dual carriageway

If you want to turn left and there's a cyclist in front of you, hold back. Wait until the cyclist has passed the junction and then turn left behind them.

396 Mark *one* answer
Ahead of you there is a moving vehicle with a flashing amber beacon. This means it is

- ☐ **A** slow moving
- ☐ **B** broken down
- ☐ **C** a doctor's car
- ☐ **D** a school crossing patrol

As you approach the vehicle, assess the situation. Due to its slow progress you will need to judge whether it is safe to overtake.

397 Mark *one* answer
What does this sign mean?

- ☐ **A** Contraflow pedal cycle lane
- ☐ **B** With-flow pedal cycle lane
- ☑ **C** Pedal cycles and buses only
- ☐ **D** No pedal cycles or buses

The picture of a cycle will also usually be painted on the road, sometimes with a different coloured surface. Leave these clear for cyclists and don't pass too closely when you overtake.

---

398 Mark *one* answer
You notice horse riders in front. What should you do FIRST?

- ☐ **A** Pull out to the middle of the road
- ☐ **B** Slow down and be ready to stop
- ☐ **C** Accelerate around them
- ☐ **D** Signal right

Be particularly careful when approaching horse riders – slow down and be prepared to stop. Always pass wide and slowly and look out for signals given by horse riders. Horses are unpredictable: always treat them as potential hazards and take great care when passing them.

399 Mark *one* answer
You must not stop on these road markings because you may obstruct

- ☐ **A** children's view of the crossing area
- ☐ **B** teachers' access to the school
- ☐ **C** delivery vehicles' access to the school
- ☐ **D** emergency vehicles' access to the school

These markings are found on the road outside schools. DO NOT stop (even to set down or pick up children) or park on them. The markings are to make sure that drivers, riders, children and other pedestrians have a clear view.

---

400 Mark *one* answer
The left-hand pavement is closed due to street repairs. What should you do?

- ☐ **A** Watch out for pedestrians walking in the road
- ☐ **B** Use your right-hand mirror more often
- ☐ **C** Speed up to get past the roadworks quicker
- ☐ **D** Position close to the left-hand kerb

Where street repairs have closed off pavements, proceed carefully and slowly as pedestrians might have to walk in the road.

401 Mark *one* answer

You are following a motorcyclist on an uneven road. You should

- ☐ **A** allow less room so you can be seen in their mirrors
- ☐ **B** overtake immediately
- ☐ **C** allow extra room in case they swerve to avoid potholes
- ☐ **D** allow the same room as normal because road surfaces do not affect motorcyclists

Potholes and bumps in the road can unbalance a motorcyclist. For this reason the rider might swerve to avoid an uneven road surface. Watch out at places where this is likely to occur.

402 Mark *one* answer

What does this sign tell you?

- ☐ **A** No cycling
- ☐ **B** Cycle route ahead
- ☐ **C** Cycle parking only
- ☐ **D** End of cycle route

With people's concern today for the environment, cycle routes are being created in our towns and cities. These are usually defined by road markings and signs. Respect the presence of cyclists on the road and give them plenty of room if you need to pass.

403 Mark *one* answer

You are approaching this roundabout and see the cyclist signal right. Why is the cyclist keeping to the left?

- ☐ **A** It is a quicker route for the cyclist
- ☐ **B** The cyclist is going to turn left instead
- ☐ **C** The cyclist thinks The Highway Code does not apply to bicycles
- ☐ **D** The cyclist is slower and more vulnerable

Cycling in today's heavy traffic can be hazardous. Some cyclists may not feel happy about crossing the path of traffic to take up a position in an outside lane. Be aware of this and understand that, although in the left-hand lane, the cyclist might be turning right.

404 Mark *one* answer

You are approaching this crossing. You should

- ☐ **A** prepare to slow down and stop
- ☐ **B** stop and wave the pedestrians across
- ☐ **C** speed up and pass by quickly
- ☐ **D** continue unless the pedestrians step out

Be courteous and prepare to stop. Do not wave people across as this could be dangerous if another vehicle is approaching the crossing.

405 Mark *one* answer
You see a pedestrian with a dog. The dog has a yellow or burgundy coat. This especially warns you that the pedestrian is

- ☐ **A** elderly
- ☐ **B** dog training
- ☐ **C** colour blind
- ☑ **D** deaf

Take extra care as the pedestrian may not be aware of vehicles approaching.

406 Mark *one* answer
At toucan crossings

- ☐ **A** you only stop if someone is waiting to cross
- ☐ **B** cyclists are not permitted
- ☐ **C** there is a continuously flashing amber beacon
- ☐ **D** pedestrians and cyclists may cross

There are some crossings where cycle routes lead the cyclists to cross at the same place as pedestrians. These are called toucan crossings. Always look out for cyclists, as they're likely to be approaching faster than pedestrians.

407 Mark *one* answer
Some junctions controlled by traffic lights have a marked area between two stop lines. What is this for?

- ☐ **A** To allow taxis to position in front of other traffic
- ☐ **B** To allow people with disabilities to cross the road
- ☐ **C** To allow cyclists and pedestrians to cross the road together
- ☐ **D** To allow cyclists to position in front of other traffic

These are known as advanced stop lines. When the lights are red (or about to become red) you should stop at the first white line. However if you have crossed that line as the lights change you must stop at the second line even if it means you are in the area reserved for cyclists.

408 Mark *one* answer
At some traffic lights there are advance stop lines and a marked area. What are these for?

- ☑ **A** To allow cyclists to position in front of other traffic
- ☐ **B** To let pedestrians cross when the lights change
- ☐ **C** To prevent traffic from jumping the lights
- ☐ **D** To let passengers get off a bus which is queuing

You should always stop at the first white line. Avoid going into the marked area which is reserved for cyclists only. However, if you have crossed the first white line at the time the signal changes to red you must stop at the second line even if you are in the marked area.

409 Mark *one* answer
When you are overtaking a cyclist you should leave as much room as you would give to a car. What is the main reason for this?

☐ **A** The cyclist might speed up
☐ **B** The cyclist might get off the bike
☐ **C** The cyclist might swerve
☐ **D** The cyclist might have to make a left turn

Before overtaking assess the situation. Look well ahead to see if the cyclist will need to change direction. Be especially aware of the cyclist approaching parked vehicles as they will need to alter course. Do not pass too closely or cut in sharply.

410 Mark *one* answer
What should you do when passing sheep on a road?

☐ **A** Briefly sound your horn
☐ **B** Go very slowly
☐ **C** Pass quickly but quietly
☐ **D** Herd them to the side of the road

Slow down and be ready to stop if you see animals in the road ahead. Animals are easily frightened by noise and vehicles passing too close to them. Stop if signalled to do so by the person in charge.

411 Mark *one* answer
At night you see a pedestrian wearing reflective clothing and carrying a bright red light. What does this mean?

☐ **A** You are approaching roadworks
☐ **B** You are approaching an organised walk
☐ **C** You are approaching a slow-moving vehicle
☐ **D** You are approaching a traffic danger spot

The people on the walk should be keeping to the left, but don't assume this. Pass slowly, make sure you have time to do so safely. Be aware that the pedestrians have their backs to you and may not know that you're there.

412 Mark *one* answer
You have just passed your test. How can you reduce your risk of being involved in a collision?

☐ **A** By always staying close to the vehicle in front
☐ **B** By never going over 40mph
☐ **C** By staying only in the left-hand lane on all roads
☐ **D** By taking further training

New drivers and riders are often involved in a collision or incident early in their driving career. Due to a lack of experience they may not react to hazards as quickly as more experienced road users. Approved training courses are offered by driver and rider training schools for people who have passed their test but want extra training.

413 Mark *one* answer

You want to reverse into a side road. You are not sure that the area behind your car is clear. What should you do?

☐ **A** Look through the rear window only
☐ **B** Get out and check
☐ **C** Check the mirrors only
☐ **D** Carry on, assuming it is clear

If you cannot be sure whether there is anything behind you, it is always safest to check before reversing. There may be a small child or a low obstruction close behind your car. The shape and size of your vehicle can restrict visibility.

414 Mark *one* answer

You are about to reverse into a side road. A pedestrian wishes to cross behind you. You should

☐ **A** wave to the pedestrian to stop
☐ **B** give way to the pedestrian
☐ **C** wave to the pedestrian to cross
☐ **D** reverse before the pedestrian starts to cross

If you need to reverse into a side road try to find a place that's free from traffic and pedestrians. Look all around before and during the manoeuvre. Stop and give way to any pedestrians who want to cross behind you. Avoid waving them across, sounding the horn, flashing your lights or giving any misleading signals that could lead them into a dangerous situation.

415 Mark *one* answer

Who is especially in danger of not being seen as you reverse your car?

☐ **A** Motorcyclists
☐ **B** Car drivers
☐ **C** Cyclists
☐ **D** Children

As you look through the rear of your vehicle you may not be able to see a small child. Be aware of this before you reverse. If there are children about, get out and check if it is clear before reversing.

416 Mark *one* answer

You are reversing around a corner when you notice a pedestrian walking behind you. What should you do?

☐ **A** Slow down and wave the pedestrian across
☐ **B** Continue reversing and steer round the pedestrian
☐ **C** Stop and give way
☐ **D** Continue reversing and sound your horn

Wait until the pedestrian has passed, then look around again before you start to reverse. Don't forget that you may not be able to see a small child directly behind your vehicle. Be aware of the possibility of hidden dangers.

417 Mark *one* answer
You want to turn right from a junction but your view is restricted by parked vehicles. What should you do?

- ☐ **A** Move out quickly, but be prepared to stop
- ☐ **B** Sound your horn and pull out if there is no reply
- ☐ **C** Stop, then move slowly forward until you have a clear view
- ☐ **D** Stop, get out and look along the main road to check

If you want to turn right from a junction and your view is restricted, STOP. Ease forward until you can see – there might be something approaching.
IF YOU DON'T KNOW, DON'T GO.

418 Mark *one* answer
You are at the front of a queue of traffic waiting to turn right into a side road. Why is it important to check your right mirror just before turning?

- ☐ **A** To look for pedestrians about to cross
- ☑ **B** To check for overtaking vehicles
- ☐ **C** To make sure the side road is clear
- ☐ **D** To check for emerging traffic

There could be a motorcyclist riding along the outside of the queue. Always check your mirror before turning as situations behind you can change in the time you have been waiting to turn.

419 Mark *one* answer
What must a driver do at a pelican crossing when the amber light is flashing?

- ☐ **A** Signal the pedestrian to cross
- ☐ **B** Always wait for the green light before proceeding
- ☐ **C** Give way to any pedestrians on the crossing
- ☐ **D** Wait for the red-and-amber light before proceeding

The flashing amber light allows pedestrians already on the crossing to get to the other side before a green light shows to the traffic. Be aware that some pedestrians, such as elderly people and young children, need longer to cross. Let them do this at their own pace.

420 Mark *one* answer
You've stopped at a pelican crossing. A disabled person is crossing slowly in front of you. The lights change to green. You should

- ☐ **A** allow the person to cross
- ☐ **B** drive in front of the person
- ☐ **C** edge forward slowly
- ☐ **D** sound your horn

At a pelican crossing the green light means you may proceed as long as the crossing is clear. If someone hasn't finished crossing, be patient and wait for them.

421 Mark *one* answer

You are driving past a line of parked cars. You notice a ball bouncing out into the road ahead. What should you do?

- ☐ **A** Continue driving at the same speed and sound your horn
- ☐ **B** Continue driving at the same speed and flash your headlights
- ☐ **C** Slow down and be prepared to stop for children
- ☐ **D** Stop and wave the children across to fetch their ball

Beware of children playing in the street and running out into the road. If a ball bounces out from the pavement, slow down and stop. Don't encourage anyone to retrieve it. Other road users may not see your signal and you might lead a child into a dangerous situation.

422 Mark *one* answer

You want to turn right from a main road into a side road. Just before turning you should

- ☐ **A** cancel your right-turn signal
- ☐ **B** select first gear
- ☐ **C** check for traffic overtaking on your right
- ☐ **D** stop and set the handbrake

Motorcyclists often overtake queues of vehicles. Make one last check in your mirror and your blind spot to avoid turning across their path.

423 Mark *one* answer

You are driving in slow-moving queues of traffic. Just before changing lane you should

- ☐ **A** sound the horn
- ☐ **B** look for motorcyclists filtering through the traffic
- ☐ **C** give a 'slowing down' arm signal
- ☐ **D** change down to first gear

In this situation motorcyclists could be passing you on either side. Always check before you change lanes or change direction.

424 Mark *one* answer

You are driving in town. There is a bus at the bus stop on the other side of the road. Why should you be careful?

- ☐ **A** The bus may have broken down
- ☐ **B** Pedestrians may come from behind the bus
- ☐ **C** The bus may move off suddenly
- ☐ **D** The bus may remain stationary

If you see a bus ahead watch out for pedestrians. They may not be able to see you if they're crossing from behind the bus.

425 Mark *one* answer
How should you overtake horse riders?

- [ ] **A** Drive up close and overtake as soon as possible
- [ ] **B** Speed is not important but allow plenty of room
- [ ] **C** Use your horn just once to warn them
- [ ] **D** Drive slowly and leave plenty of room

When you're on country roads be aware of particular dangers. Be prepared for farm animals, horses, pedestrians, farm vehicles and wild animals. Always be prepared to slow down or stop.

426 Mark *one* answer
You are driving on a main road. You intend to turn right into a side road. Just before turning you should

- [ ] **A** adjust your interior mirror
- [ ] **B** flash your headlamps
- [ ] **C** steer over to the left
- [ ] **D** check for traffic overtaking on your right

A last check in the offside mirror and blind spot will allow you sight of any cyclist or motorcyclist overtaking as you wait to turn.

427 Mark *one* answer
Why should you allow extra room when overtaking a motorcyclist on a windy day?

- [ ] **A** The rider may turn off suddenly to get out of the wind
- [ ] **B** The rider may be blown across in front of you
- [ ] **C** The rider may stop suddenly
- [ ] **D** The rider may be travelling faster than normal

If you're driving in high winds, be aware that the conditions might force a motorcyclist or cyclist to swerve or wobble. Take this into consideration if you're following or wish to overtake a two-wheeled vehicle.

428 Mark *one* answer
Where in particular should you look out for motorcyclists?

- [ ] **A** In a filling station
- [ ] **B** At a road junction
- [ ] **C** Near a service area
- [ ] **D** When entering a car park

Always look out for motorcyclists, and cyclists, particularly at junctions. They are smaller and usually more difficult to see than other vehicles.

429 Mark *one* answer

Where should you take particular care to look out for motorcyclists and cyclists?

☐ **A** On dual carriageways
☑ **B** At junctions
☐ **C** At zebra crossings
☐ **D** On one-way streets

Motorcyclists and cyclists are often more difficult to see on the road. This is especially the case at junctions. You may not be able to see a motorcyclist approaching a junction if your view is blocked by other traffic. A motorcycle may be travelling as fast as a car, sometimes faster. Make sure that you judge speeds correctly before you emerge.

430 Mark *one* answer

The road outside this school is marked with yellow zigzag lines. What do these lines mean?

☐ **A** You may park on the lines when dropping off school children
☐ **B** You may park on the lines when picking school children up
☑ **C** You must not wait or park your vehicle here at all
☐ **D** You must stay with your vehicle if you park here

Parking here would block the view of the school entrance and would endanger the lives of children on their way to and from school.

431 Mark *one* answer

You are driving past parked cars. You notice a bicycle wheel sticking out between them. What should you do?

☐ **A** Accelerate past quickly and sound your horn
☐ **B** Slow down and wave the cyclist across
☐ **C** Brake sharply and flash your headlights
☐ **D** Slow down and be prepared to stop for a cyclist

Scan the road as you drive. Try to anticipate hazards by being aware of the places where they are likely to occur. You'll then be able to react in good time, if necessary.

432 Mark *one* answer

You are dazzled at night by a vehicle behind you. You should

☐ **A** set your mirror to anti-dazzle
☐ **B** set your mirror to dazzle the other driver
☐ **C** brake sharply to a stop
☐ **D** switch your rear lights on and off

The interior mirror of most vehicles can be set to the anti-dazzle position. You will still be able to see the lights of the traffic behind you, but the dazzle will be greatly reduced.

433 Mark *one* answer

You are driving towards a zebra crossing. A person in a wheelchair is waiting to cross. What should you do?

- ☐ **A** Continue on your way
- ☐ **B** Wave to the person to cross
- ☐ **C** Wave to the person to wait
- ☐ **D** Be prepared to stop

You should slow down and be prepared to stop as you would with an able-bodied person. Don't wave them across as other traffic may not stop.

---

434 Mark *one* answer

Yellow zigzag lines on the road outside schools mean

- ☐ **A** sound your horn to alert other road users
- ☐ **B** stop to allow children to cross
- ☐ **C** you should not park or stop on these lines
- ☐ **D** you must not drive over these lines

Where there are yellow zigzag markings, you should not park, wait or stop, even to pick up or drop off children. A vehicle parked on the zigzag lines would obstruct children's view of the road and other drivers view of the pavement. Where there is an upright sign there is mandatory prohibition of stopping during the times shown.

435 Mark *one* answer

What do these road markings outside a school mean?

- ☐ **A** You may park here if you are a teacher
- ☐ **B** Sound your horn before parking
- ☐ **C** When parking, use your hazard warning lights
- ☐ **D** You should not wait or park your vehicle here

These markings are used outside schools so that children can see and be seen clearly when crossing the road. Parking here would block people's view of the school entrance. This could endanger the lives of children on their way to and from school.

436 Mark *one* answer

You are about to overtake a slow-moving motorcyclist. Which one of these signs would make you take special care?

☑ A   ☐ B

☐ C   ☐ D

In windy weather, watch out for motorcyclists and also cyclists as they can be blown sideways into your path. When you pass them, leave plenty of room and check their position in your mirror before pulling back in.

437 Mark *one* answer

You are waiting to emerge left from a minor road. A large vehicle is approaching from the right. You have time to turn, but you should wait. Why?

☐ A The large vehicle can easily hide an overtaking vehicle

☐ B The large vehicle can turn suddenly

☐ C The large vehicle is difficult to steer in a straight line

☑ D The large vehicle can easily hide vehicles from the left

Large vehicles can hide other vehicles that are overtaking, especially motorcycles which may be filtering past queuing traffic. You need to be aware of the possibility of hidden vehicles and not assume that it is safe to emerge.

438 Mark *one* answer

You are following a long vehicle. It approaches a crossroads and signals left, but moves out to the right. You should

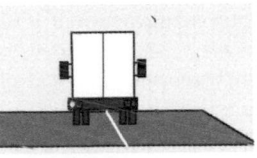

☐ A get closer in order to pass it quickly

☐ B stay well back and give it room

☐ C assume the signal is wrong and it is really turning right

☐ D overtake as it starts to slow down

A lorry may swing out to the right as it approaches a left turn. This is to allow the rear wheels to clear the kerb as it turns. Don't try to filter through if you see a gap on the nearside.

439 Mark *one* answer

You are following a long vehicle approaching a crossroads. The driver signals right but moves close to the left-hand kerb. What should you do?

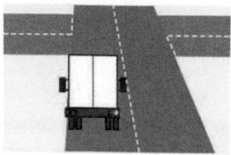

- ☐ **A** Warn the driver of the wrong signal
- ☐ **B** Wait behind the long vehicle
- ☐ **C** Report the driver to the police
- ☐ **D** Overtake on the right-hand side

When a long vehicle is going to turn right it may need to keep close to the left-hand kerb. This is to prevent the rear end of the trailer cutting the corner. You need to be aware of how long vehicles behave in such situations. Don't overtake the lorry because it could turn as you're alongside. Stay behind and wait for it to turn.

440 Mark *one* answer

You are approaching a mini-roundabout. The long vehicle in front is signalling left but positioned over to the right. You should

- ☐ **A** sound your horn
- ☐ **B** overtake on the left
- ☐ **C** follow the same course as the lorry
- ☐ **D** keep well back

At mini-roundabouts there isn't much room for a long vehicle to manoeuvre. It will have to swing out wide so that it can complete the turn safely. Keep well back and don't try to move up alongside it.

441 Mark *one* answer

Before overtaking a large vehicle you should keep well back. Why is this?

- ☐ **A** To give acceleration space to overtake quickly on blind bends
- ☐ **B** To get the best view of the road ahead
- ☐ **C** To leave a gap in case the vehicle stops and rolls back
- ☐ **D** To offer other drivers a safe gap if they want to overtake you

When following a large vehicle keep well back. If you're too close you won't be able to see the road ahead and the driver of the long vehicle might not be able to see you in their mirrors.

442 Mark *one* answer

You're travelling behind a bus that pulls up at a bus stop. What should you do?

- ☐ **A** Accelerate past the bus
- ☑ **B** Watch carefully for pedestrians
- ☐ **C** Sound your horn
- ☐ **D** Pull in closely behind the bus

There might be pedestrians crossing from in front of the bus. Look out for them if you intend to pass. Consider how many people are waiting to get on the bus - check the queue if you can. The bus might move off straight away if no one is waiting to get on

If a bus is signalling to pull out, give it priority if it's safe to do so.

443 Mark *one* answer

You are following a large lorry on a wet road. Spray makes it difficult to see. You should

- ☐ **A** drop back until you can see better
- ☐ **B** put your headlights on full beam
- ☐ **C** keep close to the lorry, away from the spray
- ☐ **D** speed up and overtake quickly

Large vehicles may throw up a lot of spray when the roads are wet. This will make it difficult for you to see ahead. Dropping back further will
- move you out of the spray and allow you to see further
- increase your separation distance. It takes longer to stop when the roads are wet and you need to allow more room.

Don't
- follow the vehicle in front too closely
- overtake, unless you can see and are sure that the way ahead is clear.

444 Mark *one* answer

You are following a large articulated vehicle. It is going to turn left into a narrow road. What action should you take?

☐ **A** Move out and overtake on the right

☐ **B** Pass on the left as the vehicle moves out

☐ **C** Be prepared to stop behind

☐ **D** Overtake quickly before the lorry moves out

Lorries are larger and longer than other vehicles and this can affect their position when approaching junctions. When turning left they may move out to the right so that they don't cut in and mount the kerb with the rear wheels.

---

445 Mark *one* answer

You keep well back while waiting to overtake a large vehicle. A car fills the gap. You should

☐ **A** sound your horn

☐ **B** drop back further

☐ **C** flash your headlights

☐ **D** start to overtake

It's very frustrating when your separation distance is shortened by another vehicle. React positively, stay calm and drop further back.

446 Mark *one* answer

You are following a long lorry. The driver signals to turn left into a narrow road. What should you do?

☐ **A** Overtake on the left before the lorry reaches the junction

☐ **B** Overtake on the right as soon as the lorry slows down

☐ **C** Do not overtake unless you can see there is no oncoming traffic

☐ **D** Do not overtake, stay well back and be prepared to stop.

When turning into narrow roads articulated and long vehicles will need more room. Initially they will need to swing out in the opposite direction to which they intend to turn. They could mask another vehicle turning out of the same junction. DON'T be tempted to overtake them or pass on the inside.

---

447 Mark *one* answer

When you approach a bus signalling to move off from a bus stop you should

☐ **A** get past before it moves

☐ **B** allow it to pull away, if it is safe to do so

☐ **C** flash your headlights as you approach

☐ **D** signal left and wave the bus on

Try to give way to buses if you can do so safely, especially when they signal to pull away from bus stops. Look out for people who've stepped off the bus, or are running to catch it, and may try to cross the road without looking. Don't try to accelerate past before it moves away or flash your lights as other road users may be misled by this signal.

448 Mark *one* answer

You wish to overtake a long, slow-moving vehicle on a busy road. You should

☐ **A** follow it closely and keep moving out to see the road ahead
☐ **B** flash your headlights for the oncoming traffic to give way
☐ **C** stay behind until the driver waves you past
☐ **D** keep well back until you can see that it is clear

If you want to overtake a long vehicle, stay well back so that you can get a better view of the road ahead. The closer you get the less you will be able to see of the road ahead. Be patient, overtaking calls for sound judgement. DON'T take a gamble, only overtake when you are certain that you can complete the manoeuvre safely.

449 Mark *one* answer

Which of these is LEAST likely to be affected by crosswinds?

☐ **A** Cyclists
☐ **B** Motorcyclists
☐ **C** High-sided vehicles
☐ **D** Cars

Although cars are the least likely to be affected, crosswinds can take anyone by surprise. This is most likely to happen after overtaking a large vehicle, when passing gaps between hedges or buildings, and on exposed sections of road.

450 Mark *one* answer

What should you do as you approach this lorry?

☐ **A** Slow down and be prepared to wait
☐ **B** Make the lorry wait for you
☐ **C** Flash your lights at the lorry
☐ **D** Move to the right-hand side of the road

When turning, long vehicles need much more room on the road than other vehicles. At junctions they may take up the whole of the road space, so be patient and allow them the room they need.

451 Mark *one* answer

You are following a large vehicle approaching crossroads. The driver signals to turn left. What should you do?

☐ **A** Overtake if you can leave plenty of room
☐ **B** Overtake only if there are no oncoming vehicles
☐ **C** Do not overtake until the vehicle begins to turn.
☐ **D** Do not overtake when at or approaching a junction.

Hold back and wait until the vehicle has turned before proceeding. Do not overtake because the vehicle turning left could hide a vehicle emerging from the same junction.

452 Mark *one* answer

Powered vehicles, such as wheelchairs or scooters, used by disabled people have a maximum speed of

- ☐ **A** 8mph
- ☐ **B** 12mph
- ☐ **C** 16mph
- ☐ **D** 20mph

These are small battery powered vehicles and include wheelchairs and mobility scooters. Some are designed for use on the pavement only and have an upper speed limit of 4mph (6km/h). Others can go on the road as well and have a speed limit of 8mph (12km/h). They are now very common and are generally used by the elderly, disabled or infirm. Take great care as they are extremely vulnerable because of their low speed and small size.

453 Mark *one* answer

Why is it more difficult to overtake a large vehicle than a car?

- ☐ **A** It takes longer to pass one
- ☐ **B** They may suddenly pull up
- ☐ **C** Their brakes are not as good
- ☐ **D** They climb hills more slowly

Depending on relevant speed, it will usually take you longer to pass a lorry than other vehicles. Some hazards to watch for include oncoming traffic, junctions ahead, bends or dips which could restrict your view, and signs or road markings that prohibit overtaking. Make sure you can see that it's safe to complete the manoeuvre before you start to overtake.

454 Mark *one* answer

In front of you is a class 3 powered vehicle (powered wheelchair) driven by a disabled person. These vehicles have a maximum speed of

- ☐ **A** 8mph (12km/h)
- ☐ **B** 18mph (29km/h)
- ☐ **C** 28mph (45km/h)
- ☐ **D** 38mph (61km/h)

These vehicles are battery powered and very vulnerable due to their slow speed, small size and low height. Some are designed for pavement and road use and have a maximum speed of 8mph (12km/h). Others are for pavement use only and are restricted to 4mph (6km/h). Take extra care and be patient if you are following one. Allow plenty of room when overtaking and do not go past unless you can do so safely.

455 Mark *one* answer

It is very windy. You are behind a motorcyclist who is overtaking a high-sided vehicle. What should you do?

- ☐ **A** Overtake the motorcyclist immediately
- ☐ **B** Keep well back
- ☐ **C** Stay level with the motorcyclist
- ☐ **D** Keep close to the motorcyclist

Motorcyclists are affected more by windy weather than other vehicles. In windy conditions, high-sided vehicles cause air turbulence. You should keep well back as the motorcyclist could be blown off course.

456 Mark *one* answer

It is very windy. You are about to overtake a motorcyclist. You should

- ☐ **A** overtake slowly
- ☑ **B** allow extra room
- ☐ **C** sound your horn
- ☐ **D** keep close as you pass

Crosswinds can blow a motorcyclist or cyclist across the lane. Passing too close could also cause a draught, unbalancing the rider.

457 Mark *one* answer

You're driving in town. Ahead of you a bus is at a bus stop. Which of the following should you do?

- ☐ **A** Flash your lights to warn the driver of your presence
- ☐ **B** Continue at the same speed but sound your horn as a warning
- ☐ **C** Watch carefully for the sudden appearance of pedestrians
- ☐ **D** Pass the bus as quickly as you possibly can

As you approach, look out for any signal the driver might make. If you pass the vehicle watch out for pedestrians attempting to cross the road from behind the bus. They will be hidden from view until the last moment.

458 Mark *one* answer

You are driving along this road. What should you be prepared to do?

- ☐ **A** Sound your horn and continue
- ☐ **B** Slow down and give way
- ☐ **C** Report the driver to the police
- ☐ **D** Squeeze through the gap

Sometimes large vehicles may need more space than other road users. If a vehicle needs more time and space to turn be prepared to stop and wait.

459 Mark *one* answer

As a driver why should you be more careful where trams operate?

- ☐ **A** Because they do not have a horn
- ☐ **B** Because they do not stop for cars
- ☐ **C** Because they do not have lights
- ☐ **D** Because they cannot steer to avoid you

You should take extra care when you first encounter trams. You will have to get used to dealing with a different traffic system.

Be aware that they can accelerate and travel very quickly and that they cannot change direction to avoid obstructions.

460 Mark *one* answer

You are towing a caravan. Which is the safest type of rear-view mirror to use?

☐ **A** Interior wide-angle mirror
☐ **B** Extended-arm side mirrors
☐ **C** Ordinary door mirrors
☐ **D** Ordinary interior mirror

Towing a large trailer or caravan can greatly reduce your view of the road behind. You need to use the correct equipment to make sure you can see clearly behind and down both sides of the caravan or trailer.

461 Mark *one* answer

You're driving in heavy traffic on a wet road. Spray makes it difficult to be seen. You should use your

☐ **A** full beam headlights
☐ **B** sidelights only
☐ **C** rear fog lights if visibility is more than 100 metres (328 feet)
☐ **D** dipped headlights

You must ensure that you can be seen by others on the road, but you don't want to dazzle them. Use your dipped headlights during the day if the visibility is bad. If appropriate, use your rear fog lights but don't forget to turn them off when the visibility improves.

462 Mark *one* answer

It is a very windy day and you are about to overtake a cyclist. What should you do?

☐ **A** Overtake very closely
☐ **B** Keep close as you pass
☐ **C** Sound your horn repeatedly
☐ **D** Allow extra room

Cyclists, and motorcyclists, are very vulnerable in crosswinds. They can easily be blown well off course and veer into your path. Always allow plenty of room when overtaking them. Passing too close could cause a draught and unbalance the rider.

463 Mark *one* answer

When may you overtake another vehicle on the left?

☑ **A** When you are in a one-way street
☐ **B** When approaching a motorway slip road where you will be turning off
☐ **C** When the vehicle in front is signalling to turn left
☐ **D** When a slower vehicle is travelling in the right-hand lane of a dual carriageway

You may pass slower traffic on their left while driving along a one-way street. Be aware of drivers who may need to change lanes and not expect faster traffic passing on their left.

464 Mark *one* answer

You are travelling in very heavy rain. Your overall stopping distance is likely to be

☐ **A** doubled
☐ **B** halved
☐ **C** up to ten times greater
☐ **D** no different

As well as visibility being reduced, the road will be extremely wet. This will reduce the grip the tyres have on the road and increase the distance it takes to stop. Double your separation distance.

465 Mark *one* answer

When overtaking at night you should

☐ **A** wait until a bend so that you can see the oncoming headlights
☐ **B** sound your horn twice before moving out
☐ **C** put headlights on full beam
☐ **D** beware of bends in the road ahead

Don't overtake if there's a possibility of a road junction, bend or brow of a bridge or hill ahead. There are many other possible hazards that may be difficult to see in the dark so only overtake if you're certain that the road ahead is clear. Don't take a chance.

466 Mark *one* answer
When may you wait in a box junction?

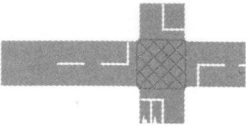

- [ ] **A** When you are stationary in a queue of traffic
- [ ] **B** When approaching a pelican crossing
- [ ] **C** When approaching a zebra crossing
- [ ] **D** When oncoming traffic prevents you turning right

The purpose of a box junction is to keep the junction clear by preventing vehicles from stopping in the path of crossing traffic.

You must not enter a box junction unless your exit is clear. But, you may enter the box and wait if you want to turn right and are only prevented from doing so by oncoming traffic.

467 Mark *one* answer
Which of these plates normally appear with this road sign?

- [ ] **A** Humps for ½ mile
- [ ] **B** Hump Bridge
- [ ] **C** Low Bridge
- [ ] **D** Soft Verge

Road humps are used to slow down the traffic. They are found in places where there are often pedestrians, such as
- in shopping areas • near schools
- in residential areas.

Watch out for people close to the kerb or crossing the road.

468 Mark *one* answer
Traffic-calming measures are used to

- [ ] **A** stop road rage
- [ ] **B** help overtaking
- [ ] **C** slow traffic down
- [ ] **D** help parking

Traffic-calming measures are used to make the roads safer for vulnerable road users, such as cyclists, pedestrians and children. These can be designed as chicanes, road humps or other obstacles that encourage drivers and riders to slow down.

469 Mark *one* answer
You are on a motorway in fog. The left-hand edge of the motorway can be identified by reflective studs. What colour are they?

- [ ] **A** Green
- [ ] **B** Amber
- [ ] **C** Red
- [ ] **D** White

Be especially careful if you're on a motorway in fog. Reflective studs are used to help you in poor visibility. Different colours are used so that you'll know which lane you are in. These are
- red on the left-hand side of the road
- white between lanes
- amber on the right-hand edge of the carriageway
- green between the carriageway and slip roads.

470 Mark *one* answer
A rumble device is designed to

- [ ] **A** give directions
- [ ] **B** prevent cattle escaping
- [ ] **C** alert you to low tyre pressure
- [ ] **D** alert you to a hazard

A rumble device consists of raised markings or strips across the road. It gives drivers an audible, visual and tactile warning. They are found along the hard shoulder on the motorway and approaching some hazards to alert drivers of the need to slow down.

471 Mark *one* answer
You have to make a journey in foggy conditions. You should

- [ ] **A** follow other vehicles' tail lights closely
- [ ] **B** avoid using dipped headlights
- [ ] **C** leave plenty of time for your journey
- [ ] **D** keep two seconds behind other vehicles

If you're planning to make a journey when it's foggy, listen to the weather reports on the radio or television. Don't travel if visibility is very poor or your trip isn't necessary.

If you do travel, leave plenty of time for your journey. If someone is expecting you at the other end, let them know that you'll be taking longer than normal to arrive.

472 Mark *one* answer
You are overtaking a car at night. You must be sure that

- [ ] **A** you flash your headlights before overtaking
- [ ] **B** you select a higher gear
- [ ] **C** you have switched your lights to full beam before overtaking
- [ ] **D** you do not dazzle other road users

To prevent your lights from dazzling the driver of the car in front, wait until you've overtaken before switching to full beam.

473 Mark *one* answer
You are on a road which has speed humps. A driver in front is travelling slower than you. You should

- [ ] **A** sound your horn
- [ ] **B** overtake as soon as you can
- [ ] **C** flash your headlights
- [ ] **D** slow down and stay behind

Be patient and stay behind the car in front. Normally you should not overtake other vehicles in traffic-calmed areas. If you overtake here your speed may exceed that which is safe along that road, defeating the purpose of the traffic-calming measures.

474 Mark *one* answer

You see these markings on the road. Why are they there?

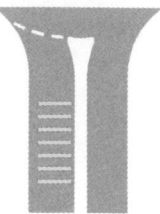

- ☐ **A** To show a safe distance between vehicles
- ☐ **B** To keep the area clear of traffic
- ☐ **C** To make you aware of your speed
- ☐ **D** To warn you to change direction

These lines may be painted on the road on the approach to a roundabout, village or a particular hazard. The lines are raised and painted yellow and their purpose is to make you aware of your speed. Reduce your speed in good time so that you avoid having to brake harshly over the last few metres before reaching the junction.

475 Mark *one* answer

Areas reserved for trams may have

- ☐ **A** metal studs around them
- ☐ **B** zigzag markings
- ☐ **C** a different surface texture
- ☐ **D** yellow hatch markings

Trams can run on roads used by other vehicles and pedestrians. The part of the road used by the trams is known as the reserved area and this should be kept clear. It often has a different surface and is usually edged with white road markings.

476 Mark *one* answer

You see a vehicle coming towards you on a single-track road. You should

- ☐ **A** go back to the main road
- ☐ **B** do an emergency stop
- ☐ **C** stop at a passing place
- ☐ **D** put on your hazard warning lights

You must take extra care when on single track roads. You may not be able to see around bends due to high hedges or fences. Proceed with caution and expect to meet oncoming vehicles around the next bend. If you do, pull into or opposite a passing place.

477 Mark *one* answer

The road is wet. Why might a motorcyclist steer round drain covers on a bend?

- ☐ **A** To avoid puncturing the tyres on the edge of the drain covers
- ☐ **B** To prevent the motorcycle sliding on the metal drain covers
- ☐ **C** To help judge the bend using the drain covers as marker points
- ☐ **D** To avoid splashing pedestrians on the pavement

Other drivers or riders may have to change course due to the size or characteristics of their vehicle. Understanding this will help you to anticipate their actions. Motorcyclists and cyclists will be checking the road ahead for uneven or slippery surfaces, especially in wet weather. They may need to move across their lane to avoid surface hazards such as potholes and drain covers.

478 Mark *one* answer

After this hazard you should test your brakes. Why is this?

- ☐ **A** You will be on a slippery road
- ☐ **B** Your brakes will be soaking wet
- ☐ **C** You will be going down a long hill
- ☐ **D** You will have just crossed a long bridge

A ford is a crossing over a stream that's shallow enough to go through. After you've gone through a ford or deep puddle the water will affect your brakes. To dry them out apply a light brake pressure while moving slowly. Don't travel at normal speeds until you are sure your brakes are working properly again.

479 Mark *one* answer

Why should you always reduce your speed when travelling in fog?

- ☐ **A** The brakes do not work as well
- ☐ **B** You will be dazzled by other headlights
- ☐ **C** The engine will take longer to warm up
- ☐ **D** It is more difficult to see events ahead

You won't be able to see as far ahead in fog as you can on a clear day. You will need to reduce your speed so that, if a hazard looms out of the fog, you have the time and space to take avoiding action.

Travelling in fog is hazardous. If you can, try and delay your journey until it has cleared.

480 Mark *one* answer

How will your vehicle be affected when you drive up steep hills?

- ☐ **A** The higher gears will pull better
- ☐ **B** The steering will feel heavier
- ☐ **C** Overtaking will be easier
- ☐ **D** The engine will work harder

The engine will need more power to pull the vehicle up the hill. When approaching a steep hill you should select a lower gear to help maintain your speed. You should do this without hesitation, so that you don't lose too much speed before engaging the lower gear.

481 Mark *one* answer

You are driving on the motorway in windy conditions. When passing high-sided vehicles you should

- ☐ **A** increase your speed
- ☐ **B** be wary of a sudden gust
- ☐ **C** drive alongside very closely
- ☐ **D** expect normal conditions

The draught caused by other vehicles could be strong enough to push you out of your lane. Keep both hands on the steering wheel to maintain full control.

482 Mark *one* answer
To correct a rear-wheel skid you should

☐ **A** not steer at all
☐ **B** steer away from it
☐ **C** steer into it
☐ **D** apply your handbrake

Prevention is better than cure, so it's important that you take every precaution to avoid a skid from starting.

If you feel the rear wheels of your vehicle beginning to skid, try to steer in the same direction to recover control. Don't brake suddenly – this will only make the situation worse.

483 Mark *one* answer
You are driving in fog. Why should you keep well back from the vehicle in front?

☐ **A** In case it changes direction suddenly
☐ **B** In case its fog lights dazzle you
☐ **C** In case it stops suddenly
☐ **D** In case its brake lights dazzle you

If you're following another road user in fog stay well back. The driver in front won't be able to see hazards until they're close and might brake suddenly. Another reason why it is important to maintain a good separation distance in fog is that the road surface is likely to be wet and slippery.

484 Mark *one* answer
You should switch your rear fog lights on when visibility drops below

☐ **A** your overall stopping distance
☐ **B** ten car lengths
☐ **C** 200 metres (656 feet)
☐ **D** 100 metres (328 feet)

If visibility falls below 100 metres (328 feet) in fog, switching on your rear fog lights will help following road users to see you. Don't forget to turn them off once visibility improves: their brightness might be mistaken for brake lights and they could dazzle other drivers.

485 Mark *one* answer
Whilst driving, the fog clears and you can see more clearly. You must remember to

☐ **A** switch off the fog lights
☐ **B** reduce your speed
☐ **C** switch off the demister
☐ **D** close any open windows

Bright rear fog lights might be mistaken for brake lights and could be misleading for the traffic behind.

486 Mark *one* answer

You have to park on the road in fog. You should

☐ **A** leave sidelights on
☐ **B** leave dipped headlights and fog lights on
☐ **C** leave dipped headlights on
☐ **D** leave main beam headlights on

If you have to park your vehicle in foggy conditions it's important that it can be seen by other road users. Try to find a place to park off the road. If this isn't possible leave it facing in the same direction as the traffic. Make sure that your lights are clean and that you leave your sidelights on.

487 Mark *one* answer

On a foggy day you unavoidably have to park your car on the road. You should

☐ **A** leave your headlights on
☐ **B** leave your fog lights on
☐ **C** leave your sidelights on
☐ **D** leave your hazard lights on

Ensure that your vehicle can be seen by other traffic. If possible, park your car off the road in a car park or driveway to avoid the extra risk to other road users.

488 Mark *one* answer

You are travelling at night. You are dazzled by headlights coming towards you. You should

☐ **A** pull down your sun visor
☐ **B** slow down or stop
☐ **C** switch on your main beam headlights
☐ **D** put your hand over your eyes

You will have additional hazards to deal with at night. Visibility may be very limited and the lights of oncoming vehicles can often dazzle you. When this happens don't close your eyes, swerve or flash your headlights, as this will also distract other drivers. It may help to focus on the left kerb, verge or lane line.

489 Mark *one* answer

Front fog lights may be used ONLY if

☐ **A** visibility is seriously reduced
☐ **B** they are fitted above the bumper
☐ **C** they are not as bright as the headlights
☐ **D** an audible warning device is used

Your vehicle should have a warning light on the dashboard which illuminates when the fog lights are being used. You need to be familiar with the layout of your dashboard so you are aware if they have been switched on in error, or you have forgotten to switch them off.

490 Mark *one* answer
Front fog lights may be used ONLY if

- ☐ **A** your headlights are not working
- ☐ **B** they are operated with rear fog lights
- ☐ **C** they were fitted by the vehicle manufacturer
- ☐ **D** visibility is seriously reduced

It is illegal to use fog lights unless visibility is seriously reduced, which is generally when you cannot see for more than 100 metres (328 feet). Check that they have been switched off when conditions improve.

491 Mark *one* answer
You are driving with your front fog lights switched on. Earlier fog has now cleared. What should you do?

- ☐ **A** Leave them on if other drivers have their lights on
- ☐ **B** Switch them off as long as visibility remains good
- ☐ **C** Flash them to warn oncoming traffic that it is foggy
- ☐ **D** Drive with them on instead of your headlights

Switch off your fog lights if the weather improves, but be prepared to use them again if visibility reduces to less than 100 metres (328 feet).

492 Mark *one* answer
Front fog lights should be used ONLY when

- ☐ **A** travelling in very light rain
- ☐ **B** visibility is seriously reduced
- ☐ **C** daylight is fading
- ☐ **D** driving after midnight

Fog lights will help others see you, but remember, they must only be used if visibility is seriously reduced to less than 100 metres (328 feet).

493 Mark *one* answer
Why should you switch off your rear fog lights when the fog has cleared?

- ☐ **A** To allow your headlamps to work
- ☐ **B** To stop draining the battery
- ☐ **C** To stop the engine losing power
- ☐ **D** To prevent dazzling following drivers

Don't forget to switch off your fog lights when the weather improves. You could be prosecuted for driving with them on in good visibility. The high intensity of rear fog lights can dazzle following drivers and make your brake lights difficult to notice.

494 Mark *one* answer
You have been driving in thick fog which has now cleared. You must switch OFF your rear fog lights because

☐ **A** they use a lot of power from the battery
☐ **B** they make your brake lights less clear
☐ **C** they will cause dazzle in your rear view mirrors
☐ **D** they may not be properly adjusted

It is essential that the traffic behind is given a clear warning when you brake. In good visibility, your rear fog lights can make it hard for others to see your brake lights. Make sure you switch off your fog lights when the visibility improves.

495 Mark *one* answer
Front fog lights should be used

☐ **A** when visibility is reduced to 100 metres (328 feet)
☐ **B** as a warning to oncoming traffic
☐ **C** when driving during the hours of darkness
☐ **D** in any conditions and at any time

When visibility is seriously reduced, switch on your fog lights if you have them fitted. It is essential not only that you can see ahead, but also that other road users are able to see you.

496 Mark *one* answer
Using rear fog lights in clear daylight will

☐ **A** be useful when towing a trailer
☐ **B** give extra protection
☐ **C** dazzle other drivers
☐ **D** make following drivers keep back

Rear fog lights shine brighter than normal rear lights so that they show up in reduced visibility. When the weather is clear they could dazzle the driver behind, so switch them off.

497 Mark *one* answer
Using front fog lights in clear daylight will

☐ **A** flatten the battery
☐ **B** dazzle other drivers
☐ **C** improve your visibility
☐ **D** increase your awareness

Fog lights can be brighter than normal dipped headlights. If the weather has improved turn them off to avoid dazzling other road users.

498 Mark *one* answer
You may use front fog lights with headlights ONLY when visibility is reduced to less than

☐ **A** 100 metres (328 feet)
☐ **B** 200 metres (656 feet)
☐ **C** 300 metres (984 feet)
☐ **D** 400 metres (1,312 feet)

It is an offence to use fog lights if the visibility is better than 100 metres (328 feet). Switch front fog lights off if the fog clears to avoid dazzling other road users, but be aware that the fog may be patchy.

499 Mark *one* answer
Chains can be fitted to your wheels to help prevent

☐ **A** damage to the road surface
☐ **B** wear to the tyres
☐ **C** skidding in deep snow
☐ **D** the brakes locking

Snow chains can be fitted to your tyres during snowy conditions. They can help you to move off from rest or to keep moving in deep snow. You will still need to adjust your driving according to the road conditions at the time.

500 Mark *one* answer

How can you use the engine of your vehicle to control your speed?

☐ **A** By changing to a lower gear
☐ **B** By selecting reverse gear
☐ **C** By changing to a higher gear
☐ **D** By selecting neutral

You should brake and slow down before selecting a lower gear. The gear can then be used to keep the speed low and help you control the vehicle. This is particularly helpful on long downhill stretches, where brake fade can occur if the brakes overheat.

501 Mark *one* answer

Why could keeping the clutch down or selecting neutral for long periods of time be dangerous?

☐ **A** Fuel spillage will occur
☐ **B** Engine damage may be caused
☐ **C** You will have less steering and braking control
☐ **D** It will wear tyres out more quickly

Letting your vehicle roll or coast in neutral reduces your control over steering and braking. This can be dangerous on downhill slopes where your vehicle could pick up speed very quickly.

502 Mark *one* answer

You are driving on an icy road. What distance should you drive from the car in front?

☐ **A** four times the normal distance
☐ **B** six times the normal distance
☐ **C** eight times the normal distance
☐ **D** ten times the normal distance

Don't travel in icy or snowy weather unless your journey is necessary.

Drive extremely carefully when roads are or may be icy. Stopping distances can be ten times greater than on dry roads.

503 Mark *one* answer

You are on a well-lit motorway at night. You must

☐ **A** use only your sidelights
☐ **B** always use your headlights
☐ **C** always use rear fog lights
☐ **D** use headlights only in bad weather

If you're driving on a motorway at night or in poor visibility, you must always use your headlights, even if the road is well-lit. The other road users in front must be able to see you in their mirrors.

504 Mark *one* answer

You are on a motorway at night with other vehicles just ahead of you. Which lights should you have on?

- ☐ **A** Front fog lights
- ☐ **B** Main beam headlights
- ☐ **C** Sidelights only
- ☐ **D** Dipped headlights

If you're driving behind other traffic at night on the motorway, leave a two-second time gap and use dipped headlights. Full beam will dazzle the other drivers. Your headlights' beam should fall short of the vehicle in front.

505 Mark *one* answer

What will affect your vehicle's stopping distance?

- ☐ **A** The speed limit
- ☐ **B** The street lighting
- ☐ **C** The time of day
- ☐ **D** The condition of the tyres

Having tyres correctly inflated and in good condition will ensure they have maximum grip on the road; how well your tyres grip the road has a significant effect on your car's stopping distance.

506 Mark *one* answer

You are on a motorway at night. You MUST have your headlights switched on unless

- ☐ **A** there are vehicles close in front of you
- ☐ **B** you are travelling below 50mph
- ☐ **C** the motorway is lit
- ☐ **D** your vehicle is broken down on the hard shoulder

Always use your headlights at night on a motorway unless you have stopped on the hard shoulder. If you break down and have to stop on the hard shoulder, switch off the headlights but leave the sidelights on so that other road users can see your vehicle.

507 Mark *one* answer

You will feel the effects of engine braking when you

- ☐ **A** only use the handbrake
- ☐ **B** only use neutral
- ☐ **C** change to a lower gear
- ☐ **D** change to a higher gear

When going downhill, prolonged use of the brakes can cause them to overheat and lose their effectiveness. Changing to a lower gear will assist your braking.

508 Mark *one* answer

Daytime visibility is poor but not seriously reduced. You should switch on

- ☐ **A** headlights and fog lights
- ☐ **B** front fog lights
- ☐ **C** dipped headlights
- ☐ **D** rear fog lights

Only use your fog lights when visibility is seriously reduced. Use dipped headlights in poor conditions.

509 Mark *one* answer
Why are vehicles fitted with rear fog lights?

☐ **A** To be seen when driving at high speed
☐ **B** To use if broken down in a dangerous position
☐ **C** To make them more visible in thick fog
☐ **D** To warn drivers following closely to drop back

Rear fog lights make it easier to spot a vehicle ahead in foggy conditions. Avoid the temptation to use other vehicles' lights as a guide, as they may give you a false sense of security.

510 Mark *one* answer
While you are driving in fog, it becomes necessary to use front fog lights. You should

☐ **A** only turn them on in heavy traffic conditions
☐ **B** remember not to use them on motorways
☐ **C** only use them on dual carriageways
☐ **D** remember to switch them off as visibility improves

It is an offence to have your fog lights on in conditions other than seriously reduced visibility, i.e. less than 100 metres (328 feet).

511 Mark *one* answer
When snow is falling heavily you should

☐ **A** only drive with your hazard lights on
☐ **B** not drive unless you have a mobile phone
☐ **C** only drive when your journey is short
☐ **D** not drive unless it is essential

Consider if the increased risk is worth it. If the weather conditions are bad and your journey isn't essential, then stay at home.

512 Mark *one* answer
You are driving down a long steep hill. You suddenly notice your brakes are not working as well as normal. What is the usual cause of this?

☐ **A** The brakes overheating
☐ **B** Air in the brake fluid
☐ **C** Oil on the brakes
☐ **D** Badly adjusted brakes

This is more likely to happen on vehicles fitted with drum brakes but can apply to disc brakes as well. Using a lower gear will assist the braking and help you to keep control of your vehicle.

513 Mark *one* answer
You have to make a journey in fog. What should you do before you set out?

☐ **A** Top up the radiator with anti-freeze
☐ **B** Make sure that you have a warning triangle in the vehicle
☑ **C** Make sure that the windows are clean
☐ **D** Check the battery

If you have to drive in fog, drive with your dipped beam headlamps on and keep your windscreen clear. You should always be able to pull up within the distance you can see ahead.

514 Mark *one* answer
You have just driven out of fog. Visibility is now good. You MUST

☐ **A** switch off all your fog lights
☐ **B** keep your rear fog lights on
☐ **C** keep your front fog lights on
☐ **D** leave fog lights on in case fog returns

You MUST turn off your fog lights if visibility is over 100 metres (328 feet). However, be prepared for the fact that the fog may be patchy.

515 Mark *one* answer
You may drive with front fog lights switched on

☐ **A** when visibility is less than 100 metres (328 feet)
☐ **B** at any time to be noticed
☐ **C** instead of headlights on high speed roads
☐ **D** when dazzled by the lights of oncoming vehicles

Only use front fog lights if the distance you are able to see is less than 100 metres (328 feet). Turn off your fog lights as the visibility improves.

516 Mark *one* answer
Why is it dangerous to leave rear fog lights on when they're not needed?

☐ **A** They may be confused with brake lights
☐ **B** The bulbs would fail
☐ **C** Electrical systems could be overloaded
☐ **D** Direction indicators may not work properly

If your rear fog lights are left on when it isn't foggy, the glare they cause makes it difficult for road users behind to know whether you are braking or you have just forgotten to turn off your rear fog lights. This can be a particular problem on wet roads and on motorways. If you leave your rear fog lights on at night, road users behind you are likely to be dazzled and this could put them at risk.

517 Mark *one* answer

Holding the clutch pedal down or rolling in neutral for too long while driving will

☐ **A** use more fuel
☐ **B** cause the engine to overheat
☐ **C** reduce your control
☐ **D** improve tyre wear

Holding the clutch down or staying in neutral for too long will cause your vehicle to freewheel. This is known as 'coasting' and it is dangerous as it reduces your control of the vehicle.

518 Mark *one* answer

You are driving down a steep hill. Why could keeping the clutch down or rolling in neutral for too long be dangerous?

☐ **A** Fuel consumption will be higher
☐ **B** Your vehicle will pick up speed
☐ **C** It will damage the engine
☐ **D** It will wear tyres out more quickly

Driving in neutral or with the clutch down for long periods is known as 'coasting'. There will be no engine braking and your vehicle will pick up speed on downhill slopes. Coasting can be very dangerous because it reduces steering and braking control.

519 Mark *one* answer

Why is it bad technique to coast when driving downhill?

☐ **A** The fuel consumption will increase
☐ **B** The engine will overheat
☐ **C** The tyres will wear more quickly
☐ **D** The vehicle will gain speed

Coasting is when you allow the vehicle to freewheel in neutral or with the clutch pedal depressed. Speed will increase as you lose the benefits of engine braking and have less control. You shouldn't coast when approaching hazards such as junctions or bends and when travelling downhill.

520 Mark *one* answer

What should you do when dealing with this hazard?

☐ **A** Switch on your hazard lamps
☐ **B** Use a low gear and drive slowly
☐ **C** Use a high gear to prevent wheelspin
☐ **D** Switch on your windscreen wipers

In normal conditions a Ford can be crossed quite safely by driving through it slowly. The water may affect your brakes, so when you're clear of the Ford test them before you resume normal driving.

521 Mark *one* answer

Why is travelling in neutral for long distances (known as 'coasting') wrong?

☐ **A** It will cause the car to skid
☐ **B** It will make the engine stall
☐ **C** The engine will run faster
☐ **D** There is no engine braking

Try to look ahead and read the road. Plan your approach to junctions and select the correct gear in good time. This will give you the control you need to deal with any hazards that occur.

You'll coast a little every time you change gear. This can't be avoided, but it should be kept to a minimum.

522 Mark *one* answer

When MUST you use dipped headlights during the day?

☐ **A** All the time
☐ **B** Along narrow streets
☐ **C** In poor visibility
☐ **D** When parking

You MUST use dipped headlights and/or fog lights in fog when visibility is seriously reduced to 100 metres (328 feet) or less.

You should use dipped headlights, but NOT fog lights, when visibility is poor, such as in heavy rain.

523 Mark *one* answer

You are braking on a wet road. Your vehicle begins to skid. It does not have anti-lock brakes. What is the FIRST thing you should do?

☐ **A** Quickly pull up the handbrake
☐ **B** Release the footbrake
☐ **C** Push harder on the brake pedal
☐ **D** Gently use the accelerator

If the skid has been caused by braking too hard for the conditions, release the brake. You may then need to reapply and release the brake again. You may need to do this a number of times. This will allow the wheels to turn and so limit the skid. Skids are much easier to get into than they are to get out of. Prevention is better than cure. Stay alert to the road and weather conditions. Drive so that you can stop within the distance you can see to be clear.

524 Mark *one* answer

Using rear fog lights on a clear dry night will

☐ **A** help oncoming drivers see you sooner
☐ **B** help your indicators to be seen more clearly
☐ **C** give a better view of the road ahead
☐ **D** make your brake lights difficult to notice

You shouldn't use rear fog lights unless visibility is seriously reduced. If you forget to turn them off when the weather improves they can
• be confused with brake lamps
• dazzle following drivers.
A warning light will show on the dashboard to indicate when your rear fog lights are on. You should know the meaning of all the lights on your dashboard and check them before you move off and as you drive.

525 Mark *one* answer
When joining a motorway you must always

- ☐ **A** use the hard shoulder
- ☐ **B** stop at the end of the acceleration lane
- ☐ **C** come to a stop before joining the motorway
- ☐ **D** give way to traffic already on the motorway

You should give way to traffic already on the motorway. Where possible they may move over to let you in but don't force your way into the traffic stream. The traffic may be travelling at high speed so you should match your speed to fit in.

526 Mark *one* answer
What is the national speed limit for cars and motorcycles in the centre lane of a three-lane motorway?

- ☐ **A** 40mph
- ☐ **B** 50mph
- ☐ **C** 60mph
- ☐ **D** 70mph

Unless shown otherwise, the speed limit on a motorway applies to all the lanes. Look out for any signs of speed limit changes due to roadworks or traffic flow control.

527 Mark *one* answer
What is the national speed limit on motorways for cars and motorcycles?

- ☐ **A** 30mph
- ☐ **B** 50mph
- ☐ **C** 60mph
- ☐ **D** 70mph

Travelling at the national speed limit doesn't allow you to hog the right-hand lane. Always use the left-hand lane whenever possible. When leaving a motorway get into the left-hand lane well before your exit. Reduce your speed on the slip road and look out for sharp bends or curves and traffic queuing at roundabouts.

528 Mark *one* answer
The left-hand lane on a three-lane motorway is for use by

- ☐ **A** any vehicle
- ☐ **B** large vehicles only
- ☐ **C** emergency vehicles only
- ☐ **D** slow vehicles only

On a motorway all traffic should use the left-hand lane unless overtaking. Use the centre or right-hand lanes if you need to overtake. If you're overtaking a number of slower vehicles move back to the left-hand lane when you're safely past. Check your mirrors frequently and don't stay in the middle or right-hand lane if the left-hand lane is free.

529 Mark *one* answer
Which of these IS NOT allowed to travel in the right-hand lane of a three-lane motorway?

☐ **A** A small delivery van
☐ **B** A motorcycle
☐ **C** A vehicle towing a trailer
☐ **D** A motorcycle and side-car

A vehicle with a trailer is restricted to 60mph. For this reason it isn't allowed in the right-hand lane as it might hold up the faster-moving traffic that wishes to overtake in that lane.

530 Mark *one* answer
You break down on a motorway. You need to call for help. Why may it be better to use an emergency roadside telephone rather than a mobile phone?

☐ **A** It connects you to a local garage
☐ **B** Using a mobile phone will distract other drivers
☐ **C** It allows easy location by the emergency services
☐ **D** Mobile phones do not work on motorways

On a motorway it is best to use a roadside emergency telephone so that the emergency services are able to locate you easily. The nearest telephone is shown by an arrow on marker posts at the edge of the hard shoulder. If you use a mobile, they will need to know your exact location. Before you call, find out the number on the nearest marker post. This number will identify your exact location.

531 Mark *one* answer
After a breakdown you need to rejoin the main carriageway of a motorway from the hard shoulder. You should

☐ **A** move out onto the carriageway then build up your speed
☐ **B** move out onto the carriageway using your hazard lights
☐ **C** gain speed on the hard shoulder before moving out onto the carriageway
☐ **D** wait on the hard shoulder until someone flashes their headlights at you

Wait for a safe gap in the traffic before you move out. Indicate your intention and use the hard shoulder to gain speed but don't force your way into the traffic.

532 Mark *one* answer
A crawler lane on a motorway is found

☐ **A** on a steep gradient
☐ **B** before a service area
☐ **C** before a junction
☐ **D** along the hard shoulder

Slow-moving, large vehicles might slow down the progress of other traffic. On a steep gradient this extra lane is provided for these slow-moving vehicles to allow the faster-moving traffic to flow more easily.

533 Mark *one* answer
What do these motorway signs show?

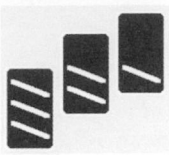

☐ **A** They are countdown markers
to a bridge
☐ **B** They are distance markers to the
next telephone
☐ **C** They are countdown markers to
the next exit
☐ **D** They warn of a police control ahead

The exit from a motorway is indicated by countdown markers. These are positioned 90 metres (100 yards) apart, the first being 270 metres (300 yards) from the start of the slip road. Move into the left-hand lane well before you reach the start of the slip road.

534 Mark *one* answer
On a motorway the amber reflective studs can be found between

☐ **A** the hard shoulder and the carriageway
☐ **B** the acceleration lane and the carriageway
☑ **C** the central reservation and the carriageway
☐ **D** each pair of the lanes

On motorways reflective studs are located into the road to help you in the dark and in conditions of poor visibility. Amber-coloured studs are found on the right-hand edge of the main carriageway, next to the central reservation.

535 Mark *one* answer
What colour are the reflective studs between the lanes on a motorway?

☐ **A** Green
☐ **B** Amber
☑ **C** White
☐ **D** Red

White studs are found between the lanes on motorways. The light from your headlights is reflected back and this is especially useful in bad weather, when visibility is restricted.

536 Mark *one* answer
What colour are the reflective studs between a motorway and its slip road?

☐ **A** Amber
☐ **B** White
☐ **C** Green
☐ **D** Red

The studs between the carriageway and the hard shoulder are normally red. These change to green where there is a slip road. They will help you identify slip roads when visibility is poor or when it is dark.

537 Mark *one* answer
You have broken down on a motorway. To find the nearest emergency telephone you should always walk

☐ **A** with the traffic flow
☐ **B** facing oncoming traffic
☐ **C** in the direction shown on the marker posts
☐ **D** in the direction of the nearest exit

Along the hard shoulder there are marker posts at 100-metre intervals. These will direct you to the nearest emergency telephone.

---

538 Mark *one* answer
You are joining a motorway. Why is it important to make full use of the slip road?

☐ **A** Because there is space available to turn round if you need to
☐ **B** To allow you direct access to the overtaking lanes
☐ **C** To build up a speed similar to traffic on the motorway
☐ **D** Because you can continue on the hard shoulder

Try to join the motorway without affecting the progress of the traffic already travelling on it. Always give way to traffic already on the motorway. At busy times you may have to slow down to merge into slow-moving traffic.

539 Mark *one* answer
How should you use the emergency telephone on a motorway?

☐ **A** Stay close to the carriageway
☐ **B** Face the oncoming traffic
☐ **C** Keep your back to the traffic
☐ **D** Stand on the hard shoulder

Traffic is passing you at speed. If the draught from a large lorry catches you by surprise it could blow you off balance and even onto the carriageway. By facing the oncoming traffic you can see approaching lorries and so be prepared for their draught. You are also in a position to see other hazards approaching.

---

540. Mark *one* answer
You are on a motorway. What colour are the reflective studs on the left of the carriageway?

☐ **A** Green
☐ **B** Red
☐ **C** White
☐ **D** Amber

Red studs are placed between the edge of the carriageway and the hard shoulder. Where slip roads leave or join the motorway the studs are green.

541 Mark *one* answer
On a three-lane motorway which lane should you normally use?

☐ **A** Left
☐ **B** Right
☐ **C** Centre
☐ **D** Either the right or centre

On a three-lane motorway you should travel in the left-hand lane unless you're overtaking. This applies regardless of the speed at which you're travelling.

542 Mark *one* answer
When going through a contraflow system on a motorway you should

☐ **A** ensure that you do not exceed 30mph
☐ **B** keep a good distance from the vehicle ahead
☐ **C** switch lanes to keep the traffic flowing
☐ **D** stay close to the vehicle ahead to reduce queues

There's likely to be a speed restriction in force. Keep to this. Don't
• switch lanes
• get too close to traffic in front of you.
Be aware there will be no permanent barrier between you and the oncoming traffic.

543 Mark *one* answer
You are on a three-lane motorway. There are red reflective studs on your left and white ones to your right. Where are you?

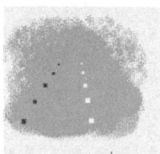

☐ **A** In the right-hand lane
☐ **B** In the middle lane
☐ **C** On the hard shoulder
☐ **D** In the left-hand lane

The colours of the reflective studs on the motorway and their locations are
• red – between the hard shoulder and the carriageway
• white – lane markings
• amber – between the edge of the carriageway and the central reservation
• green – along slip road exits and entrances
• bright green/yellow – roadworks and contraflow systems.

544 Mark *one* answer
You are approaching roadworks on a motorway. What should you do?

☐ **A** Speed up to clear the area quickly
☐ **B** Always use the hard shoulder
☐ **C** Obey all speed limits
☐ **D** Stay very close to the vehicle in front

Collisions can often happen at roadworks. Be aware of the speed limits, slow down in good time and keep your distance from the vehicle in front.

545 Mark *one* answer
Which of these must NOT use motorways?

☐ **A** Cars driven by learner drivers
☐ **B** Motorcycles over 50cc
☐ **C** Double-deck buses
☐ **D** Cars with automatic transmission

Motorways MUST NOT be used by learner drivers, pedestrians, cyclists, motorcycles under 50cc, certain slow-moving vehicles without permission, and invalid carriages weighing less than 254kg (560lbs).

546 Mark *one* answer
When using a motorway it's important that you

☐ **A** look much further ahead than you would using other roads
☐ **B** drive much faster than you would on other roads
☐ **C** clean your windscreen more often than you would on other roads
☐ **D** concentrate more than you would on other roads

Traffic on motorways usually travels faster than on other roads. You need to be looking further ahead to give yourself more time to react to any hazard that may develop.

547 Mark *one* answer
Immediately after joining a motorway you should normally

☐ **A** try to overtake
☐ **B** re-adjust your mirrors
☐ **C** position your vehicle in the centre lane
☐ **D** keep in the left-hand lane

Stay in the left-hand lane long enough to get used to the higher speeds of motorway traffic.

548 Mark *one* answer
What is the right-hand lane used for on a three-lane motorway?

☐ **A** Emergency vehicles only
☐ **B** Overtaking
☐ **C** Vehicles towing trailers
☐ **D** Coaches only

You should keep to the left and only use the right-hand lane if you're passing slower-moving traffic.

549 Mark *one* answer

What should you use the hard shoulder of a motorway for?

☐ **A** Stopping in an emergency
☐ **B** Leaving the motorway
☐ **C** Stopping when you are tired
☐ **D** Joining the motorway

Don't use the hard shoulder for stopping unless it is an emergency. If you want to stop for any other reason go to the next exit or service station.

550 Mark *one* answer

You are in the right-hand lane on a motorway. You see these overhead signs. This means

☐ **A** move to the left and reduce your speed to 50mph
☐ **B** there are roadworks 50 metres (55 yards) ahead
☐ **C** use the hard shoulder until you have passed the hazard
☐ **D** leave the motorway at the next exit

You MUST obey this sign. There might not be any visible signs of a problem ahead. However, there might be queuing traffic or another hazard which you cannot yet see.

551 Mark *one* answer

You are allowed to stop on a motorway when you

☐ **A** need to walk and get fresh air
☐ **B** wish to pick up hitchhikers
☐ **C** are told to do so by flashing red lights
☐ **D** need to use a mobile telephone

You MUST stop if there are red lights flashing above every lane on the motorway. However, if any of the other lanes do not show flashing red lights or red cross you may move into that lane and continue if it is safe to do so.

552 Mark *one* answer

You are travelling along the left-hand lane of a three-lane motorway. Traffic is joining from a slip road. You should

☐ **A** race the other vehicles
☐ **B** move to another lane
☐ **C** maintain a steady speed
☐ **D** switch on your hazard flashers

You should move to another lane if it is safe to do so. This can greatly assist the flow of traffic joining the motorway, especially at peak times.

553 Mark *one* answer
A basic rule when on motorways is

- ☐ **A** use the lane that has least traffic
- ☐ **B** keep to the left-hand lane unless overtaking
- ☐ **C** overtake on the side that is clearest
- ☐ **D** try to keep above 50mph to prevent congestion

You should normally travel in the left-hand lane unless you are overtaking a slower-moving vehicle. When you are past that vehicle move back into the left-hand lane as soon as it's safe to do so. Don't cut across in front of the vehicle that you're overtaking.

554 Mark *one* answer
On motorways you should never overtake on the left unless

- ☐ **A** you can see well ahead that the hard shoulder is clear
- ☐ **B** the traffic in the right-hand lane is signalling right
- ☐ **C** you warn drivers behind by signalling left
- ☐ **D** there is a queue of slow-moving traffic to your right that is moving more slowly than you are

Only overtake on the left if traffic is moving slowly in queues and the traffic on your right is moving more slowly than the traffic in your lane.

555 Mark *one* answer
Traffic officers are used on motorways and some 'A' class roads. In which part of the United Kingdom do they operate?

- ☐ **A** England only
- ☐ **B** England, Scotland and Wales
- ☐ **C** England and Wales
- ☐ **D** England, Wales and Northern Ireland

Traffic officers have powers to stop vehicles on safety grounds, for example if you have an insecure load, in England only. It's an offence not to comply with their directions.

556 Mark *one* answer
An Emergency Refuge Area is an area

- ☐ **A** on a motorway for use in cases of emergency or breakdown
- ☐ **B** for use if you think you will be involved in a road rage incident
- ☐ **C** on a motorway for a police patrol to park and watch traffic
- ☐ **D** for construction and road workers to store emergency equipment

Emergency Refuge Areas may be found at the side of the hard shoulder about 500 metres apart. If you break down you should use them rather than the hard shoulder if you are able. When re-joining the motorway you must remember to take extra care especially when the hard shoulder is being used as a running lane within an Active Traffic Management area. Try to match your speed to that of traffic in the lane you are joining.

557 Mark *one* answer
What is an Emergency Refuge Area on a motorway for?

☐ **A** An area to park in when you want to use a mobile phone
☐ **B** To use in cases of emergency or breakdown
☐ **C** For an emergency recovery vehicle to park in a contraflow system
☐ **D** To drive in when there is queuing traffic ahead

In cases of breakdown or emergency try to get your vehicle into an Emergency Refuge Area. This is safer than just stopping on the hard shoulder as it gives you greater distance from the main carriageway. If you are able to re-join the motorway you must take extra care, especially when the hard shoulder is being used as a running lane.

558 Mark *one* answer
Traffic officers operate on motorways and some primary routes in England. What are they authorised to do?

☐ **A** Stop and arrest drivers who break the law
☐ **B** Repair broken-down vehicles on the motorway
☐ **C** Issue fixed penalty notices
☐ **D** Stop and direct anyone on a motorway

Traffic officers do not have enforcement powers but are able to stop and direct people on motorways and some 'A' class roads. They only operate in England and work in partnership with the police at incidents providing a highly trained and visible service. They are recognised by an orange and yellow jacket and their vehicle has yellow and black markings.

559 Mark *one* answer
You are on a motorway. A red cross is displayed above the hard shoulder. What does this mean?

☐ **A** Pull up in this lane to answer your mobile phone
☐ **B** Use this lane as a running lane
☐ **C** This lane can be used if you need a rest
☐ **D** You should not travel in this lane

Active Traffic Management schemes are being introduced on motorways. Within these areas at certain times the hard shoulder will be used as a running lane. A red cross above the hard shoulder shows that this lane should NOT be used, except for emergencies and breakdowns.

560 Mark *one* answer

You are on a motorway in an Active Traffic Management (ATM) area. A mandatory speed limit is displayed above the hard shoulder. What does this mean?

- ☐ **A** You should not travel in this lane
- ☐ **B** The hard shoulder can be used as a running lane
- ☐ **C** You can park on the hard shoulder if you feel tired
- ☐ **D** You can pull up in this lane to answer a mobile phone

A mandatory speed limit sign above the hard shoulder shows that it can be used as a running lane between junctions. You must stay within the speed limit. Look out for vehicles that may have broken down and could be blocking the hard shoulder.

561 Mark *one* answer

The aim of an Active Traffic Management scheme on a motorway is to

- ☐ **A** prevent overtaking
- ☐ **B** reduce rest stops
- ☐ **C** prevent tailgating
- ☐ **D** reduce congestion

Active Traffic Management schemes are intended to reduce congestion and make journey times more reliable. In these areas the hard shoulder may be used as a running lane to ease congestion at peak times or in the event of an incident. It may appear that you could travel faster for a short distance, but keeping traffic flow at a constant speed may improve your journey time.

---

562 Mark *one* answer

You are in an Active Traffic Management area on a motorway. When the Actively Managed mode is operating

- ☐ **A** speed limits are only advisory
- ☐ **B** the national speed limit will apply
- ☐ **C** the speed limit is always 30mph
- ☐ **D** all speed limit signals are set

When an Active Traffic Management (ATM) scheme is operating on a motorway you MUST follow the mandatory instructions shown on the gantries above each lane. This includes the hard shoulder.

563 Mark *one* answer   NI

You are travelling on a motorway. A red cross is shown above the hard shoulder. What does this mean?

☐ **A** Use this lane as a rest area
☐ **B** Use this as a normal running lane
☐ **C** Do not use this lane to travel in
☐ **D** National speed limit applies in this lane

When a red cross is shown above the hard shoulder it should only be used for breakdowns or emergencies. Within Active Traffic Management (ATM) areas the hard shoulder may sometimes be used as a running lane. Speed limit signs directly ' above the hard shoulder will show that it's open.

564 Mark *one* answer

Why can it be an advantage for traffic speed to stay constant over a longer distance?

☐ **A** You will do more stop-start driving
☐ **B** You will use far more fuel
☐ **C** You will be able to use more direct routes
☐ **D** Your overall journey time will normally improve

When traffic travels at a constant speed over a longer distance, journey times normally improve. You may feel that you could travel faster for short periods but this won't generally improve your overall journey time. Signs will show the maximum speed at which you should travel.

565 Mark *one* answer

You should not normally travel on the hard shoulder of a motorway. When can you use it?

☐ **A** When taking the next exit
☐ **B** When traffic is stopped
☐ **C** When signs direct you to
☐ **D** When traffic is slow moving

Normally you should only use the hard shoulder for emergencies and breakdowns, and at roadworks when signs direct you to do so. Active Traffic Management (ATM) areas are being introduced to ease traffic congestion. In these areas the hard shoulder may be used as a running lane when speed limit signs are shown directly above.

566 Mark *one* answer

For what reason may you use the right-hand lane of a motorway?

☐ **A** For keeping out of the way of lorries
☐ **B** For travelling at more than 70mph
☐ **C** For turning right
☐ **D** For overtaking other vehicles

The right-hand lane of the motorway is for overtaking.
  Sometimes you may be directed into a right-hand lane as a result of roadworks or a traffic incident. This will be indicated by signs or officers directing the traffic.

567 Mark *one* answer

On a motorway what is used to reduce traffic bunching?

☐ **A** Variable speed limits
☐ **B** Contraflow systems
☐ **C** National speed limits
☐ **D** Lane closures

Congestion can be reduced by keeping traffic at a constant speed. At busy times maximum speed limits are displayed on overhead gantries. These can be varied quickly depending on the amount of traffic. By keeping to a constant speed on busy sections of motorway overall journey times are normally improved.

568 Mark *one* answer

When should you stop on a motorway?

☐ **A** If you have to read a map
☐ **B** When you are tired and need a rest
☐ **C** If a red cross shows above every lane
☐ **D** If your mobile phone rings

There are some occasions when you may have to stop on the carriageway of a motorway. These include when being signalled by the police or a traffic officer, when a red cross shows above every lane and in traffic jams.

569 Mark *one* answer

When may you stop on a motorway?

☐ **A** If you have to read a map
☐ **B** When you are tired and need a rest
☐ **C** If your mobile phone rings
☐ **D** In an emergency or breakdown

You should not normally stop on a motorway but there may be occasions when you need to do so. If you are unfortunate enough to break down make every effort to pull up on the hard shoulder.

570 Mark *one* answer

You are travelling on a motorway. Unless signs show a lower speed limit you must NOT exceed

☐ **A** 50mph
☐ **B** 60mph
☐ **C** 70mph
☐ **D** 80mph

The national speed limit for a car or motorcycle on the motorway is 70mph. Lower speed limits may be in force, for example at roadworks, so look out for the signs. Variable speed limits operate in some areas to control very busy stretches of motorway. The speed limit may change depending on the volume of traffic.

571 Mark *one* answer
You stop on the hard shoulder of a motorway and use the emergency telephone. Where's the best place to wait for help to arrive?

☐ **A** Next to the phone
☐ **B** Well away from the carriageway
☐ **C** With your vehicle
☐ **D** On the hard shoulder

When you're on the hard shoulder you're at risk of being injured by motorway traffic. The safest place to wait is away from the carriageway and hard shoulder, but near enough to see the emergency services arriving.

---

572 Mark *one* answer
You are on a motorway. There are red flashing lights above every lane. You must

☐ **A** pull onto the hard shoulder
☐ **B** slow down and watch for further signals
☐ **C** leave at the next exit
☐ **D** stop and wait

Red flashing lights above every lane mean you must not go on any further. You'll also see a red cross illuminated. Stop and wait. Don't
• change lanes
• continue
• pull onto the hard shoulder (unless in an emergency).

573 Mark *one* answer
You are on a three-lane motorway. A red cross is shown above the hard shoulder and mandatory speed limits above all other lanes. This means

☐ **A** the hard shoulder can be used as a rest area if you feel tired
☐ **B** the hard shoulder is for emergency or breakdown use only
☐ **C** the hard shoulder can be used as a normal running lane
☐ **D** the hard shoulder has a speed limit of 50mph

A red cross above the hard shoulder shows it is closed as a running lane and should only be used for emergencies or breakdowns. At busy times within an Active Traffic Management (ATM) area the hard shoulder may be used as a running lane. This will be shown by a mandatory speed limit on the gantry above.

574 Mark *one* answer

You are on a three-lane motorway and see this sign. It means you can use

- ☐ **A** any lane except the hard shoulder
- ☐ **B** the hard shoulder only
- ☐ **C** the three right-hand lanes only
- ☐ **D** all the lanes including the hard shoulder

Mandatory speed limit signs, above all lanes including the hard shoulder, show that you are in an Active Traffic Management (ATM) area. In this case you can use the hard shoulder as a running lane. You must stay within the speed limit shown. Look out for any vehicles that may have broken down and be blocking the hard shoulder.

575 Mark *one* answer

You are travelling on a motorway. You decide you need a rest. You should

- ☐ **A** stop on the hard shoulder
- ☐ **B** pull in at the nearest service area
- ☐ **C** pull up on a slip road
- ☐ **D** park on the central reservation

If you feel tired stop at the nearest service area. If it's too far away leave the motorway at the next exit and find a safe place to stop. You must not stop on the carriageway or hard shoulder of a motorway except in an emergency, in a traffic queue, when signalled to do so by a police or enforcement officer, or by traffic signals. Plan your journey so that you have regular rest stops.

576 Mark *one* answer

You are on a motorway. You become tired and decide you need to rest. What should you do?

- ☐ **A** Stop on the hard shoulder
- ☐ **B** Pull up on a slip road
- ☐ **C** Park on the central reservation
- ☐ **D** Leave at the next exit

Ideally you should plan your journey so that you have regular rest stops. If you do become tired leave at the next exit, or pull in at a service area if this is sooner.

577 Mark *one* answer

You are towing a trailer on a motorway. What is your maximum speed limit?

- ☐ **A** 40mph
- ☐ **B** 50mph
- ☐ **C** 60mph
- ☐ **D** 70mph

Don't forget that you're towing a trailer. If you're towing a small, light, trailer it won't reduce your vehicle's performance by very much. However, strong winds or buffeting from large vehicles might cause the trailer to snake from side to side. Be aware of your speed and don't exceed the lower limit imposed.

578 Mark *one* answer

The left-hand lane of a motorway should be used for

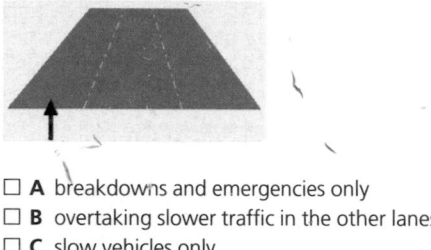

- ☐ **A** breakdowns and emergencies only
- ☐ **B** overtaking slower traffic in the other lanes
- ☐ **C** slow vehicles only
- ☐ **D** normal driving

You should keep to the left-hand lane whenever possible. Only use the other lanes for overtaking or when directed by signals. Using other lanes when the left-hand lane is empty can frustrate drivers behind you.

---

579 Mark *one* answer

You are driving on a motorway. You have to slow down quickly due to a hazard. You should

- ☐ **A** switch on your hazard lights
- ☐ **B** switch on your headlights
- ☐ **C** sound your horn
- ☐ **D** flash your headlights

Using your hazard lights, as well as brake lights, will give following traffic an extra warning of the problem ahead. Only use them for long enough to ensure that your warning has been seen.

580 Mark *one* answer

You get a puncture on the motorway. You manage to get your vehicle onto the hard shoulder. You should

- ☐ **A** change the wheel yourself immediately
- ☐ **B** use the emergency telephone and call for assistance
- ☐ **C** try to wave down another vehicle for help
- ☐ **D** only change the wheel if you have a passenger to help you

Due to the danger from passing traffic you should park as far to the left as you can and leave the vehicle by the nearside door.
   Do not attempt even simple repairs. Instead walk to an emergency telephone on your side of the road and phone for assistance. While waiting for assistance to arrive wait near your car, keeping well away from the carriageway and hard shoulder.

---

581 Mark *one* answer

You are driving on a motorway. By mistake, you go past the exit that you wanted to take. You should

- ☐ **A** carefully reverse on the hard shoulder
- ☐ **B** carry on to the next exit
- ☐ **C** carefully reverse in the left-hand lane
- ☐ **D** make a U-turn at the next gap in the central reservation

It is against the law to reverse, cross the central reservation or drive against the traffic flow on a motorway. If you have missed your exit ask yourself if your concentration is fading. It could be that you need to take a rest break before completing your journey.

582 Mark *one* answer

You are driving at 70mph on a three-lane motorway. There is no traffic ahead. Which lane should you use?

☐ **A** Any lane
☐ **B** Middle lane
☐ **C** Right lane
☐ **D** Left lane

If the left-hand lane is free you should use it, regardless of the speed you're travelling.

583 Mark *one* answer

Your vehicle has broken down on a motorway. You are not able to stop on the hard shoulder. What should you do?

☐ **A** Switch on your hazard warning lights
☐ **B** Stop following traffic and ask for help
☐ **C** Attempt to repair your vehicle quickly
☐ **D** Stand behind your vehicle to warn others

If you can't get your vehicle onto the hard shoulder, use your hazard warning lights to warn others. Leave your vehicle only when you can safely get clear of the carriageway. Do not try to repair the vehicle or attempt to place any warning device on the carriageway.

584 Mark *one* answer

Why is it particularly important to carry out a check on your vehicle before making a long motorway journey?

☐ **A** You will have to do more harsh braking on motorways
☐ **B** Motorway service stations do not deal with breakdowns
☐ **C** The road surface will wear down the tyres faster
☐ **D** Continuous high speeds may increase the risk of your vehicle breaking down

Before you start your journey make sure that your vehicle can cope with the demands of high-speed driving. You should check a number of things, the main ones being oil, water and tyres. You also need to plan rest stops if you're going a long way.

585 Mark *one* answer

You are driving on a motorway. The car ahead shows its hazard lights for a short time. This tells you that

☐ **A** the driver wants you to overtake
☐ **B** the other car is going to change lanes
☐ **C** traffic ahead is slowing or stopping suddenly
☐ **D** there is a police speed check ahead

If the vehicle in front shows its hazard lights there may be an incident or queuing traffic ahead. As well as keeping a safe distance, look beyond it to help you get an early warning of any hazards and a picture of the situation ahead.

586 Mark *one* answer

You are intending to leave the motorway at the next exit. Before you reach the exit you should normally position your vehicle

- ☐ **A** in the middle lane
- ☐ **B** in the left-hand lane
- ☐ **C** on the hard shoulder
- ☐ **D** in any lane

You'll see the first advance direction sign one mile from the exit. If you're travelling at 60mph in the right-hand lane you'll only have about 50 seconds before you reach the countdown markers. There will be another sign at the half-mile point. Move in to the left-hand lane in good time. Don't cut across traffic at the last moment and don't risk missing your exit.

587 Mark *one* answer

As a provisional licence holder you should not drive a car

- ☐ **A** over 30mph
- ☐ **B** at night
- ☐ **C** on the motorway
- ☐ **D** with passengers in rear seats

When you've passed your practical test ask your instructor to take you for a lesson on the motorway. You'll need to get used to the speed of traffic and how to deal with multiple lanes. The Pass Plus scheme has been created for new drivers, and includes motorway driving. Ask your ADI for details.

588 Mark *one* answer

Your vehicle breaks down on the hard shoulder of a motorway. You decide to use your mobile phone to call for help. You should

- ☐ **A** stand at the rear of the vehicle while making the call
- ☐ **B** try to repair the vehicle yourself
- ☐ **C** get out of the vehicle by the right-hand door
- ☐ **D** check your location from the marker posts on the left

The emergency services need to know your exact location so they can reach you as quickly as possible. Look for a number on the nearest marker post beside the hard shoulder. Give this number when you call the emergency services as it will help them to locate you. Be ready to describe where you are, for example, by reference to the last junction or service station you passed.

589 Mark *one* answer NI

You are on a three-lane motorway towing a trailer. You may use the right-hand lane when

- ☐ **A** there are lane closures
- ☐ **B** there is slow-moving traffic
- ☐ **C** you can maintain a high speed
- ☐ **D** large vehicles are in the left and centre lanes

If you are towing a caravan or trailer you must not use the right-hand lane on a motorway with three or more lanes, except in certain circumstances, such as lane closures.

590 Mark *one* answer
You are on a motorway. There is a contraflow system ahead. What would you expect to find?

☐ **A** Temporary traffic lights
☐ **B** Lower speed limits
☐ **C** Wider lanes than normal
☐ **D** Speed humps

When approaching a contraflow system reduce speed in good time and obey all speed limits. You may be travelling in a narrower lane than normal with no permanent barrier between you and the oncoming traffic. Be aware that the hard shoulder may be used for traffic and the road ahead could be obstructed by slow-moving or broken-down vehicles.

591 Mark *one* answer
On a motorway you may only stop on the hard shoulder

☐ **A** in an emergency
☐ **B** if you feel tired and need to rest
☐ **C** if you miss the exit that you wanted
☐ **D** to pick up a hitchhiker

You should only stop on the hard shoulder in a genuine emergency. DON'T stop on it to have a rest or picnic, pick up hitchhikers, answer a mobile phone or check a map. If you miss your intended exit carry on to the next, never reverse along the hard shoulder.

592 Mark *one* answer
What is the meaning of this sign?

- [ ] **A** Local speed limit applies
- [ ] **B** No waiting on the carriageway
- [ ] **C** National speed limit applies
- [ ] **D** No entry to vehicular traffic

This sign doesn't tell you the speed limit in figures. You should know the speed limit for the type of road that you're on. Study your copy of The Highway Code.

593 Mark *one* answer
What is the national speed limit for cars and motorcycles on a dual carriageway?

- [ ] **A** 30mph
- [ ] **B** 50mph
- [ ] **C** 60mph
- [ ] **D** 70mph

Ensure that you know the speed limit for the road that you're on. The speed limit on a dual carriageway or motorway is 70mph for cars and motorcycles, unless there are signs to indicate otherwise. The speed limits for different types of vehicles are listed in The Highway Code.

594 Mark *one* answer
There are no speed limit signs on the road. How is a 30mph limit indicated?

- [ ] **A** By hazard warning lines
- [ ] **B** By street lighting
- [ ] **C** By pedestrian islands
- [ ] **D** By double or single yellow lines

There is usually a 30mph speed limit where there are street lights unless there are signs showing another limit.

595 Mark *one* answer
Where you see street lights but no speed limit signs the limit is usually

- [ ] **A** 30mph
- [ ] **B** 40mph
- [ ] **C** 50mph
- [ ] **D** 60mph

The presence of street lights generally shows that there is a 30mph speed limit, unless signs tell you otherwise.

596 Mark *one* answer
What does this sign mean?

- [ ] **A** Minimum speed 30mph
- [ ] **B** End of maximum speed
- [ ] **C** End of minimum speed
- [ ] **D** Maximum speed 30mph

A red slash through this sign indicates that the restriction has ended. In this case the restriction was a minimum speed limit of 30mph.

597 Mark *one* answer
There is a tractor ahead of you. You wish to overtake but you are NOT sure if it is safe to do so. You should

- ☐ **A** follow another overtaking vehicle through
- ☐ **B** sound your horn to the slow vehicle to pull over
- ☐ **C** speed through but flash your lights to oncoming traffic
- ☐ **D** not overtake if you are in doubt

Never overtake if you're not sure whether it's safe. Can you see far enough down the road to ensure that you can complete the manoeuvre safely? If the answer is no, DON'T GO.

598 Mark *one* answer
Which vehicle is most likely to take an unusual course at a roundabout?

- ☐ **A** Estate car
- ☐ **B** Milk float
- ☐ **C** Delivery van
- ☐ **D** Long lorry

Long vehicles might have to take a slightly different position when approaching the roundabout or going around it. This is to stop the rear of the vehicle cutting in and mounting the kerb.

599 Mark *one* answer
On a clearway you must not stop

- ☐ **A** at any time
- ☐ **B** when it is busy
- ☐ **C** in the rush hour
- ☐ **D** during daylight hours

Clearways are in place so that traffic can flow without the obstruction of parked vehicles. Just one parked vehicle will cause an obstruction for all other traffic. You MUST NOT stop where a clearway is in force, not even to pick up or set down passengers.

600 Mark *one* answer
What is the meaning of this sign?

- ☐ **A** No entry
- ☐ **B** Waiting restrictions
- ☐ **C** National speed limit
- ☐ **D** School crossing patrol

This sign indicates that there are waiting restrictions. It is normally accompanied by details of when restrictions are in force.

Details of most signs which are in common use are shown in The Highway Code and a more comprehensive selection is available in Know Your Traffic Signs.

601 Mark *one* answer

You can park on the right-hand side of a road at night

- ☐ **A** in a one-way street
- ☐ **B** with your sidelights on
- ☐ **C** more than 10 metres (32 feet) from a junction
- ☐ **D** under a lamp-post

Red rear reflectors show up when headlights shine on them. These are useful when you are parked at night but will only reflect if you park in the same direction as the traffic flow. Normally you should park on the left, but if you're in a one-way street you may also park on the right-hand side.

---

602 Mark *one* answer

On a three-lane dual carriageway the right-hand lane can be used for

- ☐ **A** overtaking only, never turning right
- ☐ **B** overtaking or turning right
- ☐ **C** fast-moving traffic only
- ☐ **D** turning right only, never overtaking

You should normally use the left-hand lane on any dual carriageway unless you are overtaking or turning right.

When overtaking on a dual carriageway, look for vehicles ahead that are turning right. They're likely to be slowing or stopped. You need to see them in good time so that you can take appropriate action.

603 Mark *one* answer

You are approaching a busy junction. There are several lanes with road markings. At the last moment you realise that you are in the wrong lane. You should

- ☐ **A** continue in that lane
- ☐ **B** force your way across
- ☐ **C** stop until the area has cleared
- ☐ **D** use clear arm signals to cut across

There are times where road markings can be obscured by queuing traffic, or you might be unsure which lane you need to be in.

If you realise that you're in the wrong lane, don't cut across lanes or bully other drivers to let you in. Follow the lane you're in and find somewhere safe to turn around if you need to.

---

604 Mark *one* answer

Where may you overtake on a one-way street?

- ☐ **A** Only on the left-hand side
- ☐ **B** Overtaking is not allowed
- ☐ **C** Only on the right-hand side
- ☐ **D** Either on the right or the left

You can overtake other traffic on either side when travelling in a one-way street. Make full use of your mirrors and ensure that it's clear all around before you attempt to overtake. Look for signs and road markings and use the most suitable lane for your destination.

605 Mark *one* answer
When going straight ahead at a roundabout you should

- [ ] **A** indicate left before leaving the roundabout
- [ ] **B** not indicate at any time
- [ ] **C** indicate right when approaching the roundabout
- [ ] **D** indicate left when approaching the roundabout

When you want to go straight on at a roundabout, don't signal as you approach it, but indicate left just after you pass the exit before the one you wish to take.

---

606 Mark *one* answer
Which vehicle might have to use a different course to normal at roundabouts?

- [ ] **A** Sports car
- [ ] **B** Van
- [ ] **C** Estate car
- [ ] **D** Long vehicle

A long vehicle may have to straddle lanes either on or approaching a roundabout so that the rear wheels don't cut in over the kerb.

If you're following a long vehicle, stay well back and give it plenty of room.

607 Mark *one* answer
You may only enter a box junction when

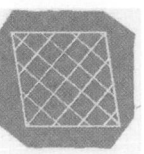

- [ ] **A** there are less than two vehicles in front of you
- [ ] **B** the traffic lights show green
- [ ] **C** your exit road is clear
- [ ] **D** you need to turn left

Yellow box junctions are marked on the road to prevent the road becoming blocked. Don't enter one unless your exit road is clear. You may only wait in the yellow box if your exit road is clear but oncoming traffic is preventing you from completing the turn.

---

608 Mark *one* answer
You may wait in a yellow box junction when

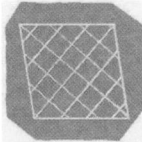

- [ ] **A** oncoming traffic is preventing you from turning right
- [ ] **B** you are in a queue of traffic turning left
- [ ] **C** you are in a queue of traffic to go ahead
- [ ] **D** you are on a roundabout

The purpose of this road marking is to keep the junction clear of queuing traffic. You may only wait in the marked area when you're turning right and your exit lane is clear but you can't complete the turn because of oncoming traffic.

609 Mark *one* answer
You MUST stop when signalled to do so by a

☐ **A** motorcyclist
☐ **B** pedestrian
☐ **C** police officer
☐ **D** bus driver

You MUST obey signals to stop given by
police and traffic officers, traffic wardens
and school crossing patrols. Failure to do so
is an offence and could lead to prosecution.

610 Mark *one* answer
**Someone is waiting to cross at a zebra
crossing. They are standing on the
pavement. You should normally**

☐ **A** go on quickly before they step
onto the crossing
☐ **B** stop before you reach the zigzag lines
and let them cross
☐ **C** stop, let them cross, wait patiently
☐ **D** ignore them as they are still on
the pavement

By standing on the pavement, the
pedestrian is showing an intention to cross.
If you are looking well down the road you
will give yourself enough time to slow down
and stop safely. Don't forget to check your
mirrors before slowing down.

611 Mark *one* answer
**At toucan crossings, apart from pedestrians
you should be aware of**

☐ **A** emergency vehicles emerging
☐ **B** buses pulling out
☐ **C** trams crossing in front
☐ **D** cyclists riding across

The use of cycles is being encouraged and
more toucan crossings are being installed.
These crossings enable pedestrians and
cyclists to cross the path of other traffic.
Watch out as cyclists will approach the
crossing faster than pedestrians.

612 Mark *one* answer
Who can use a toucan crossing?

☐ **A** Trains
☐ **B** Cyclists
☐ **C** Buses
☐ **D** Trams

Toucan crossings are similar to pelican
crossings but there's no flashing amber
phase. Cyclists share the crossing with
pedestrians and are allowed to cycle across
when the green cycle symbol is shown.

613 Mark *one* answer
At a pelican crossing, what does a flashing amber light mean?

- ☐ **A** You must not move off until the lights stop flashing
- ☐ **B** You must give way to pedestrians still on the crossing
- ☐ **C** You can move off, even if pedestrians are still on the crossing
- ☐ **D** You must stop because the lights are about to change to red

If there is no-one on the crossing when the amber light is flashing, you may proceed over the crossing. You don't need to wait for the green light to show.

614 Mark *one* answer
You are waiting at a pelican crossing. The red light changes to flashing amber. This means you must

- ☐ **A** wait for pedestrians on the crossing to clear
- ☐ **B** move off immediately without any hesitation
- ☐ **C** wait for the green light before moving off
- ☐ **D** get ready and go when the continuous amber light shows

This light allows time for the pedestrians already on the crossing to get to the other side in their own time, without being rushed. Don't rev your engine or start to move off while they are still crossing.

615 Mark *one* answer
When can you park on the left opposite these road markings?

- ☐ **A** If the line nearest to you is broken
- ☐ **B** When there are no yellow lines
- ☐ **C** To pick up or set down passengers
- ☐ **D** During daylight hours only

You MUST NOT park or stop on a road marked with double white lines (even where one of the lines is broken) except to pick up or set down passengers.

616 Mark *one* answer
You are intending to turn right at a crossroads. An oncoming driver is also turning right. It will normally be safer to

- ☐ **A** keep the other vehicle to your RIGHT and turn behind it (offside to offside)
- ☐ **B** keep the other vehicle to your LEFT and turn in front of it (nearside to nearside)
- ☐ **C** carry on and turn at the next junction instead
- ☐ **D** hold back and wait for the other driver to turn first

At some junctions the layout may make it difficult to turn offside to offside. If this is the case, be prepared to pass nearside to nearside, but take extra care as your view ahead will be obscured by the vehicle turning in front of you.

617 Mark *one* answer

You are on a road that has no traffic signs. There are street lights. What is the speed limit?

- ☐ **A** 20mph
- ☐ **B** 30mph
- ☐ **C** 40mph
- ☐ **D** 60mph

If you aren't sure of the speed limit a good indication is the presence of street lights. If there is street lighting the speed limit will be 30mph unless otherwise indicated.

618 Mark *one* answer

You're driving along a street with parked vehicles on the left-hand side. Why should you keep your speed down?

- ☐ **A** So that oncoming traffic can see you more clearly
- ☐ **B** You may set off car alarms
- ☐ **C** There may be delivery lorries on the street
- ☐ **D** Children may run out from between the vehicles

Travel slowly and carefully near parked vehicles. Beware of
- vehicles pulling out, especially bicycles and motorcycles
- pedestrians, especially children, who may run out from between cars
- drivers opening their doors.

619 Mark *one* answer

You meet an obstruction on your side of the road. You should

- ☐ **A** carry on, you have priority
- ☐ **B** give way to oncoming traffic
- ☐ **C** wave oncoming vehicles through
- ☐ **D** accelerate to get past first

Take care if you have to pass a parked vehicle on your side of the road. Give way to oncoming traffic if there isn't enough room for you both to continue safely.

620 Mark *one* answer

You're on a two-lane dual carriageway. Why would you use the right-hand lane?

- ☐ **A** To overtake slower traffic
- ☐ **B** For normal progress
- ☐ **C** When staying at the minimum allowed speed
- ☐ **D** To keep driving at a constant high speed

Normally you should travel in the left-hand lane and only use the right-hand lane for overtaking or turning right. Move back into the left lane as soon as it's safe but don't cut in across the path of the vehicle you've just passed.

621 Mark *one* answer

Who has priority at an unmarked crossroads?

☐ **A** The larger vehicle
☐ **B** No one has priority
☐ **C** The faster vehicle
☐ **D** The smaller vehicle

Practise good observation in all directions before you emerge or make a turn. Proceed only when you're sure it's safe to do so.

623 Mark *one* answer NI

You MUST NOT park

☐ **A** on a road with a 40mph speed limit
☐ **B** at or near a bus stop
☐ **C** where there is no pavement
☐ **D** within 20 metres (65 feet) of a junction

It's important not to park at or near a bus stop as this could inconvenience passengers, and may put them at risk as they get on or off the bus.

622 Mark *one* answer NI

What is the nearest you may park to a junction?

☐ **A** 10 metres (32 feet)
☐ **B** 12 metres (39 feet)
☐ **C** 15 metres (49 feet)
☐ **D** 20 metres (66 feet)

Don't park within 10 metres (32 feet) of a junction (unless in an authorised parking place). This is to allow drivers emerging from, or turning into, the junction a clear view of the road they are joining. It also allows them to see hazards such as pedestrians or cyclists at the junction.

624 Mark *one* answer

You are waiting at a level crossing. A train has passed but the lights keep flashing. You must

☐ **A** carry on waiting
☐ **B** phone the signal operator
☐ **C** edge over the stop line and look for trains
☐ **D** park and investigate

If the lights at a level crossing continue to flash after a train has passed, you should still wait as there might be another train coming. Time seems to pass slowly when you're held up in a queue. Be patient and wait until the lights stop flashing.

625 Mark *one* answer

At a crossroads there are no signs or road markings. Two vehicles approach. Which has priority?

☐ **A** Neither of the vehicles
☐ **B** The vehicle travelling the fastest
☐ **C** Oncoming vehicles turning right
☐ **D** Vehicles approaching from the right

At a crossroads where there are no 'give way' signs or road markings be very careful. No vehicle has priority, even if the sizes of the roads are different.

626 Mark *one* answer

What does this sign tell you?

☐ **A** That it is a no-through road
☐ **B** End of traffic-calming zone
☐ **C** Free parking zone ends
☐ **D** No waiting zone ends

The blue and red circular sign on its own means that waiting restrictions are in force. This sign shows that you are leaving the controlled zone and waiting restrictions no longer apply.

627 Mark *one* answer

You are entering an area of roadworks. There is a temporary speed limit displayed. You should

☐ **A** not exceed the speed limit
☐ **B** obey the limit only during rush hour
☐ **C** ignore the displayed limit
☐ **D** obey the limit except at night

Where there are extra hazards such as roadworks, it's often necessary to slow traffic down by imposing a temporary speed limit. These speed limits aren't advisory, they must be obeyed.

628 Mark *one* answer

You should NOT park

☐ **A** on a one-way street
☐ **B** near a police station
☐ **C** on a side road
☐ **D** near a school entrance

It may be tempting to park where you shouldn't while you run a quick errand. Careless parking, such as by a bus stop or outside a school, is a selfish act and could endanger other road users.

629 Mark *one* answer
You are travelling on a well-lit road at night in a built-up area. By using dipped headlights you will be able to

- [ ] **A** see further along the road
- [ ] **B** go at a much faster speed
- [ ] **C** switch to main beam quickly
- [ ] **D** be easily seen by others

You may be difficult to see when you're travelling at night, even on a well-lit road. If you use dipped headlights rather than sidelights other road users will see you more easily.

630 Mark *one* answer
The dual carriageway you are turning right onto has a very narrow central reservation. What should you do?

- [ ] **A** Proceed to the central reservation and wait
- [ ] **B** Wait until the road is clear in both directions
- [ ] **C** Stop in the first lane so that other vehicles give way
- [ ] **D** Emerge slightly to show your intentions

When the central reservation is narrow you should treat a dual carriageway as one road. Wait until the road is clear in both directions before emerging to turn right. If you try to treat it as two separate roads and wait in the middle, you are likely to cause an obstruction and possibly a collision.

631 Mark *one* answer
What is the national speed limit on a single carriageway road for cars and motorcycles?

- [ ] **A** 30mph
- [ ] **B** 50mph
- [ ] **C** 60mph
- [ ] **D** 70mph

Exceeding the speed limit is dangerous and can result in you receiving penalty points on your licence. It isn't worth it. You should know the speed limit for the road that you're on by observing the road signs. Different speed limits apply if you are towing a trailer.

632 Mark *one* answer
You park at night on a road with a 40mph speed limit. You should park

- [ ] **A** facing the traffic
- [ ] **B** with parking lights on
- [ ] **C** with dipped headlights on
- [ ] **D** near a street light

You MUST use parking lights when parking at night on a road or lay-by with a speed limit greater than 30mph. You MUST also park in the direction of the traffic flow and not close to a junction.

633 Mark *one* answer
You will see these red and white markers when approaching _

☐ **A** the end of a motorway
☐ **B** a concealed level crossing
☐ **C** a concealed speed limit sign
☐ **D** the end of a dual carriageway

If there is a bend just before the level crossing you may not be able to see the level crossing barriers or waiting traffic. These signs give you an early warning that you may find these hazards just around the bend.

634 Mark *one* answer
You are travelling on a motorway. You MUST stop when signalled to do so by which of these?

☐ **A** Flashing amber lights above your lane
☐ **B** A traffic officer
☐ **C** Pedestrians on the hard shoulder
☐ **D** A driver who has broken down

You'll find traffic officers on England's motorways. They work in partnership with the police, helping to keep traffic moving and to make your journey as safe as possible. It is an offence not to comply with the directions given by a traffic officer.

635 Mark *one* answer
At a busy unmarked crossroads, which of the following has priority?

☐ **A** Vehicles going straight ahead
☐ **B** Vehicles turning right
☐ **C** None of the vehicles
☐ **D** The vehicles that arrived first

If there are no road signs or markings do not assume that you have priority. Remember that other drivers may assume they have the right to go. No type of vehicle has priority but it's courteous to give way to large vehicles. Also look out in particular for cyclists and motorcyclists.

636 Mark *one* answer
You are going straight ahead at a roundabout. How should you signal?

☐ **A** Signal right on the approach and then left to leave the roundabout
☐ **B** Signal left after you leave the roundabout and enter the new road
☐ **C** Signal right on the approach to the roundabout and keep the signal on
☐ **D** Signal left just after you pass the exit before the one you will take

To go straight ahead at a roundabout you should normally approach in the left-hand lane. You will not normally need to signal, but look out for the road markings. At some roundabouts the left lane on approach is marked as 'left turn only', so make sure you use the correct lane to go ahead. Signal before you leave as other road users need to know your intentions.

637 Mark *one* answer
You may drive over a footpath

☐ **A** to overtake slow-moving traffic
☐ **B** when the pavement is very wide
☐ **C** if no pedestrians are near
☐ **D** to get into a property

It is against the law to drive on or over a footpath, except to gain access to a property. If you need to cross a pavement, watch for pedestrians in both directions.

638 Mark *one* answer
A single carriageway road has this sign. What is the maximum permitted speed for a car towing a trailer?

☐ **A** 30mph
☐ **B** 40mph
☐ **C** 50mph
☐ **D** 60mph

When towing trailers, speed limits are also lower on dual carriageways and motorways. These speed limits apply to vehicles pulling all sorts of trailers including caravans, horse boxes etc.

639 Mark *one* answer
You are towing a small caravan on a dual carriageway. You must not exceed

☐ **A** 50mph   ☐ **B** 40mph
☐ **C** 70mph   ☐ **D** 60mph

The speed limit is reduced for vehicles towing caravans and trailers, to lessen the risk of the outfit becoming unstable. Due to the increased weight and size of the vehicle and caravan combination, you should plan well ahead. Be extra-careful in windy weather, as strong winds could cause a caravan or large trailer to snake from side to side.

640 Mark *one* answer
You want to park and you see this sign. On the days and times shown you should

Meter ZONE
Mon - Fri
8.30 am - 6.30 pm
Saturday
8.30 am - 1.30 pm

☐ **A** park in a bay and not pay
☐ **B** park on yellow lines and pay
☐ **C** park on yellow lines and not pay
☐ **D** park in a bay and pay

Parking restrictions apply in a variety of places and situations. Make sure you know the rules and understand where and when restrictions apply. Controlled parking areas will be indicated by signs and road markings. Parking in the wrong place could cause an obstruction and danger to other traffic. It can also result in a fine.

641 Mark *one* answer

You are driving along a road that has a cycle lane. The lane is marked by a solid white line. This means that during its period of operation

☐ **A** the lane may be used for parking your car
☐ **B** you may drive in that lane at any time
☐ **C** the lane may be used when necessary
☐ **D** you must not drive in that lane

Leave the lane free for cyclists. At other times, when the lane is not in operation, you should still be aware that there may be cyclists about. Give them room and don't pass too closely.

642 Mark *one* answer

A cycle lane is marked by a solid white line. You must not drive or park in it

☐ **A** at any time
☐ **B** during the rush hour
☐ **C** if a cyclist is using it
☐ **D** during its period of operation

The cycle lanes are there for a reason. Keep them free and allow cyclists to use them.

It is illegal to drive or park in a cycle lane, marked by a solid white line, during its hours of operation. Parking in a cycle lane will obstruct cyclists and they may move into the path of traffic on the main carriageway as they ride around the obstruction. This could be hazardous for both the cyclist and other road users.

643 Mark *one* answer

While driving, you intend to turn left into a minor road. On the approach you should

☐ **A** keep just left of the middle of the road
☐ **B** keep in the middle of the road
☐ **C** swing out wide just before turning
☐ **D** keep well to the left of the road

Don't swing out into the centre of the road in order to make the turn. This could endanger oncoming traffic and may cause other road users to misunderstand your intentions.

644 Mark *one* answer

You are waiting at a level crossing. The red warning lights continue to flash after a train has passed by. What should you do?

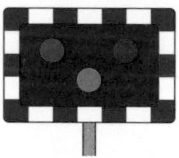

☐ **A** Get out and investigate
☐ **B** Telephone the signal operator
☐ **C** Continue to wait
☐ **D** Drive across carefully

At a level crossing flashing red lights mean you must stop. If the train passes but the lights keep flashing, wait. There may be another train coming.

645 Mark *one* answer
You are driving over a level crossing. The warning lights come on and a bell rings. What should you do?

- ☐ **A** Get everyone out of the vehicle immediately
- ☐ **B** Stop and reverse back to clear the crossing
- ☐ **C** Keep going and clear the crossing
- ☐ **D** Stop immediately and use your hazard warning lights

Keep going, don't stop on the crossing. If the amber warning lights come on as you're approaching the crossing, you MUST stop unless it is unsafe to do so. Red flashing lights together with an audible signal mean you MUST stop.

646 Mark *one* answer
You are on a busy main road and find that you are travelling in the wrong direction. What should you do?

- ☐ **A** Turn into a side road on the right and reverse into the main road
- ☐ **B** Make a U-turn in the main road
- ☐ **C** Make a 'three-point' turn in the main road
- ☐ **D** Turn round in a side road

Don't turn round in a busy street or reverse from a side road into a main road. Find a quiet side road and choose a place where you won't obstruct an entrance or exit. Look out for pedestrians and cyclists as well as other traffic.

647 Mark *one* answer
You may remove your seat belt when carrying out a manoeuvre that involves

- ☐ **A** reversing
- ☐ **B** a hill start
- ☐ **C** an emergency stop
- ☐ **D** driving slowly

Don't forget to put your seat belt back on when you've finished reversing.

648 Mark *one* answer
You must not reverse

- ☐ **A** for longer than necessary
- ☐ **B** for more than a car's length
- ☐ **C** into a side road
- ☐ **D** in a built-up area

You may decide to turn your vehicle around by reversing into an opening or side road. When you reverse, always look behind and all around and watch for pedestrians. Don't reverse from a side road into a main road. You MUST NOT reverse further than is necessary.

649 Mark *one* answer
When you are NOT sure that it is safe to reverse your vehicle you should

- ☐ **A** use your horn
- ☐ **B** rev your engine
- ☐ **C** get out and check
- ☐ **D** reverse slowly

If you can't see all around your vehicle get out and have a look. You could also ask someone reliable outside the vehicle to guide you. A small child could easily be hidden directly behind you. Don't take risks.

650 Mark *one* answer
When may you reverse from a side road into a main road?

- ☐ **A** Only if both roads are clear of traffic
- ☐ **B** Not at any time
- ☐ **C** At any time
- ☐ **D** Only if the main road is clear of traffic

Don't reverse into a main road from a side road. The main road is likely to be busy and the traffic on it moving quickly. Cut down the risks by reversing into a quiet side road.

651 Mark *one* answer
You want to turn right at a box junction. There is oncoming traffic. You should

- ☐ **A** wait in the box junction if your exit is clear
- ☐ **B** wait before the junction until it is clear of all traffic
- ☐ **C** drive on, you cannot turn right at a box junction
- ☐ **D** drive slowly into the box junction when signalled by oncoming traffic

You can move into the box junction to wait as long as your exit is clear. The oncoming traffic will stop when the traffic lights change, allowing you to proceed.

652 Mark *one* answer
You are reversing your vehicle into a side road. When would the greatest hazard to passing traffic occur?

- ☐ **A** After you've completed the manoeuvre
- ☐ **B** Just before you actually begin to manoeuvre
- ☐ **C** After you've entered the side road
- ☐ **D** When the front of your vehicle swings out

Always check road and traffic conditions in all directions before reversing into a side road. Keep a good look-out throughout the manoeuvre. Act on what you see and wait if necessary.

653 Mark *one* answer
Where is the safest place to park your vehicle at night?

- ☐ **A** In a garage
- ☐ **B** On a busy road
- ☐ **C** In a quiet car park
- ☐ **D** Near a red route

If you have a garage, use it. Your vehicle is less likely to be a victim of car crime if it's in a garage. Also in winter the windows will be free from ice and snow.

654 Mark *one* answer

You are driving on an urban clearway. You may stop only to

- ☐ **A** set down and pick up passengers
- ☐ **B** use a mobile telephone
- ☐ **C** ask for directions
- ☐ **D** load or unload goods

Urban clearways may be in built-up areas and their times of operation will be clearly signed. You should stop only for as long as is reasonable to pick up or set down passengers. You should ensure that you are not causing an obstruction for other traffic.

655 Mark *one* answer

You are looking for somewhere to park your vehicle. The area is full EXCEPT for spaces marked 'disabled use'. You can

- ☐ **A** use these spaces when elsewhere is full
- ☐ **B** park if you stay with your vehicle
- ☐ **C** use these spaces, disabled or not
- ☐ **D** not park there unless permitted

It is illegal to park in a parking space reserved for disabled users.

These spaces are provided for people with limited mobility, who may need extra space to get in and out of their vehicle.

656 Mark *one* answer

Your vehicle is parked on the road at night. When must you use sidelights?

- ☐ **A** Where there are continuous white lines in the middle of the road
- ☐ **B** Where the speed limit exceeds 30mph
- ☐ **C** Where you are facing oncoming traffic
- ☐ **D** Where you are near a bus stop

When parking at night, park in the direction of the traffic. This will enable other road users to see the reflectors on the rear of your vehicle. You MUST use your sidelights when parking on a road, or in a lay-by on a road, where the speed limit is over 30mph.

657 Mark *one* answer

You are on a road that is only wide enough for one vehicle. There is a car coming towards you. What should you do?

- ☐ **A** Pull into a passing place on your right
- ☐ **B** Force the other driver to reverse
- ☐ **C** Pull into a passing place if your vehicle is wider
- ☐ **D** Pull into a passing place on your left

Pull into the nearest passing place on the left if you meet another vehicle in a narrow road. If the nearest passing place is on the right, wait opposite it.

658 Mark *one* answer

You are driving at night with full beam headlights on. A vehicle is overtaking you. You should dip your lights

- ☐ **A** some time after the vehicle has passed you
- ☐ **B** before the vehicle starts to pass you
- ☐ **C** only if the other driver dips their headlights
- ☐ **D** as soon as the vehicle passes you

On full beam your lights could dazzle the driver in front. Make sure that your light beam falls short of the vehicle in front.

659 Mark *one* answer

When may you drive a motor car in this bus lane?

- ☐ **A** Outside its hours of operation
- ☐ **B** To get to the front of a traffic queue
- ☐ **C** You may not use it at any time
- ☐ **D** To overtake slow-moving traffic

Some bus lanes only operate during peak hours and other vehicles may use them outside these hours. Make sure you check the sign for the hours of operation before driving in a bus lane.

660 Mark *one* answer

Signals are normally given by direction indicators and

- ☐ **A** brake lights
- ☐ **B** side lights
- ☐ **C** fog lights
- ☐ **D** interior lights

Your brake lights will give an indication to traffic behind that you're slowing down. Good anticipation will allow you time to check your mirrors before slowing.

661 Mark *one* answer

You are parked in a busy high street. What is the safest way to turn your vehicle around so you can go the opposite way?

- ☐ **A** Find a quiet side road to turn round in
- ☐ **B** Drive into a side road and reverse into the main road
- ☐ **C** Get someone to stop the traffic
- ☐ **D** Do a U-turn

Make sure you carry out the manoeuvre without causing a hazard to other vehicles. Choose a place to turn which is safe and convenient for you and for other road users.

662 Mark *one* answer

To help keep your vehicle secure at night, where should you park?

- ☐ **A** Near a police station
- ☐ **B** In a quiet road
- ☐ **C** On a red route
- ☐ **D** In a well-lit area

Whenever possible park in an area which will be well lit at night.

663 Mark *one* answer

You are in the right-hand lane of a dual carriageway. You see signs showing that the right-hand lane is closed 800 yards ahead. You should

- ☐ **A** keep in that lane until you reach the queue
- ☐ **B** move to the left immediately
- ☐ **C** wait and see which lane is moving faster
- ☐ **D** move to the left in good time

Keep a look-out for traffic signs. If you're directed to change lanes, do so in good time. Don't
- push your way into traffic in another lane
- leave changing lanes until the last moment.

664 Mark *one* answer

You're driving on a road that has a cycle lane. The lane is marked by a broken white line. This means that

- ☐ **A** you should not drive in the lane unless it is unavoidable
- ☐ **B** there's a reduced speed limit for motor vehicles using the lane
- ☐ **C** cyclists can travel in both directions in that lane
- ☐ **D** the lane must be used by motorcyclists in heavy traffic

Where signs or road markings show lanes are for cyclists only, leave them free. Don't drive or park in a cycle lane unless it is unavoidable.

665 Mark *one* answer

What MUST you have to park in a disabled space?

- ☐ **A** A Blue Badge
- ☐ **B** A wheelchair
- ☐ **C** An advanced driver certificate
- ☐ **D** An adapted vehicle

Don't park in a space reserved for disabled people unless you or your passenger are a disabled badge holder. The badge must be displayed in your vehicle in the bottom left-hand corner of the windscreen.

666 Mark *one* answer

When MUST you stop your vehicle?

- ☐ **A** If you're involved in an incident that causes damage or injury
- ☐ **B** At a junction where there are Give Way lines
- ☐ **C** At the end of a one-way street
- ☐ **D** Before merging onto a motorway white lines

You MUST stop your vehicle when signalled to do so by a
- police or traffic officer
- traffic warden
- school crossing patrol
- red traffic light.
You must also stop if you're involved in an incident which causes damage or injury to any other person, vehicle, animal or property.

667 Mark *one* answer
You MUST obey signs giving orders. These signs are mostly in

- ☐ **A** green rectangles
- ☐ **B** red triangles
- ☐ **C** blue rectangles
- ☐ **D** red circles

There are three basic types of traffic sign, those that warn, inform or give orders. Generally, triangular signs warn, rectangular ones give information or directions, and circular signs usually give orders. An exception is the eight-sided 'STOP' sign.

---

668 Mark *one* answer
Traffic signs giving orders are generally which shape?

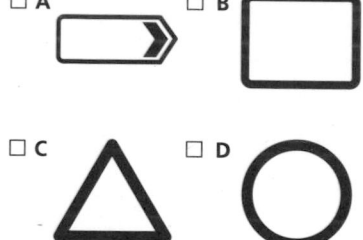

- ☐ **A**
- ☐ **B**
- ☐ **C**
- ☐ **D**

Road signs in the shape of a circle give orders. Those with a red circle are mostly prohibitive. The 'stop' sign is octagonal to give it greater prominence. Signs giving orders MUST always be obeyed.

669 Mark *one* answer
Which type of sign tells you NOT to do something?

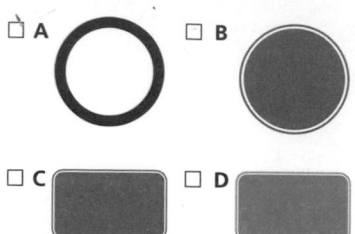

- ☐ **A**
- ☐ **B**
- ☐ **C**
- ☐ **D**

Signs in the shape of a circle give orders. A sign with a red circle means that you aren't allowed to do something. Study Know Your Traffic Signs to ensure that you understand what the different traffic signs mean.

---

670 Mark *one* answer
What does this sign mean?

- ☐ **A** Maximum speed limit with traffic calming
- ☐ **B** Minimum speed limit with traffic calming
- ☐ **C** '20 cars only' parking zone
- ☐ **D** Only 20 cars allowed at any one time

If you're in places where there are likely to be pedestrians such as outside schools, near parks, residential areas and shopping areas, you should be extra-cautious and keep your speed down.

Many local authorities have taken measures to slow traffic down by creating traffic-calming measures such as speed humps. They are there for a reason; slow down.

671 Mark *one* answer

Which sign means no motor vehicles are allowed?

☐ A   ☐ B

☐ C   ☐ D

You would generally see this sign at the approach to a pedestrian-only zone.

672 Mark *one* answer

Which of these signs means no motor vehicles?

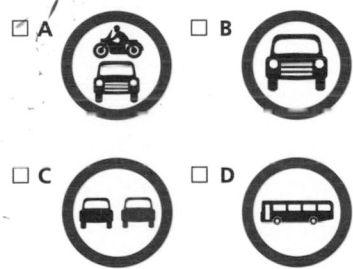

☑ A   ☐ B

☐ C   ☐ D

If you are driving a motor vehicle or riding a motorcycle you MUST NOT travel past this sign. This area has been designated for use by pedestrians.

673 Mark *one* answer

What does this sign mean?

☐ **A** New speed limit 20mph
☐ **B** No vehicles over 30 tonnes
☐ **C** Minimum speed limit 30mph
☐ **D** End of 20mph zone

Where you see this sign the 20mph restriction ends. Check all around for possible hazards and only increase your speed if it's safe to do so.

674 Mark *one* answer

What does this sign mean?

☐ **A** No overtaking
☐ **B** No motor vehicles
☐ **C** Clearway (no stopping)
☐ **D** Cars and motorcycles only

A sign will indicate which types of vehicles are prohibited from certain roads. Make sure that you know which signs apply to the vehicle you're using.

675 Mark *one* answer

What does this sign mean?

- ☐ **A** No parking
- ☐ **B** No road markings
- ☐ **C** No through road
- ☐ **D** No entry

'No entry' signs are used in places such as one-way streets to prevent vehicles driving against the traffic. To ignore one would be dangerous, both for yourself and other road users, as well as being against the law.

676 Mark *one* answer

What does this sign mean?

- ☐ **A** Bend to the right
- ☐ **B** Road on the right closed
- ☐ **C** No traffic from the right
- ☐ **D** No right turn

The 'no right turn' sign may be used to warn road users that there is a 'no entry' prohibition on a road to the right ahead.

677 Mark *one* answer

Which sign means 'no entry'?

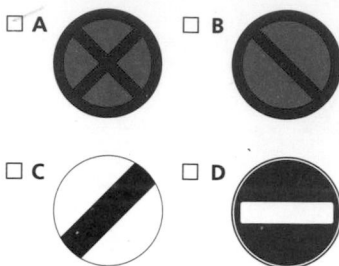

Look out for traffic signs. Disobeying or not seeing a sign could be dangerous. It may also be an offence for which you could be prosecuted.

678 Mark *one* answer

What does this sign mean?

- ☐ **A** Route for trams only
- ☐ **B** Route for buses only
- ☐ **C** Parking for buses only
- ☐ **D** Parking for trams only

Avoid blocking tram routes. Trams are fixed on their route and can't manoeuvre around other vehicles and pedestrians. Modern trams travel quickly and are quiet so you might not hear them approaching.

679 Mark *one* answer
Which type of vehicle does this sign apply to?

- ☐ **A** Wide vehicles
- ☐ **B** Long vehicles
- ☑ **C** High vehicles
- ☐ **D** Heavy vehicles

The triangular shapes above and below the dimensions indicate a height restriction that applies to the road ahead.

680 Mark *one* answer
Which sign means NO motor vehicles allowed?

☐ A    ☑ B

☐ C   ☐ D

This sign is used to enable pedestrians to walk free from traffic. It's often found in shopping areas.

681 Mark *one* answer
What does this sign mean?

- ☐ **A** You have priority
- ☐ **B** No motor vehicles
- ☐ **C** Two-way traffic
- ☐ **D** No overtaking

Road signs that prohibit overtaking are placed in locations where passing the vehicle in front is dangerous. If you see this sign don't attempt to overtake. The sign is there for a reason and you must obey it.

682 Mark *one* answer
What does this sign mean?

- ☐ **A** Keep in one lane
- ☐ **B** Give way to oncoming traffic
- ☐ **C** Do not overtake
- ☐ **D** Form two lanes

If you're behind a slow-moving vehicle be patient. Wait until the restriction no longer applies and you can overtake safely.

683 Mark *one* answer
Which sign means no overtaking?

☐ A
☐ B
☐ C
☐ D

This sign indicates that overtaking here is not allowed and you could face prosecution if you ignore this prohibition.

684 Mark *one* answer
What does this sign mean?

☐ **A** Waiting restrictions apply
☐ **B** Waiting permitted
☐ **C** National speed limit applies
☐ **D** Clearway (no stopping)

There will be a plate or additional sign to tell you when the restrictions apply.

685 Mark *one* answer
What does this sign mean?

☐ **A** End of restricted speed area
☐ **B** End of restricted parking area
☐ **C** End of clearway
☐ **D** End of cycle route

Even though you have left the restricted area, make sure that you park where you won't endanger other road users or cause an obstruction.

686 Mark *one* answer
Which sign means 'no stopping'?

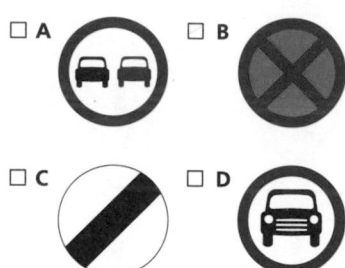

☐ A
☐ B
☐ C
☐ D

Stopping where this clearway restriction applies is likely to cause congestion. Allow the traffic to flow by obeying the signs.

687 Mark *one* answer
What does this sign mean?

- ☐ **A** Roundabout
- ☐ **B** Crossroads
- ☐ **C** No stopping
- ☐ **D** No entry

This sign is in place to ensure a clear route for traffic. Don't stop except in an emergency.

688 Mark *one* answer
You see this sign ahead. It means

- ☐ **A** national speed limit applies
- ☐ **B** waiting restrictions apply
- ☐ **C** no stopping
- ☐ **D** no entry

Clearways are stretches of road where you aren't allowed to stop unless in an emergency. You'll see this sign. Stopping where these restrictions apply may be dangerous and likely to cause an obstruction. Restrictions might apply for several miles and this may be indicated on the sign.

689 Mark *one* answer
What does this sign mean?

- ☐ **A** Distance to parking place ahead
- ☐ **B** Distance to public telephone ahead
- ☐ **C** Distance to public house ahead
- ☐ **D** Distance to passing place ahead

If you intend to stop and rest, this sign allows you time to reduce speed and pull over safely.

690 Mark *one* answer
What does this sign mean?

- ☐ **A** Vehicles may not park on the verge or footway
- ☐ **B** Vehicles may park on the left-hand side of the road only
- ☐ **C** Vehicles may park fully on the verge or footway
- ☐ **D** Vehicles may park on the right-hand side of the road only

In order to keep roads free from parked cars, there are some areas where you're allowed to park on the verge. Only do this where you see the sign. Parking on verges or footways anywhere else could lead to a fine.

691 Mark *one* answer
What does this traffic sign mean?

- ☐ **A** No overtaking allowed
- ☐ **B** Give priority to oncoming traffic
- ☐ **C** Two-way traffic
- ☐ **D** One-way traffic only

Priority signs are normally shown where the road is narrow and there isn't enough room for two vehicles to pass. These can be at narrow bridges, road works and where there's a width restriction.

Make sure that you know who has priority, don't force your way through. Show courtesy and consideration to other road users.

692 Mark *one* answer
What is the meaning of this traffic sign?

- ☐ **A** End of two-way road
- ☐ **B** Give priority to vehicles coming towards you
- ☐ **C** You have priority over vehicles coming towards you
- ☐ **D** Bus lane ahead

Don't force your way through. Show courtesy and consideration to other road users. Although you have priority, make sure oncoming traffic is going to give way before you continue.

693 Mark *one* answer
What does this sign mean?

- ☐ **A** No overtaking
- ☐ **B** You are entering a one-way street
- ☐ **C** Two-way traffic ahead
- ☐ **D** You have priority over vehicles from the opposite direction

Don't force your way through if oncoming vehicles fail to give way. If necessary, slow down and give way to avoid confrontation or a collision.

694 Mark *one* answer
What shape is a STOP sign at a junction?

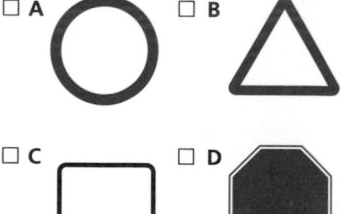

☐ A   ☐ B

☐ C   ☐ D

To make it easy to recognise, the 'stop' sign is the only sign of this shape. You must stop and take effective observation before proceeding.

695 Mark *one* answer
At a junction you see this sign partly covered by snow. What does it mean?

- ☐ **A** Crossroads
- ☐ **B** Give way
- ☐ **C** Stop
- ☐ **D** Turn right

The STOP sign is the only road sign that is octagonal. This is so that it can be recognised and obeyed even if it is obscured, for example by snow.

---

696 Mark *one* answer
What does this sign mean?

- ☐ **A** Service area 30 miles ahead
- ☐ **B** Maximum speed 30mph
- ☐ **C** Minimum speed 30mph
- ☐ **D** Lay-by 30 miles ahead

This sign is shown where slow-moving vehicles would impede the flow of traffic, for example in tunnels. However, if you need to slow down or even stop to avoid an incident or potential collision, you should do so.

697 Mark *one* answer
What does this sign mean?

- ☐ **A** Give way to oncoming vehicles
- ☐ **B** Approaching traffic passes you on both sides
- ☐ **C** Turn off at the next available junction
- ☐ **D** Pass either side to get to the same destination

These signs are often seen in one-way streets that have more than one lane. When you see this sign, use the route that's the most convenient and doesn't require a late change of direction.

---

698 Mark *one* answer
What does this sign mean?

- ☐ **A** Route for trams
- ☐ **B** Give way to trams
- ☐ **C** Route for buses
- ☐ **D** Give way to buses

Take extra care when you encounter trams. Look out for road markings and signs that alert you to them. Modern trams are very quiet and you may not hear them approaching.

699 Mark *one* answer
What does a circular traffic sign with a blue background do?

- ☐ **A** Give warning of a motorway ahead
- ☐ **B** Give directions to a car park
- ☐ **C** Give motorway information
- ☐ **D** Give an instruction

Signs with blue circles mostly give a positive instruction. These are often found in urban areas and include signs for mini-roundabouts and directional arrows.

700 Mark *one* answer
Where would you see a contraflow bus and cycle lane?

- ☐ **A** On a dual carriageway
- ☐ **B** On a roundabout
- ☐ **C** On an urban motorway
- ☐ **D** On a one-way street

In a contraflow lane the traffic permitted to use it travels in the opposite direction to traffic in the other lanes on the road.

701 Mark *one* answer
What does this sign mean?

- ☐ **A** Bus station on the right
- ☐ **B** Contraflow bus lane
- ☐ **C** With-flow bus lane
- ☐ **D** Give way to buses

There will also be markings on the road surface to indicate the bus lane. You must not use this lane for parking or overtaking.

702 Mark *one* answer
What does a sign with a brown background show?

- ☐ **A** Tourist directions
- ☐ **B** Primary roads
- ☐ **C** Motorway routes
- ☐ **D** Minor routes

Signs with a brown background give directions to places of interest. They will often be seen on a motorway directing you along the easiest route to the attraction.

703 Mark *one* answer

This sign means

- ☐ **A** tourist attraction
- ☐ **B** beware of trains
- ☐ **C** level crossing
- ☐ **D** beware of trams

These signs indicate places of interest and are designed to guide you by the easiest route. They are particularly useful if you are unfamiliar with the area.

704 Mark *one* answer

What are triangular signs for?

- ☐ **A** To give warnings
- ☐ **B** To give information
- ☐ **C** To give orders
- ☐ **D** To give directions

This type of sign will warn you of hazards ahead.

Make sure you look at each sign that you pass on the road, so that you do not miss any vital instructions or information.

705 Mark *one* answer

What does this sign mean?

- ☐ **A** Turn left ahead
- ☐ **B** T-junction
- ☐ **C** No through road
- ☐ **D** Give way

This type of sign will warn you of hazards ahead. Make sure you look at each sign and road markings that you pass, so that you do not miss any vital instructions or information. This particular sign shows there is a T-junction with priority over vehicles from the right.

706 Mark *one* answer

What does this sign mean?

- ☐ **A** Multi-exit roundabout
- ☐ **B** Risk of ice
- ☐ **C** Six roads converge
- ☐ **D** Place of historical interest

It will take up to ten times longer to stop when it's icy. Where there is a risk of icy conditions you need to be aware of this and take extra care. If you think the road may be icy, don't brake or steer harshly as your tyres could lose their grip on the road.

707 Mark *one* answer
What does this sign mean?

☐ **A** Crossroads
☐ **B** Level crossing with gate
☐ **C** Level crossing without gate
☐ **D** Ahead only

The priority through the junction is shown by the broader line. You need to be aware of the hazard posed by traffic crossing or pulling out onto a major road.

708 Mark *one* answer
What does this sign mean?

☐ **A** Ring road
☐ **B** Mini-roundabout
☐ **C** No vehicles
☐ **D** Roundabout

As you approach a roundabout look well ahead and check all signs. Decide which exit you wish to take and move into the correct position as you approach the roundabout, signalling as required.

709 Mark *one* answer
What information would be shown in a triangular road sign?

☐ **A** Road narrows
☐ **B** Ahead only
☐ **C** Keep left
☐ **D** Minimum speed

Warning signs are there to make you aware of potential hazards on the road ahead. Take note of the signs so you're prepared and can take whatever action is necessary.

710 Mark *one* answer
What does this sign mean?

☐ **A** Cyclists must dismount
☐ **B** Cycles are not allowed
☐ **C** Cycle route ahead
☐ **D** Cycle in single file

Where there's a cycle route ahead, a sign will show a bicycle in a red warning triangle. Watch out for children on bicycles and cyclists rejoining the main road.

711 Mark *one* answer

Which sign means that pedestrians may be walking along the road?

□ A

□ B

□ C

□ D

When you pass pedestrians in the road, leave plenty of room. You might have to use the right-hand side of the road, so look well ahead, as well as in your mirrors, before pulling out. Take great care if there is a bend in the road obscuring your view ahead.

712 Mark *one* answer

Which of these signs means there is a double bend ahead?

□ A

□ B

□ C

□ D

Triangular signs give you a warning of hazards ahead. They are there to give you time to prepare for the hazard, for example by adjusting your speed.

713 Mark *one* answer

What does this sign mean?

□ **A** Wait at the barriers
□ **B** Wait at the crossroads
□ **C** Give way to trams
□ **D** Give way to farm vehicles

Obey the 'give way' signs. Trams are unable to steer around you if you misjudge when it is safe to enter the junction.

714 Mark *one* answer

What does this sign mean?

□ **A** Humpback bridge
□ **B** Humps in the road
□ **C** Entrance to tunnel
□ **D** Soft verges

These have been put in place to slow the traffic down. They're usually found in residential areas. Slow down to an appropriate speed.

715 Mark *one* answer

Which of these signs means the end of a dual carriageway?

☐ **A**  ☐ **B**

☐ **C**  ☐ **D**

If you're overtaking make sure you move back safely into the left-hand lane before you reach the end of the dual carriageway.

716 Mark *one* answer

What does this sign mean?

☐ **A** End of dual carriageway
☐ **B** Tall bridge
☐ **C** Road narrows
☐ **D** End of narrow bridge

Don't leave moving into the left-hand lane until the last moment. Plan ahead and don't rely on other traffic letting you in.

717 Mark *one* answer

What does this sign mean?

☐ **A** Crosswinds
☐ **B** Road noise
☐ **C** Airport
☐ **D** Adverse camber

A warning sign with a picture of a windsock will indicate there may be strong crosswinds. This sign is often found on exposed roads.

718 Mark *one* answer

What does this traffic sign mean?

☐ **A** Slippery road ahead
☐ **B** Tyres liable to punctures ahead
☐ **C** Danger ahead
☐ **D** Service area ahead

This sign is there to alert you to the likelihood of danger ahead. It may be accompanied by a plate indicating the type of hazard. Be ready to reduce your speed and take avoiding action.

719 Mark *one* answer

You are about to overtake when you see this sign. You should

Hidden dip

- ☐ **A** overtake the other driver as quickly as possible
- ☐ **B** move to the right to get a better view
- ☐ **C** switch your headlights on before overtaking
- ☐ **D** hold back until you can see clearly ahead

You won't be able to see any hazards that might be hidden in the dip. As well as oncoming traffic the dip may conceal
- cyclists
- horse riders
- parked vehicles
- pedestrians

in the road.

720 Mark *one* answer

What does this sign mean?

- ☐ **A** Level crossing with gate or barrier
- ☐ **B** Gated road ahead
- ☐ **C** Level crossing without gate or barrier
- ☐ **D** Cattle grid ahead

Some crossings have gates but no attendant or signals. You should stop, look both ways, listen and make sure that there is no train approaching. If there is a telephone, contact the signal operator to make sure that it's safe to cross.

721 Mark *one* answer

What does this sign mean?

- ☐ **A** No trams ahead
- ☐ **B** Oncoming trams
- ☐ **C** Trams crossing ahead
- ☐ **D** Trams only

This sign warns you to beware of trams. If you don't usually drive in a town where there are trams, remember to look out for them at junctions and look for tram rails, signs and signals.

722 Mark *one* answer

What does this sign mean?

- ☐ **A** Adverse camber
- ☐ **B** Steep hill downwards
- ☐ **C** Uneven road
- ☐ **D** Steep hill upwards

This sign will give you an early warning that the road ahead will slope downhill. Prepare to alter your speed and gear. Looking at the sign from left to right will show you whether the road slopes uphill or downhill.

723 Mark *one* answer
What does this sign mean?

- ☐ **A** Uneven road surface
- ☐ **B** Bridge over the road
- ☐ **C** Road ahead ends
- ☐ **D** Water across the road

This sign is found where a shallow stream crosses the road. Heavy rainfall could increase the flow of water. If the water looks too deep or the stream has spread over a large distance, stop and find another route.

724 Mark *one* answer
What does this sign mean?

- ☐ **A** Turn left for parking area
- ☐ **B** No through road on the left
- ☐ **C** No entry for traffic turning left
- ☐ **D** Turn left for ferry terminal

If you intend to take a left turn, this sign shows you that you can't get through to another route using the left-turn junction ahead.

725 Mark *one* answer
What does this sign mean?

- ☐ **A** T-junction
- ☐ **B** No through road
- ☐ **C** Telephone box ahead
- ☐ **D** Toilet ahead

You will not be able to find a through route to another road. Use this road only for access.

726 Mark *one* answer
Which sign means 'no through road'?

☐ A    ☐ B

☐ C    ☐ D

This sign is found at the entrance to a road that can only be used for access.

727 Mark *one* answer

Which is the sign for a ring road?

☐ **A** 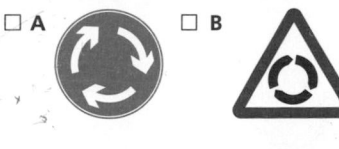 ☐ **B**

☐ **C**  ☐ **D**

Ring roads are designed to relieve congestion in towns and city centres.

728 Mark *one* answer

What does this sign mean?

☐ **A** The right-hand lane ahead is narrow
☐ **B** Right-hand lane for buses only
☐ **C** Right-hand lane for turning right
☐ **D** The right-hand lane is closed

Yellow and black temporary signs may be used to inform you of roadworks or lane restrictions. Look well ahead. If you have to change lanes, do so in good time.

729 Mark *one* answer

What does this sign mean?

☐ **A** Change to the left lane
☐ **B** Leave at the next exit
☐ **C** Contraflow system
☐ **D** One-way street

If you use the right-hand lane in a contraflow system, you'll be travelling with no permanent barrier between you and the oncoming traffic. Observe speed limits and keep a good distance from the vehicle ahead.

730 Mark *one* answer

What does this sign mean?

☐ **A** Leave motorway at next exit
☐ **B** Lane for heavy and slow vehicles
☐ **C** All lorries use the hard shoulder
☐ **D** Rest area for lorries

Where there's a long, steep, uphill gradient on a motorway, a crawler lane may be provided. This helps the traffic to flow by diverting the slower heavy vehicles into a dedicated lane on the left.

731 Mark *one* answer
A red traffic light means

- ☐ **A** you should stop unless turning left
- ☐ **B** stop, if you are able to brake safely
- ☐ **C** you must stop and wait behind the stop line
- ☐ **D** proceed with caution

Make sure you learn and understand the sequence of traffic lights. Whatever light appears you will then know what light is going to appear next and be able to take the appropriate action. For example if amber is showing on its own you'll know that red will appear next, giving you ample time to slow and stop safely.

732 Mark *one* answer
At traffic lights, amber on its own means

- ☐ **A** prepare to go
- ☐ **B** go if the way is clear
- ☐ **C** go if no pedestrians are crossing
- ☐ **D** stop at the stop line

When amber is showing on its own red will appear next. The amber light means STOP, unless you have already crossed the stop line or you are so close to it that pulling up might cause a collision.

733 Mark *one* answer
You are at a junction controlled by traffic lights. When should you NOT proceed at green?

- ☐ **A** When pedestrians are waiting to cross
- ☐ **B** When your exit from the junction is blocked
- ☐ **C** When you think the lights may be about to change
- ☐ **D** When you intend to turn right

As you approach the lights look into the road you wish to take. Only proceed if your exit road is clear. If the road is blocked hold back, even if you have to wait for the next green signal.

734 Mark *one* answer
You are in the left-hand lane at traffic lights. You are waiting to turn left. At which of these traffic lights must you NOT move on?

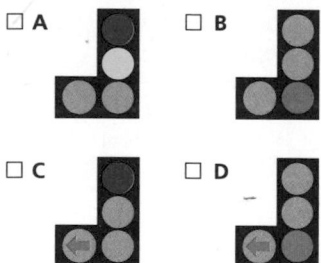

At some junctions there may be a separate signal for different lanes. These are called 'filter' lights. They're designed to help traffic flow at major junctions. Make sure that you're in the correct lane and proceed if the way is clear and the green light shows for your lane.

735 Mark *one* answer
What does this sign mean?

- ☐ **A** Traffic lights out of order
- ☐ **B** Amber signal out of order
- ☐ **C** Temporary traffic lights ahead
- ☐ **D** New traffic lights ahead

Where traffic lights are out of order you might see this sign. Proceed with caution as nobody has priority at the junction.

---

736 Mark *one* answer
When traffic lights are out of order, who has priority?

- ☐ **A** Traffic going straight on
- ☐ **B** Traffic turning right
- ☐ **C** Nobody
- ☐ **D** Traffic turning left

When traffic lights are out of order you should treat the junction as an unmarked crossroads. Be cautious as you may need to give way or stop. Keep a look out for traffic attempting to cross the junction at speed.

737 Mark *one* answer
These flashing red lights mean STOP. Where would you find them?

- ☐ **A** Pelican crossings
- ☐ **B** Motorway exits
- ☐ **C** Zebra crossings
- ☐ **D** Level crossings

These signals are found at level crossings, swing or lifting bridges, some airfields and emergency access sites. The flashing red lights mean stop whether or not the way seems to be clear.

---

738 Mark *one* answer
What do these zigzag lines at pedestrian crossings mean?

- ☐ **A** No parking at any time
- ☐ **B** Parking allowed only for a short time
- ☐ **C** Slow down to 20mph
- ☐ **D** Sounding horns is not allowed

The approach to, and exit from, a pedestrian crossing is marked with zigzag lines. You must not park on them or overtake the leading vehicle when approaching the crossing. Parking here would block the view for pedestrians and the approaching traffic.

739 Mark *one* answer

When may you cross a double solid white line in the middle of the road?

- ☐ **A** To pass traffic that is queuing back at a junction
- ☐ **B** To pass a car signalling to turn left ahead
- ☐ **C** To pass a road maintenance vehicle travelling at 10mph or less
- ☐ **D** To pass a vehicle that is towing a trailer

You may cross the solid white line to pass a stationary vehicle, pedal cycle, horse or road maintenance vehicle if they are travelling at 10mph or less. You may also cross the solid line to enter into a side road or access a property.

740 Mark *one* answer

What does this road marking mean?

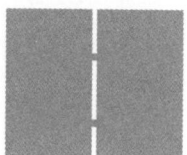

- ☐ **A** Do not cross the line
- ☐ **B** No stopping allowed
- ☐ **C** You are approaching a hazard
- ☐ **D** No overtaking allowed

Road markings will warn you of a hazard ahead. A single, broken line along the centre of the road, with long markings and short gaps, is a hazard warning line. Don't cross it unless you can see that the road is clear well ahead.

741 Mark *one* answer

Where would you see this road marking?

- ☐ **A** At traffic lights
- ☐ **B** On road humps
- ☐ **C** Near a level crossing
- ☐ **D** At a box junction

Due to the dark colour of the road, changes in level aren't easily seen. White triangles painted on the road surface give you an indication of where there are road humps.

742 Mark *one* answer

Which is a hazard warning line?

☐ A   ☐ B

☐ C   ☐ D

You need to know the difference between the normal centre line and a hazard warning line. If there is a hazard ahead, the markings are longer and the gaps shorter. This gives you advanced warning of an unspecified hazard ahead.

743 Mark *one* answer
At this junction there is a stop sign with a solid white line on the road surface. Why is there a stop sign here?

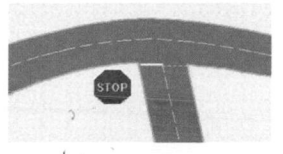

- ☐ **A** Speed on the major road is de-restricted
- ☐ **B** It is a busy junction
- ☐ **C** Visibility along the major road is restricted
- ☐ **D** There are hazard warning lines in the centre of the road

If your view is restricted at a road junction you must stop. There may also be a 'stop' sign. Don't emerge until you're sure there's no traffic approaching.
IF YOU DON'T KNOW, DON'T GO.

744 Mark *one* answer
You see this line across the road at the entrance to a roundabout. What does it mean?

- ☐ **A** Give way to traffic from the right
- ☐ **B** Traffic from the left has right of way
- ☐ **C** You have right of way
- ☐ **D** Stop at the line

Slow down as you approach the roundabout and check for traffic from the right. If you need to stop and give way, stay behind the broken line until it is safe to emerge onto the roundabout.

745 Mark *one* answer
How will a police officer In a patrol vehicle normally get you to stop?

- ☐ **A** Flash the headlights, indicate left and point to the left
- ☐ **B** Wait until you stop, then approach you
- ☐ **C** Use the siren, overtake, cut in front and stop
- ☐ **D** Pull alongside you, use the siren and wave you to stop

You must obey signals given by the police. If a police officer in a patrol vehicle wants you to pull over they will indicate this without causing danger to you or other traffic.

746 Mark *one* answer
You approach a junction. The traffic lights are not working. A police officer gives this signal. You should

- ☐ **A** turn left only
- ☐ **B** turn right only
- ☐ **C** stop level with the officer's arm
- ☐ **D** stop at the stop line

If a police officer or traffic warden is directing traffic you must obey them. They will use the arm signals shown in The Highway Code. Learn what these mean and act accordingly.

747 Mark *one* answer
The driver of the car in front is giving this arm signal. What does it mean?

- ☐ **A** The driver is slowing down
- ☐ **B** The driver intends to turn right
- ☐ **C** The driver wishes to overtake
- ☐ **D** The driver intends to turn left

There might be an occasion where another driver uses an arm signal. This may be because the vehicle's indicators are obscured by other traffic. In order for such signals to be effective all drivers should know the meaning of them. Be aware that the 'left turn' signal might look similar to the 'slowing down' signal.

748 Mark *one* answer
Where would you see these road markings?

- ☐ **A** At a level crossing
- ☐ **B** On a motorway slip road
- ☐ **C** At a pedestrian crossing
- ☐ **D** On a single-track road

When driving on a motorway or slip road, you must not enter into an area marked with chevrons and bordered by a solid white line for any reason, except in an emergency.

749 Mark *one* answer
What does this motorway sign mean?

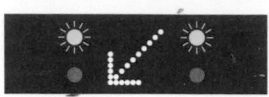

- ☐ **A** Change to the lane on your left
- ☐ **B** Leave the motorway at the next exit
- ☐ **C** Change to the opposite carriageway
- ☐ **D** Pull up on the hard shoulder

On the motorway, signs sometimes show temporary warnings due to traffic or weather conditions. They may be used to indicate
- lane closures
- temporary speed limits
- weather warnings.

750 Mark *one* answer
What does this motorway sign mean?

- ☐ **A** Temporary minimum speed 50mph
- ☐ **B** No services for 50 miles
- ☐ **C** Obstruction 50 metres (164 feet) ahead
- ☐ **D** Temporary maximum speed 50mph

Look out for signs above your lane or on the central reservation. These will give you important information or warnings about the road ahead. Due to the high speed of motorway traffic these signs may light up some distance from any hazard. Don't ignore the signs just because the road looks clear to you.

751 Mark *one* answer
What does this sign mean?

- ☐ **A** Through traffic to use left lane
- ☐ **B** Right-hand lane T-junction only
- ☑ **C** Right-hand lane closed ahead
- ☐ **D** 11 tonne weight limit

You should move into the lanes as directed by the sign. Here the right-hand lane is closed and the left-hand and centre lanes are available. Merging in turn is recommended when it's safe and traffic is going slowly, for example at road works or a road traffic incident. When vehicles are travelling at speed this is not advisable and you should move into the appropriate lane in good time.

752 Mark *one* answer
On a motorway this sign means

- ☐ **A** move over onto the hard shoulder
- ☐ **B** overtaking on the left only
- ☐ **C** leave the motorway at the next exit
- ☑ **D** move to the lane on your left

It is important to know and obey temporary signs on the motorway: they are there for a reason. You may not be able to see the hazard straight away, as the signs give warnings well in advance, due to the speed of traffic on the motorway.

753 Mark *one* answer
What does '25' mean on this motorway sign?

- ☐ **A** The distance to the nearest town
- ☐ **B** The route number of the road
- ☐ **C** The number of the next junction
- ☐ **D** The speed limit on the slip road

Before you set out on your journey use a road map to plan your route. When you see advance warning of your junction, make sure you get into the correct lane in plenty of time. Last-minute harsh braking and cutting across lanes at speed is extremely hazardous.

754 Mark *one* answer
The right-hand lane of a three-lane motorway is

- ☐ **A** for lorries only
- ☑ **B** an overtaking lane
- ☐ **C** the right-turn lane
- ☐ **D** an acceleration lane

You should stay in the left-hand lane of a motorway unless overtaking. The right-hand lane of a motorway is an overtaking lane and not a 'fast lane'.

After overtaking, move back to the left when it is safe to do so.

755 Mark *one* answer
Where can you find reflective amber studs on a motorway?

☐ **A** Separating the slip road from the motorway
☐ **B** On the left-hand edge of the road
☐ **C** On the right-hand edge of the road
☐ **D** Separating the lanes

At night or in poor visibility reflective studs on the road help you to judge your position on the carriageway.

---

756 Mark *one* answer
Where on a motorway would you find green reflective studs?

☐ **A** Separating driving lanes
☐ **B** Between the hard shoulder and the carriageway
☐ **C** At slip road entrances and exits
☐ **D** Between the carriageway and the central reservation

Knowing the colours of the reflective studs on the road will help you judge your position, especially at night, in foggy conditions or when visibility is poor.

757 Mark *one* answer
You are travelling along a motorway. You see this sign. You should

☐ **A** leave the motorway at the next exit
☐ **B** turn left immediately
☐ **C** change lane
☐ **D** move onto the hard shoulder

You'll see this sign if the motorway is closed ahead. Pull into the nearside lane as soon as it is safe to do so. Don't leave it to the last moment.

---

758 Mark *one* answer
What does this sign mean?

☐ **A** No motor vehicles
☐ **B** End of motorway .
☐ **C** No through road
☐ **D** End of bus lane

When you leave the motorway make sure that you check your speedometer. You may be going faster than you realise. Slow down and look out for speed limit signs.

759 Mark *one* answer
Which of these signs means that the national speed limit applies?

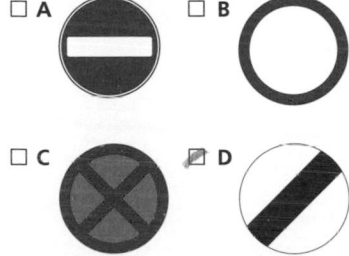

☐ A

☐ B

☐ C

☑ D

You should know the speed limit for the road on which you are travelling, and the vehicle that you are driving. The different speed limits are shown in The Highway Code.

760 Mark *one* answer
What is the maximum speed on a single carriageway road?

☐ **A** 50mph
☑ **B** 60mph
☐ **C** 40mph
☐ **D** 70mph

If you're travelling on a dual carriageway that becomes a single carriageway road, reduce your speed gradually so that you aren't exceeding the limit as you enter. There might not be a sign to remind you of the limit, so make sure you know what the speed limits are for different types of roads and vehicles.

761 Mark *one* answer
What does this sign mean?

☐ **A** End of motorway
☐ **B** End of restriction
☐ **C** Lane ends ahead
☐ **D** Free recovery ends

Temporary restrictions on motorways are shown on signs which have flashing amber lights. At the end of the restriction you will see this sign without any flashing lights.

762 Mark *one* answer
This sign is advising you to

☑ **A** follow the route diversion
☐ **B** follow the signs to the picnic area
☐ **C** give way to pedestrians
☐ **D** give way to cyclists

When a diversion route has been put in place, drivers are advised to follow a symbol which may be a triangle, square, circle or diamond shape on a yellow background.

763 Mark *one* answer

Why would this temporary speed limit sign be shown?

- ☐ **A** To warn of the end of the motorway
- ☐ **B** To warn you of a low bridge
- ☐ **C** To warn you of a junction ahead
- ☐ **D** To warn of road works ahead

In the interests of road safety, temporary speed limits are imposed at all major road works. Signs like this, giving advanced warning of the speed limit, are normally placed about three quarters of a mile ahead of where the speed limit comes into force.

764 Mark *one* answer

This traffic sign means there is

- ☐ **A** a compulsory maximum speed limit
- ☐ **B** an advisory maximum speed limit
- ☐ **C** a compulsory minimum speed limit
- ☐ **D** an advised separation distance

The sign gives you an early warning of a speed restriction. If you are travelling at a higher speed, slow down in good time. You could come across queuing traffic due to roadworks or a temporary obstruction.

765 Mark *one* answer

You see this sign at a crossroads. You should

- ☐ **A** maintain the same speed
- ☐ **B** carry on with great care
- ☐ **C** find another route
- ☐ **D** telephone the police

When traffic lights are out of order treat the junction as an unmarked crossroad. Be very careful as no one has priority and be prepared to stop.

766 Mark *one* answer

You are signalling to turn right in busy traffic. How would you confirm your intention safely?

- ☐ **A** Sound the horn
- ☐ **B** Give an arm signal
- ☐ **C** Flash your headlights
- ☐ **D** Position over the centre line

In some situations you may feel your indicators cannot be seen by other road users. If you think you need to make your intention more clearly seen, give the arm signal shown in The Highway Code.

767 Mark *one* answer
What does this sign mean?

- ☐ **A** Motorcycles only
- ☐ **B** No cars
- ☐ **C** Cars only
- ☑ **D** No motorcycles

You must comply with all traffic signs and be especially aware of those signs which apply specifically to the type of vehicle you are using.

768 Mark *one* answer
You are on a motorway. You see this sign on a lorry that has stopped in the right-hand lane. You should

- ☐ **A** move into the right-hand lane
- ☐ **B** stop behind the flashing lights
- ☑ **C** pass the lorry on the left
- ☐ **D** leave the motorway at the next exit

Sometimes work is carried out on the motorway without closing the lanes. When this happens, signs are mounted on the back of lorries to warn other road users of roadworks ahead.

769 Mark *one* answer
You are on a motorway. Red flashing lights appear above your lane only. What should you do?

- ☐ **A** Continue in that lane and look for further information
- ☐ **B** Move into another lane in good time
- ☐ **C** Pull onto the hard shoulder
- ☐ **D** Stop and wait for an instruction to proceed

Flashing red lights above your lane show that your lane is closed. You should move into another lane as soon as you can do so safely.

770 Mark *one* answer
A red traffic light means

- ☐ **A** you must stop behind the white stop line
- ☐ **B** you may go straight on if there is no other traffic
- ☐ **C** you may turn left if it is safe to do so
- ☐ **D** you must slow down and prepare to stop if traffic has started to cross

The white line is generally positioned so that pedestrians have room to cross in front of waiting traffic. Don't move off while pedestrians are crossing, even if the lights change to green.

771 Mark *one* answer
The driver of this car is giving an arm signal. What are they about to do?

- ☐ **A** Turn to the right
- ☐ **B** Turn to the left
- ☐ **C** Go straight ahead
- ☐ **D** Let pedestrians cross

In some situations drivers may need to give arm signals, in addition to indicators, to make their intentions clear. For arm signals to be effective, all road users should know their meaning.

772 Mark *one* answer
When may you sound the horn?

- ☐ **A** To give you right of way
- ☐ **B** To attract a friend's attention
- ☐ **C** To warn others of your presence
- ☐ **D** To make slower drivers move over

Never sound the horn aggressively. You MUST NOT sound it when driving in a built-up area between 11.30pm and 7am or when you are stationary, an exception to this is when another road user poses a danger. Do not scare animals by sounding your horn.

773 Mark *one* answer
You must not use your horn when you are stationary

- ☐ **A** unless a moving vehicle may cause you danger
- ☐ **B** at any time whatsoever
- ☐ **C** unless it is used only briefly
- ☐ **D** except for signalling that you have just arrived

When stationary only sound your horn if you think there is a risk of danger from another road user. Don't use it just to attract someone's attention. This causes unnecessary noise and could be misleading.

774 Mark *one* answer
What does this sign mean?

- ☐ **A** You can park on the days and times shown
- ☐ **B** No parking on the days and times shown
- ☐ **C** No parking at all from Monday to Friday
- ☐ **D** End of the urban clearway restrictions

Urban clearways are provided to keep traffic flowing at busy times. You may stop only briefly to set down or pick up passengers. Times of operation will vary from place to place so always check the signs.

775 Mark *one* answer
What does this sign mean?

- ☐ **A** Quayside or river bank
- ☐ **B** Steep hill downwards
- ☐ **C** Uneven road surface
- ☐ **D** Road liable to flooding

You should be careful in these locations as the road surface is likely to be wet and slippery. There may be a steep drop to the water, and there may not be a barrier along the edge of the road.

776 Mark *one* answer
Which sign means you have priority over oncoming vehicles?

 ☐ A ☐ B

 ☐ C  ☐ D

Even though you have priority, be prepared to give way if other drivers don't. This will help to avoid congestion, confrontation or even a collision.

777 Mark *one* answer
A white line like this along the centre of the road is a

- ☐ **A** bus lane marking
- ☐ **B** hazard warning
- ☐ **C** give way marking
- ☐ **D** lane marking

The centre of the road is usually marked by a broken white line, with lines that are shorter than the gaps. When the lines become longer than the gaps this is a hazard warning line. Look well ahead for these, especially when you are planning to overtake or turn off.

778 Mark *one* answer

What is the reason for the yellow criss-cross lines painted on the road here?

- ☐ **A** To mark out an area for trams only
- ☑ **B** To prevent queuing traffic from blocking the junction on the left
- ☐ **C** To mark the entrance lane to a car park
- ☐ **D** To warn you of the tram lines crossing the road

Yellow 'box junctions' like this are often used where it's busy. Their purpose is to keep the junction clear for crossing traffic. Don't enter the painted area unless your exit is clear. The exception to this is when you are turning right and are only prevented from doing so by oncoming traffic or by other vehicles waiting to turn right.

779 Mark *one* answer

What is the reason for the area marked in red and white along the centre of this road?

- ☐ **A** It is to separate traffic flowing in opposite directions
- ☐ **B** It marks an area to be used by overtaking motorcyclists
- ☐ **C** It is a temporary marking to warn of the roadworks
- ☐ **D** It is separating the two sides of the dual carriageway

Areas of 'hatched markings' such as these are to separate traffic streams which could be a danger to each other. They are often seen on bends or where the road becomes narrow. If the area is bordered by a solid white line, you must not enter it except in an emergency.

780 Mark *one* answer

Other drivers may sometimes flash their headlights at you. In which situation are they allowed to do this?

- ☐ **A** To warn of a radar speed trap ahead
- ☐ **B** To show that they are giving way to you
- ☐ **C** To warn you of their presence
- ☐ **D** To let you know there is a fault with your vehicle

If other drivers flash their headlights this isn't a signal to show priority. The flashing of headlights has the same meaning as sounding the horn, it's a warning of their presence.

781 Mark *one* answer

In some narrow residential streets you may find a speed limit of

- ☐ **A** 20mph
- ☐ **B** 25mph
- ☐ **C** 35mph
- ☐ **D** 40mph

In some built-up areas, you may find the speed limit reduced to 20mph. Driving at a slower speed will help give you the time and space to see and deal safely with hazards such as pedestrians and parked cars.

782 Mark *one* answer

At a junction you see this signal. It means

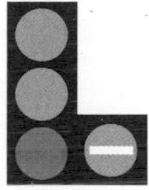

- ☐ **A** cars must stop
- ☑ **B** trams must stop
- ☐ **C** both trams and cars must stop
- ☐ **D** both trams and cars can continue

The white light shows that trams must stop, but the green light shows that other vehicles may go if the way is clear. You may not live in an area where there are trams but you should still learn the signs. You never know when you may go to a town with trams.

783 Mark *one* answer

Where would you find these road markings?

- ☐ **A** At a railway crossing
- ☐ **B** At a mini-roundabout
- ☐ **C** On a motorway
- ☐ **D** On a pedestrian crossing

These markings show the direction in which the traffic should go at a mini-roundabout.

784 Mark *one* answer

There is a police car following you. The police officer flashes the headlights and points to the left. What should you do?

- ☐ **A** Turn left at the next junction
- ☐ **B** Pull up on the left
- ☐ **C** Stop immediately
- ☐ **D** Move over to the left

You must pull up on the left as soon as it's safe to do so and switch off your engine.

785 Mark *one* answer
You see this amber traffic light ahead. Which light or lights, will come on next?

- ☐ **A** Red alone
- ☐ **B** Red and amber together
- ☐ **C** Green and amber together
- ☐ **D** Green alone

At junctions controlled by traffic lights you must stop behind the white line until the lights change to green. Red and amber lights showing together also mean stop.

You may proceed when the light is green unless your exit road is blocked or pedestrians are crossing in front of you.

If you're approaching traffic lights that are visible from a distance and the light has been green for some time they are likely to change. Be ready to slow down and stop.

786 Mark *one* answer
This broken white line painted in the centre of the road means

- ☐ **A** oncoming vehicles have priority over you
- ☐ **B** you should give priority to oncoming vehicles
- ☐ **C** there is a hazard ahead of you
- ☐ **D** the area is a national speed limit zone

A long white line with short gaps means that you are approaching a hazard. If you do need to cross it, make sure that the road is clear well ahead.

787 Mark *one* answer
You see this signal overhead on the motorway. What does it mean?

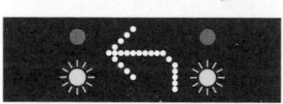

- ☐ **A** Leave the motorway at the next exit
- ☐ **B** All vehicles use the hard shoulder
- ☐ **C** Sharp bend to the left ahead
- ☐ **D** Stop, all lanes ahead closed

You will see this sign if there has been an incident ahead and the motorway is closed. You MUST obey the sign. Make sure that you prepare to leave as soon as you see the warning sign.

Don't pull over at the last moment or cut across other traffic.

788 Mark *one* answer
What is the purpose of these yellow criss-cross lines on the road?

- ☐ **A** To make you more aware of the traffic lights
- ☐ **B** To guide you into position as you turn
- ☐ **C** To prevent the junction becoming blocked
- ☐ **D** To show you where to stop when the lights change

You MUST NOT enter a box junction until your exit road or lane is clear. The exception to this is if you want to turn right and are only prevented from doing so by oncoming traffic or by other vehicles waiting to turn right.

789 Mark *one* answer
What MUST you do when you see this sign?

- ☐ **A** Stop, only if traffic is approaching
- ☐ **B** Stop, even if the road is clear
- ☐ **C** Stop, only if children are waiting to cross
- ☐ **D** Stop, only if a red light is showing

STOP signs are situated at junctions where visibility is restricted or there is heavy traffic. They MUST be obeyed. You MUST stop.
Take good all-round observation before moving off.

790 Mark *one* answer
Which shape is used for a 'give way' sign?

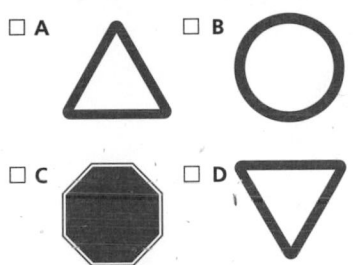

☐ **A** ☐ **B**

☐ **C** ☐ **D**

Other warning signs are the same shape and colour, but the 'give way' sign triangle points downwards. When you see this sign you MUST give way to traffic on the road which you are about to enter.

791 Mark *one* answer
What does this sign mean?

- ☐ **A** Buses turning
- ☐ **B** Ring road
- ☐ **C** Mini-roundabout
- ☐ **D** Keep right

When you see this sign, look out for any direction signs and judge whether you need to signal your intentions. Do this in good time so that other road users approaching the roundabout know what you're planning to do.

792 Mark *one* answer
What does this sign mean?

☐ **A** Two-way traffic straight ahead
☐ **B** Two-way traffic crosses a one-way road
☐ **C** Two-way traffic over a bridge
☐ **D** Two-way traffic crosses a two-way road

Be prepared for traffic approaching from junctions on either side of you. Try to avoid unnecessary changing of lanes just before the junction.

793 Mark *one* answer
What does this sign mean?

☐ **A** Two-way traffic ahead across a one-way road
☐ **B** Traffic approaching you has priority
☐ **C** Two-way traffic straight ahead
☐ **D** Motorway contraflow system ahead

This sign may be at the end of a dual carriageway or a one-way street. It is there to warn you of oncoming traffic.

794 Mark *one* answer
What does this sign mean?

☐ **A** Humpback bridge
☐ **B** Traffic-calming hump
☐ **C** Low bridge
☐ **D** Uneven road

You will need to slow down. At humpback bridges your view ahead will be restricted and the road will often be narrow on the bridge. If the bridge is very steep or your view is restricted sound your horn to warn others of your approach. Going too fast over the bridge is highly dangerous to other road users and could even cause your wheels to leave the road, with a resulting loss of control.

795 Mark *one* answer
Which of the following signs informs you that you are coming to a 'no through road'?

☐ **A**  ☐ **B**

☐ **C**  ☐ **D**

This sign is found at the entrance to a road that can only be used for access.

796 Mark *one* answer
What does this sign mean?

☐ **A** Direction to park-and-ride car park
☐ **B** No parking for buses or coaches
☐ **C** Directions to bus and coach park
☐ **D** Parking area for cars and coaches

To ease the congestion in town centres, some cities and towns provide park-and-ride schemes. These allow you to park in a designated area and ride by bus into the centre.
  Park-and-ride schemes are usually cheaper and easier than car parking in the town centre.

797 Mark *one* answer
You are approaching traffic lights. Red and amber are showing This means

☐ **A** pass the lights if the road is clear
☐ **B** there is a fault with the lights – take care
☐ **C** wait for the green light before you cross the stop line
☐ **D** the lights are about to change to red

Be aware that other traffic might still be clearing the junction. Make sure the way is clear before continuing.

798 Mark *one* answer
This marking appears on the road just before a

☐ **A** 'no entry' sign
☐ **B** 'give way' sign
☐ **C** 'stop' sign
☐ **D** 'no through road' sign

Where you see this road marking you should give way to traffic on the main road. It might not be used at junctions where there is relatively little traffic. However, if there is a double broken line across the junction the 'give way' rules still apply.

799 Mark *one* answer
At a railway level crossing the red light signal continues to flash after a train has gone by. What should you do?

☐ **A** Phone the signal operator
☐ **B** Alert drivers behind you
☐ **C** Wait
☐ **D** Proceed with caution

You MUST always obey red flashing stop lights. If a train passes but the lights continue to flash, another train will be passing soon. Cross only when the lights go off and the barriers open.

800 Mark *one* answer

You are in a tunnel and you see this sign. What does it mean?

- ☐ **A** Direction to emergency pedestrian exit
- ☐ **B** Beware of pedestrians, no footpath ahead
- ☐ **C** No access for pedestrians
- ☐ **D** Beware of pedestrians crossing ahead

If you have to leave your vehicle in a tunnel and leave by an emergency exit, do so as quickly as you can. Follow the signs directing you to the nearest exit point. If there are several people using the exit, don't panic but try to leave in a calm and orderly manner.

801 Mark *one* answer

Which of these signs shows that you are entering a one-way system?

If the road has two lanes you can use either lane and overtake on either side. Use the lane that's more convenient for your destination unless signs or road markings indicate otherwise.

802 Mark *one* answer

What does this sign mean?

- ☐ **A** With-flow bus and cycle lane
- ☐ **B** Contraflow bus and cycle lane
- ☐ **C** No buses and cycles allowed
- ☐ **D** No waiting for buses and cycles

Buses and cycles can travel in this lane. In this case they will flow in the same direction as other traffic. If it's busy they may be passing you on the left, so watch out for them. Times on the sign will show its hours of operation. No times shown, or no sign at all, means it's 24 hours. In some areas other vehicles, such as taxis and motorcycles, are allowed to use bus lanes. The sign will show these.

803 Mark *one* answer

Which of these signs warns you of a zebra crossing?

Look well ahead and check the pavements and surrounding areas for pedestrians. Look for anyone walking towards the crossing. Check your mirrors for traffic behind, in case you have to slow down or stop.

804 Mark *one* answer
What does this sign mean?

- ☐ **A** No footpath
- ☐ **B** No pedestrians
- ☐ **C** Zebra crossing
- ☐ **D** School crossing

You need to be aware of the various signs that relate to pedestrians. Some of the signs look similar but have very different meanings. Make sure you know what they all mean and be ready for any potential hazard.

805 Mark *one* answer
What does this sign mean?

- ☐ **A** School crossing patrol
- ☐ **B** No pedestrians allowed
- ☐ **C** Pedestrian zone – no vehicles
- ☐ **D** Zebra crossing ahead

Look well ahead and be ready to stop for any pedestrians crossing, or about to cross, the road. Also check the pavements for anyone who looks like they might step or run into the road.

806 Mark *one* answer
Which sign means there will be two-way traffic crossing your route ahead?

☐ A   ☑ B   ☐ C   ☐ D

This sign is found in or at the end of a one-way system. It warns you that traffic will be crossing your path from both directions.

807 Mark *one* answer
Which arm signal tells you that the car you are following is going to pull up?

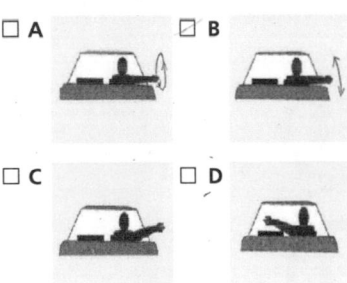

☐ A   ☑ B   ☐ C   ☐ D

There may be occasions when drivers need to give an arm signal to confirm an indicator. This could include in bright sunshine, at a complex road layout, when stopping at a pedestrian crossing or when turning right just after passing a parked vehicle. You should understand what each arm signal means. If you give arm signals, make them clear, correct and decisive.

808 Mark *one* answer
Which of these signs means turn left ahead?

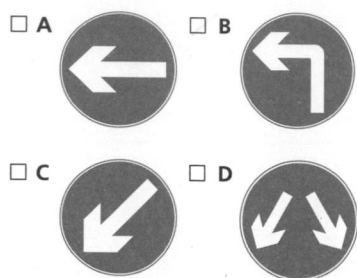

□ A   □ B

□ C   □ D

Blue circles tell you what you must do and this sign gives a clear instruction to turn left ahead. You should be looking out for signs at all times and know what they mean.

809 Mark *one* answer
Which sign shows that traffic can only travel in one direction on the road you're on?

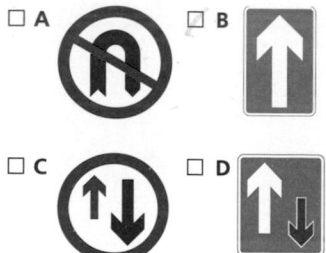

□ A   □ B

□ C   □ D

This sign means that traffic can only travel in one direction. The others show different priorities on a two-way road.

810 Mark *one* answer
You have just driven past this sign. You should be aware that

□ **A** it is a single track road
□ **B** you cannot stop on this road
□ **C** there is only one lane in use
☑ **D** all traffic is going one way

In a one-way system traffic may be passing you on either side. Always be aware of all traffic signs and understand their meaning. Look well ahead and react to them in good time.

811 Mark *one* answer
You are approaching a red traffic light. What will the signal show next?

□ **A** Red and amber
□ **B** Green alone
□ **C** Amber alone
□ **D** Green and amber

If you know which light is going to show next you can plan your approach accordingly. This can help prevent excessive braking or hesitation at the junction.

812 Mark *one* answer
What does this sign mean?

- ☐ **A** Low bridge ahead
- ☐ **B** Tunnel ahead
- ☐ **C** Ancient monument ahead
- ☐ **D** Traffic danger spot ahead

When approaching a tunnel switch on your dipped headlights. Be aware that your eyes might need to adjust to the sudden darkness. You may need to reduce your speed.

813 Mark *one* answer
You are approaching a zebra crossing where pedestrians are waiting. Which arm signal might you give?

☑ **A**   ☐ **B**

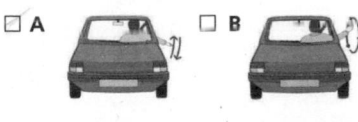

☐ **C**   ☐ **D**

A 'slowing down' signal will indicate your intentions to oncoming and following vehicles. Be aware that pedestrians might start to cross as soon as they see this signal.

814 Mark *one* answer
The white line along the side of the road

- ☐ **A** shows the edge of the carriageway
- ☐ **B** shows the approach to a hazard
- ☐ **C** means no parking
- ☐ **D** means no overtaking

A continuous white line is used on many roads to indicate the edge of the carriageway. This can be useful when visibility is restricted. The line is discontinued at junctions, lay-bys and entrances and exits from private drives.

815 Mark *one* answer
You see this white arrow on the road ahead. It means

- ☐ **A** entrance on the left
- ☐ **B** all vehicles turn left
- ☐ **C** keep left of the hatched markings
- ☐ **D** road bending to the left

Don't attempt to overtake here, as there might be unseen hazards over the brow of the hill. Keep to the left.

816 Mark *one* answer
How should you give an arm signal to turn left?

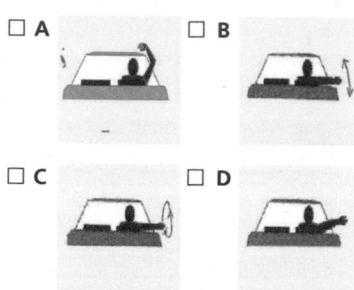

☐ A ☐ B
☐ C ☐ D

There may be occasions where other road users are unable to see your indicator, such as in bright sunlight or at a busy, complicated junction. In these cases a hand signal will help others to understand your intentions.

817 Mark *one* answer
You are waiting at a T-junction. A vehicle is coming from the right with the left signal flashing. What should you do?

☐ A Move out and accelerate hard
☐ B Wait until the vehicle starts to turn in
☐ C Pull out before the vehicle reaches the junction
☐ D Move out slowly

Other road users may give misleading signals. When you're waiting at a junction don't emerge until you're sure of their intentions.

818 Mark *one* answer
When may you use hazard warning lights when driving?

☐ A Instead of sounding the horn in a built-up area between 11.30pm and 7am
☐ B On a motorway or unrestricted dual carriageway, to warn of a hazard ahead
☐ C On rural routes, after a warning sign of animals
☐ D On the approach to toucan crossings where cyclists are waiting to cross

When there's queuing traffic ahead and you have to slow down or even stop, showing your hazard warning lights will alert following traffic to the hazard. Don't forget to switch them off as the queue forms behind you.

819 Mark *one* answer
You are driving on a motorway. There is a slow-moving vehicle ahead. On the back you see this sign. You should

☐ A pass on the right
☐ B pass on the left
☐ C leave at the next exit
☐ D drive no further

If a vehicle displaying this sign is in your lane you will have to pass it on the left. Use your mirrors and signal. When it's safe move into the lane on your left. You should always look well ahead so that you can spot any hazards early, giving yourself time to react safely.

820 Mark *one* answer
You should NOT normally stop on these markings near schools

- ☐ **A** except when picking up children
- ☐ **B** under any circumstances
- ☐ **C** unless there is nowhere else available
- ☐ **D** except to set down children

At schools you should not stop on yellow zigzag lines for any length of time, not even to set down or pick up children or other passengers.

821 Mark *one* answer
Why should you make sure that your indicators are cancelled after turning?

- ☐ **A** To avoid flattening the battery
- ☐ **B** To avoid misleading other road users
- ☐ **C** To avoid dazzling other road users
- ☐ **D** To avoid damage to the indicator relay

Leaving your indicators on could confuse other road users and may even lead to a crash. Be aware that if you haven't taken a sharp turn your indicators may not self-cancel and you will need to turn them off manually.

822 Mark *one* answer
You are driving in busy traffic. You want to pull up on the left just after a junction on the left. When should you signal?

- ☐ **A** As you are passing or just after the junction
- ☐ **B** Just before you reach the junction
- ☐ **C** Well before you reach the junction
- ☐ **D** It would be better not to signal at all

You need to signal to let other drivers know your intentions. However, if you indicate too early they may think you are turning left into the junction. Correct timing of the signal is very important to avoid misleading others.

823 Mark *one* answer
An MOT certificate is normally valid for

☐ **A** three years after the date it was issued
☑ **B** 10,000 miles
☐ **C** one year after the date it was issued
☐ **D** 30,000 miles

Make a note of the date that your MOT certificate expires. Some garages remind you that your vehicle is due an MOT but not all do. You may take your vehicle for MOT up to one month in advance and have the certificate post dated.

824 Mark *one* answer
A cover note is a document issued before you receive your

☐ **A** driving licence
☐ **B** insurance certificate
☐ **C** registration document
☐ **D** MOT certificate

Sometimes an insurance company will issue a temporary insurance certificate called a cover note. It gives you the same insurance cover as your certificate, but lasts for a limited period, usually one month.

825 Mark *one* answer
You've just passed your practical test. You don't hold a full licence in another category. Within two years you get six penalty points on your licence. What will you have to do?

☐ **A** Retake only your theory test
☐ **B** Retake your theory and practical tests
☐ **C** Retake only your practical test
☐ **D** Reapply for your full licence immediately

If you accumulate six or more penalty points within two years of gaining your first full licence it will be revoked. The six or more points include any gained due to offences you committed before passing your test. If this happens you may only drive as a learner until you pass both the theory and practical tests again.

826 Mark *one* answer
For how long is a Statutory Off Road Notification (SORN) valid?

☐ **A** Until the vehicle is taxed sold or scrapped
☐ **B** Until the vehicle is insured and MOT'd
☐ **C** Until the vehicle is repaired or modified
☐ **D** Until the vehicle is used on the road

A SORN declaration allows you to keep a vehicle off road and untaxed. SORN will end when the vehicle is taxed, sold or scrapped.

827 Mark *one* answer NI
What is a Statutory Off Road Notification (SORN)?

- ☐ **A** A notification to tell DVSA that a vehicle does not have a current MOT
- ☐ **B** Information kept by the police about the owner of the vehicle
- ☐ **C** A notification to tell DVLA that a vehicle is not being used on the road
- ☐ **D** Information held by insurance companies to check the vehicle is insured

If you want to keep a vehicle off the public road you must declare SORN. It is an offence not to do so. You then won't have to pay road tax. Your SORN is valid until your vehicle is taxed, sold or scrapped.

828 Mark *one* answer NI
What does a Statutory Off Road Notification (SORN) tell the DVLA?

- ☐ **A** That your vehicle is being used on the road but the MOT has expired
- ☐ **B** That you no longer own the vehicle
- ☐ **C** That your vehicle is not being used on the road
- ☐ **D** That you are buying a personal number plate.

By making a SORN, DVLA will know that this vehicle is being kept off the public road and does not need vehicle excise duty to be paid. Once you have made a SORN, it remains valid until you tax, sell or scrap the vehicle.

829 Mark *one* answer
What is the maximum specified fine for driving without insurance?

- ☐ **A** Unlimited
- ☐ **B** £500
- ☐ **C** £1000
- ☐ **D** £5000

It is a serious offence to drive without insurance. As well as a heavy fine you may be disqualified or incur penalty points.

830 Mark *one* answer
Who is legally responsible for ensuring that a Vehicle Registration Certificate (V5C) is updated?

- ☐ **A** The registered vehicle keeper
- ☐ **B** The vehicle manufacturer
- ☐ **C** Your insurance company
- ☐ **D** The licensing authority

It is your legal responsibility to keep the details of your Vehicle Registration Certificate (V5C) up to date. You should tell the licensing authority of any changes. These include your name, address, or vehicle details. If you don't do this you may have problems when you sell your vehicle.

831 Mark *one* answer
For which of these MUST you show your insurance certificate?

☐ **A** When making a SORN
☐ **B** When buying or selling a vehicle
☐ **C** When a police officer asks you for it
☐ **D** When having an MOT inspection

You MUST be able to produce your valid insurance certificate when requested by a police officer. If you can't do this immediately you may be asked to take it to a police station. Other documents you may be asked to produce are your driving licence and MOT certificate.

832 Mark *one* answer
Your vehicle must have valid insurance cover before you can do what?

☐ **A** Make a SORN
☐ **B** Sell the vehicle
☐ **C** Scrap the vehicle
☐ **D** Tax the vehicle

Your vehicle MUST have valid insurance cover before you can tax it. If required, it will also need to have a valid MOT certificate. You can tax your vehicle online, by phone or at certain post offices.

833 Mark *one* answer
Your vehicle needs a current MOT certificate. Until you have one you will NOT be able to

☐ **A** renew your driving licence
☐ **B** change your insurance company
☐ **C** renew your vehicle excise licence
☐ **D** notify a change of address

If your vehicle is required to have an MOT certificate you will need to make sure this is current before you are able to renew your vehicle excise licence (road tax). You can renew online, by phone or at certain post offices.

834 Mark *one* answer
Which of these is needed before you can use a vehicle on the road legally?

☐ **A** A valid driving licence
☐ **B** Breakdown cover
☐ **C** Proof of your identity
☐ **D** A vehicle handbook

Using a vehicle on the road illegally carries a heavy fine and can lead to penalty points on your licence. You MUST have
• a valid driving licence
• paid the appropriate vehicle excise duty (road tax)
• proper insurance cover

835 Mark *one* answer
What must you have when you apply to renew your vehicle excise licence?

☑ **A** Valid insurance
☐ **B** The chassis number
☐ **C** The handbook
☐ **D** A valid driving licence

The vehicle excise licence (road tax) can be renewed at post offices, vehicle registration offices, online, or by phone. When applying make sure you have all the relevant valid documents, including a valid MOT test certificate where applicable.

836 Mark *one* answer
A police officer asks to see your documents. You do not have them with you. You may be asked to take them to a police station within

☐ **A** 5 days
☐ **B** 7 days
☐ **C** 14 days
☐ **D** 21 days

You don't have to carry the documents for your vehicle around with you. If a police officer asks to see them and you don't have them with you, you may be asked to produce them at a police station within seven days.

837 Mark *one* answer
When should you update your Vehicle Registration Certificate?

☐ **A** When you pass your driving test
☐ **B** When you move house
☐ **C** When your vehicle needs an MOT
☐ **D** When you have a collision

As the registered keeper of a vehicle it is up to you to inform DVLA (DVA in Northern Ireland) of any changes in your vehicle or personal details, for example, change of name or address. You do this by completing the relevant section of the Registration Certificate and sending it to them.

838 Mark *one* answer
To drive on the road learners MUST

☐ **A** have NO penalty points on their licence
☐ **B** have taken professional instruction
☐ **C** have a signed, valid provisional licence
☐ **D** apply for a driving test within 12 months

Before you drive on the road you MUST have a valid provisional licence, for the category of vehicle that you're driving. It must show your signature, it isn't valid without it.

839 Mark *one* answer

Before driving anyone else's motor vehicle you should make sure that

- ☐ **A** the vehicle owner has third party insurance cover
- ☐ **B** your own vehicle has insurance cover
- ☐ **C** the vehicle is insured for your use
- ☐ **D** the owner has left the insurance documents in the vehicle

Driving a vehicle without insurance cover is illegal. If you cause injury to anyone or damage to property, it could be very expensive and you could also be subject to a criminal prosecution. You can arrange insurance cover with an insurance company, a broker and some motor manufacturers or dealers.

840 Mark *one* answer

Your car needs to pass an MOT test. What may be invalidated if you drive the car without a current MOT certificate?

- ☐ **A** The vehicle service record
- ☐ **B** Your insurance
- ☐ **C** The vehicle excise licence (road tax)
- ☐ **D** Your vehicle registration document

If your vehicle requires an MOT certificate, it's illegal to drive it without one and your insurance may be invalid if you do so. The only exceptions are that you may drive to a pre-arranged MOT test appointment, or to a garage for repairs required for the test.

841 Mark *one* answer

How old must you be to supervise a learner driver?

- ☐ **A** 18 years old
- ☐ **B** 19 years old
- ☐ **C** 20 years old
- ☐ **D** 21 years old

As well as being at least 21 years old you must hold a full EC/EEA driving licence for the category of vehicle being driven and have held that licence for at least three years.

842 Mark *one* answer

A newly qualified driver must

- ☐ **A** display green 'L' plates
- ☐ **B** not exceed 40mph for 12 months
- ☐ **C** be accompanied on a motorway
- ☐ **D** have valid motor insurance

It is your responsibility to make sure you are properly insured for the vehicle you are driving.

843 Mark *one* answer

You have third party insurance. What does this cover?

- ☐ **A** Damage to your vehicle
- ☐ **B** Fire damage to your vehicle
- ☐ **C** Flood damage to your vehicle
- ☐ **D** Damage to other vehicles

Third party insurance doesn't cover damage to your own vehicle or injury to yourself. If you have a crash and your vehicle is damaged you might have to carry out the repairs at your own expense.

844 Mark *one* answer

Who is responsible for paying the vehicle excise duty (road tax)?

☐ **A** The driver of the vehicle
☐ **B** The registered keeper of the vehicle
☐ **C** The car dealer
☐ **D** The Driver and Vehicle Licensing Agency (DVLA)

The registered keeper of the vehicle is responsible for paying the vehicle excise duty or making a Statutory Off-Road Notification (SORN) if the vehicle is to be kept untaxed and off the road.

---

845 Mark *one* answer

Your vehicle needs a current MOT certificate. What will you be unable to renew without this certificate?

☐ **A** Your driving licence
☐ **B** Your vehicle insurance
☐ **C** Your vehicle excise licence
☐ **D** Your vehicle registration document

If your vehicle requires a current MOT certificate you will be unable to renew your vehicle excise licence (road tax) without it.

846 Mark *one* answer

What information is found on a vehicle registration document?

☐ **A** The registered keeper
☐ **B** The type of insurance cover
☐ **C** The service history details
☐ **D** The date of the MOT

Every vehicle used on the road has a registration document. It shows vehicle details including date of first registration, registration number, previous keeper, registered keeper, make of vehicle, engine size, chassis number, year of manufacture and colour.

---

847 Mark *one* answer

You have a duty to contact the licensing authority when

☐ **A** you go abroad on holiday
☐ **B** you change your vehicle
☐ **C** your job involves travelling abroad
☐ **D** your job status changes

The licensing authority need to keep their records up to date. They send out a reminder when a vehicle's excise licence (road tax) is due for renewal. To do this they need to know the name and address of the registered keeper. Every vehicle in the country is registered, so it's possible to trace its history.

848 Mark *one* answer
You must notify the licensing authority when

☑ **A** your health affects your driving
☐ **B** your work takes you abroad
☐ **C** you intend to lend your vehicle
☐ **D** your vehicle requires an MOT certificate

The licensing authorities hold the records of all vehicles, drivers and riders in Great Britain and Northern Ireland. They need to know if you have a medical condition that might affect your ability to drive safely. Don't risk endangering your own safety or that of other road users.

849 Mark *one* answer   NI
The cost of your insurance may reduce if you

☐ **A** are under 25 years old
☐ **B** do not wear glasses
☐ **C** pass the driving test first time
☐ **D** take the Pass Plus scheme

The cost of insurance varies with your age and how long you have been driving. Usually, the younger you are the more expensive it is, especially if you are under 25 years of age.

The Pass Plus scheme provides additional training to newly qualified drivers. Pass Plus is recognised by many insurance companies and taking this extra training could give you reduced insurance premiums, as well as improving your skills and experience.

850 Mark *one* answer   NI
Which of the following may reduce the cost of your insurance?

☐ **A** Having a valid MOT certificate
☐ **B** Taking a Pass Plus course
☐ **C** Driving a powerful car
☐ **D** Having penalty points on your licence

The aim of the Pass Plus course is to build up your skills and experience. It is recognised by some insurance companies, who reward people completing the scheme with cheaper insurance premiums.

851 Mark *one* answer
To supervise a learner driver you must

☐ **A** have held a licence for at least a year
☐ **B** be at least 21 years old
☐ **C** be an approved driving instructor
☐ **D** hold an advanced driving certificate

Learner drivers benefit by combining professional driving lessons with private practice. However, you need to be at least 21 years old and have held your driving licence for at least 3 years before you can supervise a learner driver.

852 Mark *one* answer

Your car requires an MOT certificate. When is it legal to drive it without an MOT certificate?

☐ **A** Up to seven days after the old certificate has run out.

☐ **B** When driving to an MOT centre to arrange an appointment.

☐ **C** When driving the car with the owner's permission.

☑ **D** When driving to an appointment at an MOT centre.

When a car is three years old (four years old in Northern Ireland), it MUST pass an MOT test and have a valid MOT certificate before it can be used on the road. Exceptionally, you may

- drive to a pre-arranged test appointment or to a garage for repairs required for the test
- drive vehicles made before 1960 without an MOT test, but they must be in a roadworthy condition before being used on the road.

853 Mark *one* answer   **NI**

Motor cars must first have an MOT test certificate when they are

☐ **A** one year old

☐ **B** three years old

☐ **C** five years old

☑ **D** seven years old

The vehicle you drive MUST be roadworthy and in good condition. If it's over three years old it MUST pass an MOT test to remain in use on the road. Vehicles made before 1960 are exempt from the MOT test, but must be in a roadworthy condition before being driven on the road.

854 Mark *one* answer   **NI**

The Pass Plus scheme has been created for new drivers. What is its main purpose?

☑ **A** To allow you to drive faster

☐ **B** To allow you to carry passengers

☐ **C** To improve your basic skills

☐ **D** To let you drive on motorways

New drivers are far more vulnerable on the road and more likely to be involved in incidents and collisions. The Pass Plus scheme has been designed to improve new drivers' basic skills and help widen their driving experience.

855 Mark *one* answer

Your vehicle is insured third party only. This covers

☐ **A** damage to your vehicle

☐ **B** damage to other vehicles

☐ **C** injury to yourself

☐ **D** all damage and injury

This type of insurance cover is usually cheaper than comprehensive. However, it doesn't cover any damage you cause to your own vehicle or property. It only covers damage and injury you cause to others.

856 Mark *one* answer

What is the legal minimum insurance cover you must have to drive on public roads?

☐ **A** Third party, fire and theft
☐ **B** Comprehensive
☐ **C** Third party only
☐ **D** Personal injury cover

The minimum insurance required by law is third party cover. This covers others involved in a collision but not damage to your vehicle. Basic third party insurance won't cover theft or fire damage. Check with your insurance company for advice on the best cover for you and make sure that you read the policy carefully.

857 Mark *one* answer

You claim on your insurance to have your car repaired. Your policy has an excess of £100. What does this mean?

☐ **A** The insurance company will pay the first £100 of any claim
☐ **B** You will be paid £100 if you do not claim within one year
☐ **C** Your vehicle is insured for a value of £100 if it is stolen
☐ **D** You will have to pay the first £100 of the cost of repair to your car

Having an excess on your policy will help to keep down the premium, but if you make a claim you will have to pay the excess yourself, in this case £100.

858 Mark *one* answer   NI

The Pass Plus scheme is designed to

☐ **A** give you a discount on your MOT
☐ **B** improve your basic driving skills
☐ **C** increase your mechanical knowledge
☐ **D** allow you to drive anyone else's vehicle

After passing your practical driving test you can take further training. This is known as the Pass Plus scheme. It is designed to improve your basic driving skills and involves a series of modules including night time and motorway driving. The sort of things you may not have covered whilst learning.

859 Mark *one* answer   NI

By taking part in the Pass Plus scheme you will

☐ **A** never get any points on your licence
☐ **B** be able to service your own car
☐ **C** allow you to drive anyone else's vehicle
☐ **D** improve your basic driving skills

The Pass Plus scheme can be taken after you've passed your practical driving test. Ask your ADI for details. It is designed to improve your basic driving skills. By successfully completing the course you may get a discount on your insurance.

860 Mark *one* answer NI

What does the Pass Plus scheme enable newly qualified drivers to do?

☑ **A** Widen their driving experience
☐ **B** Supervise a learner driver
☐ **C** Increase their insurance premiums
☐ **D** Avoid mechanical breakdowns

The Pass Plus scheme was created for newly qualified drivers. It aims to widen their driving experience and improve basic skills. After passing the practical driving test additional professional training can be taken with an Approved Driving Instructor (ADI). Some insurance companies also offer discounts to holders of a Pass Plus certificate.

861 Mark *one* answer NI

New drivers can take further training after passing the practical test. A Pass Plus course will help to

☐ **A** get your car through its MOT test
☐ **B** widen your experience
☐ **C** increase your insurance premiums
☐ **D** get you cheaper road tax

Novice drivers are much more likely to be involved in a collision than experienced drivers. The Pass Plus scheme gives structured training to help new drivers improve basic skills and widen their experience. Approved Driving Instructors (ADIs) will be able to advise of the benefits.

862 Mark *one* answer NI

The Pass Plus Scheme is operated by DVSA for newly qualified drivers. What is it intended to do?

☑ **A** Improve your basic skills
☐ **B** Reduce the cost of your driving licence
☐ **C** Prevent you from paying congestion charges
☐ **D** Allow you to supervise a learner driver

The Pass Plus scheme provides a wide range of driving experience accompanied by a qualified instructor. There is no test and when completed you may get a reduction in insurance costs. It can help to improve basic skills, reduce the risk of having a collision and make you a safer driver.

863 Mark *one* answer

For which of these must you show your motor insurance certificate?

☐ **A** When you are taking your driving test
☐ **B** When buying or selling a vehicle
☐ **C** When a police officer asks you for it
☐ **D** When having an MOT inspection

When you take out motor insurance you'll be issued with a certificate. This contains details explaining who and what is insured. If a police officer asks to see your insurance certificate you must produce it at the time or at a police station within a specified period. You also need to have current valid insurance when renewing your vehicle excise duty (road tax).

864 Mark *one* answer
Which of these is needed before you can drive legally?

☐ **A** A vehicle handbook
☐ **B** Proper insurance cover
☐ **C** A vehicle service record
☐ **D** Breakdown cover

Make sure that you have a valid driving licence and proper insurance cover before driving any vehicle. It is also a legal requirement that the appropriate vehicle excise duty (road tax) has been paid.

865 Mark *one* answer
A friend wants to help you learn to drive. They must be

☐ **A** at least 21 and have held a full licence for at least one year
☐ **B** over 18 and hold an advanced driver's certificate
☐ **C** over 18 and have fully comprehensive insurance
☐ **D** at least 21 and have held a full licence for at least three years

Helping someone to drive is a responsible task. Before learning to drive you're advised to find a qualified Approved Driving Instructor (ADI) to teach you. This will ensure that you're taught the correct procedures from the start.

866 Mark *one* answer
Your motor insurance policy has an excess of £100. What does this mean?

☐ **A** The insurance company will pay the first £100 of any claim
☐ **B** You will be paid £100 if you do not have a crash
☐ **C** Your vehicle is insured for a value of £100 if it is stolen
☐ **D** You will have to pay the first £100 of any claim

This is a method used by insurance companies to keep annual premiums down. Generally, the higher the excess you choose to pay, the lower the annual premium you will be charged.

867 Mark *one* answer

You see a car on the hard shoulder of a motorway with a HELP pennant displayed. This means the driver is most likely to be

- ☐ **A** a disabled person
- ☐ **B** first aid trained
- ☐ **C** a foreign visitor
- ☐ **D** a rescue patrol person

If a disabled driver's vehicle breaks down and they are unable to walk to an emergency phone, they are advised to stay in their car and switch on the hazard warning lights. They may also display a 'Help' pennant in their vehicle.

868 Mark *one* answer

When should you use hazard warning lights?

- ☑ **A** When you slow down quickly on a motorway because of a hazard ahead
- ☐ **B** When you leave your car at the roadside to visit a shop
- ☐ **C** When you wish to stop on double yellow lines
- ☐ **D** When you need to park on the pavement

Hazard warning lights are fitted to all modern cars and some motorcycles. They should be used to warn
- other road users when your vehicle is causing a temporary obstruction, for example after a collision or when it's broken down
- following drivers on a motorway of a hazard or obstruction ahead.
They should not be used as an excuse for dangerous or illegal parking.

869 Mark *one* answer

When are you allowed to use hazard warning lights?

- ☐ **A** When stopped and temporarily obstructing traffic
- ☐ **B** When travelling during darkness without headlights
- ☐ **C** When parked for shopping on double yellow lines
- ☐ **D** When travelling slowly because you are lost

You must not use hazard warning lights when moving, except when slowing suddenly on a motorway or unrestricted dual carriageway to warn the traffic behind.
   Never use hazard warning lights to excuse dangerous or illegal parking.

870 Mark *one* answer

You are going through a congested tunnel and have to stop. What should you do?

- ☐ **A** Pull up very close to the vehicle in front to save space
- ☐ **B** Ignore any message signs as they are never up to date
- ☐ **C** Keep a safe distance from the vehicle in front
- ☐ **D** Make a U-turn and find another route

It's important to keep a safe distance from the vehicle in front at all times. This still applies in congested tunnels even if you are moving very slowly or have stopped. If the vehicle in front breaks down you may need room to manoeuvre past it.

871 Mark *one* answer
On the motorway, the hard shoulder should be used

- ☐ **A** to answer a mobile phone
- ☐ **B** when an emergency arises
- ☐ **C** for a short rest when tired
- ☐ **D** to check a road atlas

Pull onto the hard shoulder and use the emergency telephone to report your problem. This lets the emergency services know your exact location so they can send help. Never cross the carriageway to use the telephone on the other side.

872 Mark *one* answer
You arrive at the scene of a crash. Someone is bleeding badly from an arm wound. There is nothing embedded in it. What should you do?

- ☐ **A** Apply pressure over the wound and keep the arm down
- ☐ **B** Dab the wound
- ☐ **C** Get them a drink
- ☐ **D** Apply pressure over the wound and raise the arm

If possible, lay the casualty down. Check for anything that may be in the wound. Apply firm pressure to the wound using clean material, without pressing on anything which might be in it. Raising the arm above the level of the heart will also help to stem the flow of blood.

873 Mark *one* answer
You are at an incident where a casualty is unconscious. Their breathing should be checked. This should be done for at least

- ☐ **A** 2 seconds
- ☐ **B** 10 seconds
- ☐ **C** 1 minute
- ☐ **D** 2 minutes

Once the airway is open, check breathing. Listen and feel for breath. Do this by placing your cheek over their mouth and nose, and look to see if the chest rises. This should be done for up to 10 seconds.

874 Mark *one* answer
Following a collision someone has suffered a burn. The burn needs to be cooled. What is the shortest time it should be cooled for?

- ☐ **A** 5 minutes
- ☐ **B** 10 minutes
- ☐ **C** 15 minutes
- ☐ **D** 20 minutes

Check the casualty for shock and if possible try to cool the burn for at least ten minutes. Use a clean, cold non-toxic liquid preferably water.

875 Mark *one* answer
After a collision someone has suffered a burn. The burn needs to be cooled. What is the shortest time it should be cooled for?

- ☐ **A** 30 seconds
- ☐ **B** 60 seconds
- ☐ **C** 5 minutes
- ☐ **D** 10 minutes

It's important to cool a burn for at least ten minutes. Use a clean, cold non-toxic liquid preferably water. Bear in mind the person may also be in shock.

876 Mark *one* answer
A casualty is not breathing normally. Chest compressions should be given. At what rate?

☐ **A** 10 per minute
☐ **B** 120 per minute
☐ **C** 60 per minute
☐ **D** 240 per minute

If a casualty is not breathing normally chest compressions may be needed to maintain circulation. Place two hands on the centre of the chest and press down hard and fast – around 5-6 centimetres and about twice a second.

877 Mark *one* answer
A person has been injured. They may be suffering from shock. What are the warning signs to look for?

☐ **A** Flushed complexion
☐ **B** Warm dry skin
☐ **C** Slow pulse
☐ **D** Pale grey skin

The effects of shock may not be immediately obvious. Warning signs are rapid pulse, sweating, pale grey skin and rapid shallow breathing.

878 Mark *one* answer
You suspect that an injured person may be suffering from shock. What are the warning signs to look for?

☐ **A** Warm dry skin ☐ **B** Sweating
☑ **C** Slow pulse ☐ **D** Skin rash

Sometimes you may not realise that someone is in shock. The signs to look for are rapid pulse, sweating, pale grey skin and rapid shallow breathing.

879 Mark *one* answer
An injured person has been placed in the recovery position. They are unconscious but breathing normally. What else should be done?

☐ **A** Press firmly between the shoulders
☐ **B** Place their arms by their side
☐ **C** Give them a hot sweet drink
☐ **D** Check the airway is clear

After a casualty has been placed in the recovery position, their airway should be checked to make sure it's clear. Don't leave them alone until medical help arrives. Where possible do NOT move a casualty unless there's further danger.

880 Mark *one* answer
An injured motorcyclist is lying unconscious in the road. You should always

☐ **A** remove the safety helmet
☐ **B** seek medical assistance
☐ **C** move the person off the road
☐ **D** remove the leather jacket

If someone has been injured, the sooner proper medical attention is given the better. Send someone to phone for help or go yourself. An injured person should only be moved if they're in further danger. An injured motorcyclist's helmet should NOT be removed unless it is essential.

881 Mark *one* answer

You are on a motorway. A large box falls onto the road from a lorry. The lorry does not stop. You should

☑ **A** go to the next emergency telephone and report the hazard
☐ **B** catch up with the lorry and try to get the driver's attention
☐ **C** stop close to the box until the police arrive
☐ **D** pull over to the hard shoulder, then remove the box

Lorry drivers can be unaware of objects falling from their vehicles. If you see something fall onto a motorway look to see if the driver pulls over. If they don't stop, do not attempt to retrieve it yourself. Pull on to the hard shoulder near an emergency telephone and report the hazard.

882 Mark *one* answer

You are going through a long tunnel. What will warn you of congestion or an incident ahead?

☐ **A** Hazard warning lines
☐ **B** Other drivers flashing their lights
☐ **C** Variable message signs
☐ **D** Areas marked with hatch markings

Follow the instructions given by the signs or by tunnel officials.

In congested tunnels a minor incident can soon turn into a major one with serious or even fatal results.

883 Mark *one* answer

An adult casualty is not breathing. To maintain circulation, compressions should be given. What is the correct depth to press?

☐ **A** 1 to 2 centimetres
☐ **B** 5 to 6 centimetres
☐ **C** 10 to 15 centimetres
☐ **D** 15 to 20 centimetres

An adult casualty is not breathing normally. To maintain circulation place two hands on the centre of the chest. Then press down hard and fast – around 5 to 6 centimetres and about twice a second.

884 Mark *one* answer

You're the first to arrive at the scene of a crash. What should you do?

☐ **A** Leave as soon as another motorist arrives
☐ **B** Flag down other motorists to help you
☐ **C** Drag all casualties away from the vehicles
☐ **D** Call the emergency services promptly

At a crash scene you can help in practical ways, even if you aren't trained in first aid. Call the emergency services and make sure you don't put yourself or anyone else in danger. The safest way to warn other traffic is by switching on your hazard warning lights.

885 Mark *one* answer
At the scene of a traffic incident you should

☑ **A** not put yourself at risk
☐ **B** go to those casualties who are screaming
☐ **C** pull everybody out of their vehicles
☐ **D** leave vehicle engines switched on

It's important that people at the scene of a collision do not create further risk to themselves or others. If the incident is on a motorway or major road, traffic will be approaching at speed. Do not put yourself at risk when trying to help casualties or warning other road users.

886 Mark *one* answer
You're the first person to arrive at an incident where people are badly injured. You've switched on your hazard lights and checked all engines are stopped. What else should you do?

☑ **A** Make sure that an ambulance is called for
☐ **B** Stop other cars and ask the drivers for help
☐ **C** Try and get people who are injured to drink something
☐ **D** Move the people who are injured clear of their vehicles

If you're the first to arrive at a crash scene the first concerns are the risk of further collision and fire. Ensuring that vehicle engines are switched off will reduce the risk of fire. Use hazard warning lights so that other traffic knows there's a need for caution. Make sure the emergency services are contacted, don't assume this has already been done.

887 Mark *one* answer
You arrive at the scene of a motorcycle crash. The rider is injured. When should the helmet be removed?

☐ **A** Only when it is essential
☐ **B** Always straight away
☐ **C** Only when the motorcyclist asks
☐ **D** Always, unless they are in shock

DO NOT remove a motorcyclist's helmet unless it is essential. Remember they may be suffering from shock. Don't give them anything to eat or drink but do reassure them confidently.

888 Mark *one* answer
You arrive at a serious motorcycle crash. The motorcyclist is unconscious and bleeding. What should you do to help them?

☐ **A** Sweep up any loose debris
☐ **B** Make a list of witnesses
☐ **C** Check their breathing
☐ **D** Take the numbers of other vehicles

Further collisions and fire are the main dangers immediately after a crash. If possible get others to assist you and make the area safe. Help those involved and remember DR ABC (Danger, Response, Airway, Breathing, Compressions). This will help when dealing with any injuries.

889 Mark *one* answer
You arrive at an incident. A motorcyclist is unconscious. Your FIRST priority is the casualty's

☐ **A** breathing
☐ **B** bleeding
☐ **C** broken bones
☐ **D** bruising

At the scene of an incident always be aware of danger from further collisions or fire. The first priority when dealing with an unconscious person is to ensure they can breathe. This may involve clearing their airway if you can see an obstruction, or if they're having difficulty breathing.

890 Mark *one* answer
At an incident a casualty is unconscious. What should you check urgently?

☐ **A** Flesh wounds
☐ **B** Airway
☐ **C** Shock
☐ **D** Broken bones

Remember DR ABC (Danger, Response, Airway, Breathing, Compressions). An unconscious casualty may have difficulty breathing. Check that their airway is clear by tilting the head back gently. Unblock the airway if necessary, then make sure the casualty is breathing. Compressions may need to be given to maintain circulation.

891 Mark *one* answer
You arrive at the scene of an incident. It's just happened and someone is unconscious. What should be given urgent priority to help them?

☐ **A** Stop any heavy bleeding
☐ **B** Try to get them to drink water
☐ **C** Take the numbers of vehicles involved
☐ **D** Look for any witnesses

Make sure that the emergency services are called immediately. Remember DR ABC (Danger, Response, Airway, Breathing, Compressions) and, once first aid has been given, stay with the casualty.

892 Mark *one* answer
At an incident someone is unconscious. What would your priority be?

☐ **A** Find out their name
☐ **B** To wake them up
☐ **C** Make them comfortable
☐ **D** Check their airway is clear

Remember this procedure by saying DR ABC. (This stands for Danger, Response, Airway, Breathing, Compressions.) Give whatever first aid you can and stay with the injured person until the emergency services arrive.

893 Mark *one* answer
You've stopped at an incident to give help. What should you do?

- ☐ **A** Keep injured people warm and comfortable
- ☐ **B** Give injured people something to eat
- ☐ **C** Keep injured people on the move by walking them around
- ☐ **D** Give injured people a warm drink

There are a number of things you can do to help, even without expert training. Be aware of further danger from other traffic and fire; make sure the area is safe. People may be in shock. Don't give them anything to eat or drink. Keep them warm and comfortable and reassure them. Don't move injured people unless there is a risk of further danger.

894 Mark *one* answer
You arrive at an incident which has only just happened and someone is injured. What should be given urgent priority?

- ☐ **A** Ask for witnesses' details
- ☐ **B** Give the injured person a warm drink
- ☐ **C** Stop any severe bleeding
- ☐ **D** Note the registration numbers of vehicles involved

The first priority with a casualty is to make sure their airway is clear and they're breathing. Any wounds should be checked for objects and bleeding stemmed using clean material. Ensure the emergency services are called as they're the experts. If you're not first aid trained consider getting training. It might save a life.

895 Mark *one* answer
Which of the following should you NOT do at the scene of a collision?

- ☐ **A** Warn other traffic by switching on your hazard warning lights
- ☐ **B** Call the emergency services immediately
- ☐ **C** Offer someone a cigarette to calm them down
- ☐ **D** Ask drivers to switch off their engines

Keeping casualties or witnesses calm is important, but never offer a cigarette because of the risk of fire. Bear in mind they may be in shock. Don't offer an injured person anything to eat or drink. They may have internal injuries or need surgery.

896 Mark *one* answer
There's been a collision. A driver is suffering from shock. What should you do?

- ☐ **A** Give them a drink
- ☐ **B** Reassure them
- ☐ **C** Ask who caused the incident
- ☐ **D** Offer them a cigarette

A casualty suffering from shock may have injuries that aren't immediately obvious. Call the emergency services then stay with the person in shock, offering reassurance until the experts arrive.

897 Mark *one* answer

You have to treat someone for shock at the scene of an incident. You should

☐ A reassure them constantly
☐ B walk them around to calm them down
☐ C give them something cold to drink
☐ D cool them down as soon as possible

Stay with the casualty and talk to them quietly and firmly to calm and reassure them. Avoid moving them unnecessarily in case they are injured. Keep them warm, but don't give them anything to eat or drink.

898 Mark *one* answer

You arrive at the scene of a motorcycle crash. No other vehicle is involved. The rider is unconscious and lying in the middle of the road. The FIRST thing you should do is

☐ A move the rider out of the road
☐ B warn other traffic
☐ C clear the road of debris
☐ D give the rider reassurance

The motorcyclist is in an extremely vulnerable position, exposed to further danger from traffic. Approaching vehicles need advance warning in order to slow down and safely take avoiding action or stop. Don't put yourself or anyone else at risk. Use the hazard warning lights on your vehicle to alert other road users to the danger.

899 Mark *one* answer

At an incident a small child is not breathing. To restore normal breathing you should breathe into their mouth

☐ A sharply
☐ B gently
☐ C heavily
☐ D rapidly

If a young child has stopped breathing, first check that the airway is clear. Then give compressions to the chest using one hand (two fingers for an infant) and begin mouth-to-mouth resuscitation. Breathe very gently and continue the procedure until they can breathe without help.

900 Mark *one* answer

At an incident a casualty isn't breathing. What should you do while helping them to start breathing again?

☐ A put their arms across their chest
☐ B shake them firmly
☐ C roll them onto their side
☐ D tilt their head back gently

It's important to ensure that the airways are clear before you start mouth-to-mouth resuscitation. Gently tilt their head back and use your finger to check for and remove any obvious obstruction in the mouth.

901 Mark *one* answer

You arrive at an incident. There has been an engine fire and someone's hands and arms have been burnt. You should NOT

- ☐ **A** douse the burn thoroughly with clean cool non-toxic liquid
- ☐ **B** lay the casualty down on the ground
- ☐ **C** remove anything sticking to the burn
- ☐ **D** reassure them confidently and repeatedly

This could cause further damage and infection to the wound. Your first priority is to cool the burn with a clean, cool, non-toxic liquid, preferably water. Don't forget the casualty may be in shock.

902 Mark *one* answer

You arrive at an incident where someone is suffering from severe burns. You should

- ☐ **A** apply lotions to the injury
- ☐ **B** burst any blisters
- ☐ **C** remove anything stuck to the burns
- ☐ **D** douse the burns with clean cool non-toxic liquid

Use a liquid that is clean, cold and non-toxic, preferably water. Its coolness will help take the heat out of the burn and relieve the pain. Keep the wound doused for at least ten minutes. If blisters appear don't attempt to burst them as this could lead to infection.

903 Mark *one* answer

You arrive at an incident. A pedestrian is bleeding heavily from a leg wound. The leg isn't broken and there's nothing in the wound. What should you do?

- ☐ **A** Dab the wound to stop bleeding
- ☐ **B** Keep both legs flat on the ground
- ☐ **C** Fetch them a warm drink
- ☐ **D** Raise the leg to lessen bleeding

If there's nothing in the wound, applying a pad of clean cloth or bandage will help stem the bleeding. Raising the leg will also lessen the flow of blood. Don't tie anything tightly round the leg as this will restrict circulation and could result in long-term injury.

904 Mark *one* answer

At an incident a casualty is unconscious but still breathing. You should only move them if

- ☐ **A** an ambulance is on its way
- ☐ **B** bystanders advise you to
- ☐ **C** there is further danger
- ☐ **D** bystanders will help you to

Do not move a casualty unless there is further danger, for example, from other traffic or fire. They may have unseen or internal injuries. Moving them unnecessarily could cause further injury. Do NOT remove a motorcyclist's helmet unless it's essential.

905 Mark *one* answer

At a collision you suspect a casualty has back injuries. The area is safe. You should

- ☐ **A** offer them a drink
- ☐ **B** not move them
- ☐ **C** raise their legs
- ☐ **D** not call an ambulance

Talk to the casualty and keep them calm. Do not attempt to move them as this could cause further injury. Call an ambulance at the first opportunity.

906 Mark *one* answer

At an incident it is important to look after any casualties. When the area is safe, you should

- ☐ **A** get them out of the vehicle
- ☐ **B** give them a drink
- ☐ **C** give them something to eat
- ☐ **D** keep them in the vehicle

When the area is safe and there's no danger from other traffic or fire it's better not to move casualties. Moving them may cause further injury.

907 Mark *one* answer

A tanker is involved in a collision. Which sign shows that it is carrying dangerous goods?

☐ **A**  ☐ **B**

☐ **C** ☐ **D**

There will be an orange label on the side and rear of the tanker. Look at this carefully and report what it says when you phone the emergency services. Details of hazard warning plates are given in The Highway Code.

908 Mark *one* answer

You're involved in a collision. Afterwards, which document may the police ask you to produce?

- ☐ **A** Vehicle registration document
- ☐ **B** Driving licence
- ☐ **C** Theory test certificate
- ☐ **D** Vehicle service record

You MUST stop if you've been involved in a collision which results in injury or damage. The police may ask to see your driving licence and insurance details at the time or later at a police station.

909 Mark *one* answer

After a collision someone is unconscious in their vehicle. When should you call the emergency services?

- ☐ **A** Only as a last resort
- ☑ **B** As soon as possible
- ☐ **C** After you have woken them up
- ☒ **D** After checking for broken bones

It is important to make sure that emergency services arrive on the scene as soon as possible. When a person is unconscious, they could have serious injuries that are not immediately obvious.

910 Mark *one* answer

A casualty has an injured arm. They can move it freely but it is bleeding. Why should you get them to keep it in a raised position?

- ☐ **A** Because it will ease the pain
- ☐ **B** It will help them to be seen more easily
- ☐ **C** To stop them touching other people
- ☐ **D** It will help to reduce the blood flow

If a casualty is bleeding heavily, raise the limb to a higher position. This will help to reduce the blood flow. Before raising the limb you should make sure that it is not broken.

911 Mark *one* answer

You are going through a tunnel. What systems are provided to warn of any incidents, collisions or congestion?

- ☐ **A** Double white centre lines
- ☐ **B** Variable message signs
- ☐ **C** Chevron 'distance markers'
- ☐ **D** Rumble strips

Take notice of any instructions given on variable message signs or by tunnel officials. They will warn you of any incidents or congestion ahead and advise you what to do.

912 Mark *one* answer

A collision has just happened. An injured person is lying in a busy road. What is the FIRST thing you should do to help?

- ☐ **A** Treat the person for shock
- ☐ **B** Warn other traffic
- ☐ **C** Place them in the recovery position
- ☐ **D** Make sure the injured person is kept warm

The most immediate danger is further collisions and fire. You could warn other traffic by displaying an advance warning triangle or sign (but not on a motorway), switching on hazard warning lights or by any other means that does not put you or others at risk.

913 Mark *one* answer

At an incident a casualty has stopped breathing. You should

☐ **A** keep the head tilted forwards as far as possible

☐ **B** remove anything that is blocking the mouth

☐ **C** raise the legs to help with circulation

☐ **D** try to give the casualty something to drink

Unblocking the airway and gently tilting the head back will help the casualty to breathe. They'll then be in the correct position if mouth-to-mouth resuscitation is required. Don't move a casualty unless there's further danger.

914 Mark *one* answer

You're at the scene of an incident. Someone is suffering from shock. You should

☐ **A** reassure them confidently

☐ **B** offer them a cigarette

☐ **C** give them a warm drink

☐ **D** offer them some food

If someone is suffering from shock, try to keep them warm and as comfortable as you can. Don't give them anything to eat or drink but reassure them confidently and try not to leave them alone.

915 Mark *one* answer

There has been a collision. A motorcyclist is lying injured and unconscious. Unless it's essential, why should you usually NOT attempt to remove their helmet?

☐ **A** Because they may not want you to

☐ **B** This could result in more serious injury

☐ **C** They will get too cold if you do this

☐ **D** Because you could scratch the helmet

When someone is injured, any movement which is not absolutely necessary should be avoided since it could make injuries worse. Unless it is essential, it's generally safer to leave a motorcyclist's helmet in place.

916 Mark *one* answer

You have broken down on a two-way road. You have a warning triangle. You should place the warning triangle at least how far from your vehicle?

☐ **A** 5 metres (16 feet)

☐ **B** 25 metres (82 feet)

☐ **C** 45 metres (147 feet)

☐ **D** 100 metres (328 feet)

Advance warning triangles fold flat and don't take up much room. Use it to warn other road users if your vehicle has broken down or there's been an incident. Place it at least 45 metres (147 feet) behind your vehicle or incident on the same side of the road or verge. Place it further back if the scene is hidden by, for example, a bend, hill or dip in the road. Don't use them on motorways.

917 Mark *one* answer

You break down on a level crossing. The lights have not yet begun to flash. What's the first thing should you do?

- ☐ **A** Tell drivers behind what has happened
- ☐ **B** Leave your vehicle and get everyone clear
- ☐ **C** Walk down the track and signal the next train
- ☐ **D** Stay in your car until you're told to move

If your vehicle breaks down on a level crossing, your first priority is to get everyone out of the vehicle and clear of the crossing. Then use the railway telephone, if there is one, to tell the signal operator. If you have time before the train arrives, move the vehicle clear of the crossing, but only do this if alarm signals are not on.

918 Mark *one* answer

Your tyre bursts while you're driving. What should you do?

- ☐ **A** Pull on the handbrake
- ☐ **B** Brake as quickly as possible
- ☐ **C** Pull up slowly at the side of the road
- ☐ **D** Continue on at a normal speed

A tyre bursting can lead to a loss of control, especially if you're travelling at high speed. Using the correct procedure should help you to stop the vehicle safely.

919 Mark *one* answer

What should you do when a front tyre bursts?

- ☐ **A** Apply the handbrake to stop the vehicle
- ☐ **B** Brake firmly and quickly
- ☐ **C** Let the vehicle roll to a stop
- ☐ **D** Hold the steering wheel lightly

Try not to react by applying the brakes harshly. This could lead to further loss of steering control. Indicate your intention to pull up at the side of the road and roll to a stop.

920 Mark *one* answer

Your vehicle has a puncture on a motorway. What should you do?

- ☐ **A** Drive slowly to the next service area to get assistance
- ☐ **B** Pull up on the hard shoulder. Change the wheel as quickly as possible
- ☐ **C** Pull up on the hard shoulder. Use the emergency phone to get assistance
- ☐ **D** Switch on your hazard lights. Stop in your lane

Pull up on the hard shoulder and make your way to the nearest emergency telephone to call for assistance.

Do not attempt to repair your vehicle while it is on the hard shoulder because of the risk posed by traffic passing at high speeds.

921 Mark *one* answer
You have stalled in the middle of a level crossing and cannot restart the engine. The warning bell starts to ring. You should

☐ **A** get out and clear of the crossing
☐ **B** run down the track to warn the signal operator
☐ **C** carry on trying to restart the engine
☐ **D** push the vehicle clear of the crossing

Try to stay calm, especially if you have passengers on board. If you can't restart your engine before the warning bells ring, leave the vehicle and get yourself and any passengers well clear of the crossing.

922 Mark *one* answer
You're driving on a motorway. When can you use hazard warning lights?

☐ **A** When a vehicle is following too closely
☐ **B** When you slow down quickly because of danger ahead
☐ **C** When you're towing another vehicle
☐ **D** When you're driving on the hard shoulder

Briefly using your hazard warning lights will warn the traffic travelling behind you that there's a hazard ahead. This can reduce the chance of vehicles crashing into the back of each other.

923 Mark *one* answer
You've broken down on a motorway. When you use the emergency telephone you will be asked for

☐ **A** details about your vehicle
☐ **B** four driving licence details
☐ **C** the name of your vehicle's insurance company
☐ **D** your employer's details

Have the correct details ready before you use the emergency telephone. The operator will need to know the details of your vehicle and its fault. For your own safety always face the traffic when you speak on a roadside telephone.

924 Mark *one* answer
Before driving through a tunnel what should you do?

☐ **A** Switch your radio off
☐ **B** Remove any sunglasses
☐ **C** Close your sunroof
☐ **D** Switch on windscreen wipers

If you are wearing sunglasses you should remove them before driving into a tunnel. If you don't, your vision will be restricted, even in tunnels that appear to be well-lit.

925 Mark *one* answer
You are driving through a tunnel and the traffic is flowing normally. What should you do?

- ☐ **A** Use parking lights
- ☐ **B** Use front spot lights
- ☐ **C** Use dipped headlights
- ☐ **D** Use rear fog lights

Before entering a tunnel you should switch on your dipped headlights, as this will allow you to see and be seen. In many tunnels it is a legal requirement.

Don't wear sunglasses while driving in a tunnel. You may wish to tune your radio into a local channel.

926 Mark *one* answer
You are driving through a tunnel. Your vehicle breaks down. What should you do?

- ☑ **A** Switch on hazard warning lights
- ☐ **B** Remain in your vehicle
- ☐ **C** Wait for the police to find you
- ☐ **D** Rely on CCTV cameras seeing you

If your vehicle breaks down in a tunnel it could present a danger to other traffic. First switch on your hazard warning lights and then call for help from an emergency telephone point.

Don't rely on being found by the police or being seen by a CCTV camera. The longer the vehicle stays in an exposed position, the more danger it poses to other drivers.

927 Mark *one* answer
When driving through a tunnel you should

- ☐ **A** Look out for variable message signs
- ☐ **B** Use your air conditioning system
- ☐ **C** Switch on your rear fog lights
- ☐ **D** Always use your windscreen wipers

A minor incident in a tunnel can quickly turn into a major disaster. Variable message signs are provided to warn of any incidents or congestion. Follow their advice.

928 Mark *one* answer
What safeguard could you take against fire risk to your vehicle?

- ☐ **A** Keep water levels above maximum
- ☐ **B** Check out any strong smell of fuel
- ☐ **C** Avoid driving with a full tank of fuel
- ☐ **D** Use fuel additives

The fuel in your vehicle can be a dangerous fire hazard. If you smell fuel check out where it's coming from. Never

- use a naked flame near the vehicle if you can smell fuel
- smoke when refuelling your vehicle.

929 Mark *one* answer
You are on the motorway. Luggage falls from your vehicle. What should you do?

☑ **A** Stop at the next emergency telephone and contact the police
☐ **B** Stop on the motorway and put on hazard lights while you pick it up
☐ **C** Walk back up the motorway to pick it up
☐ **D** Pull up on the hard shoulder and wave traffic down

If any object falls onto the motorway carriageway from your vehicle pull over onto the hard shoulder near an emergency telephone and phone for assistance. Don't stop on the carriageway or attempt to retrieve anything.

930 Mark *one* answer
While driving, a warning light on your vehicle's instrument panel comes on. You should

☐ **A** continue if the engine sounds all right
☐ **B** hope that it is just a temporary electrical fault
☐ **C** deal with the problem when there is more time
☐ **D** check out the problem quickly and safely

Make sure you know what the different warning lights mean. An illuminated warning light could mean that your car is unsafe to drive. Don't take risks. If you aren't sure about the problem get a qualified mechanic to check it.

931 Mark *one* answer
You have broken down on a two-way road. You have a warning triangle. It should be displayed

☐ **A** on the roof of your vehicle
☐ **B** at least 150 metres (492 feet) behind your vehicle
☐ **C** at least 45 metres (147 feet) behind your vehicle
☐ **D** just behind your vehicle

If you need to display a warning triangle make sure that it can be clearly seen by other road users. Place it on the same side of the road as the broken down vehicle and away from any obstruction that would make it hard to see.

932 Mark *one* answer
Your engine catches fire. What should you do first?

☐ **A** Lift the bonnet and disconnect the battery
☐ **B** Lift the bonnet and warn other traffic
☐ **C** Call a breakdown service
☐ **D** Call the fire brigade

If you suspect a fire in the engine compartment you should pull up as safely and as quickly as possible. DO NOT open the bonnet as this will fuel the fire further. Get any passengers out of the vehicle and dial 999 immediately to contact the fire brigade.

933 Mark *one* answer
Your vehicle breaks down in a tunnel. What should you do?

☐ **A** Stay in your vehicle and wait for the police
☐ **B** Stand in the lane behind your vehicle to warn others
☐ **C** Stand in front of your vehicle to warn oncoming drivers
☐ **D** Switch on hazard lights then go and call for help immediately

A broken-down vehicle in a tunnel can cause serious congestion and danger to other road users. If your vehicle breaks down, get help without delay. Switch on your hazard warning lights, then go to an emergency telephone point to call for help.

934 Mark *one* answer
Your vehicle catches fire while driving through a tunnel. It is still driveable. What should you do?

☐ **A** Leave it where it is with the engine running
☐ **B** Pull up, then walk to an emergency telephone point
☐ **C** Park it away from the carriageway
☑ **D** Drive it out of the tunnel if you can do so

If it's possible, and you can do so without causing further danger, it may be safer to drive a vehicle which is on fire out of a tunnel. The greatest danger in a tunnel fire is smoke and suffocation.

935 Mark *one* answer
You are driving through a tunnel. Your vehicle catches fire. What should you do?

☐ **A** Continue through the tunnel if you can
☐ **B** Turn your vehicle around immediately
☐ **C** Reverse out of the tunnel
☐ **D** Carry out an emergency stop

The main dangers in a tunnel fire are suffocation and smoke. If you can do so safely it's better to drive a burning vehicle out of a tunnel. If you can't do this, pull over, switch off the engine, use hazard warning lights and phone immediately for help. It may be possible to put out a small fire but if it seems large do NOT tackle it!

936 Mark *one* answer
You're in a tunnel. Your vehicle is on fire and you cannot drive it. What should you do?

☐ **A** Stay in the vehicle and close the windows
☐ **B** Switch on hazard warning lights
☐ **C** Leave the engine running
☐ **D** Switch off all of your lights

It's usually better to drive a burning vehicle out of a tunnel. If you can't do this pull over and stop at an emergency point if possible. Switch off the engine, use hazard warning lights, and leave the vehicle immediately. Call for help from the nearest emergency point. If you have an extinguisher it may help to put out a small fire but don't try to tackle a large one.

937 Mark *one* answer
When approaching a tunnel it is good advice to

☐ **A** put on your sunglasses and use the sun visor
☐ **B** check your tyre pressures
☐ **C** change down to a lower gear
☐ **D** make sure your radio is tuned to the frequency shown

On the approach to tunnels a sign will usually show a local radio channel. It should give a warning of any incidents or congestion in the tunnel ahead. Many radios can be set to automatically pick up traffic announcements and local frequencies. If you have to tune the radio manually don't be distracted while doing so. Incidents in tunnels can lead to serious casualties. The greatest hazard is fire. Getting an advance warning of problems could save your life and others.

938 Mark *one* answer
Your vehicle has broken down on an automatic railway level crossing. What should you do FIRST?

☐ **A** Get everyone out of the vehicle and clear of the crossing
☐ **B** Telephone your vehicle recovery service to move it
☐ **C** Walk along the track to give warning to any approaching trains
☐ **D** Try to push the vehicle clear of the crossing as soon as possible

Firstly get yourself and anyone else well away from the crossing. If there's a railway phone use that to get instructions from the signal operator. Then if there's time move the vehicle clear of the crossing.

939 Mark *one* answer
What should you carry for use in the event of a collision?

☐ **A** Road map
☐ **B** Can of petrol
☐ **C** Jump leads
☐ **D** Fire extinguisher

Various items can provide invaluable help in the event of a collision or breakdown – such as a first aid kit and a fire extinguisher. They could even save a life.

940 Mark *one* answer
You have a collision whilst your car is moving. What is the FIRST thing you must do?

☐ **A** Stop only if someone waves at you
☐ **B** Call the emergency services
☐ **C** Stop at the scene of the incident
☐ **D** Call your insurance company

If you are in a collision that causes damage or injury to any other person, vehicle, animal or property, by law you MUST STOP. Give your name, the vehicle owner's name and address, and the vehicle's registration number to anyone who has reasonable grounds for requiring them.

941 Mark *one* answer
You're in collision with another moving vehicle. Someone is injured and your vehicle is damaged. What information should you find out?

☐ **A** Whether the other driver is licensed to drive
☑ **B** The other driver's name, address and telephone number
☐ **C** The destination of the other driver
☐ **D** The occupation of the other driver

Try to keep calm and don't rush. Make sure that you've shared all the relevant details with the other driver before you leave the scene. If possible take pictures and note the positions of all the vehicles involved.

942 Mark *one* answer   **NI**
You lose control of your car and damage a garden wall. No one is around. What must you do?

☐ **A** Report the incident to the police within 24 hours
☐ **B** Go back to tell the house owner the next day
☐ **C** Report the incident to your insurance company when you get home
☐ **D** Find someone in the area to tell them about it immediately

If the property owner is not available at the time, you MUST inform the police of the incident. This should be done as soon as possible, and within 24 hours.

943 Mark *one* answer
You are in a collision on a two-way road. You have a warning triangle with you. At what distance before the obstruction should you place the warning triangle?

☐ **A** 25 metres (82 feet)
☐ **B** 45 metres (147 feet)
☐ **C** 100 metres (328 feet)
☐ **D** 150 metres (492 feet)

This is the minimum distance to place the triangle from the obstruction. If there's a bend or hump in the road place it so that approaching traffic has plenty of time to react to the warning and slow down. You may also need to use your hazard warning lights, especially in poor visibility or at night.

944 Mark *one* answer
You have a collision while driving through a tunnel. You are not injured but your vehicle cannot be driven. What should you do FIRST?

☐ **A** Rely on other drivers phoning for the police
☐ **B** Switch off the engine and switch on hazard lights
☐ **C** Take the names of witnesses and other drivers
☐ **D** Sweep up any debris that is in the road

If you are involved in a collision in a tunnel be aware of the danger this can cause to other traffic. The greatest danger is fire. Put on your hazard warning lights straight away and switch off your engine. Then call for help from an emergency telephone point.

945 Mark *one* answer

You are driving through a tunnel. There has been a collision and the car in front is on fire and blocking the road. What should you do?

☐ **A** Overtake and continue as quickly as you can
☐ **B** Lock all the doors and windows
☐ **C** Switch on hazard warning lights
☐ **D** Stop, then reverse out of the tunnel

If the vehicle in front is on fire, you should pull over to the side and stop. Switch on your warning lights and switch off your engine. If you can locate a fire extinguisher use it to put out the fire, taking great care. Do NOT open the bonnet. Always call for help from the nearest emergency point and if possible give first aid to anyone who is injured.

946 Mark *one* answer

You're towing a small trailer on a busy three-lane motorway. All the lanes are open. You must

☐ **A** not exceed 50mph
☐ **B** not overtake
☐ **C** have a stabiliser fitted
☐ **D** use only the left and centre lanes

The motorway regulations for towing a trailer state that you MUST NOT
• use the right-hand lane of a three-lane motorway, unless directed to do so (for example at roadworks or due to a lane closure)
• exceed 60mph.

947 Mark *one* answer

If a trailer swerves or snakes when you are towing it you should

☑ **A** ease off the accelerator and reduce your speed
☐ **B** let go of the steering wheel and let it correct itself
☐ **C** brake hard and hold the pedal down
☐ **D** increase your speed as quickly as possible

Strong winds or buffeting from large vehicles can cause a trailer or caravan to snake or swerve. If this happens, ease off the accelerator. Don't brake harshly, steer sharply or increase your speed.

948 Mark *one* answer

How can you stop a caravan snaking from side to side?

☐ **A** Turn the steering wheel slowly to each side
☐ **B** Accelerate to increase your speed
☐ **C** Stop as quickly as you can
☐ **D** Slow down very gradually

Keep calm and don't brake harshly or you could lose control completely. Ease off the accelerator until the unit is brought back under control. The most dangerous time is on long downhill gradients.

949 Mark *one* answer

On which occasion should you inflate your tyres to more than their normal pressure?

☐ **A** When the roads are slippery
☐ **B** When the vehicle is fitted with anti-lock brakes
☐ **C** When the tyre tread is worn below 2mm
☐ **D** When carrying a heavy load

Check the vehicle handbook. This should give you guidance on the correct tyre pressures for your vehicle and when you may need to adjust them. If you are carrying a heavy load you may need to adjust the headlights as well. Most cars have a switch on the dashboard to do this.

950 Mark *one* answer
A heavy load on your roof rack will

- ☐ **A** improve the road holding
- ☐ **B** reduce the stopping distance
- ☐ **C** make the steering lighter
- ☐ **D** reduce stability

A heavy load on your roof rack will reduce the stability of the vehicle because it moves the centre of gravity away from that designed by the manufacturer. Be aware of this when you negotiate bends and corners.

If you change direction at speed, your vehicle and/or load could become unstable and you could lose control.

951 Mark *one* answer
You are towing a caravan along a motorway. The caravan begins to swerve from side to side. What should you do?

- ☐ **A** Ease off the accelerator slowly
- ☐ **B** Steer sharply from side to side
- ☐ **C** Do an emergency stop
- ☐ **D** Speed up very quickly

Try not to brake or steer heavily as this will only make matters worse and you could lose control altogether. Keep calm and regain control by easing off the accelerator.

952 Mark *one* answer
Overloading your vehicle can seriously affect the

- ☐ **A** gearbox
- ☐ **B** journey time
- ☐ **C** handling
- ☐ **D** battery life

Any load will have an effect on the handling of your vehicle and this becomes worse as you increase the load. You need to be aware of this when carrying passengers, heavy loads, fitting a roof rack or towing a trailer.

953 Mark *one* answer
Who is responsible for making sure that a vehicle is not overloaded?

- ☐ **A** The driver of the vehicle
- ☐ **B** The owner of the items being carried
- ☐ **C** The person who loaded the vehicle
- ☐ **D** The licensing authority

Your vehicle must not be overloaded. Carrying heavy loads will affect control and handling characteristics. If your vehicle is overloaded and it causes a crash, you'll be held responsible.

954 Mark *one* answer
You are planning to tow a caravan. Which of these will mostly help to aid the vehicle handling?

☐ **A** A jockey wheel fitted to the tow bar
☐ **B** Power steering fitted to the towing vehicle
☐ **C** Anti-lock brakes fitted to the towing vehicle
☐ **D** A stabiliser fitted to the towbar

Towing a caravan or trailer affects the way the tow vehicle handles. It is highly recommended that you take a caravan manoeuvring course. These are provided by various organisations for anyone wishing to tow a trailer.

955 Mark *one* answer
Are passengers allowed to ride in a caravan that is being towed?

☐ **A** Yes, if they are over fourteen
☐ **B** No, not at any time
☐ **C** Only if all the seats in the towing vehicle are full
☐ **D** Only if a stabiliser is fitted

Riding in a towed caravan is highly dangerous. The safety of the entire unit is dependent on the stability of the trailer. Moving passengers would make the caravan unstable and could cause loss of control.

956 Mark *one* answer
A trailer must stay securely hitched up to the towing vehicle. What additional safety device can be fitted to the trailer braking system?

☐ **A** Stabiliser
☐ **B** Jockey wheel
☐ **C** Corner steadies
☐ **D** Breakaway cable

In the event of a tow bar failure the cable activates the trailer brakes, then snaps. This allows the towing vehicle to get free of the trailer and out of danger.

957 Mark *one* answer
Why would you fit a stabiliser before towing a caravan?

☐ **A** It will help with stability when driving in crosswinds
☐ **B** It will allow heavy items to be loaded behind the axle
☐ **C** It will help you to raise and lower the jockey wheel
☐ **D** It will allow you to tow without the breakaway cable

Fitting a stabiliser to your tow bar will help to reduce snaking by the caravan especially where there are crosswinds. However, this does not take away your responsibility to ensure that your vehicle/caravan combination is loaded correctly.

Section 14 – **Vehicle loading**

958 Mark *one* answer
You wish to tow a trailer. Where would you find the maximum noseweight of your vehicle's tow ball?

- [ ] **A** In the vehicle handbook
- [ ] **B** In The Highway Code
- [ ] **C** In your vehicle registration certificate
- [ ] **D** In your licence documents

You must know how to load your trailer or caravan so that the hitch exerts a downward force onto the tow ball. This information can be found in your vehicle handbook or from your vehicle manufacturer's agent.

959 Mark *one* answer
Any load that is carried on a roof rack should be

- [ ] **A** securely fastened when driving
- [ ] **B** loaded towards the rear of the vehicle
- [ ] **C** visible in your exterior mirror
- [ ] **D** covered with plastic sheeting

The safest way to carry items on the roof is in a specially designed roof box. This will help to keep your luggage secure and dry, and also has less wind resistance than loads carried on a roof rack.

960 Mark *one* answer
You are carrying a child in your car. They are under three years of age. Which of these is a suitable restraint?

- [ ] **A** A child seat
- [ ] **B** An adult holding a child
- [ ] **C** An adult seat belt
- [ ] **D** An adult lap belt

It's your responsibility to ensure that all children in your car are secure. Suitable restraints include a child seat, baby seat, booster seat or booster cushion. It's essential that any restraint used should be suitable for the child's size and weight, and fitted to the manufacturers instructions.

Part 5: Glossary

Accelerate

To make the vehicle move faster by pressing the right-hand pedal.

Advanced stop lines

A marked area on the road at traffic lights, which permits cyclists or buses to wait in front of other traffic.

Adverse weather

Bad weather that makes driving difficult or dangerous.

Alert

Quick to notice possible hazards.

Anticipation

Looking out for hazards and taking action before a problem starts.

Anti-lock brakes

Brakes that stop the wheels locking so that you are less likely to skid on a slippery road.

Aquaplane

To slide out of control on a wet road surface.

Articulated vehicle

A long vehicle that is divided into two or more sections joined by cables.

Attitude

The way you think or feel, which affects the way you drive. Especially, whether you are patient and polite, or impatient and aggressive.

Automatic

A vehicle with gears that change by themselves as you speed up or slow down.

Awareness

Taking notice of the road and traffic conditions around you at all times.

Black ice

An invisible film of ice that forms over the road surface, creating very dangerous driving conditions.

Blind spot

The section of road behind you which you cannot see in your mirrors. You 'cover' your blind spot by looking over your shoulder before moving off or overtaking.

Brake fade

Loss of power to the brakes when you have been using them for a long time without taking your foot off the brake pedal. For example, when driving down a steep hill. The brakes will overheat and not work properly.

Braking distance

The distance you must allow to slow the vehicle in order to come to a stop.

Brow

The highest point of a hill.

Built-up area

A town, or place with lots of buildings.

Carriageway

One side of a road or motorway. A 'dual carriageway' has a central reservation.

Catalytic converter

A piece of equipment fitted in the exhaust system that changes harmful gases into less harmful ones.

Chicane

A sharp double bend that has been put into a road to make traffic slow down.

Child restraint

A child seat or special seat belt for children. It keeps them safe and stops them moving around in the car.

Clearway

A road where no stopping is allowed at any time. The sign for a clearway is a red cross in a red circle on a blue background.

Coasting

Driving a vehicle without using any of the gears. That is, with your foot on the clutch pedal and the car in neutral.

Commentary driving

Talking to yourself about what you see on the road ahead and what action you are going to take – an aid to concentration.

Comprehensive insurance

A motor insurance policy that pays for all repairs even if you cause an accident.

Concentration

Keeping all your attention on your driving.

Conditions

How good or bad the road surface is, volume of traffic on the road, and what the weather is like.

Congestion

Heavy traffic that makes it difficult to get to where you want to go.

Consideration

Thinking about other road users and not just yourself. For example, letting another driver go first at a junction, or stopping at a zebra crossing to let pedestrians cross over.

Contraflow

When traffic on a motorway follows signs to move to the opposite carriageway for a short distance because of roadworks. (During a contraflow, there is traffic driving in both directions on the same side of the motorway.)

Coolant

Liquid in the radiator that removes heat from the engine.

Defensive driving

Driving safely without taking risks, looking out for hazards and thinking for others.

Disqualified

Stopped from doing something (eg driving) by law, because you have broken the law.

Distraction

Anything that stops you concentrating on your driving, such as chatting to passengers or on your mobile phone.

Document

An official paper or card, eg your driving licence.

Dual carriageway

A road or motorway with a central reservation.

Engine braking – *see also* gears

Using the low gears to keep your speed down. For example, when you are driving down a steep hill and you want to stop the vehicle running away. Using the gears instead of braking will help to prevent brake fade.

Environment

The world around us and the air we breathe.

Equestrian crossing

An unusual kind of crossing. It has a button high up for horse riders to push.

Exceed

Go higher than an upper limit.

Exhaust emissions

Gases that come out of the exhaust pipe to form part of the outside air.

Field of vision

How far you can see in front and around you when you are driving.

Filler cap

Provides access to the vehicle's fuel tank, for filling up with petrol or diesel.

Fog lights

Extra bright rear (and sometimes front) lights which may be switched on in conditions of very poor visibility. You must remember to switch them off when visibility improves, as they can dazzle and distract other drivers.

Ford

A place in a stream or river which is shallow enough to drive across with care.

Four-wheel drive (4WD)

On a conventional vehicle, steering and engine speed affect just two 'drive' wheels. On 4WD, they affect all four wheels, ensuring optimum grip on loose ground.

Frustration

Feeling annoyed because you cannot drive as fast as you want to because of other drivers or heavy traffic.

Fuel consumption

The amount of fuel (petrol or diesel) that your vehicle uses. Different vehicles have different rates of consumption. Increased fuel consumption means using more fuel. Decreased fuel consumption means using less fuel.

Fuel gauge

A display or dial on the instrument panel that tells you how much fuel (petrol or diesel) you have left.

Gantry

An overhead platform like a high narrow bridge that displays electric signs on a motorway.

Gears

Control the speed of the engine in relation to the vehicle's speed. May be hand operated (manual) or automatically controlled. In a low gear (such as first or second) the engine runs more slowly. In a high gear (such as fourth or fifth), it runs more quickly. Putting the car into a lower gear as you drive can create the effect of engine braking – forcing the engine to run more slowly.

Handling

How well your vehicle moves or responds when you steer or brake.

Harass

To drive in away that makes other road users afraid.

Hard shoulder

The single lane to the left of the inside lane on a motorway, which is for emergency use only. You should not drive on the hard shoulder except in an emergency, or when there are signs telling you to use the hard shoulder because of roadworks.

Harsh braking (or harsh acceleration)

Using the brake or accelerator too hard so as to cause wear on the engine.

Hazard warning lights

Flashing amber lights which you should use only when you have broken down. On a motorway you can use them to warn other drivers behind of a hazard ahead.

Glossary

High-sided vehicle

A van or truck with tall sides, or a tall trailer such as a caravan or horse-box, that is at risk of being blown off-course in strong winds.

Impatient

Not wanting to wait for pedestrians and other road users.

Inflate

To blow up – to put air in your tyres until they are at the right pressures.

Instrument panel

The car's electrical controls and gauges, set behind the steering wheel. Also called the dashboard.

Intimidate

To make someone feel afraid.

Involved

Being part of something. For example, being one of the drivers in an accident.

Jump leads

A pair of thick electric cables with clips at either end. You use it to charge a flat battery by connecting it to the live battery in another vehicle.

Junction

A place where two or more roads join.

Liability

Being legally responsible.

Manoeuvre

Using the controls to make your car move in a particular direction. For example turning, reversing or parking.

Manual

By hand. In a car that is a 'manual' or has manual gears, you have to change the gears yourself.

Maximum

The largest possible; 'maximum speed' is the highest speed allowed.

Minimum

The smallest possible.

Mirrors

Modern cars have a minimum of three rear view mirrors: one in the centre of the windscreen, and one on each front door. Additional mirrors may be required on longer vehicles, or when towing a high trailer such as a caravan. Some mirrors may be curved (convex or concave) to increase the field of vision. The mirror on the windscreen can be turned to anti-dazzle position, if glare from headlights behind creates a distraction.

Mobility

The ability to move around easily.

Monotonous

Boring. For example, a long stretch of motorway with no variety and nothing interesting to see.

MOT

The test that proves your car is safe to drive. Your MOT certificate is one of the important documents for your vehicle.

Motorway

A fast road that has two or more lanes on each side and a hard shoulder. Drivers must join or leave it on the left, via a motorway junction. Many kinds of slower vehicles – such as bicycles – are not allowed on motorways.

Multiple-choice questions

Questions with several possible answers where you have to try to choose the right one.

Observation

The ability to notice important information, such as hazards developing ahead.

Obstruct

To get in the way of another road user.

Octagonal

Having eight sides.

Oil level

The amount of oil needed for the engine to run effectively. The oil level should be checked as part of your regular maintenance routine, and the oil replaced as necessary.

Pedestrian

A person walking.

Pelican crossing

A crossing with traffic lights that pedestrians can use by pushing a button. Cars must give way to pedestrians on the crossing while the amber light is flashing. You must give pedestrians enough time to get to the other side of the road.

Perception

Seeing or noticing (as in Hazard Perception).

Peripheral vision

The area around the edges of your field of vision.

Positive attitude

Being sensible and obeying the law when you drive.

Priority

The vehicle or other road user that is allowed by law to go first is the one that has priority.

Provisional licence

A first driving licence. all learner drivers must get one before they start having lessons.

Puffin crossing

A type of pedestrian crossing that does not have a flashing amber light phase.

Reaction time

The amount of time it takes you to see a hazard and decide what to do about it.

Red route

You see these in London and some other cities. Double red lines at the edge of the road tell you that you must not stop or park there at any time. Single red lines have notices with times when you must not stop or park. Some red routes have marked bays for either parking or loading at certain times.

Red warning triangle

An item of safety equipment to carry in your car in case you break down. You can place the triangle 45m behind your car on the same side of the road. It warns traffic that your vehicle is causing an obstruction. (Do not use these on motorways.)

Residential areas

Areas of housing where people live. The speed limit is 30mph or sometimes 20mph.

Road hump

A low bump built across the road to slow vehicles down. Also called 'sleeping policemen'.

Rumble strips

Raised strips across the road near a roundabout or junction that change the sound the tyres make on the road surface, warning drivers to slow down. They are also used on motorways to separate the main carriageway from the hard shoulder.

Safety margin

The amount of space you need to leave between your vehicle and the one in front so that you are not in danger of crashing into it if the driver slows down suddenly or stops. Safety margins have to be longer in wet or icy conditions.

Separation distance

The amount of space you need to leave between your vehicle and the one in front so that you are not in danger of crashing into it if the driver slows down suddenly or stops. The separation distance must be longer in wet or icy conditions.

Security coded radio

To deter thieves, a radio or CD unit which requires a security code (or pin number) to operate it.

Single carriageway

Generally, a road with one lane in each direction.

Skid

When the tyres fail to grip the surface of the road, the subsequent loss of control of the vehicle's movement is called a skid. Usually caused by harsh or fierce braking, steering or acceleration.

Snaking

Moving from side to side. This sometimes happens with caravans or trailers when you drive too fast, or they are not properly loaded.

Staggered junction

Where you drive cross another road. Instead of going straight across, you have to go a bit to the right or left.

Steering

Control of the direction of the vehicle. May be affected by road surface conditions: when the steering wheel turns very easily, steering is 'light', and when you have to pull hard on the wheel it is described as 'heavy'.

Sterile

Clean and free from bacteria.

Stopping distance

The time it takes for you to stop your vehicle – made up of 'thinking distance' and 'braking distance'.

Supervisor

Someone who sits in the passenger seat with a learner driver. They must be over 21 and have held a full driving licence for at least three years.

Tailgating

Driving too closely behind another vehicle – either to harass the driver in front or to help you in thick fog.

Thinking distance

The time it takes you to notice something and take the right action. You need to add thinking distance to your braking distance to make up your total stopping distance.

Third party insurance

An insurance policy that insures you against any claim by passengers or other persons for damage or injury to their person or property.

Toucan crossing

A type of pedestrian crossing that does not have a flashing amber light phase, and cyclists are allowed to ride across.

Tow

To pull something behind your vehicle. It could be a caravan or trailer.

Traffic-calming measures

Speed humps, chicanes and other devices placed in roads to slow traffic down.

Tram

A public transport vehicle which moves along the streets on fixed rails, usually electrically powered by overhead lines.

Tread depth

The depth of the grooves in a car's tyres that help them grip the road surface. The grooves must all be at least 1.6mm deep.

Turbulence

Strong movement of air. For example, when a large vehicle passes a much smaller one.

Two-second rule

In normal driving, the ideal minimum distance between you and the vehicle in front can be timed using the 'two-second' rule. As the vehicle in front passes a fixed object (such as a signpost), say to yourself 'Only a fool breaks the two second rule'. It takes two seconds to say it. If you have passed the same object before you finish, you are too close – pull back.

Tyre pressures

The amount of air which must be pumped into a tyre in order for it to be correctly blown up.

Vehicle Excise Duty

The tax you pay for your vehicle so that you may drive it on public roads.

Vehicle Registration Certificate

A record of details about a vehicle and its owner, also known as a log book.

Vehicle watch scheme

A system for identifying vehicles that may have been stolen.

Vulnerable

At risk of harm or injury.

Waiting restrictions

Times when you may not park or load your vehicle in a particular area.

Wheel balancing

To ensure smooth rotation at all speeds, wheels need to be 'balanced' correctly. This is a procedure done at a garage or tyre centre, when each wheel is removed for testing. Balancing may involve minor adjustment with the addition of small weights, to avoid wheel wobble.

Wheel-spin

When the vehicle's wheels spin round out of control with no grip on the road surface.

Zebra crossing

A pedestrian crossing without traffic lights. It has an orange light, and is marked by black and white stripes on the road. Drivers must stop for pedestrians to cross.

Part 6: Answers to theory test revision questions

Answers to questions

Section 1 – Alertness

1 C	2 B	3 D	4 C	5 C	6 C	7 C	8 B	9 C
10 B	11 A	12 A	13 B	14 D	15 B	16 A	17 A	18 B
19 B	20 B	21 C	22 B	23 B	24 C	25 D	26 D	27 D
28 B	29 D	30 B	31 D	32 C	33 C	34 A	35 D	36 B
37 D								

Section 2 – Attitude

38 D	39 A	40 C	41 D	42 D	43 B	44 B	45 A	46 A
47 D	48 B	49 A	50 B	51 A	52 A	53 C	54 A	55 D
56 D	57 D	58 A	59 B	60 C	61 B	62 A	63 B	64 C
65 A	66 C	67 A	68 C	69 C	70 D	71 B	72 D	73 B
74 C	75 A	76 A	77 B	78 A	79 A	80 B	81 B	82 C
83 B	84 D	85 D	86 C	87 C				

Section 3 – Safety and your vehicle

88 A	89 C	90 C	91 C	92 B	93 D	94 C	95 D	96 D
97 D	98 A	99 C	100 D	101 B	102 B	103 D	104 B	105 D
106 A	107 A	108 B	109 C	110 D	111 A	112 B	113 C	114 D
115 A	116 B	117 A	118 B	119 B	120 B	121 D	122 D	123 B
124 C	125 A	126 D	127 A	128 B	129 D	130 D	131 D	132 B
133 B	134 B	135 D	136 B	137 A	138 C	139 D	140 A	141 B
142 D	143 B	144 B	145 B	146 D	147 C	148 B	149 D	150 D
151 B	152 A	153 D	154 C	155 A	156 A	157 B	158 D	159 C
160 C	161 A	162 A	163 D	164 C	165 B	166 B	167 B	168 A
169 D	170 B	171 D	172 C	173 A	174 D	175 C	176 B	177 A
178 B	179 D	180 B	181 C	182 D	183 D	184 B	185 A	186 D
187 B	188 C	189 D	190 D	191 C	192 D	193 B	194 B	195 C
196 A	197 A	198 A	199 D					

Section 4 – Safety margins

200 D	201 D	202 D	203 A	204 B	205 D	206 B	207 D	208 C
209 C	210 B	211 B	212 C	213 A	214 C	215 A	216 D	217 A
218 B	219 A	220 B	221 D	222 C	223 B	224 B	225 D	226 A
227 C	228 A	229 C	230 B	231 B	232 C	233 B	234 B	235 C
236 C	237 B	238 D	239 C	240 D	241 D	242 A	243 D	244 B
245 D	246 A	247 D	248 A	249 A	250 C	251 B	252 C	253 B
254 B	255 B	256 C	257 D	258 C				

Section 5 – Hazard awareness

259 C	260 C	261 A	262 D	263 C	264 C	265 C	266 D	267 B
268 A	269 A	270 A	271 C	272 C	273 B	274 A	275 C	276 D
277 B	278 B	279 C	280 A	281 D	282 D	283 C	284 B	285 C
286 B	287 A	288 A	289 A	290 C	291 A	292 D	293 B	294 C
295 C	296 A	297 B	298 B	299 B	300 B	301 A	302 D	303 A
304 B	305 C	306 B	307 B	308 B	309 C	310 D	311 C	312 C
313 A	314 B	315 A	316 A	317 B	318 B	319 C	320 C	321 C
322 A	323 C	324 D	325 D	326 C	327 C	328 D	329 B	330 D
331 C	332 B	333 B	334 C	335 D	336 A	337 A	338 A	339 D
340 D	341 D	342 A	343 B	344 D	345 D	346 A	347 C	348 B
349 A	350 B	351 D	352 A	353 B	354 A			

Section 6 – Vulnerable road users

355 D	356 D	357 C	358 C	359 B	360 D	361 D	362 C	363 D
364 A	365 D	366 D	367 B	368 D	369 D	370 C	371 C	372 C
373 A	374 D	375 C	376 D	377 D	378 C	379 C	380 D	381 A
382 D	383 C	384 C	385 D	386 D	387 B	388 A	389 C	390 D
391 C	392 C	393 A	394 D	395 A	396 A	397 B	398 B	399 A
400 A	401 C	402 B	403 D	404 A	405 D	406 D	407 D	408 A
409 C	410 B	411 B	412 D	413 B	414 B	415 D	416 C	417 C
418 B	419 C	420 A	421 C	422 C	423 B	424 B	425 D	426 D
427 B	428 B	429 B	430 C	431 D	432 A	433 D	434 C	435 D

Section 7 – Other types of vehicle

436 A	437 A	438 B	439 B	440 D	441 B	442 B	443 A	444 C
445 B	446 D	447 B	448 D	449 D	450 A	451 D	452 A	453 A
454 A	455 B	456 B	457 C	458 B	459 D	460 B	461 D	462 D

Section 8 – Vehicle handling

463 A	464 A	465 D	466 D	467 A	468 C	469 C	470 D	471 C
472 D	473 D	474 C	475 C	476 C	477 B	478 B	479 D	480 D
481 B	482 C	483 C	484 D	485 A	486 A	487 C	488 B	489 A
490 D	491 B	492 B	493 D	494 B	495 A	496 C	497 B	498 A
499 C	500 A	501 C	502 D	503 B	504 D	505 D	506 D	507 C
508 C	509 C	510 D	511 D	512 A	513 C	514 A	515 A	516 A
517 C	518 B	519 D	520 B	521 D	522 C	523 B	524 D	

Answers to questions

525 D	526 D	527 D	528 A	529 C	530 C	531 C	532 A	533 C
534 C	535 C	536 C	537 C	538 C	539 B	540 B	541 A	542 B
543 D	544 C	545 A	546 A	547 D	548 B	549 A	550 A	551 C
552 B	553 B	554 D	555 A	556 A	557 B	558 D	559 D	560 B
561 D	562 D	563 C	564 D	565 C	566 D	567 A	568 C	569 D
570 C	571 B	572 D	573 B	574 D	575 B	576 D	577 C	578 D
579 A	580 B	581 B	582 D	583 A	584 D	585 C	586 B	587 C
588 D	589 A	590 B	591 A					

Section 10 – **Rules of the road**

592 C	593 D	594 B	595 A	596 C	597 D	598 D	599 A	600 B
601 A	602 B	603 A	604 D	605 A	606 D	607 C	608 A	609 C
610 C	611 D	612 B	613 B	614 A	615 C	616 A	617 B	618 D
619 B	620 A	621 B	622 A	623 B	624 A	625 A	626 D	627 A
628 D	629 D	630 B	631 C	632 B	633 B	634 B	635 C	636 D
637 D	638 C	639 D	640 D	641 D	642 D	643 D	644 C	645 C
646 D	647 A	648 A	649 C	650 B	651 A	652 D	653 A	654 A
655 D	656 B	657 D	658 D	659 A	660 A	661 A	662 D	663 D
664 A	665 A	666 A						

Section 11 – **Road and traffic signs**

667 D	668 D	669 A	670 A	671 B	672 A	673 D	674 B	675 D
676 D	677 D	678 A	679 C	680 B	681 D	682 C	683 B	684 A
685 B	686 B	687 C	688 C	689 A	690 C	691 B	692 C	693 D
694 D	695 C	696 C	697 D	698 A	699 D	700 D	701 B	702 A
703 A	704 A	705 B	706 B	707 A	708 D	709 A	710 C	711 A
712 B	713 C	714 B	715 D	716 A	717 A	718 C	719 D	720 A
721 C	722 B	723 D	724 B	725 B	726 C	727 C	728 D	729 C
730 B	731 C	732 D	733 B	734 A	735 A	736 C	737 D	738 A
739 C	740 C	741 B	742 A	743 C	744 A	745 A	746 D	747 D
748 B	749 A	750 D	751 C	752 D	753 C	754 B	755 C	756 C
757 A	758 B	759 D	760 B	761 B	762 A	763 D	764 A	765 B
766 B	767 D	768 C	769 B	770 A	771 B	772 C	773 A	774 B
775 A	776 C	777 B	778 B	779 A	780 C	781 A	782 B	783 B
784 B	785 A	786 C	787 A	788 C	789 B	790 D	791 C	792 B
793 C	794 A	795 C	796 A	797 C	798 B	799 C	800 A	801 B
802 A	803 A	804 C	805 D	806 B	807 B	808 B	809 B	810 D
811 A	812 B	813 A	814 A	815 C	816 C	817 B	818 B	819 B
820 B	821 B	822 A						

Section 12 – Documents

823 C	824 B	825 B	826 A	827 C	828 C	829 A	830 A	831 C
832 D	833 C	834 A	835 A	836 B	837 B	838 C	839 C	840 B
841 D	842 D	843 D	844 B	845 C	846 A	847 B	848 A	849 D
850 B	851 B	852 D	853 B	854 C	855 B	856 C	857 D	858 B
859 D	860 A	861 B	862 A	863 C	864 B	865 D	866 D	

Section 13 – Incidents, accidents and emergencies

867 A	868 A	869 A	870 C	871 B	872 D	873 B	874 B	875 D
876 B	877 D	878 B	879 D	880 B	881 A	882 C	883 B	884 D
885 A	886 A	887 A	888 C	889 A	890 B	891 A	892 D	893 A
894 C	895 C	896 B	897 A	898 B	899 B	900 D	901 C	902 D
903 D	904 C	905 B	906 D	907 B	908 B	909 B	910 D	911 B
912 B	913 B	914 A	915 B	916 C	917 B	918 C	919 C	920 C
921 A	922 B	923 A	924 B	925 C	926 A	927 A	928 B	929 A
930 D	931 C	932 D	933 D	934 D	935 A	936 B	937 D	938 A
939 D	940 C	941 B	942 A	943 B	944 B	945 C		

Section 14 – Vehicle loading

946 D	947 A	948 D	949 D	950 D	951 A	952 C	953 A	954 D
955 B	956 D	957 A	958 A	959 A	960 A			

Part 7:
The Highway
Code

Contents   Page

Introduction

This Highway Code applies to England, Scotland and Wales. *The Highway Code* is essential reading for everyone.

The most vulnerable road users are pedestrians, particularly children, older or disabled people, cyclists, motorcyclists and horse riders. It is important that all road users are aware of The Code and are considerate towards each other. This applies to pedestrians as much as to drivers and riders.

Many of the rules in the Code are legal requirements, and if you disobey these rules you are committing a criminal offence. You may be fined, given penalty points on your licence or be disqualified from driving. In the most serious cases you may be sent to prison. Such rules are identified by the use of the words **'MUST/MUST NOT'**. In addition, the rule includes an abbreviated reference to the legislation which creates the offence. An explanation of the abbreviations is given in Annexe 4 – The road user and the law.

Although failure to comply with the other rules of the Code will not, in itself, cause a person to be prosecuted, *The Highway Code* may be used in evidence in any court proceedings under the Traffic Acts (see Annexe 4 – The road user and the law) to establish liability. This includes rules which use advisory wording such as 'should/should not' or 'do/do not'.

Knowing and applying the rules contained in *The Highway Code* could significantly reduce road casualties. Cutting the number of deaths and injuries that occur on our roads every day is a responsibility we all share. *The Highway Code* can help us discharge that responsibility.

Rules for pedestrians

General guidance

1. Pavements (including any path along the side of a road) should be used if provided. Where possible, avoid being next to the kerb with your back to the traffic. If you have to step into the road, look both ways first. Always show due care and consideration for others.

2. If there is no pavement keep to the right-hand side of the road so that you can see oncoming traffic. You should take extra care and
• be prepared to walk in single file, especially on narrow roads or in poor light
• keep close to the side of the road.
It may be safer to cross the road well before a sharp right-hand bend so that oncoming traffic has a better chance of seeing you. Cross back after the bend.

3. Help other road users to see you. Wear or carry something light-coloured, bright or fluorescent in poor daylight conditions. When it is dark, use reflective materials (e.g. armbands, sashes, waistcoats, jackets, footwear), which can be seen by drivers using headlights up to three times as far away as non-reflective materials.

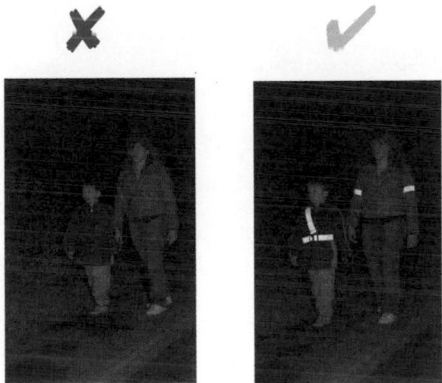

Rule 3: Help yourself to be seen

4. Young children should not be out alone on the pavement or road (see Rule 7). When taking children out, keep between them and the traffic and hold their hands firmly. Strap very young children into push-chairs or use reins. When pushing a young child in a buggy, do not push the buggy into the road when checking to see if it is clear to cross, particularly from between parked vehicles.

5. Organised walks. Large groups of people walking together should use a pavement if available; if one is not, they should keep to the left. Look-outs should be positioned at the front and back of the group, and they should wear fluorescent clothes in daylight and reflective clothes in the dark. At night, the look-out in front should show a white light and the one at the back a red light. People on the outside of large groups should also carry lights and wear reflective clothing.

6. Motorways. Pedestrians **MUST NOT** be on motorways or slip roads except in an emergency (see Rules 271 and 275).

Laws RTRA sect 17, MT(E&W)R 1982 as amended, reg 15(1)(b) & MT(S)R reg 13

Crossing the road

7. The Green Cross Code. The advice given below on crossing the road is for all pedestrians. Children should be taught the Code and should not be allowed out alone until they can understand and use it properly. The age when they can do this is different for each child. Many children cannot judge how fast vehicles are going or how far away they are. Children learn by example, so parents and carers should always use the Code in full when out with their children. They are responsible for deciding at what age children can use it safely by themselves.

A. First find a safe place to cross and where there is space to reach the pavement on the other side. Where there is a crossing nearby, use it. It is safer to cross using a subway, a footbridge, an island, a zebra, pelican, toucan or puffin crossing, or where there is a crossing point controlled by a police officer, a school crossing patrol or a traffic warden. Otherwise choose a place where you can see clearly in all directions. Try to avoid crossing between parked cars (see Rule 14), on a blind bend, or close to the brow of a hill. Move to a space where drivers and riders can see you clearly. Do not cross the road diagonally.

Rule 7: Look all around and listen for traffic before crossing

B. Stop just before you get to the kerb, where you can see if anything is coming. Do not get too close to the traffic. If there's no pavement, keep back from the edge of the road but make sure you can still see approaching traffic.

C. Look all around for traffic and listen. Traffic could come from any direction. Listen as well, because you can sometimes hear traffic before you see it.

D. If traffic is coming, let it pass. Look all around again and listen. Do not cross until there is a safe gap in the traffic and you are certain that there is plenty of time. Remember, even if traffic is a long way off, it may be approaching very quickly.

E. When it is safe, go straight across the road – do not run. Keep looking and listening for traffic while you cross, in case there is any traffic you did not see, or in case other traffic appears suddenly. Look out for cyclists and motorcyclists travelling between lanes of traffic. Do not walk diagonally across the road.

8. At a junction. When crossing the road, look out for traffic turning into the road, especially from behind you. If you have started crossing and traffic wants to turn into the road, you have priority and they should give way (see Rule 170).

9. Pedestrian Safety Barriers. Where there are barriers, cross the road only at the gaps provided for pedestrians. Do not climb over the barriers or walk between them and the road.

10. Tactile paving. Raised surfaces that can be felt underfoot provide warning and guidance to blind or partially sighted people. The most common surfaces are a series of raised studs, which are used at crossing points with a dropped kerb, or a series of rounded raised bars which are used at level crossings, at the top and bottom of steps and at some other hazards.

11. One-way streets. Check which way the traffic is moving. Do not cross until it is safe to do so without stopping. Bus and cycle lanes may operate in the opposite direction to the rest of the traffic.

12. Bus and cycle lanes. Take care when crossing these lanes as traffic may be moving faster than in the other lanes, or against the flow of traffic.

13. Routes shared with cyclists. Some cycle tracks run alongside footpaths or pavements, using a segregating feature to separate cyclists from people on foot. Segregated routes may also incorporate short lengths of tactile paving to help visually impaired people stay on the correct side. On the pedestrian side this will comprise a series of flat-topped bars running across the direction of travel (ladder pattern). On the cyclist side the same bars are orientated in the direction of travel (tramline pattern). Not all routes which are shared with cyclists are segregated. Take extra care where this is so (see Rule 62).

14. Parked vehicles. If you have to cross between parked vehicles, use the outside edges of the vehicles as if they were the kerb. Stop there and make sure you can see all around and that the traffic can see you. Make sure there is a gap between any parked vehicles on the other side, so you can reach the pavement. Never cross the road in front of, or behind, any vehicle with its engine running, especially a large vehicle, as the driver may not be able to see you.

15. Reversing vehicles. Never cross behind a vehicle which is reversing, showing white reversing lights or sounding a warning.

16. Moving vehicles. You **MUST NOT** get onto or hold onto a moving vehicle.
Law RTA 1988 sect 26

17. At night. Wear something reflective to make it easier for others to see you (see Rule 3). If there is no pedestrian crossing nearby, cross the road near a street light so that traffic can see you more easily.

Crossings

18. At all crossings. When using any type of crossing you should
• always check that the traffic has stopped before you start to cross or push a pram onto a crossing
• always cross between the studs or over the zebra markings. Do not cross at the side of the crossing or on the zig-zag lines, as it can be dangerous.
You **MUST NOT** loiter on any type of crossing.
Laws ZPPPCRGD reg 19 & RTRA sect 25(5)

19. Zebra crossings. Give traffic plenty of time to see you and to stop before you start to cross. Vehicles will need more time when the road is slippery. Wait until traffic has stopped from both directions or the road is clear before crossing. Remember that traffic does not have to stop until someone has moved onto the crossing. Keep looking both ways, and listening, in case a driver or rider has not seen you and attempts to overtake a vehicle that has stopped.

Rule 19: Zebra crossings have flashing beacons

20. Where there is an island in the middle of a zebra crossing, wait on the island and follow Rule 19 before you cross the second half of the road – it is a separate crossing.

Rule 20: Zebra crossings with a central island are two separate crossings

21. At traffic lights. There may be special signals for pedestrians. You should only start to cross the road when the green figure shows. If you have started to cross the road and the green figure goes out, you should still have time to reach the other side, but do not delay. If no pedestrian signals have been provided, watch carefully and do not cross until the traffic lights are red and the traffic has stopped. Keep looking and check for traffic that may be turning the corner. Remember that traffic lights may let traffic move in some lanes while traffic in other lanes has stopped.

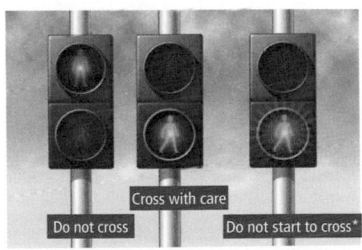

Rule 21: At traffic lights, puffin and pelican crossings
*At pelican crossings only

22. Pelican crossings. These are signal-controlled crossings operated by pedestrians. Push the control button to activate the traffic signals. When the red figure shows, do not cross. When a steady green figure shows, check the traffic has stopped then cross with care. When the green figure begins to flash you should not start to cross. If you have already started you should have time to finish crossing safely.

23. Puffin crossings differ from pelican crossings as the red and green figures are above the control box on your side of the road and there is no flashing green figure phase. Press the button and wait for the green figure to show.

24. When the road is congested, traffic on your side of the road may be forced to stop even though their lights are green. Traffic may still be moving on the other side of the road, so press the button and wait for the signal to cross.

25. Toucan crossings are light-controlled crossings which allow cyclists and pedestrians to share crossing space and cross at the same time. They are push-button operated. Pedestrians and cyclists will see the green signal together. Cyclists are permitted to ride across.

Rule 25: Toucan crossings can be used by both cyclists and pedestrians

26. At some crossings there is a bleeping sound or voice signal to indicate to blind or partially sighted people when the steady green figure is showing, and there may be a tactile signal to help deafblind people.

27. Equestrian crossings are for horse riders. They have pavement barriers, wider crossing spaces, horse and rider figures in the light panels and either two sets of controls (one higher), or just one higher control panel.

Rule 27: Equestrian crossings are used by horse riders
There is often a parallel crossing

28. 'Staggered' pelican or puffin crossings. When the crossings on each side of the central refuge are not in line they are two separate crossings. On reaching the central island, press the button again and wait for a steady green figure.

Rule 28: Staggered crossings (with an island in the middle)
are two separate crossings

29. Crossings controlled by an authorised person. Do not cross the road unless you are signalled to do so by a police officer, traffic warden or school crossing patrol. Always cross in front of them.

30. Where there are no controlled crossing points available it is advisable to cross where there is an island in the middle of the road. Use the Green Cross Code (see Rule 7) to cross to the island and then stop and use it again to cross the second half of the road.

Situations needing extra care

31. Emergency vehicles. If an ambulance, fire engine, police or other emergency vehicle approaches using flashing blue lights, headlights and/or sirens, keep off the road.

32. Buses. Get on or off a bus only when it has stopped to allow you to do so. Watch out for cyclists when you are getting off. Never cross the road directly behind or in front of a bus. Wait until it has moved off and you can see clearly in both directions.

33. Tramways. These may run through pedestrian areas. Their path will be marked out by shallow kerbs, changes in the paving or other road surface, white lines or yellow dots. Cross at designated crossings where provided. Elsewhere treat trams as you would other road vehicles and look both ways along the track before crossing. Do not walk along the track as trams may come up behind you. Trams move quietly and cannot steer to avoid you.

34. Railway level crossings. You **MUST NOT** cross or pass a stop line when the red lights show, (including a red pedestrian figure). Also do not cross if an alarm is sounding or the barriers are being lowered. The tone of the alarm may change if another train is approaching. If there are no lights, alarms or barriers, stop, look both ways and listen before crossing. A tactile surface comprising rounded bars running across the direction of pedestrian travel may be installed on the footpath approaching a level crossing to warn visually impaired people of its presence. The tactile surface should extend across the full width of the footway and should be located at an appropriate distance from the barrier or projected line of the barrier.
Law TSRGD, reg 52

35. Street and pavement repairs. A pavement may be closed temporarily because it is not safe to use. Take extra care if you are directed to walk in or to cross the road.

Rules for users of powered wheelchairs and powered mobility scooters

Powered wheelchairs and mobility scooters
(Called Invalid Carriages in law)

36. There is one class of manual wheelchair (called a Class 1 invalid carriage) and two classes of powered wheelchairs and powered mobility scooters. Manual wheelchairs and Class 2 vehicles are those with an upper speed limit of 4mph (6km/h) and are designed to be used on pavements. Class 3 vehicles are those with an upper speed limit of 8mph (12km/h) and are equipped to be used on the road as well as the pavement.

37. When you are on the road you should obey the guidance and rules for other vehicles; when on the pavement you should follow the guidance and rules for pedestrians.

On pavements

38. Pavements are safer than roads and should be used when available. You should give pedestrians priority and show consideration for other pavement users, particularly those with a hearing or visual impairment who may not be aware that you are there.

39. Powered wheelchairs and scooters **MUST NOT** travel faster than 4mph (6km/h) on pavements or in pedestrian areas. You may need to reduce your speed to adjust to other pavement users who may not be able to move out of your way quickly enough or where the pavement is too narrow.
Law UICHR 1988 reg 4

40. When moving off the pavement onto the road, you should take special care. Before moving off, always look round and make sure it's safe to join the traffic. Always try to use dropped kerbs when moving off the pavement, even if this means travelling further to locate one. If you have to climb or descend a kerb, always approach it at right angles and don't try to negotiate a kerb higher than the vehicle manufacturer's recommendations.

On the road

41. You should take care when travelling on the road as you may be travelling more slowly than other traffic (your machine is restricted to 8mph (12km/h) and may be less visible).

42. When on the road, Class 3 vehicles should travel in the direction of the traffic. Class 2 users should always use the pavement when it is available. When there is no pavement, you should use caution when on the road. Class 2 users should, where possible, travel in the direction of the traffic. If you are travelling at night when lights **MUST** be used, you should travel in the direction of the traffic to avoid confusing other road users.

Law UICHR 1988 reg 9

43. You **MUST** follow the same rules about using lights, indicators and horns as for other road vehicles, if your vehicle is fitted with them. At night, lights **MUST** be used. Be aware that other road users may not see you and you should make yourself more visible – even in the daytime and also at dusk – by, for instance, wearing a reflective jacket or reflective strips on the back of the vehicle.

Law UICHR 1988 reg 9

44. Take extra care at road junctions. When going straight ahead, check to make sure there are no vehicles about to cross your path from the left, the right, or overtaking you and turning left. There are several options for dealing with right turns, especially turning from a major road. If moving into the middle of the road is difficult or dangerous, you can
- stop on the left-hand side of the road and wait for a safe gap in the traffic
- negotiate the turn as a pedestrian, i.e. travel along the pavement and cross the road between pavements where it is safe to do so. Class 3 users should switch the vehicle to the lower speed limit when on pavements.

If the junction is too hazardous, it may be worth considering an alternative route. Similarly, when negotiating major roundabouts (i.e. with two or more lanes) it may be safer for you to use the pavement or find a route which avoids the roundabout altogether.

45. All normal parking restrictions should be observed. Your vehicle should not be left unattended if it causes an obstruction to other pedestrians – especially those in wheelchairs. Parking concessions provided under the Blue Badge scheme (see Further reading and Conversions) will apply to those vehicles displaying a valid badge.

46. These vehicles **MUST NOT** be used on motorways (see Rule 253). They should not be used on unrestricted dual carriageways where the speed limit exceeds 50mph (80km/h) but if they are used on these dual carriageways, they **MUST** have a flashing amber beacon. A flashing amber beacon should be used on all other dual carriageways (see Rule 220).

Laws RTRA sect 17(2) & (3), & RVLR reg 17(1) & 26

Rules about animals

Horse-drawn vehicles

47. Horse-drawn vehicles used on the highway should be operated and maintained in accordance with standards set out in the Department for Transport's Code of Practice for Horse-Drawn Vehicles. This Code lays down the requirements for a road driving assessment and includes a comprehensive list of safety checks to ensure that a carriage and its fittings are safe and in good working order. The standards set out in the Road Driving Assessment may be required to be met by a Local Authority if an operator wishes to obtain a local authority licence to operate a passenger-carrying service.

48. Safety equipment and clothing. All horse-drawn vehicles should have two red rear reflectors. It is safer not to drive at night but if you do, a light showing white to the front and red to the rear **MUST** be fitted.
Law RVLR 1989 reg 4

Horse riders

49. Safety equipment. Children under the age of 14 **MUST** wear a helmet which complies with the Regulations. It **MUST** be fastened securely. Other riders should also follow these requirements. These requirements do not apply to a child who is a follower of the Sikh religion while wearing a turban.
Laws H(PHYR) Act 1990, sect 1 & H(PHYR) Regulations 1992, reg 3

50. Other clothing. You should wear
- boots or shoes with hard soles and heels
- light-coloured or fluorescent clothing in daylight
- reflective clothing if you have to ride at night or in poor visibility.

Rule 50: Help yourself to be seen

51. At night. It is safer not to ride on the road at night or in poor visibility, but if you do, make sure you wear reflective clothing and your horse has reflective bands above the fetlock joints. A light which shows white to the front and red to the rear should be fitted, with a band, to the rider's right arm and/or leg/riding boot. If you are leading a horse at night, carry a light in your right hand, showing white to the front and red to the rear, and wear reflective clothing on both you and your horse. It is strongly recommended that a fluorescent/reflective tail guard is also worn by your horse.

Riding

52. Before you take a horse on to a road, you should
- ensure all tack fits well and is in good condition
- make sure you can control the horse.

Always ride with other, less nervous horses if you think that your horse will be nervous of traffic. Never ride a horse without both a saddle and bridle.

53. Before riding off or turning, look behind you to make sure it is safe, then give a clear arm signal.
When riding on the road you should
- keep to the left
- keep both hands on the reins unless you are signalling
- keep both feet in the stirrups
- not carry another person
- not carry anything which might affect your balance or get tangled up with the reins
- keep a horse you are leading to your left
- move in the direction of the traffic flow in a one-way street
- never ride more than two abreast, and ride in single file on narrow or busy roads and when riding round bends.

54. You **MUST NOT** take a horse onto a footpath or pavement, and you should not take a horse onto a cycle track. Use a bridleway where possible. Equestrian crossings may be provided for horse riders to cross the road and you should use these where available (see Crossings, Rule 27). You should dismount at level crossings where a 'horse rider dismount' sign is displayed.
Laws HA 1835 sect 72, R(S)A 1984, sect 129(5)

55. Avoid roundabouts wherever possible. If you use them you should
- keep to the left and watch out for vehicles crossing your path to leave or join the roundabout
- signal right when riding across exits to show you are not leaving
- signal left just before you leave the roundabout.

Other animals

56. Dogs. Do not let a dog out on the road on its own. Keep it on a short lead when walking on the pavement, road or path shared with cyclists or horse riders.

57. When in a vehicle make sure dogs or other animals are suitably restrained so they cannot distract you while you are driving or injure you, or themselves, if you stop quickly. A seat belt harness, pet carrier, dog cage or dog guard are ways of restraining animals in cars.

58. Animals being herded. These should be kept under control at all times. You should, if possible, send another person along the road in front to warn other road users, especially at a bend or the brow of a hill. It is safer not to move animals after dark, but if you do, then wear reflective clothing and ensure that lights are carried (white at the front and red at the rear of the herd).

Rules for cyclists

Overview

These rules are in addition to those in the following sections, which apply to all vehicles (except the Motorway section). See also Annexe 1 – You and your bicycle.

59. Clothing. You should wear
- a cycle helmet which conforms to current regulations, is the correct size and securely fastened
- appropriate clothes for cycling. Avoid clothes that may get tangled in the chain, or in a wheel or may obscure your lights
- light-coloured or fluorescent clothing which helps other road users to see you in daylight and poor light
- reflective clothing and/or accessories (belt, arm or ankle bands) in the dark.

Rule 59: Help yourself to be seen

60. At night your cycle **MUST** have white front and red rear lights lit. It **MUST** also be fitted with a red rear reflector (and amber pedal reflectors, if manufactured after 1/10/85). White front reflectors and spoke reflectors will also help you to be seen. Flashing lights are permitted but it is recommended that cyclists who are riding in areas without street lighting use a steady front lamp.
Law RVLR regs 13, 18 & 24

61. Cycle Routes and Other Facilities. Use cycle routes, advanced stop lines, cycle boxes and toucan crossings unless at the time it is unsafe to do so. Use of these facilities is not compulsory and will depend on your experience and skills, but they can make your journey safer.

62. Cycle Tracks. These are normally located away from the road, but may occasionally be found alongside footpaths or pavements. Cyclists and pedestrians may be segregated or they may share the same space (unsegregated). When using segregated tracks you **MUST** keep to the side intended for cyclists as the pedestrian side remains a pavement or footpath. Take care when passing pedestrians, especially children, older or disabled people, and allow them plenty of room. Always be prepared to slow down and stop if necessary. Take care near road junctions as you may have difficulty seeing other road users, who might not notice you.
Law HA 1835 sect 72

63. Cycle Lanes. These are marked by a white line (which may be broken) along the carriageway (see Rule 140). Keep within the lane when practicable. When leaving a cycle lane check before pulling out that it is safe to do so and signal your intention clearly to other road users. Use of cycle lanes is not compulsory and will depend on your experience and skills, but they can make your journey safer.

64. You **MUST NOT** cycle on a pavement.
Laws HA 1835 sect 72 & R(S)A 1984, sect 129

65. Bus Lanes. Most bus lanes may be used by cyclists as indicated on signs. Watch out for people getting on or off a bus. Be very careful when overtaking a bus or leaving a bus lane as you will be entering a busier traffic flow. Do not pass between the kerb and a bus when it is at a stop.

66. You should
- keep both hands on the handlebars except when signalling or changing gear
- keep both feet on the pedals
- never ride more than two abreast, and ride in single file on narrow or busy roads and when riding round bends
- not ride close behind another vehicle
- not carry anything which will affect your balance or may get tangled up with your wheels or chain
- be considerate of other road users, particularly blind and partially sighted pedestrians. Let them know you are there when necessary, for example, by ringing your bell if you have one. It is recommended that a bell be fitted.

67. You should
- look all around before moving away from the kerb, turning or manoeuvring, to make sure it is safe to do so. Give a clear signal to show other road users what you intend to do (see Signals to other road users)
- look well ahead for obstructions in the road, such as drains, pot-holes and parked vehicles so that you do not have to swerve suddenly to avoid them. Leave plenty of room when passing parked vehicles and watch out for doors being opened or pedestrians stepping into your path
- be aware of traffic coming up behind you
- take extra care near road humps, narrowings and other traffic calming features
- take care when overtaking (see Rules 162–169).

68. You **MUST NOT**
- carry a passenger unless your cycle has been built or adapted to carry one
- hold onto a moving vehicle or trailer
- ride in a dangerous, careless or inconsiderate manner
- ride when under the influence of drink or drugs, including medicine.

Law RTA 1988 sects 24, 26, 28, 29 & 30 as amended by RTA 1991

69. You **MUST** obey all traffic signs and traffic light signals.

Laws RTA 1988 sect 36 & TSRGD reg 10(1)

70. When parking your cycle
- find a conspicuous location where it can be seen by passers-by
- use cycle stands or other cycle parking facilities wherever possible
- do not leave it where it would cause an obstruction or hazard to other road users
- secure it well so that it will not fall over and become an obstruction or hazard.

71. You **MUST NOT** cross the stop line when the traffic lights are red. Some junctions have an advanced stop line to enable you to wait and position yourself ahead of other traffic (see Rule 178).

Laws RTA 1988 sect 36 & TSRGD regs 10 & 36(1)

Road junctions

72. On the left. When approaching a junction on the left, watch out for vehicles turning in front of you, out of or into the side road. Just before you turn, check for undertaking cyclists or motorcyclists. Do not ride on the inside of vehicles signalling or slowing down to turn left.

73. Pay particular attention to long vehicles which need a lot of room to manoeuvre at corners. Be aware that drivers may not see you. They may have to move over to the right before turning left. Wait until they have completed the manoeuvre because the rear wheels come very close to the kerb while turning. Do not be tempted to ride in the space between them and the kerb.

74. On the right. If you are turning right, check the traffic to ensure it is safe, then signal and move to the centre of the road. Wait until there is a safe gap in the oncoming traffic and give a final look before completing the turn. It may be safer to wait on the left until there is a safe gap or to dismount and push your cycle across the road.

75. Dual carriageways. Remember that traffic on most dual carriageways moves quickly. When crossing wait for a safe gap and cross each carriageway in turn. Take extra care when crossing slip roads.

Roundabouts

76. Full details about the correct procedure at roundabouts are contained in Rules 184–190. Roundabouts can be hazardous and should be approached with care.

77. You may feel safer walking your cycle round on the pavement or verge. If you decide to ride round keeping to the left-hand lane you should
- be aware that drivers may not easily see you
- take extra care when cycling across exits. You may need to signal right to show you are not leaving the roundabout
- watch out for vehicles crossing your path to leave or join the roundabout.

78. Give plenty of room to long vehicles on the roundabout as they need more space to manoeuvre. Do not ride in the space they need to get round the roundabout. It may be safer to wait until they have cleared the roundabout.

Crossing the road

79. Do not ride across equestrian crossings, as they are for horse riders only. Do not ride across a pelican, puffin or zebra crossing. Dismount and wheel your cycle across.

80. Toucan crossings. These are light-controlled crossings which allow cyclists and pedestrians to share crossing space and cross at the same time. They are push-button operated. Pedestrians and cyclists will see the green signal together. Cyclists are permitted to ride across.

81. Cycle-only crossings. Cycle tracks on opposite sides of the road may be linked by signalled crossings. You may ride across but you **MUST NOT** cross until the green cycle symbol is showing.
Law TSRGD regs 33(2) & 36(1)

82. Level crossings/Tramways. Take extra care when crossing the tracks (see Rule 306). You should dismount at level crossings where a 'cyclist dismount' sign is displayed.

Rules for motorcyclists

General guidance
These Rules are in addition to those in the following sections which apply to all vehicles. See also Annexe 2 – Motorcycle licence requirements.

83. On all journeys, the rider and pillion passenger on a motorcycle, scooter or moped **MUST** wear a protective helmet. This does not apply to a follower of the Sikh religion while wearing a turban. Helmets **MUST** comply with the Regulations and they **MUST** be fastened securely. Riders and passengers of motor tricycles and quadricycles, also called quadbikes, should also wear a protective helmet. Before each journey check that your helmet visor is clean and in good condition.
Laws RTA 1988 sects 16 & 17 & MC(PH)R as amended reg 4

84. It is also advisable to wear eye protectors, which **MUST** comply with the Regulations. Scratched or poorly fitting eye protectors can limit your view when riding, particularly in bright sunshine and the hours of darkness. Consider wearing ear protection. Strong boots, gloves and suitable clothing may help to protect you if you are involved in a collision.
Laws RTA sect 18 & MC(EP)R as amended reg 4

85. You **MUST NOT** carry more than one pillion passenger who **MUST** sit astride the machine on a proper seat. They should face forward with both feet on the footrests. You **MUST NOT** carry a pillion passenger unless your motorcycle is designed to do so. Provisional licence holders **MUST NOT** carry a pillion passenger.

Laws RTA 1988 sect 23, MV(DL)R 1999 reg 16(6) & CUR 1986 reg 102

86. Daylight riding. Make yourself as visible as possible from the side as well as the front and rear. You could wear a light or brightly coloured helmet and fluorescent clothing or strips. Dipped headlights, even in good daylight, may also make you more conspicuous. However, be aware that other vehicle drivers may still not have seen you, or judged your distance or speed correctly, especially at junctions.

Rule 86: Help yourself to be seen

87. Riding in the dark. Wear reflective clothing or strips to improve your visibility in the dark. These reflect light from the headlamps of other vehicles, making you visible from a longer distance. See Rules 113–116 for lighting requirements.

88. Manoeuvring. You should be aware of what is behind and to the sides before manoeuvring. Look behind you; use mirrors if they are fitted. When in traffic queues look out for pedestrians crossing between vehicles and vehicles emerging from junctions or changing lanes. Position yourself so that drivers in front can see you in their mirrors. Additionally, when filtering in slow-moving traffic, take care and keep your speed low.

Remember: Observation – Signal – Manoeuvre.

Rules for drivers and motorcyclists

Vehicle condition

89. Vehicle condition. You **MUST** ensure your vehicle and trailer comply with the full requirements of the Road Vehicles (Construction and Use) Regulations and Road Vehicles Lighting Regulations (see Annexe 4 – The road user and the law).

Fitness to drive

90. Make sure that you are fit to drive. You **MUST** report to the Driver and Vehicle Licensing Agency (DVLA) any health condition likely to affect your driving.
Law RTA 1988 sect 94

91. Driving when you are tired greatly increases your risk of collision. To minimise this risk

- make sure you are fit to drive. Do not begin a journey if you are tired. Get a good night's sleep before embarking on a long journey
- avoid undertaking long journeys between midnight and 6am, when natural alertness is at a minimum
- plan your journey to take sufficient breaks. A minimum break of at least 15 minutes after every two hours of driving is recommended
- if you feel at all sleepy, stop in a safe place. Do not stop on the hard shoulder of a motorway
- the most effective ways to counter sleepiness are to drink, for example, two cups of caffeinated coffee and to take a short nap (at least 15 minutes).

92. Vision. You **MUST** be able to read a vehicle number plate, in good daylight, from a distance of 20 metres (or 20.5 metres where the old style number plate is used). If you need to wear glasses (or contact lenses) to do this, you **MUST** wear them at all times while driving. The police have the power to require a driver to undertake an eyesight test.
Laws RTA 1988 sect 96 & MV(DL)R reg 40 & sch 8

93. Slow down, and if necessary stop, if you are dazzled by bright sunlight.

94. At night or in poor visibility, do not use tinted glasses, lenses or visors if they restrict your vision.

Alcohol and drugs

95. Do not drink and drive as it will seriously affect your judgement and abilities.

In England and Wales you **MUST NOT** drive with a breath alcohol level higher than 35 microgrammes/100 millilitres of breath or a blood alcohol level of more than 80 milligrammes/100 millilitres of blood.

In Scotland the legal limits are lower. You **MUST NOT** drive with a breath alcohol level higher than 22 microgrammes/100 millilitres of breath or a blood alcohol level of more than 50 milligrammes/100 millilitres of blood.

Alcohol will
- give a false sense of confidence
- reduce co-ordination and slow down reactions
- affect judgement of speed, distance and risk
- reduce your driving ability, even if you're below the legal limit
- take time to leave your body; you may be unfit to drive in the evening after drinking at lunchtime, or in the morning after drinking the previous evening.

The best solution is not to drink at all when planning to drive because any amount of alcohol affects your ability to drive safely. If you are going to drink, arrange another means of transport.

Law RTA 1988 sects 4, 5 & 11(2), Road Traffic Act 1988 PLSR

96. You **MUST NOT** drive under the influence of drugs or medicine. For medicines, check with your doctor or pharmacist and do not drive if you are advised that you may be impaired.

You **MUST NOT** drive if you have illegal drugs or certain medicines in your blood above specified limits. It is highly dangerous so never take illegal drugs if you intend to drive; the effects are unpredictable, but can be even more severe than alcohol and result in fatal or serious road crashes. Illegal drugs have been specified at very low levels so even small amounts of use could be above the specified limits. The limits for certain medicines have been specified at higher levels, above the levels generally found in the blood of patients who have taken normal therapeutic doses. If you are found to have a concentration of a drug above its specified limit in your blood because you have been prescribed or legitimately supplied a particularly high dose of medicine, then you can raise a statutory medical defence, provided your driving was not impaired by the medicine you are taking.

Law RTA 1988 sect 4 & 5

Before setting off

97. Before setting off. You should ensure that

- you have planned your route and allowed sufficient time
- clothing and footwear do not prevent you using the controls in the correct manner
- you know where all the controls are and how to use them before you need them. Not all vehicles are the same; do not wait until it is too late to find out
- your mirrors and seat are adjusted correctly to ensure comfort, full control and maximum vision
- head restraints are properly adjusted to reduce the risk of neck and spine injuries in the event of a collision
- you have sufficient fuel before commencing your journey, especially if it includes motorway driving. It can be dangerous to lose power when driving in traffic
- ensure your vehicle is legal and roadworthy
- switch off your mobile phone.

Rule 97: Make sure head restraints are properly adjusted

Vehicle towing and loading

98. Vehicle towing and loading. As a driver

- you **MUST NOT** tow more than your licence permits. If you passed a car test after 1 January 1997 you are restricted on the weight of trailer you can tow
- you **MUST NOT** overload your vehicle or trailer. You should not tow a weight greater than that recommended by the manufacturer of your vehicle
- you **MUST** secure your load and it **MUST NOT** stick out dangerously. Make sure any heavy or sharp objects and any animals are secured safely. If there is a collision, they might hit someone inside the vehicle and cause serious injury
- you should properly distribute the weight in your caravan or trailer with heavy items mainly over the axle(s) and ensure a downward load on the tow ball. Manufacturer's recommended weight and tow ball load should not be exceeded. This should avoid the possibility of swerving or snaking and going out of control. If this does happen, ease off the accelerator and reduce speed gently to regain control
- carrying a load or pulling a trailer may require you to adjust the headlights.

In the event of a breakdown, be aware that towing a vehicle on a tow rope is potentially dangerous. You should consider professional recovery.

Laws CUR reg 100 & MV(DL)R reg 43

Seat belts and child restraints

99. You **MUST** wear a seat belt in cars, vans and other goods vehicles if one is fitted (see table below). Adults, and children aged 14 years and over, **MUST** use a seat belt or child restraint, where fitted, when seated in minibuses, buses and coaches. Exemptions are allowed for the holders of medical exemption certificates and those making deliveries or collections in goods vehicles when travelling less than 50 metres (approx 162 feet).

Laws RTA 1988 sects 14 & 15, MV(WSB)R, MV(WSBCFS)R & MV(WSB)(A)R

Seat Belt Requirements.

This table summarises the main legal requirements for wearing seat belts in cars, vans and other goods vehicles

Seat belt requirements	Front seat	Rear seat	Who is responsible?
Driver	Seat belt **MUST** be worn if fitted		**Driver**
Child under 3 years of age	Correct child restraint **MUST** be used	Correct child restraint **MUST** be used. If one is not available in a taxi, may travel unrestrained.	**Driver**
Child from 3rd birthday up to 1.35 metres (approx 4ft 5ins) in height (or 12th birthday, whichever they reach first)	Correct child restraint **MUST** be used	Correct child restraint **MUST** be used where seat belts fitted. **MUST** use adult belt if correct child restraint is not available in a licensed taxi or private hire vehicle, or for reasons of unexpected necessity over a short distance, or if two occupied restraints prevent fitment of a third.	**Driver**
Child over 1.35 metres (approx 4ft 5ins) in height or 12 or 13 years	Seat belt **MUST** be worn if available	Seat belt **MUST** be worn if available	**Driver**
Adult passengers aged 14 and over	Seat belt **MUST** be worn if available	Seat belt **MUST** be worn if available	**Passenger**

100. The driver **MUST** ensure that all children under 14 years of age in cars, vans and other goods vehicles wear seat belts or sit in an approved child restraint where required (see table opposite). If a child is under 1.35 metres (approx 4 feet 5 inches) tall, a baby seat, child seat, booster seat or booster cushion **MUST** be used suitable for the child's weight and fitted to the manufacturer's instructions.

Laws RTA 1988 sects 14 & 15, MV(WSB)R, MV(WSBCFS)R & MV(WSB)(A)R

Rule 100: Make sure that a child uses a suitable restraint which is correctly adjusted

101. A rear-facing baby seat **MUST NOT** be fitted into a seat protected by an active frontal airbag, as in a crash it can cause serious injury or death to the child.

Laws RTA 1988 sects 14 & 15, MV(WSB)R, MV(WSBCFS)R & MV(WSB)(A)R

102. Children in cars, vans and other goods vehicles. Drivers who are carrying children in cars, vans and other goods vehicles should also ensure that

- children should get into the vehicle through the door nearest the kerb
- child restraints are properly fitted to manufacturer's instructions
- children do not sit behind the rear seats in an estate car or hatchback, unless a special child seat has been fitted
- the child safety door locks, where fitted, are used when children are in the vehicle
- children are kept under control.

General rules, techniques and advice for all drivers and riders

Overview

This section should be read by all drivers, motorcyclists, cyclists and horse riders. The rules in *The Highway Code* do not give you the right of way in any circumstance, but they advise you when you should give way to others. Always give way if it can help to avoid an incident.

Signals

103. Signals warn and inform other road users, including pedestrians (see Signals to other road users), of your intended actions. You should always

- give clear signals in plenty of time, having checked it is not misleading to signal at that time
- use them to advise other road users before changing course or direction, stopping or moving off
- cancel them after use
- make sure your signals will not confuse others. If, for instance, you want to stop after a side road, do not signal until you are passing the road. If you signal earlier it may give the impression that you intend to turn into the road. Your brake lights will warn traffic behind you that you are slowing down
- use an arm signal to emphasise or reinforce your signal if necessary. Remember that signalling does not give you priority.

104. You should also

- watch out for signals given by other road users and proceed only when you are satisfied that it is safe
- be aware that an indicator on another vehicle may not have been cancelled.

105. You **MUST** obey signals given by police officers, traffic officers, traffic wardens (see Signals by authorised persons) and signs used by school crossing patrols.

Laws RTRA sect 28, RTA 1988 sect 35, TMA 2004 sect 6, & FTWO art 3

106. Police stopping procedures. If the police want to stop your vehicle they will, where possible, attract your attention by

- flashing blue lights, headlights or sounding their siren or horn, usually from behind
- directing you to pull over to the side by pointing and/or using the left indicator.

You **MUST** then pull over and stop as soon as it is safe to do so. Then switch off your engine.
Law RTA 1988 sect 163

Other stopping procedures

107. Driver and Vehicle Standards Agency Officers have powers to stop vehicles on all roads, including motorways and trunk roads, in England and Wales. They will attract your attention by flashing amber lights

- either from the front requesting you to follow them to a safe place to stop
- or from behind directing you to pull over to the side by pointing and/or using the left indicator.

It is an offence not to comply with their directions. You **MUST** obey any signals given (see Signals by authorised persons).
Laws RTA 1988, sect 67, & PRA 2002, sect 41 & sched 5(8)

108. Highways Agency Traffic Officers have powers to stop vehicles on most motorways and some 'A' class roads, in England only. If HA traffic officers in uniform want to stop your vehicle on safety grounds (e.g. an insecure load) they will, where possible, attract your attention by

- flashing amber lights, usually from behind
- directing you to pull over to the side by pointing and/or using the left indicator.

You **MUST** then pull over and stop as soon as it is safe to do so. Then switch off your engine. It is an offence not to comply with their directions (see Signals by authorised persons).
Law RTA1988, sects 35 & 163 as amended by TMA 2004, sect 6

Traffic light signals and traffic signs

109. You **MUST** obey all traffic light signals (see Light signals controlling traffic) and traffic signs giving orders, including temporary signals & signs (see Traffic signs). Make sure you know, understand and act on all other traffic and information signs and road markings (see Road markings and Vehicle markings).
Laws RTA 1988 sect 36 & TSRGD regs 10, 15, 16, 25, 26, 27, 28, 29, 36, 38 & 40

110. Flashing headlights. Only flash your headlights to let other road users know that you are there. Do not flash your headlights to convey any other message or intimidate other road users.

111. Never assume that flashing headlights is a signal inviting you to proceed. Use your own judgement and proceed carefully.

112. The horn. Use only while your vehicle is moving and you need to warn other road users of your presence. Never sound your horn aggressively. You **MUST NOT** use your horn
* while stationary on the road
* when driving in a built-up area between the hours of 11.30pm and 7am

except when another road user poses a danger.

Law CUR reg 99

Lighting requirements

113. You **MUST**
* ensure all sidelights and rear registration plate lights are lit between sunset and sunrise
* use headlights at night, except on a road which has lit street lighting. These roads are generally restricted to a speed limit of 30mph (48km/h) unless otherwise specified
* use headlights when visibility is seriously reduced (see Rule 226).

Night (the hours of darkness) is defined as the period between half an hour after sunset and half an hour before sunrise).

Laws RVLR regs 3, 24, & 25, (In Scotland – RTRA 1984 sect 82 (as amended by NRSWA, para 59 of sched 8))

114. You **MUST NOT**
* use any lights in a way that would dazzle or cause discomfort to other road users, including pedestrians, cyclists and horse riders
* use front or rear fog lights unless visibility is seriously reduced. You **MUST** switch them off when visibility improves to avoid dazzling other road users (see Rule 226).

In stationary queues of traffic, drivers should apply the parking brake and, once the following traffic has stopped, take their foot off the footbrake to deactivate the vehicle brake lights. This will minimise glare to road users behind until the traffic moves again.

Law RVLR reg 27

115. You should also
* use dipped headlights, or dim-dip if fitted, at night in built-up areas and in dull daytime weather, to ensure that you can be seen
* keep your headlights dipped when overtaking until you are level with the other vehicle and then change to main beam if necessary, unless this would dazzle oncoming road users
* slow down, and if necessary stop, if you are dazzled by oncoming headlights.

116. Hazard warning lights. These may be used when your vehicle is stationary, to warn that it is temporarily obstructing traffic. Never use them as an excuse for dangerous or illegal parking. You **MUST NOT** use hazard warning lights while driving or being towed unless you are on a motorway or unrestricted dual carriageway and you need to warn drivers behind you of a hazard or obstruction ahead. Only use them for long enough to ensure that your warning has been observed.

Law RVLR reg 27

Control of the vehicle

Braking

117. In normal circumstances. The safest way to brake is to do so early and lightly. Brake more firmly as you begin to stop. Ease the pressure off just before the vehicle comes to rest to avoid a jerky stop.

118. In an emergency. Brake immediately. Try to avoid braking so harshly that you lock your wheels. Locked wheels can lead to loss of control.

119. Skids. Skidding is usually caused by the driver braking, accelerating or steering too harshly or driving too fast for the road conditions. If skidding occurs, remove the cause by releasing the brake pedal fully or easing off the accelerator. Turn the steering wheel in the direction of the skid. For example, if the rear of the vehicle skids to the right, steer immediately to the right to recover.

Rule 119: Rear of the car skids to the right. Driver steers to the right.

120. ABS. If your vehicle is fitted with anti-lock brakes, you should follow the advice given in the vehicle handbook. However, in the case of an emergency, apply the footbrake firmly; do not release the pressure until the vehicle has slowed to the desired speed. The ABS should ensure that steering control will be retained, but do not assume that a vehicle with ABS will stop in a shorter distance.

121. Brakes affected by water. If you have driven through deep water your brakes may be less effective. Test them at the first safe opportunity by pushing gently on the brake pedal to make sure that they work. If they are not fully effective, gently apply light pressure while driving slowly. This will help to dry them out.

122. Coasting. This term describes a vehicle travelling in neutral or with the clutch pressed down. It can reduce driver control because
- engine braking is eliminated
- vehicle speed downhill will increase quickly
- increased use of the footbrake can reduce its effectiveness
- steering response will be affected, particularly on bends and corners
- it may be more difficult to select the appropriate gear when needed.

The Driver and the Environment
123. You **MUST NOT** leave a parked vehicle unattended with the engine running or leave a vehicle engine running unnecessarily while that vehicle is stationary on a public road. Generally, if the vehicle is stationary and is likely to remain so for more than a couple of minutes, you should apply the parking brake and switch off the engine to reduce emissions and noise pollution. However it is permissible to leave the engine running if the vehicle is stationary in traffic or for diagnosing faults.
Law CUR regs 98 & 107

Speed limits
124. You **MUST NOT** exceed the maximum speed limits for the road and for your vehicle (see the table opposite). The presence of street lights generally means that there is a 30mph (48km/h) speed limit unless otherwise specified.
Law RTRA sects 81, 86, 89 & sch 6 (as amended by the MV(VSL)(E&W) regs 2014)

125. The speed limit is the absolute maximum and does not mean it is safe to drive at that speed irrespective of conditions. Driving at speeds too fast for the road and traffic conditions is dangerous. You should always reduce your speed when
- the road layout or condition presents hazards, such as bends
- sharing the road with pedestrians, cyclists and horse riders, particularly children, and motorcyclists
- weather conditions make it safer to do so
- driving at night as it is more difficult to see other road users.

Speed Limits

Types of vehicle	Built up areas* MPH (km/h)	Single carriageways MPH (km/h)	Dual carriageways MPH (km/h)	Motorways MPH (km/h)

Cars & motorcycles (including car derived vans up to 2 tonnes maximum laden weight)

30 (48)   60 (96)   70 (112)   70 (112)

Cars towing caravans or trailers (including car derived vans and motorcycles)

30 (48)   50 (80)   60 (96)   60 (96)

Buses, coaches and minibuses (not exceeding 12 metres (39 feet) in overall length)

30 (48)   50 (80)   60 (96)   70 (112)

Goods vehicles (not exceeding 7.5 tonnes maximum laden weight)

30 (48)   50 (80)   60 (96)   70† (112)

Goods vehicles (exceeding 7.5 tonnes maximum laden weight) in England and Wales

30 (48)   50‡ (80)   60§ (96)   60 (96)

---

* The 30mph (48km/h) limit usually applies to all traffic on all roads with street lighting unless signs show otherwise.

† 60mph (96km/h) if articulated or towing a trailer.

‡ 40mph (64km/h) in Scotland.

§ 50mph (80km/h) in Scotland.

126. Stopping Distances. Drive at a speed that will allow you to stop well within the distance you can see to be clear. You should

- leave enough space between you and the vehicle in front so that you can pull up safely if it suddenly slows down or stops. The safe rule is never to get closer than the overall stopping distance (see Typical Stopping Distances diagram, opposite)
- allow at least a two-second gap between you and the vehicle in front on roads carrying faster-moving traffic and in tunnels where visibility is reduced. The gap should be at least doubled on wet roads and increased still further on icy roads
- remember, large vehicles and motorcycles need a greater distance to stop. If driving a large vehicle in a tunnel, you should allow a four-second gap between you and the vehicle in front.

If you have to stop in a tunnel, leave at least a 5-metre (16 feet) gap between you and the vehicle in front.

Rule 126: Use a fixed point to help measure a two-second gap

Typical stopping distances

The distances below are a general guide. The distance will depend on your attention (thinking distance), the road surface, the weather and the condition of your vehicle at the time.

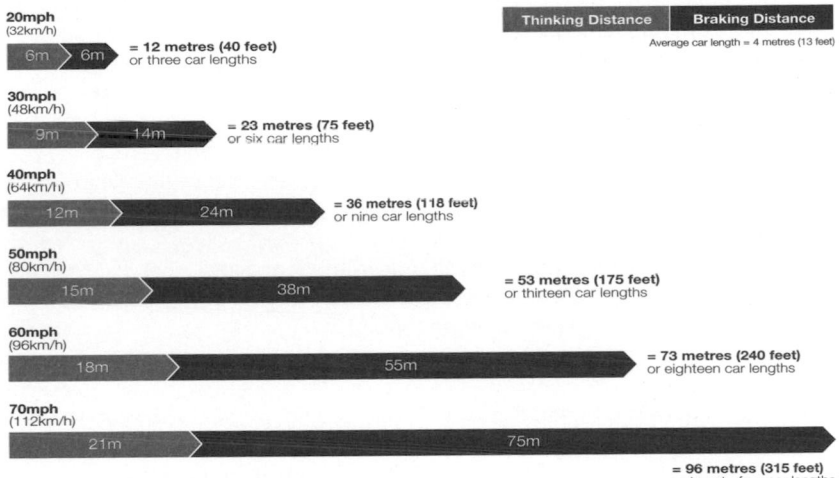

20mph (32km/h)
6m 6m
= **12 metres (40 feet)**
or three car lengths

| Thinking Distance | Braking Distance |
Average car length = 4 metres (13 feet)

30mph (48km/h)
9m 14m
= **23 metres (75 feet)**
or six car lengths

40mph (64km/h)
12m 24m
= **36 metres (118 feet)**
or nine car lengths

50mph (80km/h)
15m 38m
= **53 metres (175 feet)**
or thirteen car lengths

60mph (96km/h)
18m 55m
= **73 metres (240 feet)**
or eighteen car lengths

70mph (112km/h)
21m 75m
= **96 metres (315 feet)**
or twenty-four car lengths

Lines and lane markings on the road

Diagrams of all lines are shown in Road markings.

127. A broken white line. This marks the centre of the road. When this line lengthens and the gaps shorten, it means that there is a hazard ahead. Do not cross it unless you can see the road is clear and wish to overtake or turn off.

128. Double white lines where the line nearest to you is broken. This means you may cross the lines to overtake if it is safe, provided you can complete the manoeuvre before reaching a solid white line on your side. White direction arrows on the road indicate that you need to get back onto your side of the road.

129. Double white lines where the line nearest you is solid. This means you **MUST NOT** cross or straddle it unless it is safe and you need to enter adjoining premises or a side road. You may cross the line if necessary, provided the road is clear, to pass a stationary vehicle, or overtake a pedal cycle, horse or road maintenance vehicle, if they are travelling at 10mph (16km/h) or less.

Laws RTA 1988 sect 36 & TSRGD regs 10 & 26

130. Areas of white diagonal stripes or chevrons painted on the road. These are to separate traffic lanes or to protect traffic turning right.

- If the area is bordered by a broken white line, you should not enter the area unless it is necessary and you can see that it is safe to do so.
- If the area is marked with chevrons and bordered by solid white lines you **MUST NOT** enter it except in an emergency.

Laws MT(E&W)R regs 5, 9, 10 & 16, MT(S)R regs 4, 8, 9 & 14, RTA sect 36 & TSRGD 10(1)

131. Lane dividers. These are short, broken white lines which are used on wide carriageways to divide them into lanes. You should keep between them.

132. Reflective road studs may be used with white lines.
- White studs mark the lanes or the middle of the road.
- Red studs mark the left edge of the road.
- Amber studs mark the central reservation of a dual carriageway or motorway.
- Green studs mark the edge of the main carriageway at lay-bys and slip roads.
- Green/yellow studs indicate temporary adjustments to lane layouts, e.g. where road works are taking place.

Rule 132: Reflective road studs mark the lanes and edges of the carriageway

Multi-lane carriageways

Lane discipline

133. If you need to change lane, first use your mirrors and if necessary take a quick sideways glance to make sure you will not force another road user to change course or speed. When it is safe to do so, signal to indicate your intentions to other road users and when clear, move over.

134. You should follow the signs and road markings and get into the lane as directed. In congested road conditions do not change lanes unnecessarily. Merging in turn is recommended but only if safe and appropriate when vehicles are travelling at a very low speed, e.g. when approaching roadworks or a road traffic incident. It is not recommended at high speed.

Single carriageway

135. Where a single carriageway has three lanes and the road markings or signs do not give priority to traffic in either direction
- use the middle lane only for overtaking or turning right. Remember, you have no more right to use the middle lane than a driver coming from the opposite direction
- do not use the right-hand lane.

136. Where a single carriageway has four or more lanes, use only the lanes that signs or markings indicate.

Dual carriageways

A dual carriageway is a road which has a central reservation to separate the carriageways.

137. On a two-lane dual carriageway you should stay in the left-hand lane. Use the right-hand lane for overtaking or turning right. After overtaking, move back to the left-hand lane when it is safe to do so.

138. On a three-lane dual carriageway, you may use the middle lane or the right-hand lane to overtake but return to the middle and then the left-hand lane when it is safe.

139. Climbing and crawler lanes. These are provided on some hills. Use this lane if you are driving a slow-moving vehicle or if there are vehicles behind you wishing to overtake. Be aware of the signs and road markings which indicate the lane is about to end.

140. Cycle lanes. These are shown by road markings and signs. You **MUST NOT** drive or park in a cycle lane marked by a solid white line during its times of operation. Do not drive or park in a cycle lane marked by a broken white line unless it is unavoidable. You **MUST NOT** park in any cycle lane whilst waiting restrictions apply.
Law RTRA sects 5 & 8

141. Bus lanes. These are shown by road markings and signs that indicate which (if any) other vehicles are permitted to use the bus lane. Unless otherwise indicated, you should not drive in a bus lane during its period of operation. You may enter a bus lane to stop, to load or unload where this is not prohibited.

142. High-occupancy vehicle lanes and other designated vehicle lanes. Lanes may be restricted for use by particular types of vehicle; these restrictions may apply some or all of the time. The operating times and vehicle types will be indicated on the accompanying traffic signs. You **MUST NOT** drive in such lanes during their times of operation unless signs indicate that your vehicle is permitted (see Traffic signs).

Vehicles permitted to use designated lanes may or may not include cycles, buses, taxis, licensed private hire vehicles, motorcycles, heavy goods vehicles (HGVs) and high-occupancy vehicles (HOVs).
Where HOV lanes are in operation, they **MUST ONLY** be used by
• vehicles containing at least the minimum number of people indicated on the traffic signs
• any other vehicles, such as buses and motorcycles, as indicated on signs prior to the start of the lane, irrespective of the number of occupants.
Laws RTRA sects 5 & 8, & RTA 1988, sect 36

143. One-way streets. Traffic **MUST** travel in the direction indicated by signs. Buses and/or cycles may have a contraflow lane. Choose the correct lane for your exit as soon as you can. Do not change lanes suddenly. Unless road signs or markings indicate otherwise, you should use
• the left-hand lane when going left
• the right-hand lane when going right
• the most appropriate lane when going straight ahead.
Remember – traffic could be passing on both sides.
Laws RTA 1988 sect 36 & RTRA sects 5 & 8

General advice

144. You **MUST NOT**

- drive dangerously
- drive without due care and attention
- drive without reasonable consideration for other road users.

Law RTA 1988 sects 2 & 3 as amended by RTA 1991

145. You **MUST NOT** drive on or over a pavement, footpath or bridleway except to gain lawful access to property, or in the case of an emergency.

Laws HA 1835 sect 72 & RTA 1988 sect 34

146. Adapt your driving to the appropriate type and condition of road you are on. In particular

- do not treat speed limits as a target. It is often not appropriate or safe to drive at the maximum speed limit
- take the road and traffic conditions into account. Be prepared for unexpected or difficult situations, for example, the road being blocked beyond a blind bend. Be prepared to adjust your speed as a precaution
- where there are junctions, be prepared for road users emerging
- in side roads and country lanes look out for unmarked junctions where nobody has priority
- be prepared to stop at traffic control systems, roadworks, pedestrian crossings or traffic lights as necessary
- try to anticipate what pedestrians and cyclists might do. If pedestrians, particularly children, are looking the other way, they may step out into the road without seeing you.

147. Be considerate. Be careful of and considerate towards all types of road users, especially those requiring extra care (see Rule 204).

- You **MUST NOT** throw anything out of a vehicle; for example, food or food packaging, cigarette ends, cans, paper or carrier bags. This can endanger other road users, particularly motorcyclists and cyclists
- Try to be understanding if other road users cause problems; they may be inexperienced or not know the area well
- Be patient; remember that anyone can make a mistake
- Not allow yourself to become agitated or involved if someone is behaving badly on the road. This will only make the situation worse. Pull over, calm down and, when you feel relaxed, continue your journey
- Slow down and hold back if a road user pulls out into your path at a junction. Allow them to get clear. Do not over-react by driving too close behind to intimidate them.

Law EPA 1990 sect 87

148. Safe driving and riding needs concentration.
Avoid distractions when driving or riding such as

- loud music (this may mask other sounds)
- trying to read maps
- starting or adjusting any music or radio
- arguing with your passengers or other road users
- eating and drinking
- smoking.

You **MUST NOT** smoke in public transport vehicles or in vehicles used for work purposes in certain prescribed circumstances. Separate regulations apply to England, Wales and Scotland. In England and Wales, the driver must not smoke or allow anyone to smoke in an enclosed private vehicle carying someone under 18, including motor caravans.
Laws TSf(EV) regs, TSfP(W) regs, TPSCP(S)R regs, S-f(PVR regs & S-f(W)R regs

Mobile phones and in-vehicle technology

149. You **MUST** exercise proper control of your vehicle at all times. You **MUST NOT** use a hand-held mobile phone, or similar device, when driving or when supervising a learner driver, except to call 999 or 112 in a genuine emergency when it is unsafe or impractical to stop. Never use a hand-held microphone when driving. Using hands-free equipment is also likely to distract your attention from the road. It is far safer not to use any telephone while you are driving or riding – find a safe place to stop first or use the voicemail facility and listen to messages later.
Laws RTA 1988 sects 2 & 3 & CUR regs 104 & 110

150. There is a danger of driver distraction being caused by in-vehicle systems such as satellite navigation systems, congestion warning systems, PCs, multi-media, etc. You **MUST** exercise proper control of your vehicle at all times. Do not rely on driver assistance systems such as cruise control or lane departure warnings. They are available to assist but you should not reduce your concentration levels. Do not be distracted by maps or screen-based information (such as navigation or vehicle management systems) while driving or riding. If necessary find a safe place to stop.
Laws RTA 1988 sects 2 & 3 & CUR reg 104

151. In slow-moving traffic. You should

- reduce the distance between you and the vehicle ahead to maintain traffic flow
- never get so close to the vehicle in front that you cannot stop safely
- leave enough space to be able to manoeuvre if the vehicle in front breaks down or an emergency vehicle needs to get past
- not change lanes to the left to overtake
- allow access into and from side roads, as blocking these will add to congestion
- be aware of cyclists and motorcyclists who may be passing on either side.

Rule 151: Do not block access to a side road

Driving in built-up areas

152. Residential streets. You should drive slowly and carefully on streets where there are likely to be pedestrians, cyclists and parked cars. In some areas a 20mph (32km/h) maximum speed limit may be in force. Look out for

- vehicles emerging from junctions or driveways
- vehicles moving off
- car doors opening
- pedestrians
- children running out from between parked cars
- cyclists and motorcyclists.

153. Traffic-calming measures. On some roads there are features such as road humps, chicanes and narrowings which are intended to slow you down. When you approach these features reduce your speed. Allow cyclists and motorcyclists room to pass through them. Maintain a reduced speed along the whole of the stretch of road within the calming measures. Give way to oncoming road users if directed to do so by signs. You should not overtake other moving road users while in these areas.

Rule 153: Chicanes may be used to slow traffic down

Country roads

154. Take extra care on country roads and reduce your speed at approaches to bends, which can be sharper than they appear, and at junctions and turnings, which may be partially hidden. Be prepared for pedestrians, horse riders, cyclists, slow-moving farm vehicles or mud on the road surface. Make sure you can stop within the distance you can see to be clear. You should also reduce your speed where country roads enter villages.

155. Single-track roads. These are only wide enough for one vehicle. They may have special passing places. If you see a vehicle coming towards you, or the driver behind wants to overtake, pull into a passing place on your left, or wait opposite a passing place on your right. Give way to vehicles coming uphill whenever you can. If necessary, reverse until you reach a passing place to let the other vehicle pass. Slow down when passing pedestrians, cyclists and horse riders.

156. Do not park in passing places.

Vehicles prohibited from using roads and pavements

157. Certain motorised vehicles do not meet the construction and technical requirements for road vehicles and are generally not intended, not suitable and not legal for road, pavement, footpath, cycle path or bridleway use. These include most types of miniature motorcycles, also called mini motos, and motorised scooters, also called go peds, which are powered by electric or internal combustion engines. These types of vehicle **MUST NOT** be used on roads, pavements, footpaths or bridleways.
Laws RTA 1988 sects 34, 41a, 42, 47, 63 & 66, HA 1835, sect 72, & R(S)A sect 129

158. Certain models of motorcycles, motor tricycles and quadricycles, also called quad bikes, are suitable only for off-road use and do not meet legal standards for use on roads. Vehicles that do not meet these standards **MUST NOT** be used on roads. They **MUST NOT** be used on pavements, footpaths, cycle paths or bridleways either. You **MUST** make sure that any motorcycle, motor tricycle, quadricycle or any other motor vehicle meets legal standards and is properly registered, taxed and insured before using it on the roads. Even when registered, taxed and insured for the road, vehicles **MUST NOT** be used on pavements.
Laws RTA 1988 sects 34, 41a, 42, 47, 63, 66 & 156, HA 1835, sect 72, R(S)A sect 129, & VERA Sects 1, 29, 31A, & 43A

Using the Road

General rules

159. Before moving off you should
- use all mirrors to check the road is clear
- look round to check the blind spots (the areas you are unable to see in the mirrors)
- signal if necessary before moving out
- look round for a final check.

Move off only when it is safe to do so.

Rule 159: Check the blind spot before moving off

160. Once moving you should
- keep to the left, unless road signs or markings indicate otherwise. The exceptions are when you want to overtake, turn right or pass parked vehicles or pedestrians in the road
- keep well to the left on right-hand bends. This will improve your view of the road and help avoid the risk of colliding with traffic approaching from the opposite direction
- drive with both hands on the wheel where possible. This will help you to remain in full control of the vehicle at all times
- be aware of other road users, especially cycles and motorcycles who may be filtering through the traffic. These are more difficult to see than larger vehicles and their riders are particularly vulnerable. Give them plenty of room, especially if you are driving a long vehicle or towing a trailer
- select a lower gear before you reach a long downhill slope. This will help to control your speed
- when towing, remember the extra length will affect overtaking and manoeuvring. The extra weight will also affect the braking and acceleration.

161. Mirrors. All mirrors should be used effectively throughout your journey. You should

- use your mirrors frequently so that you always know what is behind and to each side of you
- use them in good time before you signal or change direction or speed
- be aware that mirrors do not cover all areas and there will be blind spots. You will need to look round and check.

Remember: Mirrors – Signal – Manoeuvre

Overtaking

162. Before overtaking you should make sure

- the road is sufficiently clear ahead
- road users are not beginning to overtake you
- there is a suitable gap in front of the road user you plan to overtake.

163. Overtake only when it is safe and legal to do so. You should

- not get too close to the vehicle you intend to overtake
- use your mirrors, signal when it is safe to do so, take a quick sideways glance if necessary into the blind spot area and then start to move out
- not assume that you can simply follow a vehicle ahead which is overtaking; there may only be enough room for one vehicle
- move quickly past the vehicle you are overtaking, once you have started to overtake. Allow plenty of room. Move back to the left as soon as you can but do not cut in
- take extra care at night and in poor visibility when it is harder to judge speed and distance
- give way to oncoming vehicles before passing parked vehicles or other obstructions on your side of the road
- only overtake on the left if the vehicle in front is signalling to turn right, and there is room to do so
- stay in your lane if traffic is moving slowly in queues. If the queue on your right is moving more slowly than you are, you may pass on the left
- give motorcyclists, cyclists and horse riders at least as much room as you would when overtaking a car (see Rules 211–213, 214–215).

Remember: Mirrors – Signal – Manoeuvre

Rule 163: Give vulnerable road users at least as much space as you would a car

164. Large vehicles. Overtaking these is more difficult. You should
- drop back. This will increase your ability to see ahead and should allow the driver of the large vehicle to see you in their mirrors. Getting too close to large vehicles, including agricultural vehicles such as a tractor with a trailer or other fixed equipment, will obscure your view of the road ahead and there may be another slow-moving vehicle in front
- make sure that you have enough room to complete your overtaking manoeuvre before committing yourself. It takes longer to pass a large vehicle. If in doubt do not overtake
- not assume you can follow a vehicle ahead which is overtaking a long vehicle. If a problem develops, they may abort overtaking and pull back in.

Rule 164: Do not cut in too quickly

165. You **MUST NOT** overtake
- if you would have to cross or straddle double white lines with a solid line nearest to you (but see Rule129)
- if you would have to enter an area designed to divide traffic, if it is surrounded by a solid white line
- the nearest vehicle to a pedestrian crossing, especially when it has stopped to let pedestrians cross
- if you would have to enter a lane reserved for buses, trams or cycles during its hours of operation
- after a 'No Overtaking' sign and until you pass a sign cancelling the restriction.

Laws RTA 1988 sect 36, TSRGD regs 10, 22, 23 & 24, ZPPPCRGD reg 24

166. DO NOT overtake if there is any doubt, or where you cannot see far enough ahead to be sure it is safe. For example, when you are approaching
- a corner or bend
- a hump bridge
- the brow of a hill.

167. DO NOT overtake where you might come into conflict with other road users. For example

- approaching or at a road junction on either side of the road
- where the road narrows
- when approaching a school crossing patrol
- between the kerb and a bus or tram when it is at a stop
- where traffic is queuing at junctions or roadworks
- when you would force another road user to swerve or slow down
- at a level crossing
- when a road user is indicating right, even if you believe the signal should have been cancelled. Do not take a risk; wait for the signal to be cancelled
- stay behind if you are following a cyclist approaching a roundabout or junction, and you intend to turn left
- when a tram is standing at a kerbside tram stop and there is no clearly marked passing lane for other traffic.

168. Being overtaken. If a driver is trying to overtake you, maintain a steady course and speed, slowing down if necessary to let the vehicle pass. Never obstruct drivers who wish to pass. Speeding up or driving unpredictably while someone is overtaking you is dangerous. Drop back to maintain a two-second gap if someone overtakes and pulls into the gap in front of you.

169. Do not hold up a long queue of traffic, especially if you are driving a large or slow-moving vehicle. Check your mirrors frequently, and if necessary, pull in where it is safe and let traffic pass.

Road junctions

170. Take extra care at junctions. You should

- watch out for cyclists, motorcyclists, powered wheelchairs/mobility scooters and pedestrians as they are not always easy to see. Be aware that they may not have seen or heard you if you are approaching from behind
- watch out for pedestrians crossing a road into which you are turning. If they have started to cross they have priority, so give way
- watch out for long vehicles which may be turning at a junction ahead; they may have to use the whole width of the road to make the turn (see Rule 221)
- watch out for horse riders who may take a different line on the road from that which you would expect
- not assume, when waiting at a junction, that a vehicle coming from the right and signalling left will actually turn. Wait and make sure
- look all around before emerging. Do not cross or join a road until there is a gap large enough for you to do so safely.

Rule 170: Give way to pedestrians who have started to cross

171. You **MUST** stop behind the line at a junction with a 'Stop' sign and a solid white line across the road. Wait for a safe gap in the traffic before you move off.
Laws RTA 1988 sect 36 & TSRGD regs 10 & 16

172. The approach to a junction may have a 'Give Way' sign or a triangle marked on the road. You **MUST** give way to traffic on the main road when emerging from a junction with broken white lines across the road.
Laws RTA 1988 sect 36 & TSRGD regs 10(1),16(1) & 25

173. Dual carriageways. When crossing or turning right, first assess whether the central reservation is deep enough to protect the full length of your vehicle.
*   If it is, then you should treat each half of the carriageway as a separate road. Wait in the central reservation until there is a safe gap in the traffic on the second half of the road.
*   If the central reservation is too shallow for the length of your vehicle, wait until you can cross both carriageways in one go.

Rule 173: Assess your vehicle's length and do not obstruct traffic

174. Box junctions. These have criss-cross yellow lines painted on the road (see Road markings). You **MUST NOT** enter the box until your exit road or lane is clear. However, you may enter the box and wait when you want to turn right, and are only stopped from doing so by oncoming traffic, or by other vehicles waiting to turn right. At signalled roundabouts you **MUST NOT** enter the box unless you can cross over it completely without stopping.

Law TSRGD regs 10(1) & 29(2)

Rule 174: Enter a box junction only if your exit road is clear

Junctions controlled by traffic lights

175. You **MUST** stop behind the white 'Stop' line across your side of the road unless the light is green. If the amber light appears you may go on only if you have already crossed the stop line or are so close to it that to stop might cause a collision.

Laws RTA 1988 sect 36 & TSRGD regs 10 & 36

176. You **MUST NOT** move forward over the white line when the red light is showing. Only go forward when the traffic lights are green if there is room for you to clear the junction safely or you are taking up a position to turn right. If the traffic lights are not working, treat the situation as you would an unmarked junction and proceed with great care.

Laws RTA 1988 sect 36 & TSRGD regs 10 & 36

177. Green filter arrow. This indicates a filter lane only. Do not enter that lane unless you want to go in the direction of the arrow. You may proceed in the direction of the green arrow when it, or the full green light shows. Give other traffic, especially cyclists, time and room to move into the correct lane.

178. Advanced stop lines. Some signal-controlled junctions have advanced stop lines to allow cycles to be positioned ahead of other traffic. Motorists, including motorcyclists, **MUST** stop at the first white line reached if the lights are amber or red and should avoid blocking the way or encroaching on the marked area at other times, e.g. if the junction ahead is blocked. If your vehicle has proceeded over the first white line at the time that the signal goes red, you **MUST** stop at the second white line, even if your vehicle is in the marked area. Allow cyclists time and space to move off when the green signal shows.
Laws RTA 1988 sect 36 & TSRGD regs 10, 36(1) & 43(2)

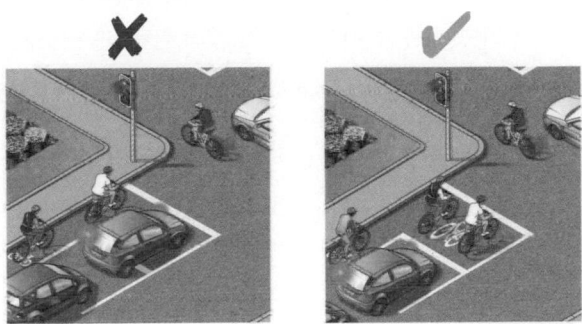

Rule 178: Do not unnecessarily encroach on the cyclists' waiting area

Turning right
179. Well before you turn right you should
- use your mirrors to make sure you know the position and movement of traffic behind you
- give a right-turn signal
- take up a position just left of the middle of the road or in the space marked for traffic turning right
- leave room for other vehicles to pass on the left, if possible.

180. Wait until there is a safe gap between you and any oncoming vehicle. Watch out for cyclists, motorcyclists, pedestrians and other road users. Check your mirrors and blind spot again to make sure you are not being overtaken, then make the turn. Do not cut the corner. Take great care when turning into a main road; you will need to watch for traffic in both directions and wait for a safe gap.
Remember: Mirrors – Signal – Manoeuvre

Rule 180: Position your vehicle correctly to avoid obstructing traffic

181. When turning right at crossroads where an oncoming vehicle is also turning right, there is a choice of two methods

- turn right side to right side; keep the other vehicle on your right and turn behind it. This is generally the safer method as you have a clear view of any approaching traffic when completing your turn
- left side to left side, turning in front of each other. This can block your view of oncoming vehicles, so take extra care. Cyclists and motorcyclists in particular may be hidden from your view. Road layout, markings or how the other vehicle is positioned can determine which course should be taken.

Rule 181: Left – Turning right side to right side.
Right – Turning left side to left side.

Turning left

182. Use your mirrors and give a left-turn signal well before you turn left. Do not overtake just before you turn left and watch out for traffic coming up on your left before you make the turn, especially if driving a large vehicle. Cyclists, motorcyclists and other road users in particular may be hidden from your view.

Rule 182: Do not cut in on cyclists

183. When turning
- keep as close to the left as is safe and practicable
- give way to any vehicles using a bus lane, cycle lane or tramway from either direction.

Roundabouts

184. On approaching a roundabout take notice and act on all the information available to you, including traffic signs, traffic lights and lane markings which direct you into the correct lane. You should
- use **Mirrors – Signal – Manoeuvre** at all stages
- decide as early as possible which exit you need to take
- give an appropriate signal (see Rule 186). Time your signals so as not to confuse other road users
- get into the correct lane
- adjust your speed and position to fit in with traffic conditions
- be aware of the speed and position of all the road users around you.

185. When reaching the roundabout you should
- give priority to traffic approaching from your right, unless directed otherwise by signs, road markings or traffic lights
- check whether road markings allow you to enter the roundabout without giving way. If so, proceed, but still look to the right before joining

- watch out for all other road users already on the roundabout; be aware they may not be signalling correctly or at all
- look forward before moving off to make sure traffic in front has moved off.

Rule 185: Follow the correct procedure at roundabouts

186. Signals and position. When taking the first exit, unless signs or markings indicate otherwise
- signal left and approach in the left-hand lane
- keep to the left on the roundabout and continue signalling left to leave.

When taking an exit to the right or going full circle, unless signs or markings indicate otherwise
- signal right and approach in the right-hand lane
- keep to the right on the roundabout until you need to change lanes to exit the roundabout
- signal left after you have passed the exit before the one you want.

When taking any intermediate exit, unless signs or markings indicate otherwise
- select the appropriate lane on approach to and on the roundabout
- you should not normally need to signal on approach
- stay in this lane until you need to alter course to exit the roundabout
- signal left after you have passed the exit before the one you want.

When there are more than three lanes at the entrance to a roundabout, use the most appropriate lane on approach and through it.

187. In all cases watch out for and give plenty of room to
- pedestrians who may be crossing the approach and exit roads
- traffic crossing in front of you on the roundabout, especially vehicles intending to leave by the next exit
- traffic which may be straddling lanes or positioned incorrectly
- motorcyclists
- cyclists and horse riders who may stay in the left-hand lane and signal right if they intend to continue round the roundabout. Allow them to do so
- long vehicles (including those towing trailers). These might have to take a different course or straddle lanes either approaching or on the roundabout because of their length. Watch out for their signals.

188. Mini-roundabouts. Approach these in the same way as normal roundabouts. All vehicles **MUST** pass round the central markings except large vehicles which are physically incapable of doing so. Remember, there is less space to manoeuvre and less time to signal. Avoid making U-turns at mini-roundabouts. Beware of others doing this.
Laws RTA 1988 sect 36 & TSRGD regs 10(1) & 16(1)

189. At double mini-roundabouts treat each roundabout separately and give way to traffic from the right.

190. Multiple roundabouts. At some complex junctions, there may be a series of mini-roundabouts at each intersection. Treat each mini-roundabout separately and follow the normal rules.

Rule 190: Treat each roundabout separately

Pedestrian crossings

191. You **MUST NOT** park on a crossing or in the area covered by the zig-zag lines. You **MUST NOT** overtake the moving vehicle nearest the crossing or the vehicle nearest the crossing which has stopped to give way to pedestrians.

Laws ZPPPCRGD regs 18, 20 & 24, RTRA sect 25(5) & TSRGD regs 10, 27 & 28

192. In queuing traffic, you should keep the crossing clear.

Rule 192: Keep the crossing clear

193. You should take extra care where the view of either side of the crossing is blocked by queuing traffic or incorrectly parked vehicles. Pedestrians may be crossing between stationary vehicles.

194. Allow pedestrians plenty of time to cross and do not harass them by revving your engine or edging forward.

195. Zebra crossings. As you approach a zebra crossing
- look out for pedestrians waiting to cross and be ready to slow down or stop to let them cross
- you **MUST** give way when a pedestrian has moved onto a crossing
- allow more time for stopping on wet or icy roads
- do not wave or use your horn to invite pedestrians across; this could be dangerous if another vehicle is approaching
- be aware of pedestrians approaching from the side of the crossing.

A zebra crossing with a central island is two separate crossings (see pictures in Crossings, Rules 18–30).

Law ZPPPCRGD reg 25

Signal-controlled crossings

196. Pelican crossings. These are signal-controlled crossings where flashing amber follows the red 'Stop' light. You **MUST** stop when the red light shows. When the amber light is flashing, you **MUST** give way to any pedestrians on the crossing. If the amber light is flashing and there are no pedestrians on the crossing, you may proceed with caution.
Laws ZPPPCRGD regs 23 & 26 & RTRA sect 25(5)

Rule 196: Allow pedestrians to cross when the amber light is flashing

197. Pelican crossings which go straight across the road are one crossing, even when there is a central island. You **MUST** wait for pedestrians who are crossing from the other side of the island.
Laws ZPPPCRGD reg 26 & RTRA sect 25(5)

198. Give way to anyone still crossing after the signal for vehicles has changed to green. This advice applies to all crossings.

199. Toucan, puffin and equestrian crossings. These are similar to pelican crossings, but there is no flashing amber phase; the light sequence for traffic at these three crossings is the same as at traffic lights. If the signal-controlled crossing is not working, proceed with extreme caution.

Reversing

200. Choose an appropriate place to manoeuvre. If you need to turn your vehicle around, wait until you find a safe place. Try not to reverse or turn round in a busy road; find a quiet side road or drive round a block of side streets.

201. Do not reverse from a side road into a main road. When using a driveway, reverse in and drive out if you can.

202. Look carefully before you start reversing. You should
- use all your mirrors
- check the 'blind spot' behind you (the part of the road you cannot see easily in the mirrors)
- check there are no pedestrians (particularly children), cyclists, other road users or obstructions in the road behind you.

Reverse slowly while
- checking all around
- looking mainly through the rear window
- being aware that the front of your vehicle will swing out as you turn.

Get someone to guide you if you cannot see clearly.

Rule 202: Check all round when reversing

203. You **MUST NOT** reverse your vehicle further than necessary.
Law CUR reg 106

Road users requiring extra care

Overview

204. The most vulnerable road users are pedestrians, cyclists, motorcyclists and horse riders. It is particularly important to be aware of children, older and disabled people, and learner and inexperienced drivers and riders.

Pedestrians

205. There is a risk of pedestrians, especially children, stepping unexpectedly into the road. You should drive with the safety of children in mind at a speed suitable for the conditions.

206. Drive carefully and slowly when

- in crowded shopping streets, Home Zones and Quiet Lanes (see Rule 218) or residential areas
- driving past bus and tram stops; pedestrians may emerge suddenly into the road
- passing parked vehicles, especially ice cream vans; children are more interested in ice cream than traffic and may run into the road unexpectedly
- needing to cross a pavement or cycle track; for example, to reach or leave a driveway. Give way to pedestrians and cyclists on the pavement
- reversing into a side road; look all around the vehicle and give way to any pedestrians who may be crossing the road
- turning at road junctions; give way to pedestrians who are already crossing the road into which you are turning
- the pavement is closed due to street repairs and pedestrians are directed to use the road
- approaching pedestrians on narrow rural roads without a footway or footpath. Always slow down and be prepared to stop if necessary, giving them plenty of room as you drive past.

Rule 206: Watch out for children in busy areas

207. Particularly vulnerable pedestrians. These include

- children and older pedestrians who may not be able to judge your speed and could step into the road in front of you. At 40mph (64km/h) your vehicle will probably kill any pedestrians it hits. At 20mph (32km/h) there is only a 1 in 20 chance of the pedestrian being killed. So kill your speed
- older pedestrians who may need more time to cross the road. Be patient and allow them to cross in their own time. Do not hurry them by revving your engine or edging forward
- people with disabilities. People with hearing impairments may not be aware of your vehicle approaching. Those with walking difficulties require more time
- blind or partially sighted people, who may be carrying a white cane or using a guide dog. They may not be able to see you approaching
- deafblind people who may be carrying a white cane with a red band or using a dog with a red and white harness. They may not see or hear instructions or signals.

208. Near schools. Drive slowly and be particularly aware of young cyclists and pedestrians. In some places, there may be a flashing amber signal below the 'School' warning sign which tells you that there may be children crossing the road ahead. Drive very slowly until you are clear of the area.

209. Drive carefully and slowly when passing a stationary bus showing a 'School Bus' sign (see Vehicle markings) as children may be getting on or off.

210. You **MUST** stop when a school crossing patrol shows a 'Stop for children' sign (see pages Signals by authorised persons and Signs giving orders).

Law RTRA sect 28

Motorcyclists and cyclists

211. It is often difficult to see motorcyclists and cyclists, especially when they are coming up from behind, coming out of junctions, at roundabouts, overtaking you or filtering through traffic. Always look out for them before you emerge from a junction; they could be approaching faster than you think. When turning right across a line of slow-moving or stationary traffic, look out for cyclists or motorcyclists on the inside of the traffic you are crossing. Be especially careful when turning, and when changing direction or lane. Be sure to check mirrors and blind spots carefully.

Rule 211: Look out for motorcyclists and cyclists at junctions

212. When passing motorcyclists and cyclists, give them plenty of room (see Rules162–167). If they look over their shoulder it could mean that they intend to pull out, turn right or change direction. Give them time and space to do so.

213. Motorcyclists and cyclists may suddenly need to avoid uneven road surfaces and obstacles such as drain covers or oily, wet or icy patches on the road. Give them plenty of room and pay particular attention to any sudden change of direction they may have to make.

Other road users

214. Animals. When passing animals, drive slowly. Give them plenty of room and be ready to stop. Do not scare animals by sounding your horn, revving your engine or accelerating rapidly once you have passed them. Look out for animals being led, driven or ridden on the road and take extra care. Keep your speed down at bends and on narrow country roads. If a road is blocked by a herd of animals, stop and switch off your engine until they have left the road. Watch out for animals on unfenced roads.

215. Horse riders and horse-drawn vehicles. Be particularly careful of horse riders and horse-drawn vehicles especially when overtaking. Always pass wide and slowly. Horse riders are often children, so take extra care and remember riders may ride in double file when escorting a young or inexperienced horse or rider. Look out for horse riders' and horse drivers' signals and heed a request to slow down or stop. Take great care and treat all horses as a potential hazard; they can be unpredictable, despite the efforts of their rider/driver.

216. Older drivers. Their reactions may be slower than other drivers. Make allowance for this.

217. Learners and inexperienced drivers. They may not be so skilful at anticipating and responding to events. Be particularly patient with learner drivers and young drivers. Drivers who have recently passed their test may display a 'new driver' plate or sticker (see Annexe 8 – Safety code for new drivers).

218. Home Zones and Quiet Lanes. These are places where people could be using the whole of the road for a range of activities such as children playing or for a community event. You should drive slowly and carefully and be prepared to stop to allow people extra time to make space for you to pass them in safety.

Other vehicles

219. Emergency and Incident Support vehicles. You should look and listen for ambulances, fire engines, police, doctors or other emergency vehicles using flashing blue, red or green lights and sirens or flashing headlights, or Highways Agency Traffic Officer and Incident Support vehicles using flashing amber lights. When one approaches do not panic. Consider the route of such a vehicle and take appropriate action to let it pass, while complying with all traffic signs. If necessary, pull to the side of the road and stop, but try to avoid stopping before the brow of a hill, a bend or narrow section of road. Do not endanger yourself, other road users or pedestrians and avoid mounting the kerb. Do not brake harshly on approach to a junction or roundabout, as a following vehicle may not have the same view as you.

220. Powered vehicles used by disabled people. These small vehicles travel at a maximum speed of 8mph (12km/h). On a dual carriageway where the speed limit exceeds 50mph (80km/h) they **MUST** have a flashing amber beacon, but on other roads you may not have that advance warning (see Rules 36–46 inclusive).
Law RVLR reg 17(1) & 26

221. Large vehicles. These may need extra road space to turn or to deal with a hazard that you are not able to see. If you are following a large vehicle, such as a bus or articulated lorry, be aware that the driver may not be able to see you in the mirrors. Be prepared to stop and wait if it needs room or time to turn.

Rule 221: Large vehicles need extra room

222. Large vehicles can block your view. Your ability to see and to plan ahead will be improved if you pull back to increase your separation distance. Be patient, as larger vehicles are subject to lower speed limits than cars and motorcycles. Many large vehicles may be fitted with speed limiting devices which will restrict speed to 56mph (90km/h) even on a motorway.

223. Buses, coaches and trams. Give priority to these vehicles when you can do so safely, especially when they signal to pull away from stops. Look out for people getting off a bus or tram and crossing the road.

224. Electric vehicles. Be careful of electric vehicles such as milk floats and trams. Trams move quickly but silently and cannot steer to avoid you.

225. Vehicles with flashing amber beacons. These warn of a slow-moving or stationary vehicle (such as a Traffic Officer vehicle, salt spreader, snow plough or recovery vehicle) or abnormal loads, so approach with caution. On unrestricted dual carriageways, motor vehicles first used on or after 1 January 1947 with a maximum speed of 25mph (40km/h) or less (such as tractors) **MUST** use a flashing amber beacon (also see Rule 220).

Law RVLR 1989, reg 17

Driving in adverse weather conditions

Overview

226. You **MUST** use headlights when visibility is seriously reduced, generally when you cannot see for more than 100 metres (328 feet). You may also use front or rear fog lights but you **MUST** switch them off when visibility improves (see Rule 236).

Law RVLR regs 25 & 27

Wet weather

227. Wet weather. In wet weather, stopping distances will be at least double those required for stopping on dry roads (see Rule 126). This is because your tyres have less grip on the road. In wet weather

*   you should keep well back from the vehicle in front. This will increase your ability to see and plan ahead
*   if the steering becomes unresponsive, it probably means that water is preventing the tyres from gripping the road. Ease off the accelerator and slow down gradually
*   the rain and spray from vehicles may make it difficult to see and be seen
*   be aware of the dangers of spilt diesel that will make the surface very slippery (see Annexe 6: Vehicle maintenance).
*   take extra care around pedestrians, cyclists, motorcyclists and horse riders.

Icy and snowy weather

228. In winter check the local weather forecast for warnings of icy or snowy weather. **DO NOT** drive in these conditions unless your journey is essential. If it is, take great care and allow more time for your journey. Take an emergency kit of de-icer and ice scraper, torch, warm clothing and boots, first aid kit, jump leads and a shovel, together with a warm drink and emergency food in case you get stuck or your vehicle breaks down.

229. Before you set off

*   you **MUST** be able to see, so clear all snow and ice from all your windows
*   you **MUST** ensure that lights are clean and number plates are clearly visible and legible
*   make sure the mirrors are clear and the windows are demisted thoroughly
*   remove all snow that might fall off into the path of other road users
*   check your planned route is clear of delays and that no further snowfalls or severe weather are predicted.

Laws CUR reg 30, RVLR reg 23, VERA sect 43 & RV(DRM)R reg 11

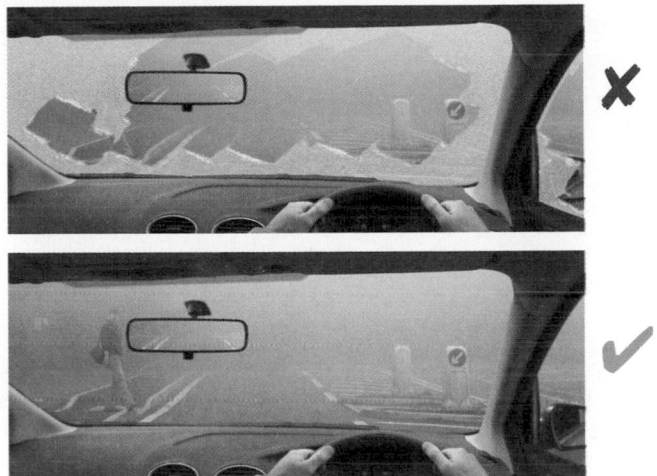

Rule 229: Make sure your windscreen is completely clear

230. When driving in icy or snowy weather
- drive with care, even if the roads have been treated
- keep well back from the road user in front as stopping distances can be ten times greater than on dry roads
- take care when overtaking vehicles spreading salt or other de-icer, particularly if you are riding a motorcycle or cycle
- watch out for snowploughs which may throw out snow on either side. Do not overtake them unless the lane you intend to use has been cleared
- be prepared for the road conditions to change over relatively short distances
- listen to travel bulletins and take note of variable message signs that may provide information about weather, road and traffic conditions ahead.

231. Drive extremely carefully when the roads are icy. Avoid sudden actions as these could cause loss of control. You should
- drive at a slow speed in as high a gear as possible; accelerate and brake very gently
- drive particularly slowly on bends where loss of control is more likely. Brake progressively on the straight before you reach a bend. Having slowed down, steer smoothly round the bend, avoiding sudden actions
- check your grip on the road surface when there is snow or ice by choosing a safe place to brake gently. If the steering feels unresponsive this may indicate ice and your vehicle losing its grip on the road. When travelling on ice, tyres make virtually no noise.

Windy weather

232. High-sided vehicles are most affected by windy weather, but strong gusts can also blow a car, cyclist, motorcyclist or horse rider off course. This can happen on open stretches of road exposed to strong crosswinds, or when passing bridges or gaps in hedges.

233. In very windy weather your vehicle may be affected by turbulence created by large vehicles. Motorcyclists are particularly affected, so keep well back from them when they are overtaking a high-sided vehicle.

Fog

234. Before entering fog check your mirrors then slow down. If the word 'Fog' is shown on a roadside signal but the road is clear, be prepared for a bank of fog or drifting patchy fog ahead. Even if it seems to be clearing, you can suddenly find yourself in thick fog.

235. When driving in fog you should
- use your lights as required (see Rule 226)
- keep a safe distance behind the vehicle in front. Rear lights can give a false sense of security
- be able to pull up well within the distance you can see clearly. This is particularly important on motorways and dual carriageways, as vehicles are travelling faster
- use your windscreen wipers and demisters
- beware of other drivers not using headlights
- not accelerate to get away from a vehicle which is too close behind you
- check your mirrors before you slow down. Then use your brakes so that your brake lights warn drivers behind you that you are slowing down
- stop in the correct position at a junction with limited visibility and listen for traffic. When you are sure it is safe to emerge, do so positively and do not hesitate in a position that puts you directly in the path of approaching vehicles.

236. You **MUST NOT** use front or rear fog lights unless visibility is seriously reduced (see Rule 226) as they dazzle other road users and can obscure your brake lights. You **MUST** switch them off when visibility improves.

Law RVLR regs 25 & 27

Hot weather

237. Keep your vehicle well ventilated to avoid drowsiness. Be aware that the road surface may become soft or if it rains after a dry spell it may become slippery. These conditions could affect your steering and braking. If you are dazzled by bright sunlight, slow down and if necessary, stop.

Waiting and parking

Waiting and parking

238. You **MUST NOT** wait or park on yellow lines during the times of operation shown on nearby time plates (or zone entry signs if in a Controlled Parking Zone) – see Traffic signs and Road markings. Double yellow lines indicate a prohibition of waiting at any time even if there are no upright signs. You **MUST NOT** wait or park, or stop to set down and pick up passengers, on school entrance markings (see Road markings) when upright signs indicate a prohibition of stopping.
Law RTRA sects 5 & 8

Parking

239. Use off-street parking areas, or bays marked out with white lines on the road as parking places, wherever possible. If you have to stop on the roadside

- do not park facing against the traffic flow
- stop as close as you can to the side
- do not stop too close to a vehicle displaying a Blue Badge: remember, the occupant may need more room to get in or out
- you **MUST** switch off the engine, headlights and fog lights
- you **MUST** apply the handbrake before leaving the vehicle
- you **MUST** ensure you do not hit anyone when you open your door. Check for cyclists or other traffic
- it is safer for your passengers (especially children) to get out of the vehicle on the side next to the kerb
- put all valuables out of sight and make sure your vehicle is secure
- lock your vehicle.

Laws CUR reg 98, 105 & 107, RVLR reg 27 & RTA 1988 sect 42

Rule 239: Check before opening your door

The Highway Code

240. You **MUST NOT** stop or park on
- the carriageway or the hard shoulder of a motorway except in an emergency (see Rule 270)
- a pedestrian crossing, including the area marked by the zig-zag lines (see Rule 191)
- a clearway (see Traffic signs)
- taxi bays as indicated by upright signs and markings
- an urban clearway within its hours of operation, except to pick up or set down passengers (see Traffic signs)
- a road marked with double white lines, even when a broken white line is on your side of the road, except to pick up or set down passengers, or to load or unload goods
- a tram or cycle lane during its period of operation
- a cycle track
- red lines, in the case of specially designated 'red routes', unless otherwise indicated by signs.

Any vehicle may enter a bus lane to stop, load or unload where this is not prohibited (see Rule 141).

Laws MT(E&W)R regs 7 & 9, MT(S)R regs 6 & 8, ZPPPCRGD regs 18 & 20, RTRA sects 5, 6 & 8, TSRGD regs 10, 26 & 27, RTA 1988 sects 21(1) & 36

241. You **MUST NOT** park in parking spaces reserved for specific users, such as Blue Badge holders, residents or motorcycles, unless entitled to do so.
Laws CSDPA sect 21 & RTRA sects 5 & 8

242. You **MUST NOT** leave your vehicle or trailer in a dangerous position or where it causes any unnecessary obstruction of the road.
Laws RTA 1988, sect 22 & CUR reg 103

243. DO NOT stop or park
- near a school entrance
- anywhere you would prevent access for Emergency Services
- at or near a bus or tram stop or taxi rank
- on the approach to a level crossing/tramway crossing
- opposite or within 10 metres (32 feet) of a junction, except in an authorised parking space
- near the brow of a hill or hump bridge
- opposite a traffic island or (if this would cause an obstruction) another parked vehicle
- where you would force other traffic to enter a tram lane
- where the kerb has been lowered to help wheelchair users and powered mobility vehicles

- in front of an entrance to a property
- on a bend
- where you would obstruct cyclists' use of cycle facilities

except when forced to do so by stationary traffic.

244. You **MUST NOT** park partially or wholly on the pavement in London, and should not do so elsewhere unless signs permit it. Parking on the pavement can obstruct and seriously inconvenience pedestrians, people in wheelchairs or with visual impairments and people with prams or pushchairs.

Law GL(GP)A sect 15

245. Controlled Parking Zones. The zone entry signs indicate the times when the waiting restrictions within the zone are in force. Parking may be allowed in some places at other times. Otherwise parking will be within separately signed and marked bays.

246. Goods vehicles. Vehicles with a maximum laden weight of over 7.5 tonnes (including any trailer) **MUST NOT** be parked on a verge, pavement or any land situated between carriageways, without police permission. The only exception is when parking is essential for loading and unloading, in which case the vehicle **MUST NOT** be left unattended.

Law RTA 1988 sect 19

247. Loading and unloading. Do not load or unload where there are yellow markings on the kerb and upright signs advise restrictions are in place (see Road markings). This may be permitted where parking is otherwise restricted. On red routes, specially marked and signed bays indicate where and when loading and unloading is permitted.

Law RTRA sects 5 & 8

Parking at night

248. You **MUST NOT** park on a road at night facing against the direction of the traffic flow unless in a recognised parking space.

Laws CUR reg 101 & RVLR reg 24

249. All vehicles **MUST** display parking lights when parked on a road or a lay-by on a road with a speed limit greater than 30mph (48km/h).

Law RVLR reg 24

250. Cars, goods vehicles not exceeding 1525kg unladen weight, invalid carriages, motorcycles and pedal cycles may be parked without lights on a road (or lay-by) with a speed limit of 30mph (48km/h) or less if they are

- at least 10 metres (32 feet) away from any junction, close to the kerb and facing in the direction of the traffic flow
- in a recognised parking place or lay-by.

Other vehicles and trailers, and all vehicles with projecting loads, **MUST NOT** be left on a road at night without lights.

Laws RVLR reg 24 & CUR reg 82(7)

251. Parking in fog. It is especially dangerous to park on the road in fog. If it is unavoidable, leave your parking lights or sidelights on.

252. Parking on hills. If you park on a hill you should
- park close to the kerb and apply the handbrake firmly
- select a forward gear and turn your steering wheel away from the kerb when facing uphill
- select reverse gear and turn your steering wheel towards the kerb when facing downhill
- use 'park' if your car has an automatic gearbox.

Rule 252: Turn your wheels away from the kerb when parking facing uphill. Turn your wheels towards the kerb when parking downhill

Decriminalised Parking Enforcement (DPE)

DPE is becoming increasingly common as more authorities take on this role. The local traffic authority assumes responsibility for enforcing many parking contraventions in place of the police. Further details on DPE may be found at the following websites:

www.trafficpenaltytribunal.gov.uk (outside London)

www.parkingandtrafficappeals.gov.uk (inside London)

Motorways

General
Many other Rules apply to motorway driving, either wholly or in part: Rules 46, 57, 83–88, 89–102, 103–126, 130–134, 139, 144, 146–151, 160–161, 219, 221–222, 225, 226–237, 274–278, 280–287 and 288–290.

253. Prohibited vehicles. Motorways **MUST NOT** be used by pedestrians, holders of provisional motorcycle or car licences, riders of motorcycles under 50cc, cyclists, horse riders, certain slow-moving vehicles and those carrying oversized loads (except by special permission), agricultural vehicles and powered wheelchairs/powered mobility scooters (see Rules 36–46 incl)
Laws HA 1980 sects 16, 17 & sch 4, MT(E&W)R regs 3(d), 4 & 11, MT(E&W)(A)R, R(S)A sects 7, 8 & sch 3, RTRA sects 17(2) & (3), & MT(S)R reg 10

254. Traffic on motorways usually travels faster than on other roads, so you have less time to react. It is especially important to use your mirrors earlier and look much further ahead than you would on other roads.

Motorway signals

255. Motorway signals (see Light signals controlling traffic) are used to warn you of a danger ahead. For example, there may be an incident, fog, a spillage or road workers on the carriageway which you may not immediately be able to see.

256. Signals situated on the central reservation apply to all lanes. On very busy stretches, signals may be overhead with a separate signal for each lane.

257. Amber flashing lights. These warn of a hazard ahead. The signal may show a temporary maximum speed limit, lanes that are closed or a message such as 'Fog'. Adjust your speed and look out for the danger until you pass a signal which is not flashing or one that gives the 'All clear' sign and you are sure it is safe to increase your speed.

258. Red flashing lights. If red lights on the overhead signals flash above your lane and a red 'X' is showing, you **MUST NOT** go beyond the signal in that lane. If red lights flash on a signal in the central reservation or at the side of the road, you **MUST NOT** go beyond the signal in any lane.
Laws RTA 1988 sect 36 & TSRGD regs 10 & 38

Joining the motorway

259. When you join the motorway you will normally approach it from a road on the left (a slip road) or from an adjoining motorway. You should

- give priority to traffic already on the motorway
- check the traffic on the motorway and match your speed to fit safely into the traffic flow in the left-hand lane
- not cross solid white lines that separate lanes or use the hard shoulder
- stay on the slip road if it continues as an extra lane on the motorway
- remain in the left-hand lane long enough to adjust to the speed of traffic before considering overtaking.

On the motorway

260. When you can see well ahead and the road conditions are good, you should

- drive at a steady cruising speed which you and your vehicle can handle safely and is within the speed limit (see Rule 124)
- keep a safe distance from the vehicle in front and increase the gap on wet or icy roads, or in fog (see Rules 126 and 235).

261. You **MUST NOT** exceed 70mph (112km/h), or the maximum speed limit permitted for your vehicle (see Speed limits tables). If a lower speed limit is in force, either permanently or temporarily, at roadworks for example, you **MUST NOT** exceed the lower limit. On some motorways, mandatory motorway signals (which display the speed within a red ring) are used to vary the maximum speed limit to improve traffic flow. You **MUST NOT** exceed this speed limit.
Law RTRA sects 17, 86, 89 & sch 6

262. The monotony of driving on a motorway can make you feel sleepy. To minimise the risk, follow the advice in Rule 91.

263. You **MUST NOT** reverse, cross the central reservation, or drive against the traffic flow. If you have missed your exit, or have taken the wrong route, carry on to the next exit.
Laws MT(E&W)R regs 6, 8 & 10 & MT(S)R regs 4, 5, 7 & 9

Lane discipline

264. You should always drive in the left-hand lane when the road ahead is clear. If you are overtaking a number of slower-moving vehicles, you should return to the left-hand lane as soon as you are safely past. Slow-moving or speed-restricted vehicles should always remain in the left-hand lane of the carriageway unless overtaking. You **MUST NOT**

drive on the hard shoulder except in an emergency or if directed to do so by the police, HA traffic officers in uniform or by signs.

Laws MT(E&W)R regs 5, 9 & 16(1)(a), MT(S)R regs 4, 8 & 14(1)(a), and RTA 1988, sects 35 & 186, as amended by TMA 2004 sect 6

265. The right-hand lane of a motorway with three or more lanes **MUST NOT** be used (except in prescribed circumstances) if you are driving
- any vehicle drawing a trailer
- a goods vehicle with a maximum laden weight exceeding 3.5 tonnes but not exceeding 7.5 tonnes, which is required to be fitted with a speed limiter
- a goods vehicle with a maximum laden weight exceeding 7.5 tonnes
- a passenger vehicle with a maximum laden weight exceeding 7.5 tonnes constructed or adapted to carry more than eight seated passengers in addition to the driver
- a passenger vehicle with a maximum laden weight not exceeding 7.5 tonnes which is constructed or adapted to carry more than eight seated passengers in addition to the driver, which is required to be fitted with a speed limiter.

Laws MT(E&W)R reg 12, MT(E&W)AR (2004), MT(S)R reg 11 & MT(S)AR (2004)

266. Approaching a junction. Look well ahead for signals or signs. Direction signs may be placed over the road. If you need to change lanes, do so in good time. At some junctions a lane may lead directly off the motorway. Only get in that lane if you wish to go in the direction indicated on the overhead signs.

Overtaking

267. Do not overtake unless you are sure it is safe and legal to do so. Overtake only on the right. You should
- check your mirrors
- take time to judge the speeds correctly
- make sure that the lane you will be joining is sufficiently clear ahead and behind
- take a quick sideways glance into the blind spot area to verify the position of a vehicle that may have disappeared from your view in the mirror
- remember that traffic may be coming up behind you very quickly. Check all your mirrors carefully. Look out for motorcyclists. When it is safe to do so, signal in plenty of time, then move out
- ensure you do not cut in on the vehicle you have overtaken
- be especially careful at night and in poor visibility when it is harder to judge speed and distance.

268. Do not overtake on the left or move to a lane on your left to overtake. In congested conditions, where adjacent lanes of traffic are moving at similar speeds, traffic in left-hand lanes may sometimes be moving faster than traffic to the right. In these conditions you may keep up with the traffic in your lane even if this means passing traffic in the lane to your right. Do not weave in and out of lanes to overtake.

269. Hard shoulder. You **MUST NOT** use the hard shoulder for overtaking. In areas where an Active Traffic Management (ATM) Scheme is in force, the hard shoulder may be used as a running lane. You will know when you can use this because a speed limit sign will be shown above all open lanes, including the hard shoulder. A red cross or blank sign above the hard shoulder means that you **MUST NOT** drive on the hard shoulder except in an emergency or breakdown. Emergency refuge areas have also been built into these areas for use in cases of emergency or breakdown.

Laws MT(E&W)R regs 5, 5A & 9, MT(S)R regs 4 & 8

Rule 269: Overhead gantry showing red cross over hard shoulder

Stopping

270. You **MUST NOT** stop on the carriageway, hard shoulder, slip road, central reservation or verge except in an emergency, or when told to do so by the police, HA traffic officers in uniform, an emergency sign or by flashing red light signals. Do not stop on the hard shoulder to either make or receive mobile phone calls.

Laws MT(E&W)R regs 5A, 7, 9, 10 & 16, MT(S)R regs 6(1), 8, 9 & 14, PRA 2002 sect 41 & sched 5(8), & RTA 1988 sects 35 & 163 as amended by TMA 2004, sect 6

271. You **MUST NOT** pick up or set down anyone, or walk on a motorway, except in an emergency.

Laws RTRA sect 17 & MT(E&W)R reg 15

Leaving the motorway

272. Unless signs indicate that a lane leads directly off the motorway, you will normally leave the motorway by a slip road on your left. You should
- watch for the signs letting you know you are getting near your exit
- move into the left-hand lane well before reaching your exit
- signal left in good time and reduce your speed on the slip road as necessary.

273. On leaving the motorway or using a link road between motorways, your speed may be higher than you realise – 50mph (80km/h) may feel like 30mph (48km/h). Check your speedometer and adjust your speed accordingly. Some slip-roads and link roads have sharp bends, so you will need to slow down.

Breakdowns and incidents

Breakdowns

274. If your vehicle breaks down, think first of all other road users and
- get your vehicle off the road if possible
- warn other traffic by using your hazard warning lights if your vehicle is causing an obstruction
- help other road users see you by wearing light-coloured or fluorescent clothing in daylight and reflective clothing at night or in poor visibility
- put a warning triangle on the road at least 45 metres (147 feet) behind your broken-down vehicle on the same side of the road, or use other permitted warning devices if you have them. Always take great care when placing or retrieving them, but never use them on motorways
- if possible, keep your sidelights on if it is dark or visibility is poor
- do not stand (or let anybody else stand) between your vehicle and oncoming traffic
- at night or in poor visibility do not stand where you will prevent other road users seeing your lights.

Additional rules for the motorway

275. If your vehicle develops a problem, leave the motorway at the next exit or pull into a service area. If you cannot do so, you should

- pull on to the hard shoulder and stop as far to the left as possible, with your wheels turned to the left
- try to stop near an emergency telephone (situated at approximately one-mile (1.6km) intervals along the hard shoulder)
- leave the vehicle by the left-hand door and ensure your passengers do the same. You **MUST** leave any animals in the vehicle or, in an emergency, keep them under proper control on the verge. Never attempt to place a warning triangle on a motorway
- do not put yourself in danger by attempting even simple repairs
- ensure that passengers keep away from the carriageway and hard shoulder, and that children are kept under control
- walk to an emergency telephone on your side of the carriageway (follow the arrows on the posts at the back of the hard shoulder) – the telephone is free of charge and connects directly to the Highways Agency or the police. Use these in preference to a mobile phone (see Rule 283). Always face the traffic when you speak on the phone
- give full details to the Highways Agency or the police; also inform them if you are a vulnerable motorist such as disabled, older or travelling alone
- return and wait near your vehicle (well away from the carriageway and hard shoulder)
- if you feel at risk from another person, return to your vehicle by a left-hand door and lock all doors. Leave your vehicle again as soon as you feel this danger has passed.

Laws MT(E&W)R reg 14 & MT(S)R reg 12

Rule 275: Keep well back from the hard shoulder

276. Before you rejoin the carriageway after a breakdown, build up speed on the hard shoulder and watch for a safe gap in the traffic. Be aware that other vehicles may be stationary on the hard shoulder.

277. If you cannot get your vehicle onto the hard shoulder
- do not attempt to place any warning device on the carriageway
- switch on your hazard warning lights
- leave your vehicle only when you can safely get clear of the carriageway.

Disabled drivers
278. If you have a disability which prevents you from following the above advice you should
- stay in your vehicle
- switch on your hazard warning lights
- display a 'Help' pennant or, if you have a car or mobile telephone, contact the emergency services and be prepared to advise them of your location.

Obstructions

279. If anything falls from your vehicle (or any other vehicle) on to the road, stop and retrieve it only if it is safe to do so.

280. Motorways. On a motorway do not try to remove the obstruction yourself. Stop at the next emergency telephone and call the Highways Agency or the police.

Incidents

281. Warning signs or flashing lights. If you see or hear emergency or incident support vehicles in the distance, be aware there may be an incident ahead (see Rule 219). Police Officers and Highways Agency Traffic Officers may be required to work in the carriageway, for example dealing with debris, collisions or conducting rolling road blocks. Police officers will use rear-facing flashing red and blue lights and HA Traffic Officers will use rear-facing flashing red and amber lights in these situations. Watch out for such signals, slow down and be prepared to stop. You **MUST** follow any directions given by Police officers or Traffic officers as to whether you can safely pass the incident or blockage.
Laws RTA1988, sects 35 & 163, and as amended by TMA 2004, sect 6

282. When passing the scene of an incident or crash do not be distracted or slow down unnecessarily (for example if an incident is on the other side of a dual carriageway). This may cause a collision or traffic congestion, but see Rule 283.

283. If you are involved in a crash or stop to give assistance
- use your hazard warning lights to warn other traffic
- ask drivers to switch off their engines and stop smoking
- arrange for the emergency services to be called immediately with full details of the incident location and any casualties (on a motorway, use the emergency telephone which allows easy location by the emergency services. If you use a mobile phone, first make sure you have identified your location from the marker posts on the side of the hard shoulder)
- move uninjured people away from the vehicles to safety; on a motorway this should, if possible, be well away from the traffic, the hard shoulder and the central reservation
- do not move injured people from their vehicles unless they are in immediate danger from fire or explosion
- do not remove a motorcyclist's helmet unless it is essential to do so
- be prepared to give first aid as shown in Annexe 7, First aid on the road
- stay at the scene until emergency services arrive.

If you are involved in any other medical emergency on the motorway you should contact the emergency services in the same way.

Incidents involving dangerous goods

284. Vehicles carrying dangerous goods in packages will be marked with plain orange reflective plates. Road tankers and vehicles carrying tank containers of dangerous goods will have hazard warning plates (see Vehicle markings).

285. If an incident involves a vehicle containing dangerous goods, follow the advice in Rule 283 and, in particular
- switch off engines and **DO NOT SMOKE**
- keep well away from the vehicle and do not be tempted to try to rescue casualties as you yourself could become one
- call the emergency services and give as much information as possible about the labels and markings on the vehicle. **DO NOT** use a mobile phone close to a vehicle carrying flammable loads.

Documentation

286. If you are involved in a collision which causes damage or injury to any other person, vehicle, animal or property, you **MUST**
- stop
- give your own and the vehicle owner's name and address, and the registration number of the vehicle, to anyone having reasonable grounds for requiring them
- if you do not give your name and address at the time of the collision, report it to the police as soon as reasonably practicable, and in any case within 24 hours.

Law RTA 1988 sect 170

287. If another person is injured and you do not produce your insurance certificate at the time of the crash to a police officer or to anyone having reasonable grounds to request it, you **MUST**

- report it to the police as soon as possible and in any case within 24 hours
- produce your insurance certificate for the police within seven days.

Law RTA 1988 sect 170

Roadworks, level crossings and tramways

Roadworks

288. When the 'Road Works Ahead' sign is displayed, you will need to be more watchful and look for additional signs providing more specific instructions. Observe all signs – they are there for your safety and the safety of road workers.

- You **MUST NOT** exceed any temporary maximum speed limit.
- Use your mirrors and get into the correct lane for your vehicle in good time and as signs direct.
- Do not switch lanes to overtake queuing traffic.
- Take extra care near cyclists and motorcyclists as they are vulnerable to skidding on grit, mud or other debris at roadworks.
- Where lanes are restricted due to roadworks, merge in turn (see Rule 134).
- Do not drive through an area marked off by traffic cones.
- Watch out for traffic entering or leaving the works area, but do not be distracted by what is going on there. Concentrate on the road ahead, not the roadworks.
- Bear in mind that the road ahead may be obstructed by the works or by slow moving or stationary traffic.
- Keep a safe distance – there could be queues in front. To obtain further information about roadworks see Conversions and Further Reading.

Law RTRA sect 16

Additional rules for high-speed roads

289. Take special care on motorways and other high-speed dual carriageways.

- One or more lanes may be closed to traffic and a lower speed limit may apply.
- Works vehicles that are slow moving or stationary with a large 'Keep Left' or 'Keep Right' sign on the back are sometimes used to close lanes for repairs, and a flashing light arrow may also be used to make the works vehicle more conspicuous from a distance and give earlier warning to drivers that they need to move over to the next lane.

- Check mirrors, slow down and change lanes if necessary.
- Keep a safe distance from the vehicle in front (see Rule 126).

290. Contraflow systems mean that you may be travelling in a narrower lane than normal and with no permanent barrier between you and oncoming traffic. The hard shoulder may be used for traffic, but be aware that there may be broken-down vehicles ahead of you. Keep a good distance from the vehicle ahead and observe any temporary speed limits.

Level crossings

291. A level crossing is where a road crosses a railway or tramway line. Approach and cross it with care. Never drive onto a crossing until the road is clear on the other side and do not get too close to the car in front. Never stop or park on, or near a crossing.

292. Overhead electric lines. It is dangerous to touch overhead electric lines. You **MUST** obey the safe height warning road signs and you should not continue forward onto the railway if your vehicle touches any height barrier or bells. The clearance available is usually 5 metres (16 feet 6 inches) but may be lower.

Laws RTA 1988 sect 36, TSRGD 2002 reg 17(5)

293. Controlled Crossings. Most crossings have traffic light signals with a steady amber light, twin flashing red stop lights (see Light signals controlling traffic and Traffic signs) and an audible alarm for pedestrians. They may have full, half or no barriers.
- You **MUST** always obey the flashing red stop lights.
- You **MUST** stop behind the white line across the road.
- Keep going if you have already crossed the white line when the amber light comes on.
- Do not reverse onto or over a controlled crossing.
- You **MUST** wait if a train goes by and the red lights continue to flash. This means another train will be passing soon.
- Only cross when the lights go off and barriers open.
- Never zig-zag around half-barriers, they lower automatically because a train is approaching.
- At crossings where there are no barriers, a train is approaching when the lights show.

Laws RTA 1988 sect 36 & TSRGD regs 10 & 40

Rule 293: Stop when the traffic lights show

294. Railway telephones. If you are driving a large or slow-moving vehicle, a long, low vehicle with a risk of grounding, or herding animals, a train could arrive before you are clear of the crossing. You **MUST** obey any sign instructing you to use the railway telephone to obtain permission to cross. You **MUST** also telephone when clear of the crossing if requested to do so.

Laws RTA 1988 sect 36 & TSRGD regs 10 & 16(1)

295. Crossings without traffic lights. Vehicles should stop and wait at the barrier or gate when it begins to close and not cross until the barrier or gate opens.

296. User-operated gates or barriers. Some crossings have 'Stop' signs and small red and green lights. You **MUST NOT** cross when the red light is showing, only cross if the green light is on. If crossing with a vehicle, you should

- open the gates or barriers on both sides of the crossing
- check that the green light is still on and cross quickly
- close the gates or barriers when you are clear of the crossing.

Laws RTA 1988 sect 36 & TSRGD regs 10 & 52(2)

297. If there are no lights, follow the procedure in Rule 295. Stop, look both ways and listen before you cross. If there is a railway telephone, always use it to contact the signal operator to make sure it is safe to cross. Inform the signal operator again when you are clear of the crossing.

298. Open crossings. These have no gates, barriers, attendant or traffic lights but will have a 'Give Way' sign. You should look both ways, listen and make sure there is no train coming before you cross.

299. Incidents and breakdowns. If your vehicle breaks down, or if you have an incident on a crossing you should

- get everyone out of the vehicle and clear of the crossing immediately
- use a railway telephone if available to tell the signal operator. Follow the instructions you are given
- move the vehicle clear of the crossing if there is time before a train arrives. If the alarm sounds, or the amber light comes on, leave the vehicle and get clear of the crossing immediately.

Tramways

300. You **MUST NOT** enter a road, lane or other route reserved for trams. Take extra care where trams run along the road. You should avoid driving directly on top of the rails and should take care where trams leave the main carriageway to enter the reserved route, to ensure you do not follow them. The width taken up by trams is often shown by tram lanes marked by white lines, yellow dots or by a different type of road surface. Diamond-shaped signs and white light signals give instructions to tram drivers only.

Law RTRA sects 5 & 8

301. Take extra care where the track crosses from one side of the road to the other and where the road narrows and the tracks come close to the kerb. Tram drivers usually have their own traffic signals and may be permitted to move when you are not. Always give way to trams. Do not try to race or overtake them or pass them on the inside, unless they are at tram stops or stopped by tram signals and there is a designated tram lane for you to pass.

302. You **MUST NOT** park your vehicle where it would get in the way of trams or where it would force other drivers to do so. Do not stop on any part of a tram track, except in a designated bay where this has been provided alongside and clear of the track. When doing so, ensure that all parts of your vehicle are outside the delineated tram path. Remember that a tram cannot steer round an obstruction.

Law RTRA sects 5 & 8

303. Tram stops. Where the tram stops at a platform, either in the middle or at the side of the road, you **MUST** follow the route shown by the road signs and markings. At stops without platforms you **MUST NOT** drive between a tram and the left-hand kerb when a tram has stopped to pick up passengers. If there is no alternative route signed, do not overtake the tram – wait until it moves off.

Law RTRA sects 5 & 8

304. Look out for pedestrians, especially children, running to catch a tram approaching a stop.

305. Always give priority to trams, especially when they signal to pull away from stops, unless it would be unsafe to do so. Remember that they may be carrying large numbers of standing passengers who could be injured if the tram had to make an emergency stop. Look out for people getting off a bus or tram and crossing the road.

306. All road users, but particularly cyclists and motorcyclists, should take extra care when driving or riding close to or crossing the tracks, especially if the rails are wet. You should take particular care when crossing the rails at shallow angles, on bends and at junctions. It is safest to cross the tracks directly at right angles. Other road users should be aware that cyclists and motorcyclists may need more space to cross the tracks safely.

307. Overhead electric lines. Tramway overhead wires are normally 5.8 metres above any carriageway, but can be lower. You should ensure that you have sufficient clearance between the wire and your vehicle (including any load you are carrying) before driving under an overhead wire. Drivers of vehicles with extending cranes, booms, tipping apparatus or other types of variable height equipment should ensure that the equipment is fully lowered. Where overhead wires are set lower than 5.8 metres (19 feet), these will be indicated by height clearance markings – similar to 'low bridge' signs. The height clearances on these plates should be carefully noted and observed. If you are in any doubt as to whether your vehicle will pass safely under the wires, you should always contact the local police or the tramway operator. Never take a chance as this can be extremely hazardous.

Light signals controlling traffic

Traffic Light Signals

  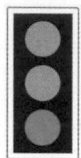 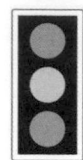 

RED means 'Stop'. Wait behind the stop line on the carriageway	RED AND AMBER also means 'Stop'. Do not pass through or start until GREEN shows	GREEN means you may go on if the way is clear. Take special care if you intend to turn left or right and give way to pedestrians who are crossing	AMBER means 'Stop' at the stop line. You may go on only if the AMBER appears after you have crossed the stop line or are so close to it that to pull up might cause an accident	A GREEN ARROW may be provided in addition to the full green signal if movement in a certain direction is allowed before or after the full green phase. If the way is clear you may go but only in the direction shown by the arrow. You may do this whatever other lights may be showing. White light signals may be provided for trams

Flashing red lights

Alternately flashing red lights mean YOU MUST STOP

At level crossings, lifting bridges, airfields, fire stations, etc.

Motorway signals

You **MUST NOT** proceed further in this lane

Change lane

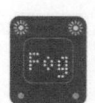

Reduced visibility ahead

Lane ahead closed

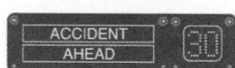

Temporary maximum speed advised and information message

Leave motorway at next exit

Temporary maximum speed advised

End of restriction

Lane control signals

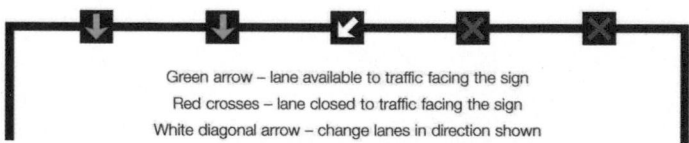

Green arrow – lane available to traffic facing the sign

Red crosses – lane closed to traffic facing the sign

White diagonal arrow – change lanes in direction shown

Signals to other road users

Direction indicator signals

I intend to move out to the
right or turn right

I intend to move in to the left
or turn left or stop on the left

Brake light signals

Reversing light signals

I am applying the brakes

I intend to reverse

These signals should not be used except for the purposes described.

Arm signals

For use when direction indicator signals are not used, or when necessary to reinforce direction indicator signals and stop lights. *Also for use by pedal cyclists and those in charge of horses.*

I intend to move in to
the left or turn left

I intend to move out to
the right or turn right

I intend to slow
down or stop

Signals by authorised persons

Police officers

Stop

Traffic approaching from the front

Traffic approaching from both front and behind

Traffic approaching from behind

To beckon traffic on

From the side

From the front

From behind*

Arm signals to persons controlling traffic

I want to go straight on

I want to turn left; use either hand

I want to turn right

* In Wales, bilingual signs appear on emergency services vehicles and clothing

Driver & Vehicle Standards Agency (DVSA) officers and traffic officers

Traffic officer

DVSA officer

These officers now have new powers to stop/direct vehicles and will be using hand signals and light signals similar to those used by police. You **MUST** obey any signals given (see Rules 107 and 108).

School Crossing Patrols

Not ready to cross pedestrians

Barrier to stop pedestrians crossing

Ready to cross pedestrians, vehicles must be prepared to stop

All vehicles must stop

Traffic signs

Signs giving orders

**Signs with red circles are mostly prohibitive.
Plates below signs qualify their message.**

Entry to
20mph zone

End of
20mph zone

Maximum
speed

National speed
limit applies

School crossing
patrol

Stop and
give way

Give way to
traffic on
major road

Manually operated temporary
STOP and GO signs

No entry for
vehicular traffic

No vehicles
except bicycles
being pushed

No cycling

No motor
vehicles

No buses
(over 8
passenger
seats)

No
overtaking

No
towed
caravans

No vehicles
carrying
explosives

No vehicle or
combination of
vehicles over
length shown

No vehicles
over
height shown

No vehicles
over
width shown

Give priority to
vehicles from
opposite
direction

No right turn

No left turn

No
U-turns

No goods vehicles
over maximum
gross weight
shown (in tonnes)
except for loading
and unloading

Note: Although *The Highway Code* shows many of the signs commonly in use, a comprehensive explanation of our signing system is given in the Department's booklet *Know Your Traffic Signs*, which is on sale at booksellers. The booklet also illustrates and explains the vast majority of signs the road user is likely to encounter. The signs illustrated in *The Highway Code* are not all drawn to the same scale. In Wales, bilingual versions of some signs are used including Welsh and English versions of place names. Some older designs of signs may still be seen on the roads.

No vehicles over maximum gross weight shown (in tonnes)

Parking restricted to permit holders

No stopping during period indicated except for buses

No stopping during times shown except for as long as necessary to set down or pick up passengers

No waiting

No stopping (Clearway)

Signs with blue circles but no red border mostly give positive instruction.

Ahead only

Turn left ahead (right if symbol reversed)

Turn left (right if symbol reversed)

Keep left (right if symbol reversed)

Vehicles may pass either side to reach same destination

Mini-roundabout (roundabout circulation – give way to vehicles from the immediate right)

Route to be used by pedal cycles only

Segregated pedal cycle and pedestrian route

Minimum speed

End of minimum speed

Buses and cycles only

Trams only

Pedestrian crossing point over tramway

One-way traffic (note: compare circular 'Ahead only' sign)

With-flow bus and cycle lane

Contraflow bus lane

With-flow pedal cycle lane

Warning signs

Mostly triangular

Distance to 'STOP' line ahead

Dual carriageway ends

Road narrows on right (left if symbol reversed)

Road narrows on both sides

Distance to 'Give Way' line ahead

Crossroads

Junction on bend ahead

T-junction with priority over vehicles from the right

Staggered junction

Traffic merging from left ahead

The priority through route is indicated by the broader line.

Double bend first to left (symbol may be reversed)

Bend to right (or left if symbol reversed)

Roundabout

Uneven road

Plate below some signs

Two-way traffic crosses one-way road

Two-way traffic straight ahead

Opening or swing bridge ahead

Low-flying aircraft or sudden aircraft noise

Falling or fallen rocks

Traffic signals not in use

Traffic signals

Slippery road

Steep hill downwards

Steep hill upwards

Gradients may be shown as a ratio i.e. 20% = 1:5

Tunnel ahead

Trams crossing ahead

Level crossing with barrier or gate ahead

Level crossing without barrier or gate ahead

Level crossing without barrier

Warning signs – continued

School crossing patrol ahead (some signs have amber lights which flash when crossings are in use)

Frail (or blind or disabled if shown) pedestrians likely to cross road ahead

Pedestrians in road ahead

Zebra crossing

Overhead electric cable; plate indicates maximum height of vehicles which can pass safely

Available width of headroom indicated

Sharp deviation of route to left (or right if chevrons reversed)

Light signals ahead at level crossing, airfield or bridge

Miniature warning lights at level crossings

Cattle

Wild animals

Wild horses or ponies

Accompanied horses or ponies

Cycle route ahead

Risk of ice

Traffic queues likely ahead

Distance over which road humps extend

Other danger; plate indicates nature of danger

Soft verges

Side winds

Hump bridge

Worded warning sign

Quayside or river bank

Risk of grounding

Direction signs

Mostly rectangular

Signs on motorways – blue backgrounds

At a junction leading directly into a motorway (junction number may be shown on a black background)

On approaches to junctions (junction number on black background)

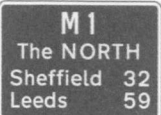

Route confirmatory sign after junction

Downward pointing arrows mean 'Get in lane'
The left-hand lane leads to a different destination from the other lanes.

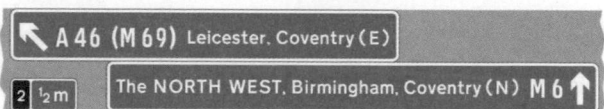

The panel with the inclined arrow indicates the destinations which can be reached by leaving the motorway at the next junction

Signs on primary routes - green backgrounds

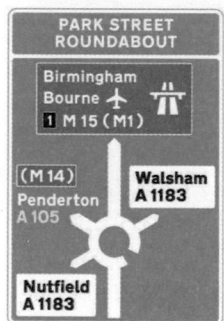

On approaches to junctions

At the junction

On approaches to junctions

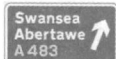

On approach to a junction in Wales (bilingual)

A 46
The SOUTH
Nottingham 17
Leicester 32
(M1 South) 35

Route confirmatory sign after junction

Blue panels indicate that the motorway starts at the junction ahead.
Motorways shown in brackets can also be reached along the route indicated.
White panels indicate local or non-primary routes leading from the junction ahead.
Brown panels show the route to tourist attractions.
The name of the junction may be shown at the top of the sign.
The aircraft symbol indicates the route to an airport.
A symbol may be included to warn of a hazard or restriction along that route.

Green background signs – continued

Primary route forming part of a ring road

Signs on non-primary and local routes - black borders

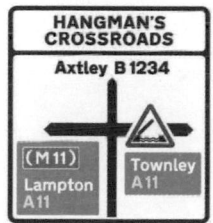

On approaches to junctions

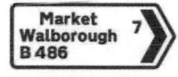

At the junction

Direction to toilets with access for the disabled

Green panels indicate that the primary route starts at the junction ahead.
Route numbers on a blue background show the direction to a motorway.
Route numbers on a green background show the direction to a primary route.

Other direction signs

Picnic site

Ancient monument in the care of English Heritage

Direction to a car park

Tourist attraction

Direction to camping and caravan site

Advisory route for lorries

Route for pedal cycles forming part of a network

Recommended route for pedal cycles to place shown

Route for pedestrians

Symbols showing emergency diversion route for motorway and other main road traffic

Diversion route

Information signs

All rectangular

Entrance to controlled parking zone

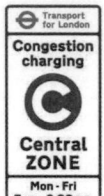

Entrance to congestion charging zone

End of controlled parking zone

Advance warning of restriction or prohibition ahead

Parking place for solo motorcycles

With-flow bus lane ahead which pedal cycles and taxis may also use

Lane designated for use by high occupancy vehicles (HOV) - see rule 142

Vehicles permitted to use an HOV lane ahead

End of motorway

Start of motorway and point from which motorway regulations apply

Appropriate traffic lanes at junction ahead

Traffic on the main carriageway coming from right has priority over joining traffic

Additional traffic joining from left ahead. Traffic on main carriageway has priority over joining traffic from right hand lane of slip road

Traffic in right hand lane of slip road joining the main carriageway has prority over left hand lane

'Countdown' markers at exit from motorway (each bar represents 100 yards to the exit). Green-backed markers may be used on primary routes and white-backed markers with black bars on other routes. At approaches to concealed level crossings white-backed markers with red bars may be used. Although these will be erected at equal distances the bars do not represent 100 yard intervals.

Motorway service area sign showing the operator's name

Information signs – continued

Traffic has priority over oncoming vehicles

Hospital ahead with Accident and Emergency facilities

Tourist information point

No through road for vehicles

Recommended route for pedal cycles

Home Zone Entry

Area in which cameras are used to enforce traffic regulations

Bus lane on road at junction ahead

Roadworks signs

Road works

Loose chippings

Temporary hazard at roadworks

Temporary lane closure (the number and position of arrows and red bars may be varied according to lanes open and closed)

Slow-moving or stationary works vehicle blocking a traffic lane. Pass in the direction shown by the arrow.

Mandatory speed limit ahead

Roadworks 1 mile ahead

End of roadworks and any temporary restrictions including speed limits

Signs used on the back of slow-moving or stationary vehicles warning of a lane closed ahead by a works vehicle. There are no cones on the road.

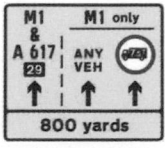

Lane restrictions at roadworks ahead

One lane crossover at contraflow roadworks

Road markings

Across the carriageway

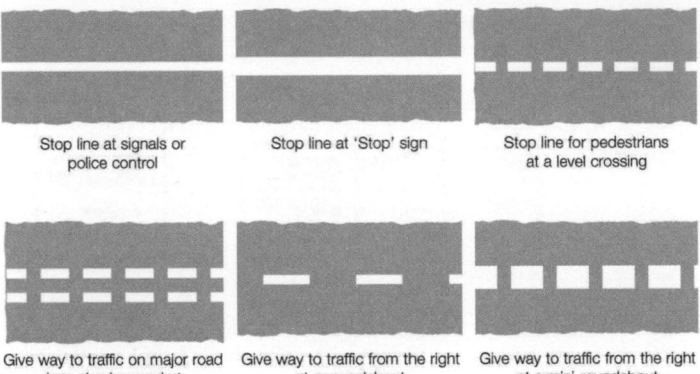

Stop line at signals or police control

Stop line at 'Stop' sign

Stop line for pedestrians at a level crossing

Give way to traffic on major road (can also be used at mini roundabouts)

Give way to traffic from the right at a roundabout

Give way to traffic from the right at a mini-roundabout

Along the carriageway

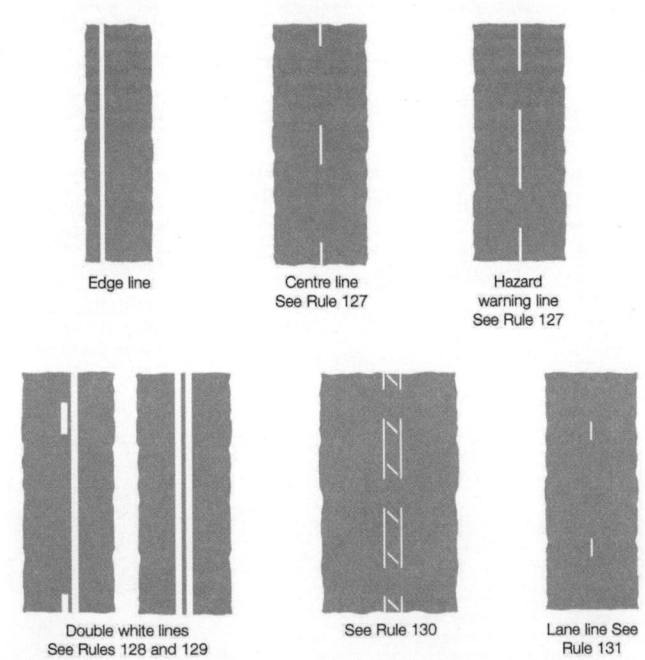

Edge line

Centre line
See Rule 127

Hazard
warning line
See Rule 127

Double white lines
See Rules 128 and 129

See Rule 130

Lane line See
Rule 131

Along the edge of the carriageway

Waiting restrictions

Waiting restrictions indicated by yellow lines apply to the carriageway, pavement and verge. You may stop to load or unload (unless there are also loading restrictions as described below) or while passengers board or alight. Double yellow lines mean no waiting at any time, unless there are signs that specifically indicate seasonal restrictions. The times at which the restrictions apply for other road markings are shown on nearby plates or on entry signs to controlled parking zones. If no days are shown on the signs, the restrictions are in force every day including Sundays and Bank Holidays. White bay markings and upright signs (see below) indicate where parking is allowed.

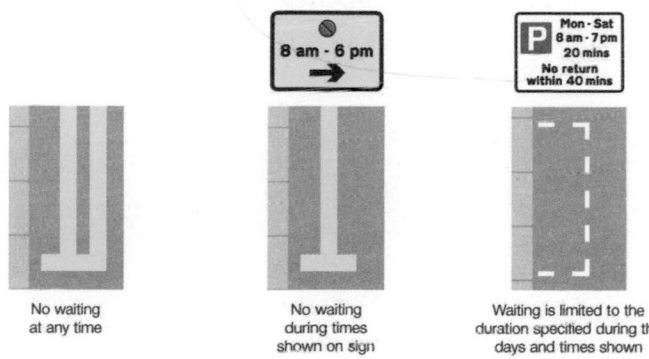

No waiting at any time

No waiting during times shown on sign

Waiting is limited to the duration specified during the days and times shown

Red Route stopping controls

Red lines are used on some roads instead of yellow lines. In London the double and single red lines used on Red Routes indicate that stopping to park, load/unload or to board and alight from a vehicle (except for a licensed taxi or if you hold a Blue Badge) is prohibited. The red lines apply to the carriageway, pavement and verge. The times that the red line prohibitions apply are shown on nearby signs, but the double red line ALWAYS means no stopping at any time. On Red Routes you may stop to park, load/unload in specially marked boxes and adjacent signs specify the times and purposes and duration allowed. A box MARKED IN RED indicates that it may only be available for the purpose specified for part of the day (e.g. between busy peak periods). A box MARKED IN WHITE means that it is available throughout the day.

RED AND SINGLE YELLOW LINES CAN ONLY GIVE A GUIDE TO THE RESTRICTIONS AND CONTROLS IN FORCE AND SIGNS, NEARBY OR AT A ZONE ENTRY, MUST BE CONSULTED.

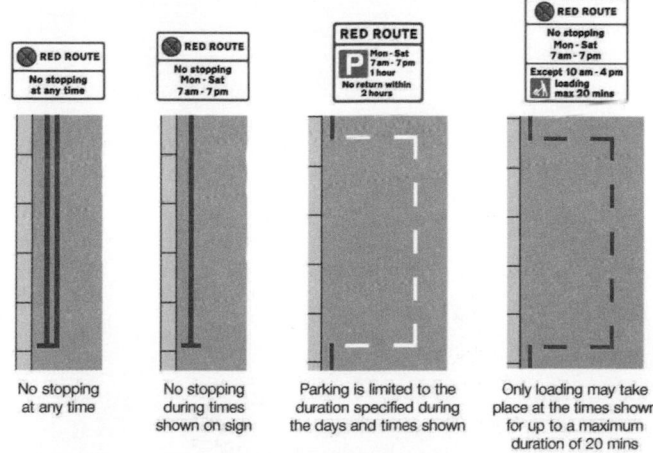

No stopping at any time

No stopping during times shown on sign

Parking is limited to the duration specified during the days and times shown

Only loading may take place at the times shown for up to a maximum duration of 20 mins

On the kerb or at the edge of the carriageway

Loading restrictions on roads other than Red Routes

Yellow marks on the kerb or at the edge of the carriageway indicate that loading or unloading is prohibited at the times shown on the nearby black and white plates. You may stop while passengers board or alight. If no days are indicated on the signs the restrictions are in force every day including Sundays and Bank Holidays.

ALWAYS CHECK THE TIMES SHOWN ON THE PLATES.

Lengths of road reserved for vehicles loading and unloading are indicated by a white 'bay' marking with the words 'Loading Only' and a sign with the white on blue 'trolley' symbol. This sign also shows whether loading and unloading is restricted to goods vehicles and the times at which the bay can be used. If no times or days are shown it may be used at any time. Vehicles may not park here if they are not loading or unloading.

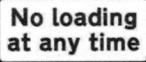

No loading or unloading
at any time

No loading or unloading
at the times shown

Loading bay

Other road markings

Keep entrance clear of stationary vehicles, even if picking up or setting down children

Warning of 'Give Way'
just ahead

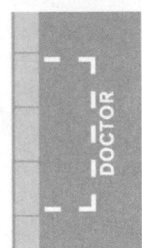

Parking space reserved
for vehicles named

See Rule 243

See Rule 141

Box junction - See Rule 174

Do not block that part of
the carriageway indicated

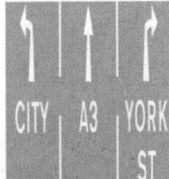

Indication of traffic lanes

Vehicle markings

Large goods vehicle rear markings

Motor vehicles over 7500 kilograms maximum gross weight and trailers over 3500 kilograms maximum gross weight

Left   Right

LONG VEHICLE

Central

The vertical markings are also required to be fitted to builders' skips placed in the road, commercial vehicles or combinations longer than 13 metres (optional on combinations between 11 and 13 metres)

Hazard warning plates

Certain tank vehicles carrying dangerous goods must display hazard information panels

The panel illustrated is for flammable liquid. Diamond symbols indicating other risks include:

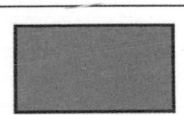

The above panel will be displayed by vehicles carrying certain dangerous goods in packages

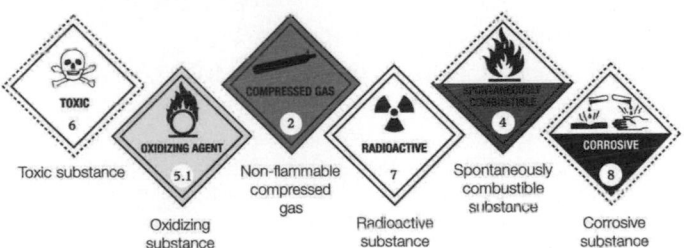

Toxic substance

Oxidizing substance

Non-flammable compressed gas

Radioactive substance

Spontaneously combustible substance

Corrosive substance

Projection markers

Side marker   End marker

Both required when load or equipment (eg crane jib) overhangs front or rear by more than two metres

Other

School bus
(displayed in front or rear window of bus or coach)

Annexes

1. You and your bicycle

Make sure that you feel confident of your ability to ride safely on the road. Be sure that

- you choose the right size and type of cycle for comfort and safety
- lights and reflectors are kept clean and in good working order
- tyres are in good condition and inflated to the pressure shown on the tyre
- gears are working correctly
- the chain is properly adjusted and oiled
- the saddle and handlebars are adjusted to the correct height.

It is recommended that you fit a bell to your cycle.

You **MUST**

- ensure your brakes are efficient
- at night, use lit front and rear lights and have a red rear reflector.

Laws PCUR regs 6 & 10 & RVLR reg 18

Cycle training can help both children and adults, especially those adults returning to cycling to develop the skills needed to cycle safely on today's roads. A new national cycle training standard has been developed which the Government is promoting and making funding available for delivery in schools.

All cyclists should consider the benefits of undertaking cycle training. For information, contact your local authority.

2. Motorcycle licence requirements

If you have a provisional motorcycle licence, you **MUST** satisfactorily complete a Compulsory Basic Training (CBT) course.

You can then ride unaccompanied on the public road a motorcycle up to 125cc, with a power output not exceeding 11kW, with L plates (in Wales either D plates or L plates, or both, can be used), for up to two years.

To ride a moped, learners **MUST**:

- be 16 or over
- have a provisional moped licence
- complete CBT training.

You can then ride unaccompanied on the public road a two-wheeled vehicle with a maximum design speed of 45km/h (28mph), with L plates (in Wales either D plates or L plates, or both, can be used), for up to two years.

You **MUST** first pass the theory test for motorcycles and then the moped practical test to obtain your full moped licence.

If you passed your car driving test before 1 February 2001 you are qualified to ride a moped without L plates (and/or D plates in Wales), although it is recommended that you complete CBT before riding on the road. If you passed your car driving test after this date you **MUST** complete CBT before riding a moped on the road.

Licence categories for mopeds and motorcycles

Category AM (moped) – minimum age 16

- two-wheeled vehicle with a maximum design speed of 45km/h (28mph)
- three- or four-wheeled vehicle with a maximum design speed over 25km/h (15.5mph), up to 50cc and with a power output not exceeding 4 kW.

Category A1 – minimum age 17
- motorcycles up to 125cc, with a power output not exceeding 11kW
- tricycles with a power output not exceeding 15kW.

Category A2 – minimum age 19
- motorcycles with a power output not exceeding 35kW.

Category A
- unrestricted motorcycles with a power output over 35kW (minimum age 24 under direct access, or 21 under progressive access)
- tricycles with a power output over 15kW (minimum age 21).

Progressive access is a process that allows a rider to take a higher-category practical test if they already have at least two years' experience on a lowercategory motorcycle. For example, if you have held a category A2 licence for a minimum of two years, you can take the category A practical test at age 21. There is no requirement to take another theory test.

If you want to learn to ride motorcycles larger than 125cc and with a power output over 11kW, you **MUST** meet the minimum age requirements, satisfactorily complete a CBT course and be accompanied by an approved instructor on another motorcycle in radio contact.

To obtain your full moped or motorcycle licence you **MUST** pass a motorcycle theory test and modules 1 and 2 practical tests on a two-wheeled motorcycle.

You **MUST NOT** carry a pillion passenger or pull a trailer until you have passed your test. Also see Rule 253 covering vehicles prohibited from motorways.
Law MV(DL)R reg 16

3. Motor vehicle documentation and learner driver requirements

Documents

Driving licence. You **MUST** have a valid driving licence for the category of motor vehicle you are driving. You **MUST** inform the Driver and Vehicle Licensing Agency (DVLA) if you change your name and/or address.
Law RTA 1988 sects 87 & 99(4)

Holders of non-European Community licences who are now resident in the UK may only drive on that licence for a maximum of 12 months from the date they become resident in this country. To ensure continuous driving entitlement

* a British provisional licence should be obtained and a driving test(s) passed before the 12-month period elapses, or
* in the case of a driver who holds a licence from a country which has been designated in law for licence exchange purposes, the driver should exchange the licence for a British one.

MOT. Cars and motorcycles **MUST** normally pass an MOT test three years from the date of the first registration and every year after that. You **MUST NOT** drive a motor vehicle without an MOT certificate when it should have one. Exceptionally, you may drive to a pre-arranged test appointment or to a garage for repairs required for the test. Driving an unroadworthy motor vehicle may invalidate your insurance. From November 2012, motor vehicles manufactured before 1960 will be exempted from an MOT requirement, although they can still be submitted for a test voluntarily. Owners are still legally required to ensure their vehicle is safe and roadworthy.
Law RTA 1988 sects 45, 47, 49 & 53

Insurance. To use a motor vehicle on the road, you **MUST** have a valid insurance policy. This **MUST** at least cover you for injury or damage to a third party while using that motor vehicle. Before driving any motor vehicle, make sure that it has this cover for your use or that your own insurance provides adequate cover. You **MUST NOT** drive a motor vehicle without insurance. Also, be aware that even if a road traffic incident is not your fault, you may still be held liable by insurance companies.
Law RTA 1988 sect 143

Uninsured drivers can now be automatically detected by roadside cameras. Further to the penalties for uninsured driving listed in Annexe 5, Penalties, an offender's vehicle can now be seized by the Police, taken away and crushed.

Law RTA 1988, sects 165a & 165b

The types of cover available are indicated below:

Third-Party insurance – this is often the cheapest form of insurance, and is the minimum cover required by law. It covers anyone you might injure or whose property you might damage. It does not cover damage to your own motor vehicle or injury to yourself.

Third-Party, Fire and Theft insurance – similar to third-party, but also covers you against your motor vehicle being stolen, or damaged by fire.

Comprehensive insurance – this is the most expensive but the best insurance. Apart from covering other persons and property against injury or damage, it also covers damage to your own motor vehicle, up to the market value of that vehicle, and personal injury to yourself.

Registration certificate. Registration certificates (also called harmonised registration certificates) are issued for all motor vehicles used on the road, describing them (make, model, etc) and giving details of the registered keeper. You **MUST** notify the Driver and Vehicle Licensing Agency in Swansea as soon as possible when you buy or sell a motor vehicle, or if you change your name or address.
For registration certificates issued after 27 March 1997, the buyer and seller are responsible for completing the registration certificates. The seller is responsible for forwarding them to DVLA. The procedures are explained on the back of the registration certificates.

Law RV(R&L)R regs 21, 22, 23 & 24

Vehicle Excise Duty (VED). Vehicle Excise Duty **MUST** be paid on all motor vehicles used or kept on public roads.

Law VERA sects 29 and 33

Statutory Off-Road Notification (SORN). This is a notification to the DVLA that a motor vehicle is not being used on the road. If you are the vehicle keeper and want to keep a motor vehicle untaxed and off the public road you **MUST** declare SORN – it is an offence not to do so. The vehicle will remain SORN until you sell, tax or scrap it. If your vehicle is uninsured or off the road it **MUST** have either a SORN declaration or valid insurance.

Law RV(RL)R 2002, reg 26 sched 4

Production of documents. You **MUST** be able to produce your driving licence, a valid insurance certificate and (if appropriate) a valid MOT certificate, when requested by a police officer. If you cannot do this you may be asked to take them to a police station within seven days.

Law RTA 1988 sects 164 & 165

Learner drivers

Learners driving a car **MUST** hold a valid provisional licence. They **MUST** be supervised by someone at least 21 years old who holds a full EC/EEA licence for that type of car (automatic or manual) and has held one for at least three years.

Laws MV(DL)R reg 16 & RTA 1988 sect 87

Vehicles. Any vehicle driven by a learner **MUST** display red L plates. In Wales, either red D plates, red L plates, or both, can be used. Plates **MUST** conform to legal specifications and **MUST** be clearly visible to others from in front of the vehicle and from behind. Plates should be removed or covered when not being driven by a learner (except on driving school vehicles).

Law MV(DL)R reg 16 & sched 4

You **MUST** pass the theory test (if one is required) and then a practical driving test for the category of vehicle you wish to drive before driving unaccompanied.

Law MV(DL)R reg 40

4. The road user and the law

Road traffic law

The following list can be found abbreviated throughout The Code. It is not intended to be a comprehensive guide, but a guide to some of the important points of law. For the precise wording of the law, please refer to the various Acts and Regulations (as amended) indicated in The Code. Abbreviations are listed below.

Most of the provisions apply on all roads throughout Great Britain, although there are some exceptions. The definition of a road in England and Wales is 'any highway and any other road to which the public has access and includes bridges over which a road passes' (RTA 1988 sect 192(1)). In Scotland, there is a similar definition which is extended to include any way over which the public have a right of passage (R(S)A 1984 sect 151(1)).

It is important to note that references to 'road' therefore generally include footpaths, bridleways and cycle tracks, and many roadways and driveways on private land (including many car parks). In most cases, the law will apply to them and there may be additional rules for particular paths or ways. Some serious driving offences, including drink-driving offences, also apply to all public places, for example public car parks.

Acts and regulations from 1988 can be viewed on the UK legislation (www.legislation.gov.uk) site. Acts and regulations prior to 1988 are only available in their original print format which may be obtained from The Stationery Office (www.tsoshop.co.uk).

Acts and regulations prior to 1988

Chronically Sick & Disabled Persons Act 1970	CSDPA
Functions of Traffic Wardens Order 1970	FTWO
Greater London (General Powers) Act 1974	GL(GP)A
Highway Act 1835 or 1980 (as indicated)	HA
Motorways Traffic (England & Wales) Regulations 1982	MT(E&W)R
Motorways Traffic (England & Wales) Amended Regulations	MT(E&W)(A)R
Pedal Cycles (Construction & Use) Regulations 1983	PCUR
Public Passenger Vehicles Act 1981	PPVA
Road Traffic Act 1984	RTA
Road Traffic Regulation Act 1984	RTRA
Road Vehicles (Construction & Use) Regulations 1986	CUR
Roads (Scotland) Act 1984	R(S)A

continued overleaf

Acts and Regulations from 1988 onwards

Environmental Protection Act 1990	EPA
Horses (Protective Headgear for Young Riders) Act 1990	H(PHYR)A
Horses (Protective Headgear for Young Riders) Regulations 1992	H(PHYR)R
Motor Cycles (Eye Protectors) Regulations 1999	MC(EP)R
Motor Cycles (Protective Helmets) Regulations 1998	MC(PH)R
Motorways Traffic (Scotland) Regulations 1995	MT(S)R
Motor Vehicles (Driving Licences) Regulations 1999	MV(DL)R
Motor Vehicles (Variation of Speed Limits) (England & Wales) Regulations 2014	MV(VSL)(E&W)
Motor Vehicles (Wearing of Seat Belts) Regulations 1993	MV(WSB)R
Motor Vehicles (Wearing of Seat Belts) (Amendment) Regulations 2006	MV(WSB)(A)R
Motor Vehicles (Wearing of Seat Belts by Children in Front Seats) Regulations 1993	MV(WSBCFS)R
New Roads and Streetworks Act 1991	NRSWA
Powers of Criminal Courts (Sentencing) Act 2000	PCC(S)A
Police Reform Act 2002	PRA
Prohibition of Smoking in Certain Premises (Scotland) Regulations 2006 (SI no 90)	PSCP(S)R*
Road Safety Act 2006	RSA
Road Traffic Act 1988	RTA
Road Traffic Act 1991	
Road Traffic Act 1988 (Prescribed Limit) (Scotland) Regulations 2014	PLSR
Road Traffic (New Drivers) Act 1995	RT(ND)A
Road Traffic Offenders Act 1988	RTOA
Road Vehicles (Display of Registration Marks) Regulations 2001	RV(DRM)R
Road Vehicles Lighting Regulations 1989	RVLR
Road Vehicles (Registration & Licensing) Regulations 2002	RV(R&L)R
Smoke-free (Exemptions and Vehicles) Regulations 2007	TSf (EV)*
Smoke-free premises etc (Wales) Regulations 2007	TSfP(W)R*
Traffic Management Act 2004	TMA
Traffic Signs Regulations & General Directions 2002	TSRGD
Use of Invalid Carriages on Highways Regulations 1988	UICHR
Vehicle Excise and Registration Act 1994	VERA
Zebra, Pelican and Puffin Pedestrian Crossings Regulations and General Directions 1997	ZPPPCRGD

*Specific legislation applies to smoking in vehicles which constitute workplaces. For information, visit
www.smokefreeengland.co.uk
www.clearingtheairscotland.com
www.smokingbanwales.co.uk

5. Penalties and The Highway Code

Parliament sets the maximum penalties for road traffic offences.
The seriousness of the offence is reflected in the maximum penalty.
It is for the courts to decide what sentence to impose according to
circumstances.

The penalty table on the next page indicates some of the main offences,
and the associated penalties. There is a wide range of other more
specific offences which, for the sake of simplicity, are not shown here.
The penalty points and disqualification system is described below.

Penalty points and disqualification

The penalty point system is intended to deter drivers and motorcyclists
from following unsafe motoring practices. Certain non-motoring
offences, e.g. failure to rectify vehicle defects, can also attract penalty
points.

The court **MUST** order points to be endorsed on the licence according
to the fixed number or the range set by Parliament. The accumulation
of penalty points acts as a warning to drivers and motorcyclists that they
risk disqualification if further offences are committed.
Law RTOA sects 44 & 45

A driver or motorcyclist who accumulates 12 or more penalty points
within a three-year period **MUST** be disqualified. This will be for a
minimum period of six months, or longer if the driver or motorcyclist
has previously been disqualified.
Law RTOA sect 35

For every offence which carries penalty points the court has a
discretionary power to order the licence holder to be disqualified. This
may be for any period the court thinks fit, but will usually be between a
week and a few months.

In the case of serious offences, such as dangerous driving and drink-
driving, the court **MUST** order disqualification. The minimum period is
12 months, but for repeat offenders or where the alcohol level is high,
it may be longer. For example, a second drink-drive offence in the space
of 10 years will result in a minimum of three years' disqualification.
Law RTOA sect 34

The Highway Code

Penalty Table

Offence	Maximum Penalties			
	Imprisonment	Fine	Disqualification	Penalty Points
*Causing death by dangerous driving	14 years	Unlimited	Obligatory – 2 years minimum	3–11 (if exceptionally not disqualified)
*Dangerous driving	2 years	Unlimited	Obligatory	3–11 (if exceptionally not disqualified)
*Causing death by careless driving under the influence of drink or drugs	14 years	Unlimited	Obligatory – 2 years minimum	3–11 (if exceptionally not disqualified)
Careless and inconsiderate driving	-	Unlimited	Discretionary	3–9
Driving while unfit through drink or drugs or with excess alcohol; or failing to provide a specimen for analysis	6 months	Unlimited	Obligatory	3–11 (if exceptionally not disqualified)
Failing to stop after an accident or failing to report an accident	6 months	Unlimited	Discretionary	5–10
Driving when disqualified	6 months (12 months in Scotland)	Unlimited	Discretionary	6
Driving after refusal or revocation of licence on medical grounds	6 months	Unlimited	Discretionary	3–6
Driving without insurance	-	Unlimited	Discretionary	6–8
Using a vehicle in a dangerous condition	-	£2,500 (Unlimited for LGV or PCV)	Obligatory within 3 years of previous conviction for similar offence – 6 months minimum. Otherwise discretionary	3 in each case
Failure to have proper control of vehicle or full view of the road and traffic ahead, or using a hand-held mobile phone when driving	-	£1,000 (£2,500 for PCV or goods vehicle)	Discretionary	3
Driving otherwise than in accordance with a licence	-	£1,000	Discretionary	3–6
Speeding	-	£1,000 (£2,500 for motorway offences)	Discretionary	3–6 or 3 (fixed penalty)
Traffic light offences	-	£1,000	Discretionary	3
No MOT certificate	-	£1,000	-	-
Seat belt offences	-	£500	-	-
Dangerous cycling	-	£1,000	-	-
Careless cycling	-	£1,000	-	-
Cycling on pavement	-	£500	-	-
Failing to identify driver of a vehicle	-	£1,000	Discretionary	6

*Where a court disqualifies a person on conviction for one of these offences, it must order an extended retest. The courts also have discretion to order a retest for any other offence which carries penalty points, an extended retest where disqualification is obligatory, and an ordinary test where disqualification is not obligatory.

New drivers

Special rules as set out below apply for a period of two years from the date of passing their first driving test, to drivers and motorcyclists from

- the UK, EU/EEA, the Isle of Man, the Channel Islands or Gibraltar who passed their first driving test in any of those countries
- other foreign countries who have to pass a UK driving test to gain a UK licence, in which case the UK driving test is treated as their first driving test; and
- other foreign countries who (without needing a test) exchanged their licence for a UK licence and subsequently passed a UK driving test to drive another type of vehicle, in which case the UK driving test is treated as their first driving test. For example a driver who exchanges a foreign licence (car) for a UK licence (car) and who later passes a test to drive another type of vehicle (e.g. an HGV) will be subject to the special rules.

Where a person subject to the special rules accumulates six or more penalty points before the end of the two-year period (including any points acquired before passing the test) their licence will be revoked automatically. To regain the licence they must reapply for a provisional licence and may drive only as a learner until they pass a further driving test (also see Annexe 8 – Safety code for new drivers.)

Law RT(ND)A

Note. This applies even if they pay for offences by fixed penalty. Drivers in the first group (UK, EU/EEA etc.) who already have a full licence for one type of vehicle are not affected by the special rules if they later pass a test to drive another type of vehicle.

Other consequences of offending

Where an offence is punishable by imprisonment then the vehicle used to commit the offence may be confiscated.

Law PCC(S)A, sect 143

In addition to the penalties a court may decide to impose, the cost of insurance is likely to rise considerably following conviction for a serious driving offence. This is because insurance companies consider such drivers are more likely to be involved in a collision.

Drivers disqualified for drinking and driving twice within 10 years, or once if they are over two and a half times the legal limit, or those who refused to give a specimen, also have to satisfy the Driver and Vehicle Licensing Agency's Medical Branch that they do not have an alcohol problem and are otherwise fit to drive before their licence is returned at the end of their period of disqualification. Persistent misuse of drugs or alcohol may lead to the withdrawal of a driving licence.

6. Vehicle maintenance, safety and security

Take special care that lights, brakes, steering, exhaust system, seat belts, demisters, wipers and washers are all working. Also

- lights, indicators, reflectors, and number plates **MUST** be kept clean and clear
- windscreens and windows **MUST** be kept clean and free from obstructions to vision
- lights **MUST** be properly adjusted to prevent dazzling other road users. Extra attention needs to be paid to this if the vehicle is heavily loaded
- exhaust emissions **MUST NOT** exceed prescribed levels
- ensure your seat, seat belt, head restraint and mirrors are adjusted correctly before you drive
- ensure that items of luggage are securely stowed.

Laws RVLR 1989 regs 23 & 27 & CUR 1986, regs 30 & 61

Warning displays

Make sure that you understand the meaning of all warning displays on the vehicle instrument panel. Do not ignore warning signs, they could indicate a dangerous fault developing.

- When you turn the ignition key, warning lights will be illuminated but will go out when the engine starts (except the handbrake warning light). If they do not, or if they come on while you are driving, stop and investigate the problem, as you could have a serious fault.
- If the charge warning light comes on while you are driving, it may mean that the battery isn't charging. This should also be checked as soon as possible to avoid loss of power to lights and other electrical systems.

Window tints

You **MUST NOT** use a vehicle with excessively dark tinting applied to the windscreen, or to the glass in any front window to either side of the driver. Window tinting applied during manufacture complies with the Visual Light Transmittance (VLT) standards. There are no VLT limits for rear windscreens or rear passenger windows.

Laws RTA 1988 sect 42 & CUR reg 32

Tyres

Tyres **MUST** be correctly inflated to the vehicle manufacturer's specification for the load being carried. Always refer to the vehicle's handbook or data. Tyres should also be free from certain cuts and other defects. Cars, light vans and light trailers **MUST** have a tread depth of at least 1.6 mm across the central three-quarters of the breadth of the tread and around the entire circumference. Motorcycles, large vehicles and passenger-carrying vehicles **MUST** have a tread depth of at least 1 mm across three-quarters of the breadth of the tread and in a continuous band around the entire circumference. Mopeds should have visible tread. Be aware that some vehicle defects can attract penalty points.

Law CUR reg 27

If a tyre bursts while you are driving, try to keep control of your vehicle. Grip the steering wheel firmly and allow the vehicle to roll to a stop at the side of the road.

If you have a flat tyre, stop as soon as it is safe to do so. Only change the tyre if you can do so without putting yourself or others at risk – otherwise call a breakdown service.

Tyre pressures

Check weekly. Do this before your journey, when tyres are cold. Warm or hot tyres may give a misleading reading.

Your brakes and steering will be adversely affected by under-inflated or over-inflated tyres. Excessive or uneven tyre wear may be caused by faults in the braking or suspension systems, or wheels which are out of alignment. Have these faults corrected as soon as possible.

Fluid levels

Check the fluid levels in your vehicle at least weekly. Low brake fluid may result in brake failure and a crash. Make sure you recognise the low fluid warning lights if your vehicle has them fitted.

Before winter

Ensure that the battery is well maintained and that there are appropriate anti-freeze agents in your radiator and windscreen bottle.

Other problems

If your vehicle
- pulls to one side when braking, it is most likely to be a brake fault or incorrectly inflated tyres. Consult a garage or mechanic immediately
- continues to bounce after pushing down on the front or rear, its shock absorbers are worn. Worn shock absorbers can seriously affect the operation of a vehicle and should be replaced

- smells of anything unusual such as burning rubber, petrol or an electrical fault; investigate immediately. Do not risk a fire.

Overheated engines or fire

Most engines are water-cooled. If your engine overheats you should wait until it has cooled naturally. Only then remove the coolant filler cap and add water or other coolant.

If your vehicle catches fire, get the occupants out of the vehicle quickly and to a safe place. Do not attempt to extinguish a fire in the engine compartment, as opening the bonnet will make the fire flare. Call the fire brigade.

Petrol stations/fuel tank/fuel leaks

Ensure that, when filling up your vehicle's tank or any fuel cans you are carrying, you do not spill fuel on the forecourt. Any spilled fuel should be immediately reported to the petrol station attendant. Diesel spillage is dangerous to other road users, particularly motorcyclists, as it will significantly reduce the level of grip between the tyres and road surface. Double-check for fuel leaks and make sure that

- you do not overfill your fuel tank
- the fuel cap is fastened securely
- the seal in the cap is not torn, perished or missing
- there is no visual damage to the cap or the fuel tank

Emergency fuel caps, if fitted, should form a good seal.

Never smoke, or use a mobile phone, on the forecourt of petrol stations as these are major fire risks and could cause an explosion.

Vehicle security

When you leave your vehicle you should

- remove the ignition key and engage the steering lock
- lock the car, even if you only leave it for a few minutes
- close the windows completely
- never leave children or pets in an unventilated car
- take all contents with you, or lock them in the boot. Remember, for all a thief knows a carrier bag may contain valuables
- never leave vehicle documents in the car.

For extra security fit an anti-theft device such as an alarm or immobiliser. If you are buying a new car it is a good idea to check the level of built-in security features. Consider having your registration number etched on all your car windows. This is a cheap and effective deterrent to professional thieves.

7. First Aid on the road

The following information may be of general assistance, but there's no substitute for proper training. Any first aid given at the scene of an incident should be looked on only as a temporary measure until the emergency services arrive. If you haven't had any first aid training, the following points could be helpful.

1. Deal with danger

Further collisions and fire are the main dangers following a crash. Approach any vehicle involved with care. Switch off all engines and, if possible, warn other traffic. Stop anyone from smoking.

2. Get help

Try to get the assistance of bystanders. Get someone to call the appropriate emergency services on 999 or 112 as soon as possible. They will need to know the exact location of the incident and the number of vehicles involved. Try to give information about the condition of any casualties, e.g. if anyone is having difficulty breathing, is bleeding heavily or does not respond when spoken to.

3. Help those involved

DO NOT move casualties still in vehicles unless there is the threat of further danger. **DO NOT** remove a motorcyclist's helmet unless it is essential. Remember the casualty may be suffering from shock. **DO NOT** give them anything to eat or drink. **DO** try to make them warm and as comfortable as you can. Protect them from rain or snow, but avoid unnecessary movement. **DO** give reassurance confidently and try not to leave them alone or let them wander into the path of other traffic.

4. Provide emergency care

Remember the letters **D R A B C:**

D Danger Check that you are not in danger.

R Response Try to get a response by asking questions and gently shaking their shoulders.

A Airway If the person is not talking and the airway may be blocked, then place one hand under the chin and lift the chin up and forward. If they are still having difficulty with breathing then gently tilt the head back.

B Breathing Normal breathing should be established. Once the airway is open check breathing for up to 10 seconds.

C Compressions If they have no signs of life and there is no pulse, then chest compressions should be administered. Place two hands in the centre of the chest and press down hard and fast – 5–6cm and about twice a second. You may only need one hand for a child and shouldn't press down as far. For infants, use two fingers in the middle of the chest when delivering compressions and don't press down too far.

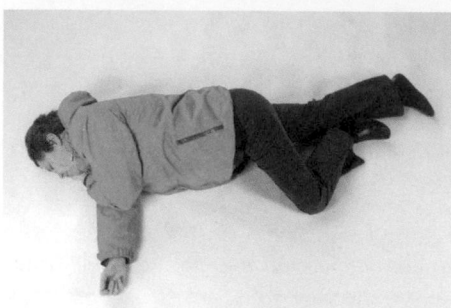

If the casualty is unconscious and breathing, place them in the recovery position until medical help arrives.

Bleeding. First, check for anything that may be in the wound, such as glass. Taking care not to press on the object, build up padding on either side of the object. If there's nothing embedded, apply firm pressure over the wound to stem the flow of blood. As soon as practical, fasten a pad to the wound with a bandage or length of cloth. Use the cleanest material available. If a limb is bleeding but not broken, raise it above the level of the heart to reduce the flow of blood. Any restriction of blood circulation for more than a short time could cause long-term injuries.

Burns. Check the casualty for shock, and if possible, try to cool the burn for at least 10 minutes with plenty of clean, cold water or other non-toxic liquid. Don't try to remove anything that's sticking to the burn.

5. Be prepared
Always carry a first aid kit – you might never need it, but it could save a life. Learn first aid – you can get first aid training from a qualified organisation such as St John Ambulance and Brigade, St Andrew's First Aid, British Red Cross Society or any suitable qualified body (see Useful websites for contact details).

8. Safety code for new drivers

Once you have passed the driving test you will be able to drive on your own. This will provide you with lots of opportunities but you need to remain safe. Even though you have shown you have the skills you need to drive safely, many newly qualified drivers lack experience. You need to continue to develop your skills, especially anticipating other road users' behaviour to avoid having a collision. As many as one driver in five has some kind of collision in their first year of driving. This code provides some assistance to help you get the through the first 12 months after passing the driving test, when you are most vulnerable, as safely as possible.

- Many of the worst collisions happen at night. Between midnight and 6am is a time of high risk for new drivers. Avoid driving then unless it's really necessary.
- If you are driving with passengers, you are responsible for their safety. Don't let them distract you or encourage you to take risks. Tell your passengers that you need to concentrate if you are to get to your destination safely.
- Never show off or try to compete with other drivers, particularly if they are driving badly.
- Don't drive if you have consumed any alcohol or taken drugs. Even over-the-counter medicines can affect your ability to drive safely – read the label to see if they may affect your driving.
- Make sure everyone's wearing a seat belt throughout the journey.
- Keep your speed down – many serious collisions happen because the driver loses control, particularly on bends.
- Most new drivers have no experience of driving high-powered or sporty cars. Unless you have learnt to drive in such a vehicle you need to get plenty of experience driving on your own before driving a more powerful car.
- Driving while uninsured is an offence. See Annex 3 for information on types of insurance cover.

REMEMBER that under the New Drivers Act you will have your licence revoked if you get six penalty points on your licence within two years of passing your first driving test. You will need to pass both the theory and practical tests again to get back your full licence.

You could consider taking further training such as Pass Plus, which could save you money on your insurance, as well as helping you reduce your risk of being involved in a collision. There are three ways to find out more: internet – www.gov.uk; telephone – 0115 936 6504; email – passplus@dsa.gsi.gov.uk

Other information

Metric conversions

The conversions given throughout *The Highway Code* are rounded but a detailed conversion chart is shown below.

Miles	Kilometres	Miles	Kilometres
1.00	1.61	40.00	64.37
5.00	8.05	45.00	72.42
10.00	16.09	50.00	80.47
15.00	24.14	55.00	88.51
20.00	32.19	60.00	96.56
25.00	40.23	65.00	104.60
30.00	48.28	70.00	112.65
35.00	56.33		

Useful websites

www.sja.org.uk (St John Ambulance)
www.firstaid.org.uk (St Andrew's First Aid)
www.redcross.org.uk (British Red Cross)
www.roadsafetygb.org.uk
www.askthe.police.uk
www.trafficpenaltytribunal.gov.uk (outside London)
www.parkingandtrafficappeals.gov.uk (inside London)
www.gov.uk/government/organisations/highways-england
www.trafficscotland.org
www.traffic-wales.com
www.cyclestreets.net
maps.google.co.uk
www.theaa.com/route-planner
www.traveline.info
ec.europa.eu/transport/road_safety/going_abroad

Further reading

The Blue Badge Scheme

Get information about the Blue Badge Scheme from your council:
www.gov.uk/blue-badge-scheme-information-council.

Code of Practice for Horse-Drawn Vehicles

A Code of Practice has been published by the Department for Transport,
Transport: www.gov.uk/government/publications/code-of-practice-for-
horse-drawn-vehicles.

Index

References are to rule numbers, except those
numbers in *bold italics*, which refer to the annexes

Notes

Notes

Personal Information

My driver number

_____

Driving instructor's name and
phone number

_____

Driving instructor's number

_____

Theory test date and time

_____

Theory test pass date

_____

Theory test certificate number

_____

Driving school code

_____

Practical test date and time

_____